D1599695

The Cambridge Companion to Sibelius

Jean Sibelius has gradually emerged as one of the most striking and influential figures in twentieth-century music, yet his work is only just beginning to receive the critical attention that its importance deserves. This *Companion* provides an accessible and vivid account of Sibelius's work in its historical and cultural context. Leading international scholars, from Finland, the United States and the UK, examine Sibelius's music from a range of critical perspectives, including nationalism, eroticism and the exotic, music and landscape, reception and musical influence. There are also chapters on recording and interpretation that offer fascinating insights into the performance of Sibelius's work. The book includes much new material, drawing on recent scholarship, as well as providing a comprehensive introduction to Sibelius's major musical achievements.

DANIEL M. GRIMLEY is a Lecturer in Music at the University of Nottingham. He is co-editor of *The Cambridge Companion to Elgar* (forthcoming), and has written articles on the music of Carl Nielsen in *Music Analysis* and *The Musical Quarterly.* Current projects include books on Grieg and on landscape in Nordic music, 1890–1930.

The Cambridge Companion to

SIBELIUS

· · · · · · · · · · · ·

EDITED BY
Daniel M. Grimley

CAMBRIDGE
UNIVERSITY PRESS

PUBLISHED BY THE PRESS SYNDICATE OF THE UNIVERSITY OF CAMBRIDGE
The Pitt Building, Trumpington Street, Cambridge, United Kingdom

CAMBRIDGE UNIVERSITY PRESS
The Edinburgh Building, Cambridge CB2 2RU, UK
40 West 20th Street, New York, NY 10011–4211, USA
477 Williamstown Road, Port Melbourne, VIC 3207, Australia
Ruiz de Alarcón 13, 28014 Madrid, Spain
Dock House, The Waterfront, Cape Town 8001, South Africa

http://www.cambridge.org

First published 2004

Printed in the United Kingdom at the University Press, Cambridge

Typeface Minion 10.75/14pt.   *System* LaTeX 2_ε [TB]

A catalogue record for this book is available from the British Library

Library of Congress Cataloguing in Publication data
The Cambridge companion to Sibelius / edited by Daniel M. Grimley.
    p.   cm. – (Cambridge companions to music)
Includes bibliographical references (p. 263) and index.
ISBN 0 521 81552 5 – ISBN 0 521 89460 3 (pb.)
1. Sibelius, Jean, 1865–1957 – Criticism and interpretation.   I. Grimley, Daniel M.   II. Series.
ML410.S54C36   2003   780′.92 – dc21   2003051521

ISBN 0 521 81552 5 hardback
ISBN 0 521 89460 3 paperback

Contents

Part IV: Interpreting Sibelius

Notes on contributors

Julian Anderson studied composition with John Lambert, Tristan Murail and Alexander Goehr. His compositions include *The Stations of the Sun* and *Imagin'd Corners*, both for orchestra, *Khorovod* and *Alhambra Fantasy* for ensemble, and *Poetry Nearing Silence* for septet. He is currently Composer in Association with the City of Birmingham Symphony Orchestra, and Head of Composition at the Royal College of Music, London. He has published numerous articles on a wide variety of new music in both English and French.

Stephen Downes is Senior Lecturer in Music at the University of Surrey. His publications include two monographs on Szymanowski, and articles on Rossini, Beethoven, Schumann, Bartók, and Penderecki. He is currently working on a book entitled *The Muse as Eros: Musical Constructions of Inspiration and Desire from Romantic Idealism to Modernist Anxiety.*

Peter Franklin is Reader in Music at the University of Oxford, where he is a Fellow of St Catherine's College. His published work includes *Mahler Symphony no. 3* (1991) and *The Life of Mahler* (1997). He also writes on early-twentieth-century opera and classical Hollywood film music.

Glenda Dawn Goss, formerly Professor of Musicology at the University of Georgia (Athens), has been Editor-in-Chief of the complete edition *Jean Sibelius Works* since 2000. She is editor and author of various books on Sibelius including *Jean Sibelius and Olin Downes: Music, Friendship, Criticism* (1995), *The Sibelius Companion* (1996) and *Jean Sibelius: A Guide to Research* (1998), as well as a volume of correspondence, *The Hämeenlinna Letters. Jean Sibelius ungdomsbrev* (1997).

Daniel M. Grimley wrote his doctoral dissertation on the music of Carl Nielsen at King's College, Cambridge (1998), and is Lecturer in Music at the University of Nottingham. Current projects include co-editing *The Cambridge Companion to Elgar* with Julian Rushton, and books on Grieg and on landscape in Nordic music, 1890–1930.

James Hepokoski is Professor of Music History at Yale University and is the co-editor of the journal *Nineteenth-Century Music*. His most recent publications include the entry on Sibelius in the second edition of the *New Grove Dictionary of Music and Musicians* (2001). In collaboration with Warren Darcy he has completed a book on classical musical structure, *Elements of Sonata Theory: Norms, Types, and Deformations in the Late-Eighteenth-Century Sonata*, forthcoming.

Matti Huttunen gained his doctorate from the University of Turku in 1993, and has been Professor of Music History at the Sibelius Academy since 1998. His work includes a broad range of articles and papers on music historiography, nationalism, and Finnish music, as well as a book, *Jean Sibelius: Pienoiselämänkerta/An Illustrated Life* (1999).

Jeffrey Kallberg is Professor of Music History at the University of Pennsylvania. He publishes widely on the music and cultural contexts of Chopin; his current projects include a study of Scandinavian song in the first half of the twentieth century.

Bethany Lowe is Lecturer in Music at the University of Newcastle-upon-Tyne. Her research interests include Sibelius, British symphonic composition, music analysis, and the relationship between analysis and performance. Her doctoral dissertation examined the structural aspects of forty-one recorded performances of Sibelius's Fifth Symphony. Bethany is also Assistant Editor to the journal *Music Analysis* and an active conductor.

Tomi Mäkelä completed his doctorate, *Virtuosität und Werkcharakter* (Katzbichler: München-Salzburg 1989), in Berlin (with Carl Dahlhaus) in 1988, and his *Habilitation* in Helsinki (a book on 1920s chamber music) in 1990. He has been Professor of Musicology at the University of Magdeburg since 1996, and has recently written articles on music of the nineteenth (Wieniawski) and early twentieth centuries (Reger, Schoenberg, Sibelius, Stravinsky, urbanity, musical exile, film music, Finnish topics).

Veijo Murtomäki is Professor of Music History at the Sibelius Academy in Helsinki and author of *Symphonic Unity: the Development of Formal Thinking in the Symphonies of Sibelius* (Helsinki, 1993). With Professor Timothy L. Jackson, he was co-editor of *Sibelius Studies* (Cambridge University Press, 2001), and editor of two Sibelius Conference Reports (Helsinki, 1995 and 2000). He is a member of the Editorial Board of the *Jean Sibelius Complete Works* (1996–), and has published many articles on the music of the classical–Romantic era, especially Sibelius, in Finnish, Swedish, German, English and French.

Ilkka Oramo studied musicology under Erik Tawaststjerna (Helsinki) and Carl Dahlhaus (Berlin), and wrote his dissertation on the music of Béla Bartók (1977). He has published articles on music theory, aesthetics of music, Bartók and Finnish composers, especially Sibelius, in scholarly publications in many countries. Since 1984 he has been Professor of Music Theory at the Sibelius Academy in Helsinki.

Jukka Tiilikainen has edited Sibelius's complete solo songs with piano for the *Jean Sibelius Works*. The first of three volumes, *JSW* VIII/2, received Das Deutschen Musikeditions Preis in 1999 (Wissenschaftliche Notenausgaben [Gesamtausgaben] category). Tiilikainen's research interests centre around Sibelius's creativity and how it manifests itself in the composer's musical manuscripts. Tiilikainen is currently preparing his doctorate on the creative process in Sibelius's songs.

Arnold Whittall is Professor Emeritus of Music Theory and Analysis at King's College London. He remains active as lecturer, reviewer and concert presenter, and has written widely on nineteenth- and twentieth-century music. Recent publications include *Exploring Twentieth-Century Music* (Cambridge University Press, 2003) and contributions to the *Cambridge Companions* on Debussy and Stravinsky.

Acknowledgements

Thanks must first and foremost go to the contributors to this volume, for their scholarship, enthusiasm and patience. The idea for this project was first broached after the Third International Jean Sibelius Conference at the Sibelius Academy, Helsinki, 7–10 December 2000, and the sense of creativity, excitement and discovery that characterised that meeting also pervades much of the discussion in this volume. I am also particularly grateful to Sir Colin Davis and Osmo Vänskä for generously agreeing to take part in the final chapter. Penny Souster has been a constant source of support, guidance and encouragement at every stage of the project.

I should like to thank the following for their help during the preparation of this book: Glenda Dawn Goss, Alison Glaister, Matti Huttunen, Timothy L. Jackson, Anna Krohn, Veijo Murtomäki, Ingrid Sykes, Dominique Toennesmann and the Finnish Music Information Centre.

Extracts from the Sibelius manuscripts held in the State Archives, University of Helsinki, are reproduced by kind permission of the Trustees of the Sibelius Estate, Finland.

Copyright permission to reproduce all music examples is gratefully acknowledged to Breitkopf & Härtel, except for the following where permission has been sought: Sibelius, 'Aus banger Brust', op. 50/4 (Exx. 8.8 and 8.9) from Robert Lienau; Sibelius, 'The Forest Lake', op. 114/2 (Ex. 9.3) from Edition Fazer; Uuno Klami, *The Adventures of Lemminkäinen on the Island* (Ex. 10.1) courtesy of the Finnish Cultural Foundation; Sibelius, Symphony no. 5 (Ex. 13.2), from Edition Wilhelm Hansen.

Chronology of Sibelius's life and career

Year	Sibelius's life and career	Contemporary political events
1865	Sibelius born on 8 December into middle-class Swedish-speaking family in Hämeenlinna (Tavastehus), son of Christian and Maria Sibelius (née Borg). Christened Johan Julius Christian.	(Finland autonomous duchy under Russian rule.)
1868	Father dies of typhus. Sibelius brought up by his mother; summers spent in Loviisa (Baltic sea port).	
1876	Enrols in Hämeenlinna Normaalilyseo (Finnish-language grammar school).	
1880	Begins violin lessons with Gustav Levander, bandmaster at Hämeenlinna.	
1881	First surviving composition[?], *Vattendroppar* ('Water drops') for violin and cello.	Coronation of Tsar Alexander III.
1882		Martin Wegelius founds Helsinki Music Institute. Robert Kajanus founds first Finnish orchestra.
1885	Enrols at Helsinki University, initially to study law. Joins Music Institute, 15 September, principal study violin.	
1887	Begins composition lessons with Wegelius.	
1889	Graduates from the Music Institute, 31 May. Begins studies in Berlin with Albert Becker.	Newspaper *Päivälehti* (later renamed *Helsingin Sanomat*) founded by Young Finns to promote radical nationalist ideas.
1890	Returns from Berlin to Finland. Leaves for Vienna, October, to study with Karl Goldmark and Robert Fuchs. Hears Bruckner's Symphony no. 3 in D minor, 21 December.	Finnish Post Office placed under direct Russian control.

1891   Returns from Vienna. Working on *Kullervo* Symphony. Meets runic singer Larin Paraske in Borgå, November (and possibly earlier in the summer) and 'listened to her with great attention and made notes on her inflections and rhythms'.

1892   Conducts premiere of *Kullervo*, 28 April, greeted with immense popular and critical acclaim. Marries Aino Järnefelt, June. Honeymoon in Karelia collecting folksongs.

1893   Birth of first daughter, Eva, March. Aunt Eva in Lovisa dies, June. Begins opera, *The Building of the Boat* (*Veneen luominen*). Project later abandoned, but prelude becomes *The Swan of Tuonela*. Conducts premiere of *Karelia* music, 13 November, Viipuri Students Gala, Helsinki University.

1894   Composes *Vårsång (La tristesse du printemps)*, premiered 21 June at open-air festival concert in Vaasa. Travels to Bayreuth, July, hears *Parsifal*, *Die Walküre*, *Siegfried*, *Götterdämmerung*, *Tannhäuser*, *Die Meistersinger* and *Lohengrin*. Travels to Italy for first time. On return, stops in Berlin to study Liszt's *Faust Symphony*, sees performances of *Carmen*, *The Bartered Bride*, *Falstaff*.

Coronation of Tsar Nicholas II.

1895   *Skogsrået* premiered, 17 April. Works on collection of Finnish folksong with A. A. Borenius-Lähteenkorvas.

1896   *Four Lemminkäinen Legends* premiered, 13 April. Composes one-act opera, *The Maiden in the Tower*, libretto by Rafael Hertzberg, premiered 9 November, and Cantata for the Coronation of Nicholas II. Applies for post of Professor of Music at Helsinki

University, and reads lecture entitled, 'Some reflections on folk music and its influence on the development of art music', 25 November. Position finally offered to Robert Kajanus after controversial appeal.

1897 Composes *The Rapid-shooter's Brides* (*Koskenlaskijan morsiamet*), ballad for voice and orchestra. Plans for symphonic poem based on Heine poem 'Ein Fichtenbaum steht einsam'. Sibelius awarded state pension.

1898 Music for Adolf Paul's play *King Christian II*, premiered 24 February. Trip to Berlin with Aino and brother, Christian. Begins work on First Symphony.

Hard-line General Nikolai Bobrikov (1839–1904) appointed Governor-General of Finland. Pursues aggressive policy of 'Russification'.

1899 Sibelius composes *Song of the Athenians* as political protest. Premiered alongside First Symphony, 26 April. First version of *Finlandia* performed as part of Press Pension celebrations, 4 November.

Nicholas II issues *February Manifesto*, curbing legislative powers of Finnish parliament. Finnish Labour Party founded.

1900 On European tour with Kajanus and Helsinki Philharmonic Orchestra, concerts in Lübeck, Berlin, Amsterdam, Brussels and Paris. Travels to Italy via Berlin, October.

1901 Sketches Second Symphony in Italy. Returns to Finland in May. Conducts *The Swan of Tuonela* and *Lemminkäinen's Return* at Heidelberg Festival.

Finnish army conscripts placed under direct Russian military command.

1902 Second Symphony premiered, 8 March. Writes cantata, *The Origin of Fire*, premiered at Finnish National Theatre, 9 April. Conducts revised version of *En saga* in Helsinki, 2 November, and Berlin, 15 November.

Eliel Saarinen builds *art nouveau* villa complex at Hvitträsk.

1903	Composed incidental music for Arvid Järnefelt's play *Kuolema* ('Death'). Premiered 2 December. Sketches Violin Concerto.	Finnish army abolished.
1904	Second Symphony performed in Chicago, January. First version of the Violin Concerto premiered, 8 February. Moves from Helsinki to villa, Ainola, in Järvenpää, 24 September.	Bobrikov assassinated by Eugene Schauman, 16 June.
1905	Conducts successful performance of Second Symphony in Berlin, January. Hears Strauss, *Ein Heldenleben* and *Sinfonia domestica*. Incidental music for *Pelléas et Mélisande* premiered, Swedish theatre, Helsinki, 17 March. First visit to England, at invitation of Granville Bantock, conducts First Symphony and *Finlandia* in Liverpool, 2 December. Meets Rosa Newmarch. Return trip includes visit to Paris.	Finnish General Strike. *November Manifesto* passed, 4 November, repeals much of earlier legislation.
1906	Sibelius's sister, Linda, succumbs to insanity, June. Projected orchestral tone poem, 'Luonnotar', becomes *Pohjola's Daughter*, premiered in St Petersburg, 29 December.	Wegelius dies, 22 March.
1907	First Symphony performed by Felix Weingartner, Berlin, 1 January. Third Symphony premiered, Helsinki, September. Meets Mahler in Helsinki, 29 October. Travels to St Petersburg, November, to attend Siloti performance of new symphony.	200-member parliament ('Eduskunta') elected.
1908	Conducts Third Symphony in London, Spring. Writes music for Strindberg's *Swanwhite*, premiered 8 April. Travels to Berlin for major throat operation. Composes *Nightride and Sunrise*, begins string quartet *Voces intimae*.	
1909	*Nightride and Sunrise* premiered, St Petersburg, January. Conducts *En saga* and *Finlandia* at Queen's Hall, London,	

13 February. Meets Debussy following performance of *Prélude à l'après-midi d'un faune* and *Nocturnes*. Trip to Koli, northern Karelia, September.

1910   Finishes *In memoriam*, March. *Voces intimae* premiered, Helsinki Conservatory, 25 April. *In memoriam* and *The Dryad* premiered, Christiania (Oslo), 8 October.

1911   Fourth Symphony premiered, Helsinki, 3 April. Greeted with critical incomprehension. Visits Paris, November.

1912   Revises *Rakastava* for string orchestra and percussion. Offered position of Professor of Composition at Akademie für Musik und darstellende Kunst, Vienna. Composed Three Sonatinas for piano, Op. 67. Visits England to conduct the Fourth Symphony at the Birmingham festival, performed after premiere of Elgar's *The Music Makers*.

Russians granted Finnish citizenship.

1913   *The Bard* premiered, 27 March (revised version premiered 9 January 1916). *Luonnotar* premiered by Aino Ackté at Gloucester festival, 10 September.

1914   Composes first version of *The Oceanides* in Berlin. Travels to United States at invitation of Carl Stoeckel, to conduct premiere at Norfolk festival, Connecticut, 4 June. Visits New York, Niagara, and receives honorary doctorate from Yale University. Returns 18 June, before outbreak of war. Begins first version of Fifth Symphony.

Outbreak of First World War.

1915   Conducts Second and Fourth Symphonies and *The Oceanides* in Gothenburg, March. Celebrations for fiftieth birthday include premiere of first version of the Fifth Symphony, 8 December.

1916	Oskar Fried conducts Fourth Symphony at Freie Volksbühne, Berlin, Spring. Composes incidental music for production of Hoffmannsthal's *Everyman*, premiered 6 November. Conducts revised version of Fifth Symphony, December.	
1917	Composes March for the Finnish Jaeger Battalion.	Tsar overthrown in Russian revolution. Many Finnish political exiles return from Siberia, including Pehr Evind Svinhufvud (1861–1944). Svinhufvud issues formal declaration of Finnish independence, 6 December.
1918	Sibelius and family temporarily forced to leave Järvenpää.	Civil war breaks out between right-wing (White) and left-wing (Red) forces, January. German forces land, 3 April, to assist White Army. War over by 16 May as General Mannerheim, commander of the White Army, orders victory parade in Helsinki.
1919	Sibelius conducts Second Symphony at Nordic Music Days, Copenhagen, 18 June. Final version of Fifth Symphony premiered, November.	Death of Axel Carpelan, 24 March. Finnish independence recognised by Britain and USA, 3 May. Kaarlo Juho Ståhlberg elected first Finnish president.
1920	Composes setting of Eino Leino's *Maan virsi* ('Hymn to the Earth'). Sibelius offered Chair of Composition at Eastman School of Music.	Finland signs Tartu peace treaty with Russian republic, October.

Kajanus conducts Third Symphony at Salle Gaveaux, Paris, 13 May, without critical success.

1921   Tour of England. Meets Vaughan Williams at reception, 10 February, conducts Fifth Symphony at Queen's Hall, 12 February. Second Symphony premiered in Italy, 1 May, conducted by Busoni. Turns down offer of post at Eastman School of Music, 9 May.

League of Nations supports Finland's territorial claim to the Åland islands.

1922   Incidental music for *Scaramouche* premiered at Royal Theatre, Copenhagen, 12 May. Brother, Christian, dies, 2 July.

1923   Sixth Symphony premiered, 19 February.

1924   Seventh Symphony premiered, Stockholm, 24 March.

Death of Busoni.

1926   Incidental music for *The Tempest* premiered at Royal Theatre, Copenhagen, 15 March. *Tapiola* premiered by Walther Damrosch, New York, 26 December.

1927   Works on Eighth Symphony.

Death of Wilhelm Stenhammar.

1931   Death of Akseli Gallen-Kallela, 7 March. Sibelius composes *Sorgmusik* ('Funeral Music') for organ, possibly using material derived from work on Eighth Symphony.

1933   First movement of Eighth Symphony copied by Paul Voigt. Continues to work on Symphony until *c.* 1935, but the manuscript and drafts eventually lost (presumably burnt) by Sibelius at Ainola in the mid-1940s.

1935   Revised versions of *Lemminkäinen and the Maidens of the Island* and *Lemminkäinen in Tuonela* premiered by Kalevala Society, Helsinki, 1 March.

1939	Sibelius conducts performance of *Andante festivo* for short-wave radio broadcast.	Russian Army attacks Finland, 30 November. Beginning of 'Winter War'. Invasion initially repelled, but finally successful in 1940, following signing of Treaty of Moscow, March.
1941		Finland joins Germany against Russia in Continuation War. Britain declares war on Finland, December.
1943	Sibelius hears performance of Vaughan Williams's Fifth Symphony (dedicated to him 'without permission'), broadcast on wireless from Stockholm, 30 September.	
1944		Finland signs peace treaty with Moscow, August. Marshal Mannerheim elected president.
1946		Juho Kusti Paasikivi elected president.
1955		Finland joins Nordic Council and United Nations.
1956		Urho Kaleva Kekkonen elected president (remains in office until 1981).
1957	Sibelius dies, 20 September.	

Introduction

In his poignantly titled short story, *The Silence*, Julian Barnes describes a
composer in his old age, alone and isolated, reflecting with whimsical bitterness on his past musical triumphs in an age before the world was swept by
the carnage of world war and the angular sounds of musical modernism.[1]
Largely fictional, though based heavily on the final volume of the English
translation of Erik Tawaststjerna's biography,[2] Barnes's story nevertheless
reveals much about the way in which, outside Finland at least, our perception of Sibelius is still shadowed by the long twilight of his career. Many of
the photographs taken of Sibelius at *Ainola* during his eighties, half-lit and
austere, serve to reinforce Arnold Bax's famous description of the composer
as 'an arresting, formidable-looking fellow, born of dark rock and northern
forest',[3] explicitly eliding national topography and the composer's individual
physiognomy with a sense of intense creative alienation. From this perspective, Sibelius's apparently conservative, peripheralised position on the very
edge of the Continental European musical tradition seems strikingly at odds
with the continued popularity and vitality of his music in the concert hall.

   Recent Sibelius scholarship, however, has begun to deconstruct this image. As James Hepokoski has written, the study of the various historical
reactions to Sibelius's music has revealed 'some of the most ideologically
charged moments in twentieth-century reception history'.[4] Balilla Pratella,
writing in a 'Manifesto of Futurist Musicians' in 1910, hailed Sibelius as a
leading musical futurist, a dynamic youthful image far removed from the
backward-looking figure of Barnes's narrative.[5] Perceived in his full historical context, Sibelius emerges as a key player in a rich cultural milieu
that embraced both the birth of Finnish nationalism and the emergence of
a distinctively Nordic modernism at the beginning of the twentieth century. During his early years in Berlin, Sibelius's contemporaries included
August Strindberg and Edvard Munch. Though Sibelius's uncomfortable
relationship with Germany during the Second World War, surely dictated
by Finland's precarious position on the edge of the Soviet Union, contributed significantly to the relative decline in his international reputation
in the 1950s, Sibelius's work has once again re-emerged as a highly influential
force in twentieth-century music. Sibelius's music thus challenges our received view of twentieth-century musical development as a straightforward
linear progression from late Romanticism through modernism to serialism
and the avant-garde. Furthermore, Sibelius's work forces us to re-engage
with the way in which we understand the construction of national identity

in music. The precise relationship between Sibelius's work and Finnish musical identity is a complex and constantly shifting one, as the meaning and significance of his music is interpreted and reassessed by each succeeding generation.

The contributions in this volume respond positively to this richer and more diverse perception of Sibelius's life and career. The chapters are grouped into discussions of biography, Sibelius's works, their reception and interpretation. Though a number of recurrent themes run throughout the book, especially notions of landscape and ideology, gender and eroticism, and musical influence, the critical approaches adopted are deliberately wide-ranging. Matti Huttunen's discussion places Sibelius within the context of Finnish musical life in the nineteenth century, and examines his emergence as a 'national composer' from a theoretical and historical perspective. Glenda Dawn Goss, whose work on Sibelius and the American music critic Olin Downes revealed one of the most compelling episodes in Sibelius reception, examines Sibelius's critical year in Vienna in 1890–1. Sibelius's youthful encounter with Viennese modernism, Goss suggests, catalysed his composition of *Kullervo*, his musical breakthrough and a work that was subsequently hailed as the birth of a truly Finnish musical style.

Stephen Downes's analysis of Sibelius's early symphonic works offers a striking new perspective on some of Sibelius's most familiar music, hearing it as suffused with an intense musical eroticism but at the same time fractured by a 'modernist sublime'. The mythic (male) heroic voice of Sibelius's early music, despite its seemingly confident assertion of Finnish national identity, is ultimately a tragic one. Meanwhile, Arnold Whittall, in his discussion of the later symphonies, acknowledges the tension in Sibelius's music between the conflicting polarities of late Romantic modernism and neoclassicism, but suggests that the apparent contradiction between these musical impulses may have had a positive, creative impact. The fundamental formal drive in Sibelius's later symphonies, Whittall argues, is towards synthesis, but the continuing outward growth of Sibelius's formal and expressive syntax leads irrevocably towards the silence of the final years. Jukka Tiilikainen's detailed account of the genesis of Sibelius's Violin Concerto likewise offers a fascinating insight into Sibelius's compositional activity. The two different versions of the work trace Sibelius's changing attitude towards composing for the violin. Far from the sense of improvisational fluency that much of the music inspires, Sibelius's creative imagination emerges through his various rewritings, drafts and revisions of the concerto as an often dark and difficult one.

Since his monograph on the Fifth Symphony,[6] James Hepokoski's work has redefined Sibelius's place within the symphonic canon. Here, in his discussion of Sibelius's most popular work, *Finlandia*, Hepokoski draws attention to the tone poem's innovative musical language and its complex cultural context. Heard as part of a series of musical *tableaux vivants*, as it was originally intended, the narrative unfolded in *Finlandia* seems even more vivid and compelling than before. Daniel M. Grimley's survey of the tone poems focuses on the role of landscape within Sibelius's music. Landscape is as much a subjective as pictorial presence in Sibelius's work, and landscape processes offer a powerful analogy for the temporal lines of perspective that run through Sibelius's music. The intention is to shift the idea of landscape from the domain of reception to that of musical perception and signification. Jeffrey Kallberg places Sibelius's songs in the context of a modernist eroticism. From the epic Karelianist scale of the early Runeberg settings to the more concentrated expression of the op. 50 collection, Sibelius's songs reveal an intense preoccupation with characteristically *fin-de-siècle* themes of longing, desire and the exotic.

In his extensive survey of Sibelius's work in smaller genres, Veijo Murtomäki argues urgently for a critical reassessment of Sibelius's achievement as a miniaturist. Too often, Murtomäki suggests, Sibelius's miniatures have been regarded as of lesser quality and importance than his symphonic works. As Murtomäki demonstrates, closer attention to Sibelius's smaller-scale works can reveal new sides to his complex musical personality. The conventional understanding of Sibelius's miniatures as 'potboilers' is an opinion born as much from particular musical prejudices (against certain kinds of popular musics, perhaps) as from a thorough engagement with the works themselves.

The discussions of reception begin with Ilkka Oramo's fascinating account of Sibelius's ambivalent relationship with the younger generation of Finnish composers. As the 'national composer', Sibelius cast a long shadow over twentieth-century Finnish music. Outside Finland, the work of such figures as Leevi Maadetoja, Uuno Klami and Aare Merikanto, some of the most individual voices in Finnish music, is barely known yet deserves greater recognition. Tomi Mäkelä's essay addresses the most problematic issue in Sibelius reception. From his persistent attempts to achieve critical success in Berlin in the early 1900s, to his distanced relationship with the Third Reich and the subsequent backlash against the Anglo-American Sibelius cult of the 1930s, Germany emerges as a central theme in Sibelius's life and career. The German construction of 'Nordic music' in the early twentieth century, and its implications for Nordic composers themselves, remains a significant area for future historical research. Peter Franklin's discussion offers a complementary account of the British reception of Sibelius's work. Though the ideological lines here may seem less sinister, given the fate of Sibelius's music in Germany, they are no less powerfully drawn. The significance of Sibelius's work in Britain during the early twentieth century was the product of a complex web of aesthetic and political factors, not least of which was the sheer sonorous impact of Sibelius's music. It is the sonic surface of Sibelius's work, as well as his innovative approach to large-scale structure, that Julian Anderson identifies as being among the crucial components of Sibelius's influence on contemporary music. In the last twenty years, Sibelius has re-emerged as one of the most important sources of inspiration for composers working across the broadest range of contemporary musical styles.

The two final chapters offer contrasting views on the interpretation of Sibelius's work. Bethany Lowe's discussion of recorded interpretations of Sibelius's music draws on recent developments in performance scholarship, as well as a more multivalent definition of interpretative authenticity, to discuss the ways in which a distinctively Sibelian performing tradition has changed and evolved. In the closing chapter, two leading international conductors, Sir Colin Davis and Osmo Vänskä, offer their thoughts on the interpretation of Sibelius's music. The fact that their views often seem to collide, or, at least, lead in widely different interpretative directions, attests to the continuing vitality and richness of Sibelius's work in the concert hall.

Though no single consensus emerges from these individual contributions as to the meaning or 'truth' of Sibelius's work, they are nevertheless guided by a fundamental acknowledgement of Sibelius's centrality in twentieth-century music. Though the image presented by Julian Barnes's short story is a striking and evocative one, it is only a small part of the infinitely more complex cultural context in which Sibelius's music was created, performed, and understood. As we continue to reassess our conventional understanding of musical modernism from an increasingly distant historical perspective, the continuing relevance and significance of Sibelius's work will surely emerge ever more strongly than before.

PART ONE

Forging a voice: perspectives on Sibelius's biography

1 The national composer and the idea of Finnishness: Sibelius and the formation of Finnish musical style

MATTI HUTTUNEN

Sibelius as a nineteenth-century and post-nineteenth-century composer

Sibelius's historical position is tricky to define. He continued the tradition of harmonic tonality well into the 1920s, but in a way that was far removed from the neo-tonalities of Stravinsky, Hindemith or Les Six. When reading historical accounts of Sibelius's music, it is easy to recognise a sense of embarrassment with regard to Sibelius's work. He is sometimes compared with Beethoven, and sometimes included in the same category as modernist composers such as Gustav Mahler, Richard Strauss, Hugo Wolf, and Max Reger.[1] The comparison with Strauss is not an implausible one. Both composers approached atonality around 1910: Strauss in *Salome* (1903/1905) and *Elektra* (1909) and Sibelius in his Fourth Symphony (1911) and *Luonnotar* (1912). Neither composer, however, followed Schoenberg's line of development, but turned instead to a more tonal musical style. For Strauss the turning point was *Der Rosenkavalier* (1911), and for Sibelius *The Oceanides* (1914) and the Fifth Symphony (1914–19).[2] Thus, the idea of placing Sibelius in the same historical category as Mahler and Strauss can be defended from the point of view of technical musical details such as tonality, but if ideological and cultural factors are considered, a more elastic categorisation is needed.

Unlike Strauss or Mahler, Sibelius was regarded as a 'national' composer. Sibelius's early masterpieces of the 1890s were strongly national in character, and, even if he later attempted to distance himself from the national romantic idiom, he remained strongly associated with the idea of the national composer. This does not mean that his music should necessarily be understood solely in terms of nineteenth-century musical aesthetics. But in general, and at least from the Finnish point of view, his music can (and historically should) be understood with reference to the reception of his early works. The reception of Sibelius's music in Finland was essentially national in character up to the Second World War. New ideas appeared already in the 1930s, and from the 1940s Sibelius scholarship concentrated largely on the structural features of his symphonies. In this chapter, I shall try to elucidate the origins and the most important characteristics of the national Sibelius cult before the Second World War, and his significance in the formation of a Finnish musical identity. Many of the ideas that originated in the 1880s and 1890s are still present in writings on Sibelius to the present day.

The concept of Finnish nationalism

Oskar Merikanto (pseudonym 'O'), music critic of the newspaper *Päivälehti*, summarised the essence of the national reception of Sibelius's work with the single sentence, 'we recognise these [tones] as ours, even if we have never heard them as such'. The quotation is taken from an article that appeared on the same day, 28 April 1892, that Sibelius's *Kullervo* was premiered in Helsinki. Merikanto was himself a composer of popular songs and operas as well as a competent organist and conductor. He did not, however, regard himself as the young genius's competitor, but rather tried to encourage Finnish music's rising star. Merikanto's statement contains two important ideas: first, the sense of ownership and possession ('we recognise these tones as ours'), and second the unconscious means of perception ('even if we have never heard them as such'). According to Merikanto, the understanding of national music is – and should be – immediate and intuitive. For Merikanto, an ideal listener should recognise the national character of the music in *Kullervo* spontaneously, without what Merikanto regarded as unnecessary analytical or (in the pejorative sense) intellectual effort. The idea of ownership is also crucial. Possession is permanent in the sense that no one who owns something can be forced to give away what he or she owns against his or her own will. Merikanto's seemingly innocent utterance has a clear reference to the idea of national independence, to something that was merely a dream in 1892 but which was eventually attained in 1917.

Merikanto's expression 'even if we have never heard them as such' also refers to the historical importance of Sibelius's work, as well as to the originality of Sibelius's compositional process. In *Kullervo*, and in the works that followed it, Sibelius created something new. Nowadays, national art can easily be perceived as old-fashioned and aesthetically weary, but in the 1890s national art was new and modern. As we shall see later, the idea that Sibelius created Finnish national music even had a Hegelian significance in the minds of early-twentieth-century Finnish writers. But Sibelius's creation was also original in a purely aesthetic sense. As has been often observed, the idea of originality contains two suppositions: firstly, that an original work of art was created through inspiration, and secondly that originality referred to innovation.[3] An original work of art created something that had never been heard or seen before, or, in Merikanto's words, never previously 'heard as such'. Sibelius's work – from the early pieces of his student years to the Seventh Symphony (1924) and *Tapiola* (1926) – was created within the national aesthetic atmosphere described by Merikanto. But this does not necessarily mean that all aspects of Sibelius's output should be understood as expressions of aesthetic originality.

Preceding events

After Finland became an autonomous Russian grand duchy in 1809, the first stirrings of nationalism emerged in a cultural-political movement called 'Turku Romanticism', based in the old Finnish capital in south-western Finland. Musically, Turku Romanticism was characterised by the formation of student choral societies. The idea of student choirs had spread to Finland from Sweden in the early nineteenth century.[4] Later, in the 1890s, student choirs premiered an important number of Sibelius's early choral works. The leading figures in the Turku Romantic movement imagined a choral music that would be sung in the Finnish language. Most of the choir members were Swedish-speaking, however, and consequently unable to sing in Finnish. Turku Romanticism strove to promote the common destiny of Finland and Sweden as a pan-nationalist ideal, and direct artistic attacks against Russia came only later. In 1828 the Turku Academy was moved to Helsinki, where it became the city's university and occupied impressive new buildings designed by the German architect Carl Engel on Senate Square. As a result, the centre of Finnish musical culture shifted to the new capital.

From 1835, the outstanding figure in Helsinki's musical life was Fredrik (originally Friedrich) Pacius. Pacius was a German-born composer, who had received a solid musical education in Kassel under Ludwig Spohr and Moritz Hauptmann. After playing violin for a few years at the Stockholm Court Orchestra, he was appointed to the post of music teacher at the University of Helsinki in 1835. He swiftly took the capital's whole musical life under his directorship. Pacius's most important works were the opera *Kung Karls Jakt* ('King Karl's Hunt', 1851), which vividly upheld the ideal of Finnish–Swedish unification, and the hymn *Vårt land* ('Fatherland', 1848), which later became the Finnish national anthem. To be sure, the tone of Pacius's operas and songs – *Vårt land*, for instance – refers obviously to German Romanticism. Weber, Mendelssohn and Spohr are the composers who are most easily associated with Pacius's works. This does not, however, diminish the immanent national value of Pacius's music, and its importance in the subsequent formation of a Finnish musical style.

Arguably the most important symbolic event in the development of Finnish national identity in the nineteenth century was the publication in 1835 of the national epic, the *Kalevala*, a collection of folk tales transcribed and edited by Elias Lönnrot. The *Kalevala* had a strong national significance especially for Finnish-speaking Finns, because it was believed to present evidence of the long cultural history of the Finnish people. Nowadays, the *Kalevala* is more often seen as an essentially literary work of Lönnrot's own creation, rather than an ethnographically genuine collection of folk poetry. This does not detract, however, from the volume's tremendous formative influence on Finnish artists, writers and musicians. The earliest orchestral work to use subject matter drawn from the *Kalevala* was Filip von Schantz's *Kullervo* overture of 1860. Schantz's overture was premiered at the opening celebration of the New [Swedish] Theatre in Helsinki on 28 November 1860, when the theatre orchestra was conducted by Schantz himself. Though Schantz's work depicts its subject with characteristically bold and sombre gestures, the general style of the overture is again close to that of German models, rather than announcing a distinctively Finnish musical voice. Later on, *Kalevala* motives were used by Robert Kajanus, the founder of the Helsinki Philharmonic Orchestra. The most well-known of Kajanus's orchestral works is the symphonic poem *Aino* of 1885. *Aino* was clearly steeped in Wagnerian late Romanticism, but, significantly for the genesis of Sibelius's *Kullervo*, the work ends with a section in which a chorus is added to the orchestra.[5]

In studying the formation of a Finnish musical style, it is important to remember that musical compositions were not simply objects of aesthetic contemplation, but live performance events that became vital points of focus for national expression. Pacius's *King Karl's Hunt*, for example, inspired Helsinki's musical circles mostly on account of its sense of occasion. Similarly, his hymn *Fatherland* would not have achieved its status outside Helsinki's academic circles had it not been taken up and popularised by the singer Bror Broms. On his concert tours, which extended throughout the whole of Finland, Broms sang *Fatherland* theatrically, dressed in the costume of a Finnish farmer in a hay field. It was against this background, of music as an increasingly intense form of cultural-political practice, that Sibelius's work first emerged in the early 1890s.

The two music cultures of Helsinki
In 1885, Sibelius became a student of the Helsinki Music Institute (nowadays known as the Sibelius Academy). At this time, Helsinki's musical culture was characterised by a schism between the city's two leading musical personalities, Martin Wegelius and Robert Kajanus. When Wegelius founded his Music Institute in 1882, he hoped to promote himself as the leading figure in the capital's musical life. His ambition, however, was seriously challenged when Robert Kajanus, who was ten years younger, founded the Helsinki Orchestral Society (from 1914 known as the Helsinki City Orchestra, and nowadays the Helsinki Philharmonic) in the same year. During the following years, Kajanus succeeded in establishing his orchestra as the first permanent

professional orchestra in Finland, but at first Wegelius's students were not permitted to visit the orchestra's concerts. Superficially, the conflict between Wegelius and Kajanus was simply a personal struggle for power. On a deeper level, however, the conflict concerned the fundamental aims and objectives of Finnish musical culture in Helsinki. As musical personalities, Wegelius and Kajanus were deeply opposed. Before Wegelius devoted himself to music, he had taken a Masters degree in aesthetics at the University of Helsinki. Kajanus, in contrast, had not even graduated from the high school. Both men were ambitious, but their aspirations were totally different. As a result, the Music Institute and the Orchestral Society were very different kinds of organisations. Before the Music Institute was founded, the Finnish Senate had proposed the establishment of a multidisciplinary Academy of Arts. The plan did not materialise, and Wegelius founded his specialist School of Music instead. Kajanus's orchestra did not have a correspondingly 'official' origin, but was driven rather by Kajanus's own personality. Nevertheless, a greater sense of national feeling was identified with the orchestra than with the Music Institute, not least because it was the orchestra that performed the first great national works in Finnish music.

All of the students at the Helsinki Music Institute were required to attend lectures in music theory and history, mostly given by Wegelius himself. (Later, Sibelius taught Finnish-language music theory at the Institute for a few years.) Wegelius wrote several textbooks for his institute, and this, in fact, represented the beginnings of academic writing on music in Finland. In 1885, Kajanus founded an 'Orchestral School', which aimed to educate practical musicians for the orchestra. At a later stage, he added music theory to the school's curriculum, but the school's aims were still much more practical than those of Wegelius's Music Institute. At his best, Kajanus could enchant an audience with his dramatic interpretations. A sense of the vivid intensity of his conducting can be felt when listening to the recordings he made of Sibelius's music in London in the early 1930s. His conducting technique, however, was clumsy, as witnessed by the fact that he was not a very good accompanist. The fact that the Orchestral Society took a leading position in Helsinki's musical life was the cause of great bitterness for Wegelius. At the same time, however, his Music Institute played an important role by providing recitals of chamber music, lieder and solo repertoire.

Adapting the title of August Halm's famous book, *Von zwei Kulturen der Musik* (1913), we can therefore speak of two different music cultures in Helsinki at the end of the nineteenth century. The one was Wegelius's educational system, and the other was Kajanus's more practically oriented promotion of orchestral music. Fundamentally, the difference between Wegelius's and Kajanus's activities reflected the difference between the two leading genres of instrumental music, namely the string quartet and the symphony.

Kajanus represented the culture of the symphony, and Wegelius the culture of the string quartet. Since its birth in the eighteenth century, the symphony was the genre of the rising bourgeoisie. It was extrovert music, relatively 'easy' to understand, and to a certain extent it was possible to use external effects in a symphony (well-known examples are the 'Turkish' percussion effects of some Viennese classical symphonies). In contrast, the string quartet was the genre of connoisseurs and experts. The music was more introverted in the sense that it presupposed a greater degree of 'listener competence', that the listener focused on the rational discussion between the instruments.

Sibelius shifted decisively between these two genres as he discovered his own individual musical voice. The first public performances of Sibelius's music, namely the Theme and Variations for string trio and the String Quartet in C♯ minor, took place in 1888–9 in the Student Concerts at the Music Institute. These works were partly exercises in voice-leading techniques, and partly independent free compositions. Sibelius wrote a handful of 'bolder' and more romantic works during his student days, but did not dare show them to Wegelius. When Sibelius sent his first two orchestral works, the *Ballet Scene* and the Overture in E Major, to Kajanus from Vienna in 1891, he became a symphonic composer almost overnight. But it was ultimately *Kullervo* that marked his breakthrough as a national composer, and defined the national-romantic musical style he was to develop for the first part of his professional career.

During spring 1892, the newspapers in Helsinki reported that Sibelius was writing a new, revolutionary work for two soloists, chorus and orchestra. On the day that the work was to receive its premiere, 28 April 1892, the press coverage was massive, including Merikanto's famous presentation of the work that contained the passage cited above. Swedish-language newspapers were also inspired, even if the work's subject was drawn from the *Kalevala*. Sibelius's move from Wegelius's Music Institute to Kajanus's Orchestral Society was not merely an external step. In the process, Sibelius effectively unified Helsinki's two musical cultures. In abstract terms, *Kullervo* was a synthesis of the 'cultures' of the string quartet and the symphony. On the one hand, it was an 'academic' work, difficult to understand, and its harmony and orchestration were regarded as especially challenging (if also sometimes ham-fisted). On the other, it was a national musical work, full of dynamic energy and drive. *Kullervo*'s premiere was perhaps one of the most important national events in Helsinki before Finnish independence in 1917. The audience in the university's Great Hall was full to capacity, and the work received a tremendous reception.[6] Reports revealed that the performance was far from perfect. Sibelius was not an experienced conductor, and the part of Kullervo's sister was too low for the soloist, Emmy Achté. This did not prevent *Kullervo* from becoming a national myth. In subsequent writings on Sibelius and the history of Finnish music, the premiere of *Kullervo* was mentioned time after time as the birth of a new, truly Finnish music. Sibelius withdrew the work from the public domain after only five performances in Helsinki in 1892 and 1893. But for the Finnish national consciousness it was nevertheless an event of crucial importance, which played a fundamental part in Finland's growing national musical culture.

Sibelius's crisis after *Kullervo*

After *Kullervo*, Sibelius underwent a profound creative crisis. His attempt to compose a Wagnerian music drama entitled *Veneen luominen* ('The Building of the Boat') foundered, and the work never materialised. The opera's musical material was later recycled in some sections of the *Lemminkäinen* suite (1896–7), though precisely how the opera's motifs and themes were reused remains unclear. We know only that the suite's best-known movement, *Tuonelan joutsen* ('The Swan of Tuonela'), was based on the opera's planned overture. Erik Tawaststjerna explains Sibelius's crisis in largely biographical terms.[7] Sibelius travelled to Germany with his Wagnerian brother-in-law, the composer and conductor Armas Järnefelt, but he was disappointed with the superficial nature of the Wagnerian cult that he encountered in Bayreuth. He also realised, Tawaststjerna argues, that the creation of music drama on an epic Wagnerian scale lay outside his capabilities and that his destiny was rather to be a composer of orchestral music and songs. Sibelius's operatic plans were also flawed by their subject matter. Sibelius prepared the libretto in collaboration with Jalmari Finne, a popular author of both children's and serious novels as well as an influential figure in Finnish national culture, but the completed text was criticised by Kaarlo Bergbom, the director of the Finnish Theatre, for being too lyrical.[8] Arguably, however, Sibelius's crisis can also be explained in terms of social history.[9] Both Tibor Kneif and Carl Dahlhaus have maintained the idea that the sociology of music should be a theory of musical genres.[10] This broader approach offers interesting possibilities for social historical research, even if recent scholarship has tended to focus on narrativity, microhistory, and the biographies of 'ordinary men' over more structuralist approaches.

Kullervo does not belong to any well-established genre. In some senses it is a choral symphony of the type represented by Berlioz's *Roméo et Juliette* (1839) or Mahler's Second Symphony (1894). In the nineteenth century, however, the choral symphony did not have such a pregnant status as the ordinary symphony or the piano sonata. Berlioz's choral symphonies, like those of Liszt, were attempts to solve the generic problem of programme music rather than to create a new independent musical genre. The real programmatic genre of late Romantic music was the symphonic poem; significantly, Sibelius used the term 'symphonic poem' ('sinfoonillinen ru- noelma') in the advertisements for the premiere of *Kullervo*. This generic context seems to have had a significant impact on the reception of *Kullervo*. *Kullervo* was a 'flat-out' work for both Sibelius and his audience, but for Sibelius it was not possible to continue along that same line.

After his student years in Berlin and Vienna, Sibelius's place in Finnish musical life remained uncertain. Being a teacher did not suit him. The com- poser Otto Kotilainen described how Sibelius sometimes let his students go out to enjoy good weather, and how he once lectured about an overtone series he had heard in a field.[11] In 1896 Sibelius applied for a job at the Uni- versity of Helsinki, following the retirement of the former lecturer of music, Richard Faltin. After considerable confusion, and an administrative scan- dal, the post was offered to Kajanus, but a year later Sibelius was awarded a state pension sufficient, for a short while, to enable him to concentrate on composition.[12] But Sibelius's position as a composer at the forefront of Finnish musical life remained ambivalent. Sibelius's creativity presupposed experimentation, and inevitably led to conflicts between the young com- poser and the expectation horizons of his audience. In Helsinki's cultural life, there was a great demand for simple patriotic songs, but not so much for more challenging and original artistic creations. Sibelius's operatic projects offer compelling evidence of this imbalance. If *The Building of the Boat* did not succeed, Sibelius's second operatic work, a one-act piece entitled *Jungfrun i tornet* ('The Maiden in the Tower', 1896), was performed in a soirée organised to support the Orchestral Society. In such circumstances, a large-scale operatic work could only be a utopian dream. Helsinki had not had a permanent opera house since 1879 (the Finnish Theatre had a 'Song Department' from 1873 to 1879). Though it might have been possible to perform *The Building of the Boat* a few times on special occasions, opera as a genre did not offer Sibelius much opportunity for future development within Finland.

Sibelius's greatest artistic achievements during the years immediately fol- lowing the premiere of *Kullervo* were symphonic poems, but even these were characterised by continual withdrawals and corrections. The *Lemminkäinen* suite, for example, appeared in two versions. The *Karelia* music (1893) and *Finlandia* (1899) have become familiar parts of the repertoire only in their modified versions. *Skogsrået* ('The Wood Nymph', 1895), which re- mained practically unperformed until the 1990s, is symbolic in many ways of Sibelius's compositional practice in the 1890s. We should not imagine that the way forward for Sibelius was obvious. Rather, Helsinki's musical culture was generally in a state of confusion. On the one side there were the highly artistic ambitions of Sibelius (who, since *Kullervo*, had become a national hero), and on the other side there were many other kinds of national and aesthetic horizons towards which Sibelius sought to orient himself.

The harshest, and the most bizarre example of a conflict between Sibelius's aspirations and critical expectation was Karl Flodin's critique of the second version of the *Lemminkäinen* suite. Flodin described the work in *Nya Pressen* on 2 November 1897 as being excessively 'sombre' and difficult to understand. *Lemminkäinen*'s bold, contemporary musical style clearly did not meet with Flodin's implicit demand for light, entertaining and positively inspiring national music. Flodin's review, in line with much other documentary evidence, proves that Sibelius did not necessarily satisfy every critical preconception of how Finnish music should develop. Though there was a sense of great national expectation in the air, Sibelius actively created a new idea of a Finnish national music, rather than simply fulfilling preconceived notions of what it might be. As stated earlier, nationalism was essentially a modern phenomenon, and Sibelius, as a composer in crisis in the 1890s, was in many respects a true trailblazer.

The 'national concert'

Concerts and other public musical events were of critical importance in the development of a Finnish national music in the nineteenth century. Such performances were largely responsible for the rise of national composition, inspired by the Turku Romantics or works such as Pacius's *King Karl's Hunt*. It is often difficult to say whether performance or composition was more significant for the formation of a national musical tradition in Finland. *Kullervo* is a good example. The work's premiere was a major national event, adorned with laurel wreaths as symbols of national pride. At the same time, the work itself became a myth in Finnish music historical consciousness: unheard after the run of early performances, *Kullervo* nevertheless represented, in the critical imagination, the birth of Finnish music. In the late nineteenth and early twentieth centuries, some great performers became national heroes whereas others did not. Sometimes it is difficult to say exactly why a particular performer succeeded in becoming a national hero. Robert Kajanus, for example, continues to be regarded as a figure of national and historical importance, whereas his younger colleague, Georg Schnéevoigt, who was also a great conductor of Sibelius's works, has never achieved a similar status.

Some performers who became national heroes achieved their status through success outside their home countries: Jenny Lind, 'the Swedish Nightingale', or Ole Bull, the Norwegian violinist, for example. Other performers gained their status by being popular within their home countries.

The Finnish singer Abraham Ojanperä is an example of a performer who seldom appeared outside Finland but was nevertheless a highly influential figure in Finnish musical culture at the turn of the twentieth century. Ojanperä sang the title role in *Kullervo*'s five performances in 1892–3. On occasions, the artistic level of a national musical figure might not be very high. Bror Broms, for example, was very popular in Finland in the mid-nineteenth century, but was evidently not a great singer even by local standards: contemporary reviews complained continually about the hoarsening of his voice during concerts. Ida Ekman and Abraham Ojanperä were particularly successful singers in Finland, who had an immensely important role in performing the songs of Sibelius, but neither of them were primarily opera singers. Ida Ekman's career was closely related to that of her husband, the pianist and conductor Karl Ekman. The Ekman recordings of Sibelius's songs, made around 1906, still have a dramatic aura of authenticity, and it is widely supposed that Sibelius regarded Ida Ekman as his favourite singer. Besides being a famous performer, Ojanperä was also a prominent teacher at the Helsinki Music Institute. He taught several generations of singers and formed an important link in the Finnish vocal tradition that stemmed from the days of such singers as Johanna von Schoultz, Alma Fohström, Filip Forstén, and Emmy Achté (the mother of the famous singer Aino Ackté).

In discussions of nineteenth-century concert culture, the kinds of concerts that form the basis of our current contemporary concert life, namely symphony concerts and Lisztian recitals, are often privileged. Public musical events in the nineteenth century were, however, much more varied than we often tend to assume. Pot-pourri concerts, for instance, were immensely popular in Paris and London.[13] In such events, piano virtuosos played anything from Mozart sonatas to arrangements of famous sections from Wagner's music dramas. Specifically 'national' concerts likewise need to be considered as a specific sub-genre within nineteenth-century musical culture. National concerts to some extent resembled pot-pourri concerts, but they also shared similarities with virtuoso recitals and soirée-like events where theatre, music and even the visual arts were combined. Though they evidently took different forms in different countries, it is possible to outline at least some of the characteristic traits of the national concert in Finland. Several factors were typically mixed in this kind of event. Ideally, the national concert had four aims: aesthetic ambitions, national aspirations, social participation, and entertainment. Theatrical elements were often combined with music, as happened when Bror Broms performed Pacius's *Fatherland*. A very good example of a Finnish national concert was the premiere of Sibelius's *Karelia* music in 1893. The work was composed as background music for a series of national *tableaux vivants* performed at a feast of the Viipuri students' union. The patriotic and social aims of the event were clear: the idea of the evening was to support the public education of the Viipuri region. The event was also intended simply to provide entertainment: the evening was restricted to a relatively small academic group, whose members enjoyed food and alcohol during the course of the performance. The fact that the music has survived as a concert suite, however, underlines the seriousness with which Sibelius treated the project. For both audience and composer, the music remained of central importance.

The present national hero

Those concerts in which Sibelius himself conducted his symphonies and other large-scale orchestral works constituted a special kind of national event. He conducted almost all the premieres of his orchestral works in Helsinki, the major exceptions being the Seventh Symphony, which Sibelius premiered in Stockholm, and *Tapiola*, which was premiered by Walter Damrosch in New York. In a sense, one can claim that the premiere of the First Symphony in 1899 solved the compositional crisis described above. It arranged the various musical genres within Sibelius's output thus far in hierarchical order, and gave rise to the notion that Sibelius's 'musical life story' could be heard primarily through his symphonies. The symphony concert was a fulfilment of the idea of a national concert. It combined nineteenth-century aesthetic ideals, especially the apotheosis of symphonic monumentality, and national aspirations.

As a symphonic composer, Sibelius is clearly a national hero in Finland, but the nature of his status has changed during the twentieth century. As early as 1891, Ilmari Krohn (pseudonym 'Cis'), a composer and one of the founders of Finnish musicology, wrote that in Sibelius's early String Quartet in B♭ major, 'the composer has described the struggles of his country, both the inner and outer; when shall the hymn of victory sound?'[14] Far from sounding especially national, to modern ears the work rather gives the impression of being written by a conscientious student in the German classical-romantic style. Krohn's expectations were so high, it seems, that he was unable to perceive the classical tone of the quartet, but wanted to label the work as national – at any cost, as it were. The premiere of *Kullervo* and the major symphony concerts that followed during Sibelius's career had a common factor: Sibelius as conductor. In fact, Sibelius's physical presence was one of the determining features of these concerts, up to the mid-1920s when Sibelius began to withdraw from public appearances. Sibelius himself was an object of immediate idolisation: he was very much a living force in Finnish musical culture. Sibelius's physical presence could provide material for further studies in the fields of psychology and philosophy. Here, it is sufficient to note that this phase of Sibelius's idolisation culminated in the official events surrounding his fiftieth birthday. In December 1915, Sibelius conducted a whole series of concerts where, for instance, the first version of his Fifth Symphony was premiered. A 'citizens' dinner' was organised after the festival concert on 8 December, before which the concert audience spontaneously formed a guard of honour in the university's great hall.

The Hegelian view

Sibelius's role as a national hero was closely bound up with a Hegelian view of national history. According to Hegel, national historiography contains two important ideas: first, the nation's history is stretched back to the Middle Ages or even further into the past in order to demonstrate the ancient roots of the national culture; second, the nation's history is seen as a steady evolution of the national spirit (*Volksgeist*). Finnish musicology started almost from scratch in 1899, when Ilmari Krohn defended his doctoral thesis *Über die Art und Entstehung der geistlichen finnischen Volksmelodien* ('On the Nature and Origins of Finnish Spiritual Folk Songs'). At the same time, a group of young scholars and critics, including Otto Andersson, Karl Flodin, Aksel Törnudd, and Heikki Klemetti, began to study the history of Finnish music. Their view of history was strongly nationalist and had a clear Hegelian tone, un-surprisingly since the greatest Finnish historians, philosophers and national ideologists of the nineteenth century, such as J. V. Snellman, Z. Topelius and Y. S. Yrjö-Koskinen, were all Hegelians. Finnish musical scholarship pro-ceeded along the two principal lines of Hegelian nationalist historiography. First, it sought to demonstrate the antiquity of Finnish musical culture as evidenced by the study of medieval Finnish manuscripts. Klemetti and his younger colleague Toivo Haapanen studied old medieval chant sources that were collected in Helsinki University Library. In 1924, Haapanen defended his doctoral dissertation on Finnish medieval neume fragments. Second, Finnish musicology attempted to support the development of a national culture towards the attainment of genuine cultural and political indepen-dence. In Finnish scholarship, Sibelius gained the position of a Hegelian 'great man', whose early national works, especially *Kullervo*, embodied the breakthrough of Finnish art music in the strong sense of the word. Nowa-days, the image of such 'great men' is often ridiculed, but it is worth re-membering that, for audiences in the 1890s, Sibelius's music was strikingly fresh. In Aristotelian terms, great men were a dynamic force in history. Their importance in late Romantic musical culture is undiminished by the fact that their canonisation has been increasingly criticised from the perspec-tives of New Musicology or feminism. Though it is impossible to cite all the texts that mention Sibelius as the creator of a truly Finnish national music, three milestones in Finnish nationalist historiography can be easily identified: the concert booklet written by Karl Flodin for the Helsinki Philharmonic Society's European concert tour in 1900,[15] Erik Furuhjelm's Sibelius biography (1916),[16] and Toivo Haapanen's book *Suomen säveltaide* ('The Music of Finland', 1940).[17] At the same time, Otto Andersson, professor of music and folklore at the Åbo Akademi University of Turku, made a start in source studies concerning Sibelius's music.[18] Flodin's booklet was the first text to mention Sibelius as the Hegelian great man of Finnish music history. The extent to which this text influenced early foreign writings on the composer remains open to speculation. Furuhjelm based his biography on the nationalist idea, and as a Swedish-speaking author he emphasised the connection between Sibelius's music and Finnish nature rather than the *Kalevala* aspect of Sibelius's work. For Furuhjelm, landscape offered a more neutral metaphor for national identity than language, given the contemporary Finnish political context. Haapanen was a versatile musician and scholar who, during his short but intensive career, worked as principal conductor of the Finnish Radio Orchestra and as professor of musicology at the University of Helsinki after Krohn. Haapanen's writings, part of which appeared outside Finland (such as in Guido Adler's *Handbuch der Musikgeschichte*, 1924), represented the culmination of nationalistic Finnish music historiography. In 1940, in *Suomen säveltaide*, Haapanen claimed that 'the result of the young composer's first adventure in the Finnish mythology [*Kullervo*] was no more and no less than the birth of true Finnish music'.[19] It is interesting to see which traits of Sibelius's music were treated as specifically 'Finnish'.

Nationalist music historians defined Finnish music in a variety of ways. An affinity with folk music, the representation of the *Kalevala* and Finnish landscape, and the expression of the national feelings of the Finnish people were the features most often mentioned as the essence of national art. Often, such writers were content with vague, indefinite statements, a trend that attests to the diverse range of contemporary ideas about Finnish music. Whichever characteristics were mentioned, however, the statements always pointed to the same (contentious) conclusion, that Sibelius's music was an original art, free of any conscious use of folk music or other calculated nationalistic effects. A central trait in Finnish nationalist historiography was the conviction that Sibelius's originality did not only depend on his great talent, but was also the result of a centuries-long evolution. Correspondingly, nationalism in music was regarded not merely as a superficial phenomenon, but as something more profound. National identity was constructed as an innate musical characteristic that could not be achieved by learning or by false intellectual means. And, like political independence, musical nationalism was symbolically perceived as immortal; a permanent state that would endure for ever in the Finnish cultural imagination. Music's national tone did not necessarily hinder its international recognition. On the contrary, national character was needed in order to achieve international status. In the dialectic between nationalism and cosmopolitanism, the positive opposite of Finnish music was a universal but still nationally coloured art, best represented by Austro-German music. From the Finnish point of view, such music was not inimical, even if Austro-Germans often regarded the music of the so-called European periphery as 'local' in the pejorative sense of the word.

A national institution: the Eighth Symphony as a social-historical problem

In the 1920s, Finnish musical culture reached a new state of institutionalisation. At first, this process was characterised by the foundation of the main musical institutions in the capital (the founding of the Finnish Opera in 1911 followed the Helsinki Music Institute and Orchestra in 1882). Later, such institutionalisation spread both socially and regionally. City orchestras were founded (Turku 1927, Tampere 1929), and the Radio Orchestra was founded in 1927. Several 'folk conservatoires' were founded by Armas Launis in Helsinki, Vaasa and Pori. During this period, as musical culture spread nationally, Sibelius began to withdraw from public view. His seventieth birthday in 1935 is usually mentioned as his last public appearance, but he gave a radio interview in the early 1940s and received guests at his villa, *Ainola*, almost up to the end of his life. This withdrawal from the public sphere did not affect Sibelius's lofty national position, but it changed its character. Earlier, the composer's national importance had been based on his physical presence in Finnish musical life. Now, however, he became a national institution. He was no longer the struggling hero; his position, like that of other institutions, was secure, defined, as it were, by the common agreement of other people.

It is no accident that the first institutions to be associated with Sibelius's name were founded just before the Second World War. The Sibelius Quartet was founded in 1933, and the Sibelius Academy adopted its current name in 1939. After the war, they were followed by Sibelius Weeks, Sibelius Museums, Sibelius Violin and Conducting Competitions, Finlandia House and so forth. The institutionalisation of Sibelius's position was also a necessary condition for the birth of formal Sibelius scholarship. The earlier nationalistic and literary-inspired activity continued up to Haapanen's *Suomen säveltaide*, but in the 1930s it began to be accompanied by an interest in the structures and forms of Sibelius's symphonies. In 1936, the composer and musicologist Eino Roiha published an article in which he presented new British Sibelius analyses, and in 1941 he defended his analytical doctoral dissertation, *Die Symphonien von Jean Sibelius*. Scholars began to understand Sibelius's historical position outside its Finnish context. The British author

Cecil Gray saw Sibelius as the saviour of music amid the turmoil of modernism, and compared Sibelius's achievements even to those of Beethoven.[20] Roiha, for his part, compared Sibelius with Paul Hindemith.

Sibelius's compositions after 1919 (that is, after the final version of the Fifth Symphony) mirrored the general development of Finnish musical life. The Sixth Symphony was the last orchestral work that was premiered under the composer's baton in Finland. The planned premiere of the Eighth Symphony was scheduled to take place outside Finland: the initial commission came from Boston, and performing rights to the premiere were reserved by London and Leipzig. Sibelius's withdrawal into the 'silence of Järvenpää' certainly offered the composer much-needed peace and solitude, but it also drew him away from the focus of Finnish musical culture. In fact, there was no longer such a single point of focus, which would have enabled Sibelius to maintain a comparable presence to that which was possible before Finnish independence. The riddle of the Eighth Symphony has fascinated scholars up to the present day. Most research on the subject has so far concerned musical sources and the biographical facts of Sibelius's life.[21] Here I shall mention only three social-historical facts that possibly explain the work's fate. First, Sibelius lost his influence in the musical culture that surrounded him. Instead, he was faced with estrangement. As Sibelius withdrew to *Ainola*, the musical culture around him expanded and established itself. This made Sibelius uncertain, and, to an extent, he lost touch with the musical culture of the years that preceded the end of the First World War. Even though those years had been stressful, the new, post-independence epoch was an era of even greater uncertainty. Second, Sibelius's national symphonies no longer occupied a unique place in Finnish musical culture. The national symphony concerts conducted by Sibelius and, to a lesser extent, by Kajanus lost their importance and were replaced by a more general symphony-concert culture. In this context, the premieres of the Seventh Symphony and *Tapiola* can almost be seen as attempts to escape from Finland. The domestic importance of concerts conducted by Sibelius himself had greatly diminished. The performances of major works outside Finland could have inspired Sibelius again, but in reality they made him ever more anxious. Third, up to the 1920s Sibelius had been regarded as the trailblazing figure in Finnish national art, and the single-handed creator of Finnish national identity in music. Now he had to react to the changing context of Finnish musical culture. Opera did not suit his character, and the symphonic poem was taken over by a younger generation led by composers such as Aarre Merikanto and Uuno Klami. Sibelius found himself in a deadlock that must have felt all the more stressful because it was a socially oppressed situation. The image of Sibelius as national hero, and of the formation of a Finnish musical style, had finally begun to enter the domain of historical myth.

2 Vienna and the genesis of *Kullervo*: 'Durchführung zum Teufel!'[1]

GLENDA DAWN GOSS

When Jean Sibelius, approaching the age of twenty-five, left Finland in October 1890 to study in Vienna, he had never composed anything on a symphonic scale. His teachers, Martin Wegelius in Helsinki and Albert Becker in Berlin, had restricted him to the writing of contrapuntal exercises and chamber works. The young man's experience with orchestral instruments was largely defined by his knowledge of the strings, although he had produced a few works for brass septet. *Kullervo*, an enormous five-movement symphony for full romantic orchestra, baritone and soprano soloists, and male choir, marked an astonishing technical as well as creative breakthrough. Because *Kullervo* was begun in Vienna, attention has naturally fallen on that city and the composer's experiences there as marking a creative turning point for Sibelius. His love for Aino Järnefelt, to whom he had just become engaged, his awakening to the *Kalevala*, Elias Lönnrot's great collection of epic poetry, and the music he heard have been considered the most important shaping events of those months. Yet Vienna itself was one of the most intellectually fertile cities of the nineteenth century, and the composer's teeming sketchbooks and lively correspondence strikingly attest to its milieu. When studied against their Viennese background, these sources suggest a far richer experience for Sibelius in the Austrian capital than has been portrayed. They also lead to some surprising insights about the most important product of that stay, Sibelius's first symphony, *Kullervo*.[2]

The psychological atmosphere

From the moment he set foot in Vienna, Sibelius responded powerfully to its atmosphere. His reactions are registered unmistakably in letters to Aino and to Martin Wegelius.[3] The day he arrived, Sibelius wrote to his former teacher, 'I always thought I was melancholy, but now I believe God made me for joy.'[4] A few weeks later, in November, the dreariest month of the year in Finland, Sibelius was again writing joyfully to Martin, 'Just imagine, for example, Vienna in the afternoon sun and warm, a letter from Aino, and letters of recommendation and money from you.'[5]

[22]

Yet even though Vienna initially delighted Sibelius and left him 'mad for joy', the city soon affected him in other ways. He was sobered by disappointments, among them the disastrous violin audition with Jacob Grün in early January 1891. The composer's self-confidence suffered further injury under Karl Goldmark's criticism: he bridled when told that his themes were 'contrived' (*machen*, as he complained to Wegelius on 12 February 1891), and he came to appreciate how arrogant the Germanic mind could be in its conviction of its musical superiority, patronising condescension towards outsiders, and stereotyping of men from the Nordic countries as barbarians. (Yet Vienna was notorious for devaluing even its own. At the end of 1897, on visiting the city where Mozart created his greatest works, Mark Twain interviewed one of its citizens who famously claimed that 'there exists no Austrian who has made an enduring name for himself which is familiar all around the globe'.)[6] How a man deals with such experiences shows his mettle, and Sibelius showed that his was made of steel.[7]

The Viennese fascination with death and the pervading sense of impending doom further affected Sibelius.[8] The year before he moved to the city, the suicide of Crown Prince Rudolf in January 1889 had sent shock waves through society, the most notable of a number of suicides that rocked the public. But death was far from a new Viennese preoccupation. Almost exactly a century earlier Mozart had written to his father, 'I never lie down at night without reflecting that – young as I am – I may not live to see another day.'[9] At the end of the nineteenth century a sense of foreboding tinged much of Austrian literature and, within weeks, imbued Sibelius's letters. Writing to Wegelius in changed tones at the end of November 1890, the young man complained that he felt as though he had lost himself: 'Where could Sibelius be?' he asked plaintively, continuing, 'I think someone is standing behind me. Could it be Death which lies in wait?'[10] Even his musical manuscripts reflect the mood: on a page of his Vienna sketchbook on which he had notated *Kullervo*'s opening theme, Sibelius jotted down the names of his father and uncles – and the dates of their deaths.[11]

That, in the full flush of youth, Sibelius's breakthrough was a work culminating in its hero's death bears full witness to the atmosphere in Vienna. Leading Austrian intellectuals, including writers Hermann Bahr (1863–1934) and Arthur Schnitzler (1862–1931) and later, the Vienna-born Anton Ehrenzweig (1908–66), a lawyer and painter, propounded a link between the death instinct and a high level of creative inspiration. In the thinking of these men, death provided 'a simulacrum of creativity . . . the dark underside of life, which every artist, like a Baroque saint, must conquer'.[12] No Baroque saint, Sibelius nevertheless expressed his fear of death again and again over his (ironically) long life, suggesting that, for him, the psychological duel with death – or its personification, the Devil – released great artistic energy. Vivid traces of these duels remain in his sketches: across two folios containing *Kullervo*'s first-movement development section, Sibelius fiercely scrawled the words *Durchführung zum Teufel* ('Development to the Devil').[13]

During the months Sibelius studied in Vienna, the city was home to Sigmund Freud (1856–1939).[14] No direct personal connection, of course, has been found between the composer and this creator of modern psychological thinking. Rather Freud's importance here lies in symbolising the various issues related to sexuality swirling through late-nineteenth-century society, from the psychological importance of mythic archetypes and the role of women in society to an increasingly open psychological and sexual awareness, all of which converged in his work. Sibelius's very choice of the *Kullervo* story, which portrays a mythic figure from Finland's national epic, the *Kalevala*, reflects these concerns. Kullervo is endowed from youth with Herculean power, but is sold into slavery after his family is supposedly killed by murderous relatives. Yet unknown to him, the family has survived, a circumstance that leads to the young man's unwitting seduction of his own sister. Kullervo avenges the violence against his clan with yet more violence, but ultimately returns to the place of incest to take his own life.

In Sibelius's symphonic rendering, the illicit love scene between brother and sister comprises the most powerful movement (the third) as well as the longest (591 bars) of the entire symphony. This emphasis marks a startling departure from previous interpretations of the *Kullervo* story. Only twice before had *Kullervo* received musical settings: Filip von Schantz's *Kullervo* overture (1860) and Robert Kajanus's *Death of Kullervo* (1881), neither of which portrays the incestuous brother–sister relationship. Among other intellectuals in Finland, writers such as Fredrik Cygnaeus, Zachris Topelius, and Aleksis Kivi as well as artists Robert Ekman, Carl Eneas Sjöstrand, and Axel Gallén had either avoided the incest scene or minimised it, preferring to interpret the drama's turning-point as the moment when Kullervo breaks his knife on a stone baked into his bread loaf by Ilmarinen's cruel wife. Sibelius, by contrast, omitted the knife scene. He shifted the drama's turning-point instead to the brother's seduction of the unknown maiden. This critical movement, which dramatically sets the stage for Kullervo's suicide at the symphony's end, culminates with 'Kullervo's Lament', the hero's anguished outpouring as he realises that the maiden to whom he has just made love is his sister. In more than six hundred compositions Sibelius never composed a more powerful psychological drama than he did here. It beggars belief that the origin of such a work in Vienna, the home of modern psychology, should be merely coincidence.

Approaching *Kullervo* from its Viennese context also helps to explain why Sibelius chose to compose so flawed a subject into music at a time when he was deeply in love. Other *Kalevala* figures, such as the Finnish Orpheus

Väinämöinen, or even the *Kalevala*'s Aino, whose story provides drama and conflict, offered equally viable possibilities for realising the national goal of a Finnish music. Yet it was Kullervo's life and death that Sibelius chose for his first symphony. In his hands *Kullervo* became a symbol of the forbidden sexual freedom so widely explored at the end of the nineteenth century and the hero's death – through suicide – a terrible but necessary price. Whether that death should be interpreted as a Freudian expurgation of guilt for its composer's excesses or a saintly simulacrum of creativity is ultimately of less importance than the great imaginative energy it so clearly unleashed.

Musical experiences

The vital importance of the music Sibelius experienced in Vienna has occasioned considerable comment.[15] What emerges from the study of the young composer's music manuscripts and letters is the fundamental importance of the symphonists Beethoven and Bruckner, particularly their Ninth and Third Symphonies respectively; affinities with the music of his Vienna teachers, Karl Goldmark and, to a lesser degree, Robert Fuchs; and Sibelius's discovery, in the midst of Austro-German music-making, of the importance of his Finnish musical and literary heritage. In addition, a close reading of the letters Sibelius wrote to Aino Järnefelt, the newly recovered original letters written to Martin Wegelius, and materials in the Sibelius Collection of the Helsinki University Library disclose other, previously unremarked, musical events that have an important bearing on *Kullervo* and its genesis.

Sibelius's principal reason in going to Austria was to learn orchestration. This desire runs like a leitmotif through his letters. What has not been realised is that in addition to the instruction with Goldmark and Fuchs, there was another kind of instruction: within two weeks of his arrival, Sibelius had purchased a copy of François-Auguste Gevaert's *Neue Instrumenten-Lehre* from a Viennese bookshop.[16] Gevaert (1828–1908), composer, teacher, and former music director of the Paris Opéra, was in 1890 Director of the Music Conservatory in Brussels. His *Traité général d'instrumentation*, written in 1863 and revised in 1885 as *Nouveau traité d'instrumentation*, was highly regarded in the world of music as a 'monument of universal knowledge'. It was also widely translated, there being even a Russian text by Pyotr Ilyich Tchaikovsky. Sibelius purchased the German translation by the respected Dr Hugo Riemann, distributed (propitiously, in view of his own future publishing relationships) by Breitkopf und Härtel.[17] When on 13 November 1890 Sibelius wrote to Wegelius that he had purchased the text, he added that he had already 'gone through it'. Thereafter, he seems to have proceeded

Example 2.1 Sibelius, *Kullervo* Symphony, III (bars 262–74)

from its study to the more pragmatic solution of persuading various instrumentalists to play for him (as he described to Wegelius on 11 January 1891). Although Sibelius made no annotations in his copy of Gevaert's text, there are various physical signs of its use – smudges, smears, ossified crumbs – above all, in the sections on winds and percussion, instruments with which Sibelius had the least experience. His shortcomings continued to plague him in *Kullervo*, where he was still writing impossibly long passages for wind players and, worse, faulty transpositions.

Yet Sibelius could write with great sensitivity for these instruments. In *Kullervo*'s third movement the composer created an instrumental love duet (bars 262–77) for Kullervo and his sister, who have not yet realised that they are related, and which functions as a kind of 'secret' communication to Aino, his beloved. Rather than selecting clarinets or violas, instruments that have often been associated with love and lovers, Sibelius chose oboes (Ex. 2.1).

Significantly, Gevaert had observed of the oboes, 'The basic feature of their essence is open-heartedness. No other instrument expresses itself with such convincing truth.'[18] Some months later, Sibelius expressed himself in similar terms to Aino, 'You will see that my new opus will make a furore with you, Angel. Everything in it is Truth.'[19]

Gevaert's section on percussion instruments, from its varying types of timpani tremolos to the array of instruments described, is of particular value for understanding Sibelius's notation, which shows very little in common with the notational styles of either Goldmark's or Fuchs's manuscripts. Gevaert includes castanets, for instance, which he describes as 'native Spanish'.[20] Sibelius introduced castanets into one of his compositions for the first time in the wake of his Gevaert study – in the *Scène de ballet*, completed in Vienna in the spring of 1891. Although one of the least Sibelian-sounding works imaginable, thanks to those castanets, in the context of Gevaert's remark their presence points to yet another ingredient that, in the magical alchemy of Vienna's special ambience, worked its golden spell on Sibelius. Unlike Berlin where Sibelius had studied the previous year, Vienna had an extraordinary mix of cultures, including an

Example 2.2 Ilmari Krohn, *Paimenessa* (bars 1–9)

authentic folk culture. It is clear from correspondence with Aino (although not with the Swedish-speaking Wegelius) that in Vienna Sibelius awoke to the value of Finnish-language culture for his own creativity. This awakening has been attributed to two things: the young composer's love for Aino, who like the rest of her family was an ardent Fennomane (supporter of the Finnish language), and nationalistic currents back home, where the more progressive voices were calling for a national art through such mouthpieces as the newly founded newspaper *Päivälehti*.

As important as these influences were, they fell on fertile soil during Sibelius's months in Vienna. There, authentic folk culture had tradition and value. Both Goldmark and Fuchs encouraged their pupil to explore his 'barbaric' roots. Sibelius received confirmation of their perceptions in the delighted reactions of a Bulgarian cellist, 'Diminico', for whom he composed melodies, 'all Finnish folk melodies or based on them'.[21] And he heard its effects in the music around him – in Mascagni's new opera, *Cavalleria rusticana* (which he heard on 14 April 1891) and even in the Turkish march in Beethoven's Ninth Symphony, which, as Sibelius told Aino on 13 April 1891, moved him to tears only three days before he began *Kullervo*.

In the midst of these congruences, there came into Sibelius's hands a song with Finnish text, *Paimenessa* ('Shepherd's Song'), by his compatriot Ilmari Krohn (1867–1960), which Sibelius described as 'really good'.[22] His enthusiasm could hardly have come from the harmonic content, which is conventional in the extreme. What is fresh is that, in composing the song to Finnish words, Krohn had found a means to capture the flexibility of the language. Some bars are lyrically rendered to the syllable 'tuu'; others are declamatory and quite recitative-like. A prevailing time signature of 5/4 now and then gives way to other metres, enhancing the overall elastic treatment of the Finnish text (Ex. 2.2).

Sibelius would soon put all of these ideas to powerful use in *Kullervo*. Already in *Drömmen*, completed in January 1891, Sibelius had created a pliant setting of Johan Ludvig Runeberg's Swedish-language verses as supple and as melancholy as any rune song (Ex. 2.3).

Example 2.3 Sibelius, *Drömmen* (bars 1–5), *Jean Sibelius Works*, VIII/2

Although its metre is 3/4, phrasing shapes the beats into groups of five, while the generally narrow melodic contour emphasises a single mood. Now here was Krohn's *Paimenessa*, demonstrating how successfully similar ideas could be used with Finnish texts. Long before the celebrated contact with the *Kalevala* singer Larin Paraske, Sibelius was finding models to guide him in his musical settings of the Finnish language.

Literary influences

Among the non-musical impulses essential to the creation of *Kullervo*, literature is unquestionably of greatest importance, and the literature of clearest significance was the *Kalevala*. Elias Lönnrot's great anthology of traditional folk poetry had been collected from singers and shamans in the eastern parts of Finland and Archangel Karelia in the early years of the nineteenth century. Not surprisingly, Sibelius's portrayal of the *Kalevala*'s most tragic figure, with its powerful settings of Finnish poetry in two movements, was closely identified from its first performances with Finnish national identity and with the movement later called Karelianism.[23] Critics hailed the composition as the 'first living Finnish musical work' and 'Finnish from beginning to end'. Yet to limit *Kullervo* to Karelian neo-Romanticism is to proscribe its fullest meanings. For while Sibelius created a work that was surely 'Finnish from beginning to end', he was simultaneously depicting other vistas from the greater world of ideas in the landscape of his first symphony.

One of the most important was realism. Even before he wrote to Aino about his 'discovery' of the *Kalevala*, Sibelius described the poetry of the

Finnish-Swede Runeberg, which he was composing into Op. 13, as 'the most real of everything I've read up to now'.[24] On Christmas Eve 1890, telling Aino of plans for a new orchestral work, he explained, 'I'm thinking of doing the thing much more "realistically" than before. In realism there is also much music.'[25] Such comments abound throughout his Vienna letters.

Sibelius's interest in realism coincided with broad intellectual concerns of the 1890s. In the first issue of *Moderne Dichtung*, published in Leipzig, Vienna, and Brno on 1 January 1890, Hermann Bahr had proclaimed a kind of literary manifesto:

> We cannot promise the kingdom of heaven. All we wish is that falsehood should cease, falsehood propounded daily from podium, pulpit and throne, for such things are ugly and evil. We have but one law, and that is the truth as perceived by each of us. To that we are beholden. It is not our fault if the truth is harsh and brutal and often cruel and scornful. We are obedient to its demands alone.[26]

The preoccupations with realism and naturalism (whose distinctions Bahr soon refined in his essay 'Die Überwindung des Naturalismus', 1891) were not limited to writers and by no means limited to Austria. Realism had emerged in Finnish literature and in Finnish art during the 1880s with works of Minna Canth, Juhani Aho, and Akseli Gallen-Kallela.[27] And throughout Europe the writings of Émile Zola had been exercising the minds of intellectuals for some time. Sibelius was fully aware of these trends. On 13 December 1890 he observed to Aino that Zola's *Thérèse Raquin*, which he had just read, was quite to his taste. On 9 April 1891, only days before *Kullervo* was begun, he wrote: 'Have you read anything by Zola? This man I like.'[28] And after having read Gottfried Keller's *Der grüne Heinrich*, Sibelius even compared himself to Zola: 'It's a shame that I no longer read such fine literature without comparing myself to Zola and consorts.'[29]

Zola's realism often bristled with frank and blatant sexuality, especially *Nana*, the realist novel about a Parisian prostitute that its author once described as a 'poem of male desires'.[30] When on 1 April 1891 Sibelius sent to his beloved a copy of Pushkin's *Eugene Onegin*, he urged her not to read everything that Zola had written, and above all, to avoid *Nana*. Perhaps the reason was that, like most young men, Sibelius had accumulated his fair share of sexual experiences. In a surprisingly frank letter to Wegelius he confided his desire to be 'clean' for Aino and worried over whether he might have become impotent, while during the last stages of completing *Kullervo* Sibelius reassured Aino about his health, promising that he had been vaccinated for her sake.[31]

Although most discussion and interpretation of *Kullervo* has dwelled on its quintessential Finnish traits and its composer's response to Karelianism, Sibelius's personal anxieties and preoccupations at the time he created the work as well as his many literary enthusiasms point to unsuspected features of this vast score. They help to explain why, intertwined with the more obvious Karelian neo-romanticism – the opening horn call (played by the strings), the rune-like lullaby of the slow movement, the chanting of Finnish texts in the third and fifth movements – there occur some of the most shockingly realistic moments that Sibelius ever composed. The first soloist to sing the Sister's role, Emmy Achté, even years afterwards remarked on the startling realism of her part.[32] And few can miss the graphic orchestral portrayal of the scene of forbidden love between the brother and sister, fifty-three bars (third movement, bars 274–327) as explicit as Shostakovich's notorious passage from *The Lady Macbeth of the Mtsensk District* that so offended Stalin some forty years later.

There was no precedent for such stark, erotic realism in Finnish music. But there was in Finnish literature: Juhani Aho's *Yksin* ('Alone'), a novella in which the main female character 'Anna' is a stand-in for Aino Järnefelt, with whom Aho, like Sibelius, had fallen in love. *Yksin* contains a potent mix of realism, romanticism, and some of the most vivid eroticism that had ever been set forth in Finnish writing.[33] And into this mix Aho stirred one ingredient more – a motto in the typical trochaic tetrameter of the *Kalevala*: 'Soitto on suruista tehty / murheista muovaeltu' (Music was from grief created / From great sorrow has been moulded). Sibelius reacted powerfully to *Yksin*, which he read the December before he began *Kullervo*. On Christmas Day 1890, he wrote to Aino of the disturbing effect the novel had on him. The following day he took up the subject again. Claiming that he was now reading the *Kalevala* fluently and in *Yksin* understood Finnish better than ever, he asserted: 'These words from the *Kalevala* (Soitto on murehista [sic] tehty) are magnificent.'[34] He immediately followed these claims with one of the most elaborate statements he ever made about the *Kalevala*, beginning with, 'In my view the *Kalevala* is completely modern. I think it is only music, theme with variations.' The circumstances show clearly, if somewhat incongruously, how reading Aho's *Yksin* decisively heightened the composer's desire to read Finnish fluently, and perhaps even triggered his new-found appreciation of *Kalevala* poetry. Nor did the fascination with *Yksin* diminish. Fully two months later, Sibelius was writing, 'Yesterday I read *Yksin*, I think, for the tenth time.'[35] The subject of the novella continued to surface in his correspondence, even as much as a year later. It is thus especially ironic that *Yksin*'s motto, 'Soitto on suruista tehty / murheista muovaeltu', which Sibelius so admired and which inspired him to articulate his much-quoted viewpoint of the *Kalevala* as 'theme with variations', is not found in the *Kalevala* at all. It comes from the first poem of the *Kanteletar*, Lönnrot's collection of lyric poetry (first published in 1840–1). The poem is not even original folk poetry, but rather an invention of Lönnrot, which he entitled

'The Kantele' and appended to the collection. No wonder Sibelius found the *Kalevala* 'completely modern'. Yet the lines' inauthenticity as folk poetry does not diminish Sibelius's perception of them as genuine ancient verse, nor alter their apparent effectiveness for him as a fitting epigraph for Aho's novella. Rather they confirm how powerful a stimulus literature – from whatever source – could be for this composer.

Sibelius discovered *Yksin*, although no monument to nineteenth-century literature, at a time and in a city where its realism, Romanticism, and eroticism were thoroughly part of the *Zeitgeist* and furthermore were closely bound up with his own life. Whether in a brash attempt to outdo a rival or from appreciation of Aho's artistic ideal of synthesis or, as seems more likely, from the combined pressures of the prevailing social and intellectual atmosphere, Sibelius, in turning for the first time in his life to the *Kalevala* for musical inspiration, treated the mythic *Kullervo* with a psychological realism and a luscious eroticism that had never previously been applied to Finland's epic poetry. Even more important, the *Kullervo* Symphony marks the first time that Sibelius worked out on a grand scale what is arguably his most outstanding and valuable trait: the ability to find the unity within apparently dissimilar elements and to work them into a convincing whole. If his ambitions outran his abilities – how else to describe the daring combination of Germanic symphony with Finland's Swedish-language male-choir tradition to portray a psychologically disturbed and suicidal mythic archetype speaking an exotic tongue, the whole portrayed in glorious sounds ranging from the ravishingly sensuous to the starkly primitive and glowingly Slavic? – nevertheless the first crucial step had been taken on a journey that would lead to undisputed masterpieces of symphonic literature.

Sibelius's months in Vienna have rightly been identified as crucial for his development as an artist. For a mind that is open and seeking, as Sibelius's letters and music manuscripts undeniably show his to have been, inspiration and ideas frequently come from unaccountable and altogether unexpected sources. The whole range of surviving primary materials shows that, in addition to all the usual reasons given for the richness of Sibelius's study in Vienna, many more influences, musical, psychological and literary, entered the composer's imagination at a critical time in his creative life. Above all, *Kullervo*, the great early achievement that was the finest product of this stay, splendidly and often movingly illustrates how Sibelius learned to weave whole cloth from the full array of human experience.

PART TWO

Musical works

3 Pastoral idylls, erotic anxieties and heroic subjectivities in Sibelius's *Lemminkäinen and the Maidens of the Island* and first two symphonies

STEPHEN DOWNES

The encounter of a young, virile, and heroic male subject with an alluring, seductive yet dangerous feminine 'Other' is an archetypal mythic narrative. It is an erotic topos that is repeatedly evoked in musical works of the Romantic and early modern period and is a crucial one in the early symphonic works of Sibelius. *Lemminkäinen and the Maidens of the Island*, Op. 22/1 (1895–6), based on the episode in the *Kalevala* recounting the hero's adventures with the young virgins of the island, is one of the most overt of such examples. Features of this work relate closely to the musical character of the first two symphonies, so that the apparently 'absolute' symphonies can persuasively be heard to engage with a similar nexus of meanings.

In the symphonic poem, first performed in 1896 but withheld from publication until after the Second World War, an opening horn call is followed by an *Allegro* first-subject group initially rather plaintive and yearning but which leads to playful, pastoral figures characterised by an increasing rhythmic energy over harmonic stasis. A long held tonic Eb pedal finally moves to Db, which enharmonically turns to C♯ (Fig. H; bar 127) as a contrasting thematic character is introduced. When the accompaniment turns to pulsating syncopated chords in strings and woodwind a surging melody in the cellos reaches the 'heights of sensuousness'.[1] Two features drive this increasingly erotic thematic process. First, the expansion of arabesque decorations into ardent melodic turns. In the first thematic group the melodic turn figure had been rather discreetly, even apologetically introduced by the triplet decorative tailpiece to the oboe melody (Fig. A; bars 13–16). It then became a central melodic aspect of the playful, dance-like woodwind figures from Fig. C (bars 44ff) and the more sentimental cello melody at Fig. D (bars 63ff). In the erotic *melos* of the second group the cello theme twice moves off its lingering initial note B via a decorative turn figure before building to emphatically and expansively expressive turns. The second crucial feature is now brought into play: at the highpoints in the melodic curve the repeated use of a striking expressive harmony is produced by the combination of a pungent dissonance with a diminished chord (Ex. 3.1). The sequential climaxes that emerge in this thematic group, a marked contrast to the harmonic

Example 3.1 Sibelius, *Lemminkäinen and the Maidens of the Island*, op. 22/1 (bars 140–4).

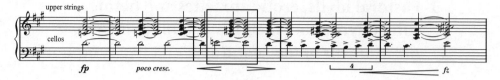

Example 3.2 Wagner, Sirens' chorus, *Tannhäuser*, Act I

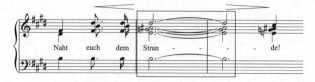

stasis of the opening, recall the world of Wagner's *Tristan und Isolde*, which of course became a *locus classicus* of erotic musical expression in the late Romanticism and early modernism of the 1880s, 1890s and beyond.[2] However, the harmonic character of this depiction of the hero's mythic-erotic encounter with young women resembles perhaps more strongly the chorus of Sirens in the first act of *Tannhäuser*, the seductive effect of which is largely achieved by the repeated use, at the top of each melodic wave, of the same dissonance that distinguishes Sibelius's theme. Already by Wagner's early maturity the diminished chord itself is rather atrophied, but the suspended dissonance imbues the harmony with erotic yearning and hints of danger (Ex. 3.2). Another feature linking the musical depiction of Lemminkäinen's adventures with the maidens with Wagner's Venusberg scene is the fact that in both pieces the seductive song and the dance elements are unified. Wagner does this by using in both the same heightened diminished chords: in the Sibelius the turn figures generate similar unity between the sensual song and the dance (in its restatement the latter acquiring, according to Tawaststjerna, a 'Dionysian perspective', as it is 'caught up in a frenzied and furious pace').[3]

The seductive second theme in *Lemminkäinen* builds to a *forte* arrival on a second-inversion dominant of the home Eb, part of the main structural process of the work, which can be heard as a prolonged and repeated attempt to reach conclusive final resolution in the tonic. This exemplifies what Timothy Jackson has identified as Sibelius's preoccupation with 'crystallization' – the gradual formation of ideas towards revelatory conclusion – and its failure, 'entropy', both of which, he argues, 'possess sexual connotations related to [Sibelius's] concept of Woman' and the 'hero's libidinal struggle' for 'sexual union'.[4] In the work's climactic cadence 'crystallization' seems to be achieved, but in the final bars the harmony of the pastoral material is curiously coloured by an insistent Db (the flattened seventh of the tonic Eb), the pitch which underpinned the transition from the static tonic of the first-subject group to the chromatic sequences of the erotic 'Other' second group. This suggests that in the encounter with the young maidens the hero's self-assurance has been undermined. Lemminkäinen has been called the 'Finnish Don Juan' and Strauss's tone poem (1888–9), which Sibelius heard in its first performance in Berlin, is often cited as a likely model for *Lemminkäinen and the Maidens of the Island*. Both suggest the interaction of formal archetypes and multi-movement contrasts within a single span and they have similar narratives of desire for erotic possession leading, in ad-mittedly different degrees, to the hero's undoing. Sibelius's First Symphony, although 'not explicitly programmatic', as James Hepokoski has noted, is based upon 'allusions' to and 'deformations' of the 'standard *per aspera ad astra* symphonic plot'[5] and therefore clearly invites interpretation accord-ing to the interrogation of heroic paradigms. In particular it can again be heard to invoke a narrative of the delights and dangers of the hero's erotic adventures.

Sibelius began work on the First Symphony in Berlin at the end of April 1898 (he initially envisaged a programmatic symphonic work based on Heine or Juhani Aho's *Panu*). According to Tawaststjerna, with this work Sibelius 'altered course away from the Wagnerian and Lisztian sirens' which had so seduced him in preceding years, and the overriding influence dis-cernible is now Tchaikovsky.[6] Timothy Howell hears a 'Tchaikovskian' ten-dency to 'indulge' in 'seductive melody' as at root a possible reaction against Austro-German symphonic style.[7] For Lionel Pike, similarly, the First Sym-phony 'relies primarily on the "sound of music"', on foreground, surface features rather than the 'unifying connections' in background 'symphonic logic', so that it is an 'immature' work in which 'dramatic gestures, brass crescendi, sensuous chromatic harmony, long dominant ninths, big tunes and harp arpeggios abound in place of the intellectual underpinning'.[8] All of which contrasts with Tawaststjerna's opinion that 'the impression is one of organic continuity'[9] and Jackson's view that the symphonic ideals of Brahms and Bruckner are more potent backgrounds for the work.[10] Indeed, delight in sensual moments and allusions to processes that suggest organic teleology can be heard to coexist in this work, and this has significant implications for its narrative meaning.

In his discussion of Tchaikovskian resemblances in the symphony Joseph Kraus hears a 'profound integration of motive and tonal plan'. On the large-scale level of tonal structure Kraus identifies a 'main polarity' of E and C which is operative across all four movements of the symphony. In the first movement the E minor–G major relation provides 'early cohesion', but the finale provides clarification of the overriding E–C tonal pair. To demonstrate this Kraus provides a Schenkerian reading of the voice-leading structure across the complete symphony with the E♭ and C keys of the middle movements functioning as massive embellishing chords under the structural top voice G. As an aspect of unity at the motivic level Kraus identifies recurrent reinterpretations of a 5–♯5–6–♭6–5 chromatic motion and the associated pattern of resolution of a diminished seventh to a six-three chord. He is particularly concerned to show how this feature, so often cited as the symphony's most 'Tchaikovskian', differs from the Russian model.[11] Veijo Murtomäki, who by contrast with Kraus hears the E–G relationship as the work's 'fertilizing agent',[12] rather unconvincingly hears the 5–♯5–6–♭6–5 chromatic motion as the basis of the whole development section, as an extension of his preoccupation with 'organic' unity across different levels of structure. Tawaststjerna, amongst others, has plotted the recurrences of this chromatic figure and its associated decorated diminished seventh, what Hepokoski calls the '*Pathétique*' dissonance (a 'sonic ideogram', or 'object for contemplative immersion'[13]) in many of the symphony's themes. This chromatic 'signature' of the symphony has, however, yet to be deciphered completely, for none of these readings offers a fully detailed and convincing interpretation of its function in the work's poetic and psychological content. Hepokoski does find the main tonal argument psychologically suggestive: 'the symphony's reigning idea seems to be that its musical narrative is obliged to unfold in a negative tonic, E minor – apparently an "imposed" or oppressive tonic subjugating a more "ideal" tonic, G major . . . the E minor is a persistent, unwelcome distortion of a desired, but unsustainable, G major'.[14] Those commentators, however, who have a rather singularly organic focus underplay the significance within this tonal structure of encounters with the sensual seductive sound of the chromatic signature. Wagnerian precedents are again powerful. Tarasti points to the E–G as comparable with the A–C 'double tonic complex' of the first act of *Tristan*.[15] This music drama is of course most famous for its fetishization of a sensuous chromatic chord. The similarly erotically charged chromatic signature of Sibelius's symphony is, furthermore, another version of the 'Sirens' chord from the Venusberg music of *Tannhäuser*. Sibelius's first movement might then be read as the opening act in an erotic symphonic drama that moves between the demands of the organic and the orgasmic. The music's sensuous moments and narratives of seduction leading to possession or destruction interact with and 'deform' the symphonic paradigms of development, synthesis and resolution.

After a slow introduction prophetically evocative of lament, an *Allegro energico* of enormous vitality launches the main sonata structure. It needs little expertise in the nineteenth-century romantic symphonic tradition to hear this as the music of a young, full-blooded and heroic subject. The

Example 3.3 Sibelius, Symphony no. 1, I (bars 41–3)

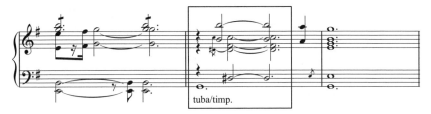

theme's urgent dotted and triplet figures lead to the first statement of the chromatic signature, thrusting up from a timpani and tuba thunderbolt (Ex. 3.3). From the start, however, the tonality is ambiguously poised between E minor and G major and over a G pedal the music's virility declines rapidly after the chromatic chord. Sequential waves rebuild the energy until a restatement of the hero's opening gesture subsides once more, this time to F♯ major (the dominant of the dominant). The modal harp chords and bird-like woodwind figures of the transition evoke a mythic–pastoral world whose idyllic possibilities are emphasised by the *Tranquillo* tempo and slow harmonic pace at the start of the second group. This leads to a stretto and crescendo evocative of the initiation of an orgiastic dance, but it is cut dramatically short by a curt staccato resolution on a unison dominant to end the exposition. The development is somewhat over-reliant on obvious sequential patterns until the erotic–idyllic tone returns (Fig. L) with two amorously intertwining solo violins recalling not only the lyrical stasis of the second theme but also the emotive diminished harmony of the chromatic signature. The development then builds in swirls of chromatic contrary motions that move to an early example of the kind of seamless flow into a 'foreshortened' recapitulation which have long been admired in Sibelius. There is no firm cadence in the tonic to mark the point of recapitulatory return: instead, the heroic first-subject group is gradually reasserted to build to the high point of the movement, a *fff tutta forza* resolution of the chromatic signature which recedes even more rapidly than in Ex. 3.3 to a string of sinking resolutions (Ex. 3.4). The moment is suggestive of the romantic sublime – of the resolution of previously apparently intractable dissonance – as its diminuendo leads to the reprise of the lyrical second thematic group over the movement's final structural dominant of E minor. There is little that is triumphantly victorious about the closing section, however, where brass chorales are coloured by whirling chromatic scales recalling the development's wildest moments, and the final bars consist of a deathly, angry gesture in low registers over which lamenting pizzicato chords state the G–E minor third. All the energetic striving of the hero's first subject has led only to doubts about his future success.

Example 3.4 Sibelius, Symphony no. 1, I (8 bars after Fig. W)

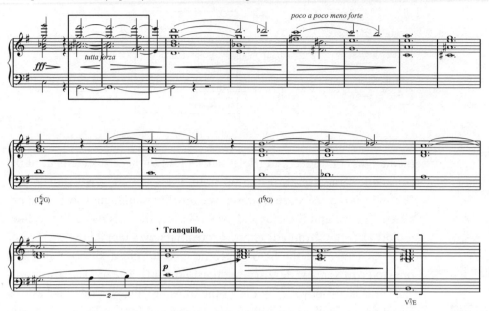

The *Andante* second movement is in E♭, a move down a semitone from the key of the first movement which Tarasti hears as 'a transference or sinking into the timelessness of the mythic world', the timbre (harp and horn pedals) reinforcing the impression of entering into a different heroic realm, a 'Finnish Valhalla'.[16] The movement, which may be read as a rondo or as an 'arch' form,[17] begins *semplice* with a theme whose rather sentimental expression offers a new emotional variant on the chromatic signature. There are stormy and passionate contrasts, but the '*Waldweben*' scene clearly relates this to the idyllic world of the first movement's second theme.[18] Its erotic quality lies in the insistent play on a sinuous chromatic inner line which may be taken as a variant of the Russian *nega*, indeed this is one of the symphony's ideas that has often been labelled as especially indebted to Tchaikovsky, Glazunov and Borodin.[19] The line's rise and fall is suggestive of hopes succeeded by frustration, and in later versions its harmonies evoke exotic luxuriance (♭VI, C♭) followed by troubled anxiety (iv, vi; A♭ and C minor), all in tonalities which are hinted at by the chromaticisms in the initial version of the theme (Ex. 3.5).

The C major main section of the third movement, which may be described as a 'primitivistic variant of a robust Viennese-Classical scherzo',[20] is a naive, energetic, Siegfried-like subject, galloping unknowingly towards his destiny. The E major Trio marks a return to the sound-world of a 'dream-like idyll'.[21] Its horn theme is based upon a new variant of the chromatic

Example 3.5 Sibelius, Symphony no. 1, II (bars 3–9)

signature, now gently yearning and leading to fluttering flutes but also somewhat minatory drum rolls – if this is a communion with nature's forest
murmurs then it is a fragile and vulnerable spiritual state. By now the narrative of the symphony has become clearly focused on repeated encounters
with the chromatic, dissonant signature chord. (In *Siegfried* the augmented
triad plays a comparable role, first associated with the testing of the young
hero, then with fear which he had not yet felt until his erotic encounter with
Woman in the figure of the awakening Brünnhilde.) The key relationships
(C and E) and contrast between physical boisterousness and quasi-erotic
reverie strengthen the *Siegfried* resonances: is this a stage towards sexual
union of the young hero with the feminine Other as celebrated in Act 3
scene iii of Wagner's music drama, an erotic re-energising of the young
hero, a redemption from his trials of the opening movement?

The symphony can be read as a post-*Siegfried* or post-*Tannhäuser* work
in which the young heroic subject ultimately meets his demise. The last
movement, which Jackson reads as a sonata-form design with an overarching telos towards a final 'catastrophe' and closure,[22] begins with an emphatic, impassioned return of the melody of the slow introduction to the
first movement which Tarasti sees as a 'mythico-musical device', an example of paradigmatic structuring outside symphonic, developmental time.[23]
This return suggests we are about to embark on a rewriting of the narrative
of the first movement after the experience of pastoral idylls and naive energies in the two middle movements. The *Allegro molto* which follows begins
dynamically over the dominant, B, but for Murtomäki the transition from
the introduction to the main *Allegro* is tonally unstable, contributing to his
reading that the 'kinetic forces' of the whole symphony build towards the
finale's lyrical second theme.[24] After a sudden jolt on the dominant, this
'goal' theme is introduced, over a long pedal, in the submediant, C major.
It is based on yet another variant of the chromatic signature and builds to
heights of *affettuoso* expression. The subsequent recapitulation of this theme
begins on a rather insecure second-inversion A♭ (enharmonically the major
mediant, symmetrically balancing its first appearance in C) and becomes
more chromatically unstable (Ex. 3.6), but this moves to a further, more

Example 3.6 Sibelius, Symphony no. 1, IV (bars 354–62)

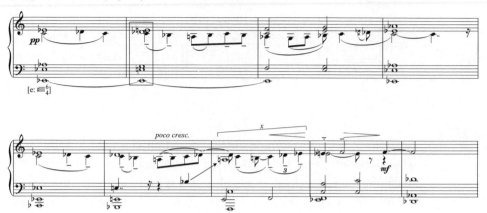

stable statement at the climactic arrival of the long awaited final structural dominant: the theme thus acquires a potentially redemptive function, as closure and completion are now most ardently anticipated.

The first movement built to a moment suggestive of the transcendental possibilities of the post-Kantian romantic sublime, the resolution of traumatic equilibrium as heard in heroic–symphonic paradigms of Beethoven and Bruckner.[25] In the finale's move towards the apparent apotheosis of the lyrical second theme this sublime experience returns – but it is now more deeply troubled. At Fig. X the resolution seems to be accomplished but the symphony's most highly dissonant chord marks a moment of catastrophe from which chromatic sequences precede a plunge into turmoil (Ex. 3.7). In response, the defiance of the symphony's final gestures, as E minor is restored, seems desperate and fatally weakened. For this Finnish Don Juan the bliss of erotic union or victory of 'possession' of the Other is not achieved: as in Strauss's tone poem, the apotheosis is problematised and resolution undermined, provoking a formal and teleological crisis.[26] This confirms that though the sublime is 'intended to evolve from the beautiful, but then to raise it by several powers', and is 'structured by the investigation into beauty', it leads to 'violation of conventional charm, and disruptions to our normal comfort'.[27] The searing dissonance at the moment of catastrophic collapse is actually a distortion of the previously so seductive chromatic signature chord. This undermines the upper line's attempts to return to the saving beauty of the second theme: indeed the turmoil of the collapse had been hinted at by the preceding chromaticised version of the theme (compare Ex. 3.6 and 3.7). This is a move to the 'modern sublime' which for Lyotard is an experience in which the unrepresentable idea of the coincidence of pleasure and pain means that the solace of good forms is denied. This may

Example 3.7 Sibelius, Symphony no. 1, IV (Fig. X, bars 405–11)

lead to 'neurosis', 'masochism', melancholic nostalgia for lost narratives or, as here, a futile attempt, 'in spite of everything', to reimpose the strivings of the 'will'.[28] The waves of emotion in the climactic recapitulation of the *affettuoso* theme, where the symphony's recurring turn idea achieves its most ardent form, suggest the 'oceanic feeling' of blissful union or Freudian regression to the Mother; but the catastrophe plunges the hero into the dark waters of a turbulent Tuonela or casts him off the coast of the isle of the dead.

The finale is subtitled 'Quasi una Fantasia'. The discontinuities, secret coherences and hidden meanings attributed to the dream had long become characteristic elements of the 'externalization of the inner life of the composer' attributed to the fantasia genre.[29] In his sketches for this movement Sibelius wrote the name of Berlioz and we might therefore recall the *Symphonie fantastique*'s troubled narrative of the relationship with the beloved muse, embodied as its *idée fixe*, an 'Episode from the Life of an Artist' which moves from reveries and amorous passions to the madness and delirium of nightmares. The attempt to possess the desired feminine Other, the hero's muse, leads to catastrophic consequences. As Lisa Rado writes, 'ultimately the perilous strategy of incorporating a construction of the opposite sex within the creative self or mind involves a level of anxiety and crisis that recalls nothing less than the powerful and terrifying experience of the sublime'. In such experiences Romantic notions of 'empowerment', of 'interjection', 'ecstasy' and 'transport', are replaced with 'despair', 'panic', 'collapse' and 'engulfment'; the loss of heroic, subjective authority leads to hyperbole, irony, nostalgic yearning, or a masochistic desire to repeat the pain of the encounter.[30] Sibelius would have known the psychological exploration of the encounter with the desired 'Other' in Knut Hamsun's *Hunger* (1890) where, struggling to find the inspiration to write, the wandering, desperate man of the streets becomes deluded and deranged, and 'She' who may become his Muse is pictured in his imagination as either a mythic princess or as destitute and debased as himself.[31] One also thinks of the three images of the feminine depicted in Munch's *The Women* (1894): pure beauty, sexual threat, and sinister wraith line up with increasing proximity to a darkly despondent male figure. The undermining of male heroic energies in the encounter with the sirenic, sensuous, yet destructive Other engages not only with this Scandinavian artistic tradition but also with a wider European symphonic legacy: it may, for example, be compared with Brahms's Third Symphony (1883), in which a recollection of the Sirens of Wagner's Venusberg (which may be heard as symbolic of Brahms's own contest with Wagner's seductive music) is part of a protracted interrogation of the heroic narrative paradigm.[32] As at the end of the tragic incestuous narrative of the third movement of *Kullervo* one may hear that in Sibelius's First the heroic quest has 'turned assertiveness against political oppression into a story of sexual trauma that threatens the stability of culturally constructed gender roles and their symbolic reflection in patriarchal narrative'.[33]

The Second Symphony, begun in the summer of 1901 and completed the following winter, has, from Robert Kajanus's report on the first performance, through Ilmari Krohn's famous 1945 reading and beyond, often been labelled a 'liberation' symphony.[34] Sibelius was acutely aware of the contemporary political situation (tensions between Finland and Russia were heightened as Sibelius sketched the work) and the burden this placed on Finnish artists. The symphony's 'heroic' apotheosis – for Kajanus a triumphant nationalist vision of the future – concludes the work in a strikingly different tone to the First. Musical analysts, meanwhile, have long praised the 'organic' processes of the first movement, where the exposition of fragmentary material gradually evolves into coherent melodic utterance, formal economy (in particular in the superimpositions and foreshortenings in the recapitulation), and a dynamic tonal structure based on a symmetrical 'axis' of D–F♯–B♭/A♯ (an extension of the mediant relationships often found in nineteenth-century music).[35] To some degree both political hermeneutic readings and analyses in terms of 'organic' teleology are tied to attempts to justify the length and bombast of the finale, which is interpreted as resolving the 'axial tensions' or closing a vast cadential progression initiated in the preceding movements.[36] The symphony's trajectory to final apotheosis seems, after the catastrophe of the First, to revert to the 'Romantic' sublime, where all tensions and disequilibria are ultimately reasoned out. The first two movements, however, continue the engagement with issues of a threatened pastoral idyll and critique of 'heroic' subjectivity that generated the erotic anxieties and catastrophic experience of the sublime in the First Symphony.

Example 3.8 Sibelius, Symphony no. 2, I (bars 11–16)

Example 3.9 Sibelius, Symphony no. 2, I (28 bars after Fig. A)

The opening establishes a gentle, pastoral character with rising string chords and a light dancing woodwind theme over a secure tonic D pedal. Into this apparently Arcadian world the expressively augmented 'echo' in the horns (bars 14–16) sentimentally emphasises the melodic turn figure which forms one of the central motifs in the organic process underlying the apparent fragmentation (Ex. 3.8). This has been called a 'lyricization of preceding neutral material' which 'introduces the lyrical persona'.[37] Significantly, it cadences on E minor, the first suggestion of melancholy and loss. What Tawaststjerna calls the 'pastoral play' then resumes, but only to come to a cadence which is paused and emptied of all but two clarinet notes. After that there is a hollow silence (it is hardly a pregnant pause) after which flutes invert the turn figure over a chromatic line whose Bb offers the first questioning of diatonic D major. The idyll is already shadowed, an elegiac tone intrudes as a deathly voice: 'Et in Arcadia Ego'. The timpani roll that asserts the dominant also now sounds minatory, and above it the flutes trill melancholic, ghostly Bbs and false-relation C♮s. The long violin melody that follows, whether it is labelled a transition or the beginning of the second thematic group, reasserts the subjective–expressive eloquence of turn figures. But its unaccompanied, 'solo' setting marks it as an isolated, vulnerable voice and its ending – slow and mournful in E minor (recalling the melancholic horns of Ex. 3.8) – leads to yet another questioning aporia. The second group continues with yearning string gestures more overtly expressive of a desire for lost idyllic pleasures (Ex. 3.9) and woodwind trills which lead to darkening diminished sevenths. Rising pizzicato string sequences pick up the speed to lead into the final thematic group of the exposition – a bolder theme suggesting F♯ tonal regions, over the return of the opening's rising string chords and urging scales, which leads to the codetta material and the cadence in the dominant, A. This idea has been called a 'masculine' '*thème conclusif*',[38] but though the exposition has an aura of structural 'mastery' its tone is often ambivalent and the teleological control of the heroic paradigm is only partially dominant.

The development is structured as a series of waves, first moving towards a darkened Db, and then more passionately through passages based on diminished-seventh harmony. Bb, the third part of the symmetrical tonal axis, plays an increasingly prominent role and as the high point (at Fig. M) is approached the bass descends through the augmented triad D–Bb–F♯. Now the melodic build-up powers on, based on the previously vulnerable and isolated secondary violin theme, to reach the structural dominant. Superimposition of material, so often remarked on in the recapitulation, already begins here: trills, previously mournfully dissonant in character (bars 39–42) but now diatonic, build from forest murmurs to ecstatic calls to accompany a powerful brass chorale version of the eloquent theme and the cadence in D – all promising the moment when the desired restoration of unity between the subject and nature might be achieved. The superimposition of the playful pastoral woodwind with the yearning secondary theme in the recapitulation perhaps further suggests this reunion through a revelation of their common harmonic aspects. Already in the second bar of the Tempo I, however, Bb had coloured the D major, and the first return of the pastoral woodwind figures, although counterpointed by the expressive subjective solo horn, is also clouded by Bb–C♯–E–G diminished sevenths. The vulnerable 'solo' string theme, which played a prominent role in the final sections of the development, is omitted and the 'masculine' 'closing theme' brings the tonality firmly to cadence in D – but diminished sevenths and Bb continue to haunt the final bars of the movement. As in *Lemminkäinen and the Maidens of the Island*, the subject's pastoral security is unsettled by the quest for desired unity.

The motivic economy, organic process, D–F♯–Bb tonal relationships and above all the fusion of themes in the recapitulation of this opening movement has led to Brahms's Second Symphony (1877) being cited as a possible model. The comparison can perhaps even more usefully be made on hermeneutic grounds. In Brahms's opening movement the idyllic lyrical D major is rather quickly questioned by a dark timpani roll and trombone diminished sevenths. As Reinhold Brinkmann has written, 'the idyllic nature-metaphor' is 'charged with history' and 'highly complex, artistically'. He notes a 'skeptically broken quality to this music . . . bound up with the awareness of an historical loss', so that the 'idyllicizing expresses mourning for a lost possession'.[39] In Sibelius's movement it is possible to hear an attempt to redress or repress brokenness and loss through formal concision, the search

Example 3.10 Sibelius, Symphony no. 2, II (3 bars after Fig. C)

for 'organic' relationships and a certain ascetic control. Sub-surface anxieties and frustrated desires seem to coexist alongside the latent unity which organicist readings so delight in revealing. Contra Adorno's infamous 1938 attack, this then is no conservative restoration of a 'dull', 'rigid' and colourless Nature. Neither does it exemplify what Adorno condemns as an 'asceticism of impotence'.[40] Tarasti has noted three aspects of desire in Sibelius's music: 1) the 'actorial desires' of Sibelius's themes, for example 'masculine virility'; 2) where desire is 'neutralized by a process of sublimation that transmutes it', not in a 'straightforward repression of desire, but rather a stymying, freezing, depersonalization and de-actorialization of it', a 'neutralization of the subject of desire' signified by its absence in an empty landscape; and 3) where the 'category of desire' arises in the moves between 'euphoria' and 'dysphoria'.[41] The first and third are clearly foundational in the First Symphony's catastrophic collapse of the heroic subject's desire to possess the other. The deeply ambivalent first movement of the Second Symphony sits ambiguously amongst all three: the actorial desire is not yet neutralised, for the subject remains a figure of desire in the pastoral landscape, and the closing bars are uncertainly poised between the potential for ultimately euphoric or dysphoric conclusion.

In his national-liberation reading of the symphony Kajanus described the *Andante* second movement in terms of a 'broken-hearted protest', but such desperation could equally be heard in more personal, subjective terms as the transmuting of desire takes a more inward turn. As is well known, thematic ideas for this movement originate in sketches Sibelius made during a stay in Italy in 1901 for a projected orchestral work on the *Divine Comedy*, where they are notated as 'Death singing for Don Juan' and 'Christus'.[42] All these allegorical figures can be seen as internalised within a single lyrical subject,[43] but one, given the underlying dualisms of Eros/Thanatos and Eros/Agape, which is a fractured, even schizophrenic soul. The lugubrious, mythic D minor modal theme is succeeded by 'eruptive' references to *Tristan* which Hepokoski hears as a 'modern-primitivist reworking' of Wagner in which 'erotic desire' is transformed 'into an anguished attempt to writhe free from the prison house of D minor'[44] (Ex. 3.10). At the first crisis point, *Molto largamente*, there is a collapse on a low, deathly *fortissimo* version of the *Tristan* chord. This latest Finnish Don Juan is in a desolate state, condemned by his erotic past. After a long silence the 'Christus' theme appears in radiant F♯ major, but then rugged, unsympathetic bass figures seem to cast aside any promise of redemption. The second half of the movement recapitulates the thematic procession, now beginning with the initial modal theme in F♯ minor and ending with a prolonged, poignant D minor. Just as the movement seems to be subsiding there is a *con forza* scream of defiance or torrent of pain in the strings and the closing pizzicato chords curiously recall the end of the first movement of the First Symphony: we should not yet mourn the hero's death.

The third movement is a Scherzo (*Vivacissimo* in B♭) and Trio (*Lento e soave* in the flat submediant G♭) whose alternation of energy and pastoral idyll parallels the equivalent movement of the First Symphony. It leads, *attacca*, to the Finale. Again comparison with Brahms's Second Symphony is instructive: in both symphonies the vigour of the last movement evokes the romantic sublime in a post-Beethovenian apotheosis, as part of an attempt, across the symphony as a whole, to unite the 'internalizing lyrical and an extensive monumentality'.[45] Sibelius's themes are elemental and resolutely straightforward and the tonal scheme is again based upon the symmetrical mediant or 'axial' relationships: D to F♯ in the exposition, with a long dominant pedal preceding the tonic restitution at the recapitulation which then 'balances' the exposition with D to B♭ and finally turns tonic minor to major. Tawaststjerna hears a defiant heroism from Sibelius: 'in the first movement . . . he broke the norms and challenged them; in the finale he clings fast to them "in spite of everything".'[46] If this is a restoration of order, a resurrection of the mythic hero, then the questioning of the hero's powers, as at the end of *Lemminkäinen and the Maidens of the Island*, or the catastrophic collapse in the face of the erotic sublime, as in the First Symphony, has been evaded or overcome. It is significant, then, that amongst the Italian sketches of 1901 which emerge in the Second Symphony there is material which eventually surfaced in the symphonic fantasy *Pohjola's Daughter*, completed in 1906, in which the hero's suffering at rejection by the maiden, because of his creative failure, is a stage towards a renewal of purpose.[47] It seems, then, that at this time Sibelius was seeking musical narratives expressing an affirmative passage out of traumatic experience. Potent, reinvigorated and apparently triumphant, the heroic subject of the Second Symphony emerges from the desires and laments of the empty pastoral landscape and the anxieties and turmoils of condemnation and solitary confinement as a kind of Nordic *Übermensch* bestriding the Karelian wilderness.

4 The later symphonies

ARNOLD WHITTALL

Beginnings

One way of surveying the history of musical composition in the twentieth century is through consideration of the ways in which the time-honoured aesthetic aspiration to balance innovation and conservation, the individual voice and the common language, was carried forward. The idea that innovation and conservation are wholly opposed in the music of any era is simplistic fantasy, and the reality of an intricate interaction between divergent tendencies affecting form and style, technique and expression, has been increasingly acknowledged by commentators alert to the strategies by which composers – even when they disclaim all conscious intention – manage to exploit that interaction.

For some years after his death, Sibelius was generally regarded as more representative of the long nineteenth century, and of late Romanticism, than of the newly progressive twentieth century, with the implication that the reasons why he was so highly praised by influential critics like Donald Tovey and Constant Lambert were also the reasons why his influence on younger composers was harmful – inhibiting rather than liberating, dedicated to conservation and rejecting innovation. In this context, even Schoenberg's accolade that Sibelius – with Shostakovich – had 'the breath of symphonists'[1] could be construed as a coded warning about the need for music to move beyond such tradition-enshrining categories: and awareness, after 1970, that tonality was showing a new capacity to adapt as well as to survive, increased the conviction that contemporary tonal music needed to avoid debilitating associations with late Romantic idioms and formal strategies.

With the argument, led since the 1990s by James Hepokoski, that Sibelius was perhaps less of a late Romantic, more of a modern classicist, a crucial stage in the reformulation of Sibelius interpretation was reached.[2] As noted above, this new phase emerged in a critical and musicological climate in which the separation of categories – musical from cultural, progressive from conservative, classic from Romantic, national from international, personal from collective – was seen as less satisfactory than the exploration of interactions and syntheses, even if those 'syntheses' seemed to embrace more of ambiguity and instability – hence the 'modern' component – than classical, stable unity of the kind achieved in pre-1830 Vienna.

An indication of how this works for Sibelius, at what is generally perceived to be the point of his breakthrough to full maturity, is provided by the first movement of his Third Symphony, completed in 1907, his forty-second year. Here a C major tonality, and a sonata-form scheme, are the sources of an intensely personal utterance. As the cliché has it, this music could be by no one else: and it is pointless to try to move from hermeneutic perceptions about its character – confident, purposeful, eloquent – to formalist description of the nature of its materials and technical procedures in ways which exclude the former from the latter. Hepokoski's summary analysis is exemplary: as an 'anti-monumental . . . counter-response to Mahler's expansive Fifth Symphony, which he had studied in 1905', Sibelius's Third 'strives to recover both the diatonic melodic fragment and the pure triad as meaningful modern utterances by presenting them in non-normative ways'.[3] At the start of the first movement, a 'diatonic melodic fragment' is offered which combines folk-like directness[4] – nothing could be less portentous – with immense developmental potential, and the work of analysis can begin with pinning down the evolutionary energy of that first seven-bar phrase, in which repetitions, extensions and variations avoid the predictable as easily as they engage listeners in positive expectations of an exhilarating musical experience. When Hepokoski writes of the composer's 'unusual aim – the defamiliarisation of the diatonic and the consonant' and a 'dogged, non-ironized retention of the triadic',[5] he emphasises the modern context of Sibelius's thinking. Nevertheless, listeners a century after the Third Symphony was composed can increasingly rely on familiarity with the music's own particular processes to promote a response which centres on an authentically classical coherence – a coherence so cumulative that moments of maximum contrast, like the movement into second-subject material at Fig. 3, create expectations of contrasted but connected continuation radically different from the proto-modernist disjunctions of late Romantic and expressionist formal alignments.

The long tradition of using the vocabulary of organicism in Sibelius studies is an acknowledgement of this aspect, and the dominance of continuity and cumulation suggests that the music is most 'dramatic' when the risk of harmonic enrichment turning into subversion is admitted. Even Murtomäki, who seeks to stress tonal ambivalence as fundamental, accepts that 'the key relationships of the symphony form a firm net governed by the tonic',[6] and although the role of F♯ in the first movement is felt to be 'disturbing', and not 'totally resolved' until the finale, the character of the first movement's ending, in which the initial, dance-like emphasis is transmuted into hymn-like lyricism, suggests that tonal stability (as an analogy for social cohesion) acquires even more intensity of feeling than the agitated and questing tendencies which it resolves. The 'non-normative' role of the triad is counterpointed by allusions to those essentials of tonal practice which had to remain non-negotiable if the concept of tonality itself was to remain valid.

The opening of the Third Symphony's second movement (*Andantino con moto, quasi allegretto*) embodies a lyricism distinct in manner from that which ends the first movement – not least because it is even more understated. The firmly rooted harmony, swaying rhythm and scalic melodic elements also reinvent the folk-like premises of the first movement's first idea. In the second movement the dance-like generic context is initially more relaxed, less rugged, but the evolving thematic process, as it emphasises darker orchestral timbres and explores greater rhythmic tension between bass and melody (after Fig. 4), prepares for the emergence after Fig. 6 of a short, more solemn chorale-like idea (compare the first movement's coda). The more richly textured recapitulation section then intensifies both the eloquence and sense of slightly easy-going nostalgia, as if a happy experience from the past were being recalled in a doubtful, even sceptical way. The concise, downbeat ending neatly summarises this ambiguity, with the smooth, openly lyrical codetta material in the woodwind intercut with string cadences which unfussily round off the recollected dance. There is more than a touch of the *valse triste* here, and the way Sibelius manages to equate understatement with soulful yet never sentimental expressions of intense feeling is remarkable – and easy to underestimate. The rhetoric of the Fourth Symphony, so often hailed as innovatory and unprecedented, has its roots here.

If the Third Symphony's central intermezzo is subtly introverted, the last movement can seem exuberant and extrovert, with an ebullient, turbulent scherzo eventually giving way to an expansive song of affirmation which breathes stability and fulfilment. There is also an obvious deepening of expression and shift of perspective: the scherzo can be read as a tone poem depicting a ride through a storm-tossed landscape or seascape, the final section as a hymn of thanksgiving for safe passage. In both parts of the movement Sibelius brings off with apparent effortlessness the difficult feat of stating essences at the outset, then unfolding an elaboration (with minimal intervening contrast) which seems as inevitable as it is absorbing. The song-finale is certainly no less dynamic than the tone-poem scherzo, projected forwards by the kind of syncopation that was also fundamental to the middle movement, and using a dialogue between degrees of harmonic rootedness (including bass pedals) and motivic variation which stresses the contingencies of the moment, as well as the integrative logic which ensures that the symphony functions as an organic whole. The cumulative power of the closing stages might seem relatively lightweight compared to the majestically building tensions and explosive resolution of the Fifth Symphony's finale. But it could have been the ending of the Third, and particularly those violin ascents from leading-note to tonic, beginning seven bars after Fig. 20, which was in the composer's mind when he devised the ending of his Seventh.

Perspectives on the classical

Veijo Murtomäki has provided a useful survey of the various ways in which the notion of the classical entered Sibelius studies, and the probable impulse for it, as far as Sibelius himself was concerned, in conversations with Busoni during 1905. Well before Hepokoski introduced his seminal concept of modern classicism, a range of commentators attempted to balance features which include what (with reference to the Third Symphony) Murtomäki terms 'the de-romanticisation of orchestral sound'[7] against the composer's distinctly 'unclassical' observations about writing symphonic fantasies in which he could 'move freely without feeling the weight of tradition', while conceding that he did after all write symphonies: it was simply that 'the concept must be expanded'.[8]

Expanding the concept while constraining the timescale is a process carried forward to quite spectacular effect in the Fourth Symphony. This fundamental tension between opposites has discouraged commentators from pigeon-holing the work as a simple continuation of the Third Symphony's classicising tendencies, and a similar awareness underpins the frequently encountered idea of the work's exemplary confrontation between classicism and modernism. Even if the dark character of the music were more a response to domestic 'misery' – sickness and poverty – than to the parlous state of contemporary music as it was thrown into upheaval in 1909 by Schoenbergian expressionism and atonality, no historian of early-twentieth-century musical developments can resist the kind of contextualisation that characterises Sibelius as defiantly defensive in face of the imminent collapse of those musical and cultural values he held most dear. The implacable yet understated A minor cadence at the end of the Fourth Symphony's finale therefore becomes a declaration of faith, a gesture of absolute commitment to a mode of expression and a means of construction which the earlier movements had shown to be under threat as never before.

The effectiveness of that final gesture is all the greater because it is not grafted on to something alien, or asserted in juxtaposition with materials and processes moving in the opposite direction. The A minor ending is the consequence, and resolution, of a symphonic argument in which an inherent organicism creates stability out of instability, and in which the connectedness which underpins the hierarchic layering of true classical tonality survives, strengthened, any local tendency to formal disruption and discontinuity. No analyst has sought to explore the implications of such thinking with more rigour than Edward Laufer, in support of his belief that each of Sibelius's symphonies 'is concerned with integration of contrasts and with cumulation over the entire span'. Laufer also believes that 'perhaps in no work is this accomplished with such cohesiveness and concentration as in the Fourth Symphony'.[9] Even the exclusion of the tonic note from the first movement's introductory material, and the general avoidance of it as an explicit bass note, before the later stages of the central ('development') section, is not so much an expression of 'doubts' about tonality as a recognition (common to 'Romantic' composers) that tonality can be enhanced with special effectiveness if its most essential aspects only gradually assume centre-stage.

As a skilled symphonic dramatist, Sibelius ensures that the clarification of the tonic A at the end of the first movement goes hand in hand with an atmosphere of reticence and even retreat. This is a very long way from the austere confidence of the fourth movement's conclusion, and while the scherzo (coming second) makes a strong move in the direction of a more active and positive mood, its dissolving ending, avoiding diatonic cadencing in F major, gives priority to the kind of classicism-resisting extended tonality which the third movement then carries over into different emotional territory. 'Brooding' and 'drifting' are two of the adjectives most commonly applied to the opening of the *Largo*, but this basic mood is complemented by the symphony's decisive shift of tone, in hymn-like melodic phrases whose repetitions intensify the sense of building determination and aspiration, of striving to look beyond those domestic miseries. The last of these great melodic surges (from Fig. G) can even be categorised as sublimely overconfident in the sense that it fails to provoke an immediate and complete change of direction for the work, but instead subsides into a final cadence similar to the first movement's: stable in structural terms but dark and depressed in mood.

By beginning the fast finale in the strings from the same octave C♯s with which the *Largo* ended, Sibelius is able to suggest that 'immediate and complete change of direction' in a more subtle way. This finale is indeed a 'classical' response to the introspection and precarious stability of what has gone before, rhythmically lithe and robustly determined, so that the 'tonal drama', and even the 'catastrophe' of an episode that 'loses gradually all sense of a tonal centre',[10] are calculated to propel the symphonic process forwards, rather than decisive gestures of radical disruption. The battle for ultimate resolution and stability may be as hard-won as in Mahler. Yet the way in which Sibelius manages the transition from the movement's tonally unresolved high point (before Fig. S) to its gently asserted closure is masterly in technique and wholly personal in expression. While the chromatic descents of the thematic phrases speak very directly of lament, and the ghostly string tremolo on the bridge at Fig. W even hints at Webern's stifled expressionism, the increasingly stable assertions of the A minor tonic triad have nothing despairing or doubtful about them. If it is 'tragic',[11] then the sense is of acceptance of inevitable realities, and of a stoical refusal to subside into inertia. This, the music seems to be saying, will be – sooner or later – the real music of the future.

Conflict or consolidation?

Crossing the tritone from icy A minor to glowing E♭ major can easily suggest the image of drawing a line before a new beginning. The substantial differences between Sibelius's Fourth and Fifth Symphonies do not rule out all connections, all continuity. Yet Hepokoski seems to welcome the idea of significant separation, declaring that only after the Fourth Symphony does Sibelius's music resist 'such shopworn binary oppositions' as conservative/progressive.[12] For Hepokoski, the Fourth is 'the climactic utterance of his modern-classical style – broken, despairingly contemplative, irretrievably lonely in tone, the product of much compositional struggle and, above all, a resolute statement of the separatist side of his conflicted artistic persona'. Hepokoski believes that 'the modernist/anti-modernist contradiction driving the Fourth Symphony is irreconcilable', and that, after the experience of struggle involved, 'Sibelius sought to forge musical structures less dependent on traditional musical shapes than on the non-systematic, intuitive logic of the musical materials selected for any given composition'.[13]

It will be clear from my own interpretation that I believe Hepokoski exaggerates the gulf between what the Fourth Symphony stands for and what followed it. That is certainly not to deny the interrelatedness of the last three symphonies (and *Tapiola*), 'four tableaux of a comprehensive vision of the spiritual presences animating the Northern forest-world'.[14] I would simply suggest that we need to move beyond the 'shopworn binary opposition' which deems the Fourth Symphony 'pessimistic' and the Fifth 'triumphalist', and to acknowledge that those 'spiritual presences' may be as palpable in the Fourth Symphony as they are in its successors. Equally, the role of 'traditional musical shapes' might be shown to be rather more positive and fundamental than Hepokoski wishes to concede – though clearly much depends on precisely what 'traditional' implies in such a complex context, and how what Hepokoski calls 'the modernist/anti-modernist contradiction' might also be seen as a 'modernist/anti-modernist' convergence.

Where the Fifth Symphony is concerned, we might also question how useful it is to equate the 'intuitive', as this affects the 'logic' whereby the materials chosen for pieces 'grow by moment-to-moment motivic transformations as spontaneously and self-assuredly as frost patterns', with the 'non-systematic'. However persuasive the general claim that 'the tonal and rhetorical layout of sonata form (or even "free sonata form"), which had governed the outer movements of Symphonies nos. 1–4, seems much less determinative of *The Oceanides* or the outer movements of the Fifth',[15] the implied opposition between the role of 'system' in the earlier works and its rejection in the later seems unnecessarily absolute. Somewhere between Hepokoski's claim, and Murtomäki's no less confident assertion that 'the essential feature about the Fifth Symphony is the way Sibelius continues the classical attitude he adopted in the preceding symphony',[16] we might find a more appealing, more sustainable truth.

Where these differences converge is in perceptions about organicism and unity. Murtomäki's claim – written before the publication of Hepokoski's 1993 analysis – that 'the [three] movements of the Fifth Symphony have been tied together by an unbroken chord of thought'[17] obviously implies a more determined suppression of any 'modernist' qualities than Hepokoski's relatively cautious judgement that the work's 'local details become clear only when considered within the workings of a single purpose being pursued throughout all of the movements'.[18] But 'single purpose' and 'unbroken chord' speak the same language. That 'single purpose' was not to re-establish traditional classicism, but the possibility of pursuing the 'modernist/anti-modernist' dialogues of the Fourth Symphony within a very different emotional world can also be detected in the formal ambiguities which result from Sibelius's 'new commitment to content-based forms'.[19] If it is indeed the case that 'each major composition after the Fourth Symphony represents a relatively unmoored structural experiment that seeks its own course in uncharted formal waters',[20] it is not inappropriate to detect a persistent tension, both exhilarating and alarming, as a way forward is found, and the charting of the uncharted proceeds. Given Murtomäki's contention that 'the entire symphony evolved out of the impulses produced by the themes of the Finale',[21] the drama, for Sibelius, was in giving that 'evolution' an aura of excitement as well as inevitability, so that the 'musical allegory of celestial order and beauty'[22] should also embody some of the traumas, messiness, and occasional heroic enterprise of real life.

Sibelius 'identified the central finale theme with the splendour of the migrating swans sighted seasonally around *Ainola* . . . Nor, apparently, was the swan-related imagery (encompassing swans, cranes and wild geese – including their cries – as disclosers of "nature mysticism and life's *Angst!*") confined to the finale.'[23] With the admission of 'life's *Angst*' Sibelius brought human striving alongside the grandeur of nature, and the Fifth Symphony's modern dimension surely resides in the sense that it is about the human perception of, and response to, the phenomena of nature. Notions of the grand and the mystical are human, not 'natural', and the character of the Fifth Symphony, far from a passive charting of natural marvels, suggests an epic human struggle to respond adequately to what nature has to offer. Only something defiantly heroic in man can do justice to the 'splendour' of those swans, and for this reason alone it is far from banal to deem Sibelius's Fifth his 'Eroica'.

Hepokoski's arguments that 'much of the work is "about" the difficulty of crystallizing out an unequivocal, successfully functional dominant',[24] and that 'the final V–I, E flat cadences of the first and last movements are no mere default conclusions but hard-won victories of tonal clarification', are verbally characterised to underline the music's 'angst' – its stress and drama. To describe that harmonic process as a 'laboured search for what had once been a self-evident, frictionless principle', and to claim that 'the symphony takes up as a primary topic the difficulty . . . of attaining a valid utterance of something (a stable cadence) that in earlier times . . . had been simplicity itself' reinforces the interpretative rhetoric. Yet in characterising the first movement as 'a gradual process that transforms circular weakness or inactivity into linear strength and rapid, forceful activity',[25] Hepokoski risks depriving the music's stable dimension of dynamism and sense of purpose. The harmonic language of the movement's initial *Molto moderato* section is not so much 'weak' as polarised between stabilising and destabilising impulses, the former 'in dialogue' with the latter just as, in Hepokoski's analysis, the overall form involves dialogue between 'a series of four broad and increasingly free rotations through a patterned set of materials' and 'a sonata deformation of the breakthrough type'.[26] The reason traditional *Formenlehre* labels are inadequate on their own is that they make it more difficult to do justice to the interplay between a harmonic and thematic organicism tending to classical integration, and more modernist multiplicities and ambiguities: and the recovery of 'the banished language of cadences' in the transition to the scherzo section brilliantly compensates for the modernist generic irony of the fact that the movement can only find closure by ceasing to be the expansive *Molto moderato* in which that 'language' was lost. Rather than Hepokoski's transformation of circular weakness into rapid, forceful activity, this can be seen as a transformation of slow-moving yet aspirational activity into a blithely exuberant display, which rejects the aspirational depth of feeling so palpable from the very first bar for unreflective excitement. The symphony will only achieve satisfying and convincing closure when it allows these two worlds of feeling to converge, rather than forcing them further apart.

This is a process which starts in the second movement, *Andante mosso, quasi allegretto*, which Hepokoski rightly sees in binary terms as an

'intentionally naive, idyllic surface' which never wholly suppresses 'the complexities within'. And because 'its larger purpose is to generate the leading
rhythms, metres, timbres, motives, and themes of the finale to come',[27] the
convergence of idyll and complexity must not only be incomplete: the music
must revert to divergence at the end of the movement, the dark songfulness
of the final string phrases turning more serene, the woodwind conclusion
gently untroubled. Only in the finale is the tendency to seek resolution by
affirming explicit polarities called into question.

Again, Hepokoski's 'rotational/teleological structure, and its [rather
tenuous] secondary dialogue with the sonata-deformational principle',[28]
provides a suitably schematic background for a process which is emphatically not a simple reversal of the first movement's motion from striving to
carefree rejoicing. The opening of the finale is exuberant, certainly, but with
a touch of turbulence which the first appearance of the Swan Hymn theme
has no difficulty in dissipating, not least with its heartwarming modulation
to C major. The return of energetic busyness, still at relatively quiet dynamic levels, could therefore be intended to prepare the ground for a more
grandiose affirmation of the material and expressive states which have already been introduced. What Sibelius does instead is astonishingly imaginative and powerful, darkening the mood and tonality, so that the Swan Hymn
returns, after Fig. L, in understated reflectiveness. Then comes the moment
where the prospect of a reversal of the first movement's strategy seems most
strongly implied. The tempo broadens progressively, the Hymn's melodic
stratum expands into an utterance of profound tragic grandeur (the strings
remaining muted, a master stroke). Yet despite the incitement to revert to
the questing, ultimately calm perspectives of the first movement's opening,
Sibelius combines a decisive perfect cadence with a change of mode from
minor to major and a return of the Hymn's contrapuntal essence – '*dolce
e nobile*'. This is the huge consummation and resolution of crisis that the
final section embodies – in Hepokoski's 'final revelation . . . the unshakable
regrasping of the "historically eclipsed" cadential harmony that was initially
represented as ungraspable in the first movement's opening two bars'.[29] But
the supreme integration of depth and exultation in the finale's conclusion
is complementary to the first movement's strong, almost innocent polarity.
It could even be claimed that the 'highest' purpose of the finale is to make
the first movement seem inadequate. But that is not the same thing as 'aesthetically redundant', and it is perhaps Sibelius's greatest achievement in the
Fifth Symphony to make that preliminary demonstration of what can and
must be gone beyond seem so inspired and inspiring, in its own terms, that
the power and persuasiveness of that which does 'go beyond' it – the finale –
becomes doubly miraculous.

Extremes?

Absolute oppositions – heroic/pastoral, epic/lyric – spring readily to mind
when the differences between Sibelius's Fifth and Sixth Symphonies are
contemplated. But the ways in which recent commentators have discussed
matters of form tends to give priority to continuities, influenced no doubt
by the knowledge that all these relatively late works seem to have been
conceived at the same time. For Murtomäki, there is no conflict in the
proposition that 'the relatively free applications of traditional forms in the
Sixth Symphony . . . are undoubtedly realizations of Sibelius's plans of
symphonic fantasies and of stepping across the boundaries of symphony'.[30]
Hepokoski gives even more emphasis to those 'relatively free applications
of traditional forms', claiming that 'the Sixth marked an even more radical
break from sonata-form practice than had the Fifth; it veered further away
from sonata norms and scarcely seems in dialogue even with extreme sonata
deformations'.[31] This follows on from the composer's own comments that
the Sixth was 'built, like the Fifth, on linear rather than harmonic foundations . . . [Its] four movements . . . are formally completely free and do not
follow the ordinary sonata scheme.' Yet it was a consequence of Sibelius's
classicising impulses that formal freedom did not promote enhanced discontinuity or instability, and Murtomäki is right when he notes that 'the
movements are linked with one another in a remarkably coherent way'.[32]

Difficulties can nevertheless arise when attempts are made to harmonise
aesthetic notions of classicism with Sibelius's 'nature-mysticism' in the Sixth
Symphony, and as far as the general character of the music is concerned, it
might well seem more fitting to emphasise such concepts as 'contemplative
circularity' than is the case with the Fifth Symphony. This is Hepokoski's
diagnosis, when he claims that 'in [the] post-Fifth-Symphony years his concerns seem to have become even more contemplative, more circular, more
"vertical" – in short, less compatible with the linear symphonic tradition'.[33]
But there is a clear dividing line between a response to the music which
finds 'profound tensions between . . . opposing tendencies' to the circular
and the processual, creating 'the nearly insurmountable problem of trying
to unite fundamentally opposed conceptions of the musical process', and a
response that believes that Sibelius relished the opportunity to explore ways
in which these conflicting tendencies could converge. This latter response,
which I adopt here, is in part the result of finding Hepokoski's emphasis on
what he terms 'stasis' in the Fifth Symphony's first movement a less than
convincing term for the way the music actually moves forward.

Hepokoski can also appear to exaggerate the effects of what he calls
'the lost world of simple dominants and tonics',[34] as if a key which is not
'stabilized' in the traditional way is undermined, rather than 'extended' or

'floating', to use Schoenbergian terms. Just as the spirit of the Fifth Symphony can appear to progress quite explicitly from aspiration and striving to fulfilment and resolution, so that of the Sixth can be felt to generate a profound and satisfying repose from its diverse tendencies to contemplation and action. So even if, as Hepokoski argues, the finale of the Sixth Symphony is 'a spiritualized representation of elemental Finnish landscape, a wintry struggle between "the [feminine] pine spirit and the wind" ',[35] the ending is not so much a matter of 'declining into extinction' or 'inevitable decay': rather, it achieves a resolution, an equilibrium, even a degree of Apollonian serenity, and this sense of fulfilling enrichment also relates to what Murtomäki describes as the way Sibelius 'enlarges decisively the concept of tonality by means of modality, thus creating a specifically modal-tonal symphonic thinking'.[36] Hepokoski's tendency to exaggerate the 'dissolution' side of the dissolution / resolution polarity is evidently motivated by his reading of the life-and-works drama of which this particular symphony is seen as a vital part. But other 'constructions' are possible, and my own commentary does not seek to contradict the accounts of musical form given by other writers, rather to complement their hermeneutic aspects.

The first movement of the Sixth Symphony is marked *Allegro molto moderato* – a direction which is not so much ambiguous as an indication of a synthesis whereby the music can move from contemplative to active within the same basic pulse, shifting emphasis (where the overall resultant rhythm is concerned) from minim and crotchet movement to quaver and semiquaver movement. Sibelius indicates no modifications of this tempo before the brief passages marked *poco allargando* and *allargando* near the end, and the *poco tranquillo* he requests for the last four bars – devices which reinforce a sense of closure established more basically by other means.

This fundamental rhythmic/metric technique of allowing contrast to evolve within continuity can be paralleled motivically, harmonically and formally in the Sixth Symphony's first movement. Similarly, action evolves from contemplation, tension (as local instability and dissonance) from fundamental consonance, centring on the association between D and F as modal/tonal centres. The confrontation which occurs just before Fig. B, and focuses on the C♯/C♮ dissonance, evolves by way of the linear processes which the composer himself underlined, and can be interpreted as the transformation of contemplative serenity into a tension which resolves into the more active, light-hearted qualities of the music from Fig. B. Development involves darkening, action itself becomes more stressful, but the cyclic process leads logically to a moment of resolution and the reassertion of a more positive mood, with the 'recapitulation' beginning in the bars before Fig. H. This essentially active music continues to Fig. K, but Sibelius refuses to end the movement in this vein: renewed darkening, and the movement's most explicitly discontinuous textures, not only dramatise the formal and spiritual crisis, but also promote the famously 'provisional' ending, in which the modal harmonic shift from C to D involves a parallel shift from 'active' to 'passive', forceful to gentle. These qualities will be present at the ending of the fourth movement too, and opinions inevitably vary as to the extent to which the finale provides a more 'decisive' resolution, in terms of both mood and harmony, than the first movement.

The second movement, *Allegretto moderato*, modulates the first movement's rhythmic characteristics into the contrast between hesitant and decisive motives. Nevertheless, the triple metre signifies the potential for more dance-like qualities (the *valse* is inevitably on the *triste* side), and the regularity of dance is offset, first by the relative complexity of the rhythmic counterpoint between Figs. E and F, then by the overtly destabilising effect of the abrupt change of texture and tempo at Fig. G. This has the typical Sibelian consequence of suggesting that the formal bonds of the movement might have been irrevocably broken, and the final, four-bar return to the first tempo, with a cadence alluding to earlier material, is certainly insufficient to counter the movement's disruptive tendencies conclusively. At this stage, therefore, the implication is that action can indeed turn anarchic – perhaps especially when it moves into the more 'urban' environment of dance styles far removed from those of folk music. The role of the two remaining movements will be to confirm or counter this 'progression'.

At the outset the *Poco vivace* third movement is more exuberantly dance-like than the *Allegretto moderato*, and some sense of a scherzo with pastoral qualities seems valid, suggested by the piping flute idea between Figs. A and B, and even more strongly by the almost Vaughan Williams-like theme first heard in the flutes at Fig. C. This unified effect is enhanced but not seriously threatened by an element of textural and harmonic drama in the final stages (after Fig. I).

The relative absence of lyric aspiration from the Sixth Symphony's central movements (neither of them slow, of course) opens a gap in the discourse that the finale will fill. As an *Allegro molto*, without the first movement's qualifying 'moderato', dynamic propulsion might be expected to be more determined: and despite some brief *poco rallentando* bars in the later stages (between Figs. I and K) the basic tempo is inflected to *Allegro assai* at Fig. L, then restrained even more determinedly by the broadening *doppio più lento* of the coda. It is bound to appear as if the more reflective, even hymn-like eloquence of this closing section has been implied but held in check from the beginning of the fourth movement, and of the whole work. The active core of the finale has a sharply etched exuberance which easily shades into hints of panic and disturbance – after Fig. F, for example – then building to the descent into darkness at Fig. I, the movement's climactic moment of drama which, however, provokes a powerful assertion of 'classical' discipline as Sibelius restores the predominant tonal, motivic and rhythmic elements with a minimum of delay and a maximum of continuity. Echoes of this turbulence, of tragic disintegration avoided only at the last moment, can certainly be heard in the intense harmonic expansions of the coda, but it is difficult to argue that these darkenings destabilise the aspiring, celebratory atmosphere, or that they are not completely dissolved into the quiet, gentle but very pure D-centred cadence at the end. Resolution, not dissolution, is coupled with a degree of understatement appropriate to a musical at-mosphere in which the generative role of action is celebrated, but shown to stem from, and return to, the spiritual source of creative contemplation – an 'inaction' which is serene and potentially sublime, for as long as it manages to keep insidious anxieties at bay.

Ending: subversion or serenity?

The continuum between action and contemplation might appear to be a concept general enough to have relevance for any work of art whose qualities are primarily classical, and therefore to suit Sibelius's last symphony as well as those which precede it. Yet it is with the Seventh Symphony, above all, that different interpretative nuances arise to challenge the usefulness of 'classicism' – paired with 'organicism' – as a defining context for the musical discourse. To start at a point of maximum agreement between authorities, Hepokoski's declaration that the Seventh Symphony 'is surely Sibelius's most remarkable compositional achievement' is evidently the result of its success in fusing fundamental elements of tradition with freedom and flexibility: 'Sibelius provided it with the architectural satisfactions and expressive depth of an abstract symphony while breaking away from references to sonata form and other traditional formal models.'[37]

Hepokoski's emphasis on an 'ad hoc structure' which 'emerges link-by-link from the transformational processes of the musical ideas themselves – a content-based form in the process of becoming'[38] – is not in conflict with an interpretation of the music as the apotheosis of classical continuity and interconnectedness, a definitive rejection of modernist fragmentation and centrifugal dispersal. But does this mean that the Seventh takes still further the Sixth's tendency towards sublime repose? As soon as we turn to Timothy L. Jackson's analysis, we encounter a more complex nexus of interpretative elements which seem to subvert the classicising thrust of the music at the same time as they aspire to enhance it.[39]

The governing poetic idea – or organic process – laid down for Sibelius by Jackson is that of 'crystallization and entropy', which Jackson sees as embodying 'the devolution of order into chaos'. This parallels Jackson's claim that, in the Fourth Symphony's finale, 'entropy triumphs and the hero's life inexorably ebbs and dissipates back into chaos and nothingness'.[40] But it is questionable whether such a singular, unambiguous reading – comparable to Hepokoski's stark assessment that the Sixth Symphony is an example of 'declining into extinction' – does justice to the elements of tonal closure and resolution which the music also displays. Jackson also links closure with catastrophe and disaster in the Seventh Symphony – the work often seen – spiritually, if not also structurally – as the polar opposite of the Fourth: and there is a very great contrast in Jackson's analysis between the organicising impulse of his voice-leading reductions, searching Schenkerianly for the ultimate linear interconnectedness at the highest structural levels, and the effect of what he terms the 'theologized domestic drama'[41] which Sibelius's annotations of his compositional drafts reveal. Somehow the 'crystallization' process, in which the association between Sibelius's wife Aino and the symphony's thrice-heard trombone theme might seem to suggest a supreme harmony between the composer's domestic environment and his creative aspirations, has to be paralleled by the opposing tendency to 'entropy', which presumably means not only structural disintegration in the creative sphere, but domestic unease and disillusion as well.

Jackson's claim that 'matrimonial and nationalist issues intertwine in Sibelius's music from *Kullervo* to the Seventh Symphony and *Tapiola*'[42] is a characteristically bold declaration of the way he aims to synthesise his interpretation of Sibelius's character and development. Yet there is a paradox in Jackson's work, in that the wider he casts his interpretative net, the more reductive (and non-dialectical) his readings become. There is no hint of how the 'public' symphonic rhetoric of Sibelius's Seventh interacts with the hidden domestic, personal, autobiographical element, which – even if we accept the logic of translating the trombone theme's heroic, expansive, positive tone into a portrait of a loved domestic companion – we can only 'hear' after we've been persuaded (by the physical evidence of what is found on paper) that the composer put it there. It seems no less plausible to argue that assertions of personal identity which centre on Aino represent a compositorial need for self-expression which is fundamentally – subversively – at odds with the process of communication from composer to listeners and interpreters (performers and musicologists alike).

From this perspective, one of the most remarkable aspects of the Seventh Symphony is the sense in which it subverts the essentials of symmetrical stability while never completely losing sight of positive, affirmative modes of expression: balancing modernism and classicism, in other words. Much effort has been devoted in the Sibelius literature to explaining how, on the one hand, the work alludes to the traditions of single-movement symphonic design, while – Murtomäki argues – being definable neither as 'a gigantic movement in sonata form nor several movements put together into a single movement in the manner of Liszt's B minor Sonata'.[43] The ambiguity is in the interaction of these divergent processes – whether we call them 'fantasia' and 'symphony', or 'symphony' and 'non-symphony' – and it is difficult to go all the way with Murtomäki's claim that 'it is something new and revolutionary in the history of symphony' when it remains quite so close to old tonal principles (despite the small number of firm cadential progressions) and motivic processes. Rather, the strength and originality of the music might be attributed principally, if not exclusively, to the contrast between the strong architecture of the three trombone statements, which provide the most explicit thematic and tonal pillars of the unified design, and the processes leading towards and away from these statements, where imbalance and instability become more evident.

In an earlier study of the Seventh Symphony,[44] which I reformulate here, I developed an interpretation in terms of two distinct levels of form and genre. First, there is the 'slow' music – introduction and trombone theme, at bar 60: central, varied recurrence of trombone theme (bar 221): recapitulation of theme (bar 475) and coda. Second, there is the 'fast' music – a 'scherzo' (bars 156–208), which is paralleled by the *Vivace* (bars 409–49) heard immediately before the build-up to the final return of the trombone theme. With transitions mediating between these extremes, we seem to have a near-symmetrical arch form. Yet one section of the work remains unaccounted for: the extended *Allegro molto moderato* (bars 258–408), which follows on from the second, C minor trombone statement, and which is itself ternary with an introduction. To the extent that the material of this section derives from previously stated motives, it might be regarded as enhancing the symphony's unity as some kind of developmental contrast. But it also serves to prevent the overall form from falling into 'predictable' symmetry, while seeming to mediate between the extremes of tempo and mood which the 'arch form' elements propose. If mediation is one factor, postponement is another, for the interpolation performs a function not dissimilar to that of the non-recurring central part of the 'exposition' (bars 22–59) in ensuring that the last statement of the main theme of the whole work is placed in the most telling and satisfying position.

Tonally, the function of the *Allegro molto moderato* is equally essential to the dramatic yet organic unpredictability of the structure. It restores a pristine C major to counter the *Sturm und Drang* of the central, minor-mode trombone statement and its hectic but transitional aftermath. Yet its own middle section recalls that aftermath, and the tonality darkens, so that the main material returns in a diatonic Eb major (at bar 375). Thus this episode does not merely postpone the clinching return of the main theme, but prepares the ground for the most dramatic tonal event of the entire symphony: the recovery of C-tonality after its displacement by E♭, a situation prefigured as early as the resolution of the dramatically accented A♭ minor chord in bar 3, yet not fully realised by either the first 'scherzo' or by the central trombone statement. This new function ensures that the second scherzo is no carbon copy of the first, but a still more urgent search for the stability necessary to end the symphony: and that stability is not only prepared with powerful inevitability, but strengthened by those locally enriching or destabilising details which give the clue for those commentators who wish to give subversive entropy the decisive voice.

Underlying my own interpretation of the Seventh Symphony is the belief that modern classicism (as distinct from classicism proper, rooted in diatonic tonality, as also from a more genuinely modernistic neo-classicism) involves the tendency to subvert structural fundamentals (both formal and harmonic) as well as the effort to affirm them. The nearest Jackson seems to get to this feature is in his view of 'apparently "strong" tonics' being 'devalued'. But in the end he is so committed to the principle of 'an overarching V–I auxiliary cadence' controlling 'the entire structure'[45] that the possibility of more flexible, less rigorously integrated or consistently hierarchical processes gaining the upper hand is never seriously considered. One of Jackson's first thoughts is his best: 'unlike those commentators who interpret the Seventh as a triumphant work, I understand it, like the Fourth, as dualistic, simultaneously embodying crystallization and its failure'.[46] Even this probably goes too far: for 'failure' substitute subversion, challenging, enriching: and for voice-leading reduction to a single structural level, substitute a Hepokoskian view of the succession of formal rotations.

Similarly, Edward Laufer's even more orthodox prolongational reduction of the Seventh Symphony, engineered to support the claim that 'the effect of the formal design, with its synthesis of contrasts, is to create a single entity, one vast sweep, of culmination, of renewal and completion',[47] involves too consistent an erasure of what is modern to make what is claimed as classical convincing. Murtomäki is no less eager to yield to the seductions of an approach which he links to Sibelius's comment about a Mozart allegro as 'the most perfect model for a symphonic movement. Think of its wonderful unity and homogeneity! It is like an uninterrupted flowing, where nothing stands out and nothing encroaches upon the rest.' Yet Murtomäki also accepts that 'despite the maximal unity of the symphony its form is equivocal',[48] and to the extent that this 'equivocal' approach to form provides a modern dimension, it also serves to draw interpretative response away from the subverted classicism of the music's unstable organicism.

Even if we do not go as far as Jackson in accepting that the music moves through recapitulation towards a 'catastrophe' and a coda which 'composes the retrospective "collapse" of motives associated with both Aino and [Sibelius's daughter] Ruth', we can surely agree that the specific tensions which Jackson associates with catastrophe and collapse cast a subversive ambivalence over the closural impetus which drives the music to that final C major chord. The ending is triumphantly abrupt – neither serene nor despairing, still less Jackson's 'living death'[49] – but poised between past and future. After 1924, Sibelius could take real and substantial pride in what he had achieved, especially in the later symphonies: and even if that achievement could not compensate him for his inability to add to his symphonic output, the continued appreciation of that achievement is decisive evidence of its greatness.

5 The genesis of the Violin Concerto

A week before Sibelius first mentioned the Violin Concerto, his thoughts returned to his youthful dream of becoming a violin virtuoso:

> I try to work but have not succeeded in shaping the routine in a way that would please me, that is now my main goal. More at the writing-table – less with the piano. Yet, I once wanted to become a violin virtuoso, and this 'performing' element always takes such strange forms within me. Tinkling on the piano and partying. It all comes from the same root. That's quite clear to me now.[1]

Becoming a violin virtuoso had been Sibelius's first priority ever since he started to study the instrument in the autumn of 1881 at the age of fifteen. 'When I play [the violin], I am filled with a strange feeling; it is as though the insides of the music opened up to me', he wrote two years later.[2] Along with violin playing he had also started to compose, and year by year his compositional activity increased. During his early years, however, composing was not given first place.

Barely a year before the completion of *Kullervo*, Sibelius still planned public appearances as a violinist: 'I play the violin every day. I think I should perform in Helsinki some time in the coming year,' he wrote to his fiancée Aino from Vienna.[3] He also auditioned for the Vienna Philharmonic Orchestra, but the result was not what he had hoped for: the jury regarded his playing as 'not at all bad', but nevertheless recommended him against playing the violin because of his nerves.[4] Thus, at the beginning of the 1890s, Sibelius's dreams of becoming a violinist ultimately had to give way to his work as a composer.

Sibelius composed about sixty works for violin during his compositional career. The first half were composed during the years 1884–94, but there then followed a pause for almost a decade until he began the concerto. A similar period of time followed the completion of the concerto before he started to write regularly for the instrument again in 1914. The next thirty pieces were composed between then and 1930. A great deal of the works are small character pieces for violin and piano (there are only two youthful sonatas), many of which depart from the traditional Romantic salon style in their austerity and aphoristic-like qualities. For violin and orchestra,

Sibelius composed two *Serenades* (op. 69), six *Humoresques* (opp. 87 and 89), and, of course, the Violin Concerto in D minor (op. 47).

The idea of composing a violin concerto had occupied Sibelius's mind for years. In 1890, for example, he wrote from Vienna that 'yesterday I saw Don Giovanni at the opera, and as usual I composed afterwards until four o'clock in the morning . . . I made a sketch for a violin concerto.' Later, in 1898, he again mentioned plans for composing a violin concerto.[5] The Violin Concerto itself was eventually completed in 1904 and revised in 1905, but in 1915 Sibelius planned a second concerto, provisionally subtitled *concerto lirico*. However, the sketch material for this planned concerto was eventually used in the Sixth Symphony.[6]

The history of the Violin Concerto

The compositional history of the Violin Concerto can be easily summarised up to the date of its premiere. In June 1900, Sibelius's admirer Axel Carpelan wrote: 'Dare we hope for a violin concerto or fantasy with orchestra?' Sibelius evidently appreciated Carpelan's opinion, since he began work on the Violin Concerto only two years later. The actual catalyst for the work may have originated in Sibelius's journey to Berlin in summer 1902. In Berlin, Sibelius met the famous virtuoso Willy Burmester, whom he knew well from the second half of the 1890s when the violinist worked in Helsinki as a concertmaster. Erik Tawaststjerna assumes that Burmester urged Sibelius to compose a concerto, and, significantly, the earliest known reference to the concerto dates from September 1902. In a letter to his wife Aino from Tvärminne in the archipelago of the Gulf of Finland, Sibelius confided, 'I have got some marvellous themes for a violin concerto.' From that point on, Sibelius worked on the concerto in between other projects and his frequent socialising in Helsinki, and by September 1903 the first two movements were ready in piano score. Sibelius sent these almost immediately to Burmester. The third movement was completed in December, by which time Sibelius had already orchestrated the first two movements and notified Carpelan that he would soon attend to the orchestration of the finale.[7]

According to press announcements, Sibelius had promised the work's premiere to Burmester in 1903. Here, however, the work's difficulties began. By the end of the year, Sibelius had decided that the work would be premiered earlier than the date agreed with Burmester, and that the violinist on this occasion would be Viktor Nováček, a teacher at the Helsinki Music School, and a violinist of relatively modest talent. When Burmester heard about this, he blew a fuse and wrote that he would never play the concerto. Sibelius placated him by explaining that the concert date had necessarily been advanced because of his financial difficulties, and that he planned to perform the work later in Helsinki and Berlin with Burmester as soloist. Burmester remained hopeful that he would be able to perform the work a few months after its premiere. As is now well known, however, Sibelius decided to revise the work immediately after its first performance, and noted, 'I will withdraw my concerto; it will appear only after two years. This is my hidden sorrow at present.' Burmester was thus set aside for the second time.[8] By the early summer, 1905, Sibelius was working on the revised version of the concerto sooner than he had anticipated. His new publisher, Robert Lienau, made immediate plans for the first performances of the new version: it would be premiered in Berlin with Richard Strauss as the conductor and with the concertmaster of the Berlin Orchestra, Karel Halíř, as the soloist. Sibelius agreed to this plan, commenting that 'if [Burmester] is not going to play in Berlin this autumn, it will not be possible to wait any longer'. Passed over three times, Burmester never played the Sibelius concerto throughout his career.[9]

The genesis of the 'marvellous themes'

Although the idea of composing the concerto dates from autumn 1902, Sibelius may have composed some of the concerto's themes earlier. The finale's first subject, for example, and the violin's answer to the second subject (Fig. 3 in the Eulenburg score), had presumably been sketched as early as 1899–1900, where they are accompanied by themes used in the Second Symphony.[10] There is no indication in these sketches that Sibelius would have been thinking of a violin concerto at the time. Furthermore, the second movement's first subject may also have appeared before Sibelius began to compose the concerto in September. In a sketch block (HUL 1570), dated 'Kervo [Kerava] 3/VI 1902', there is a plan for a four-movement work, listing the movements' principal keys: I: F major, II: A minor, III: D♭ major and IV: F major; for the third movement, Sibelius sketched the opening notes of what was to become the slow movement's first subject in the Violin Concerto.[11]

The nucleus of the first movement's first subject seems to have occurred to Sibelius as early as 1901 in Rapallo, Italy, during the time when he was working on the Second Symphony. In a sketch booklet (HUL 1550), beneath the annotation 'bells in Rapallo', the melody given as Ex. 5.1 appears.

While composing the Violin Concerto, however, the main theme 'bothered' Sibelius.[12] This concern is evident in the sources: the theme was first sketched in G♯ minor, without the nucleus seen in the previous example (Ex. 5.2).

Below, on the same page, is another sketch (Ex. 5.3), where the essential beginning of the theme occurs.

Example 5.1 Sibelius, Violin Concerto, sketch for opening theme (HUL 1550/p. [4])

Example 5.2 Sibelius, Violin Concerto, sketch for opening theme (HUL 0444/p. [1])

Example 5.3 Sibelius, Violin Concerto, sketch for opening theme (HUL 0444/p. [1])

Example 5.4 Sibelius, Violin Concerto, sketch for opening theme (HUL 0449)

Example 5.5 Sibelius, Violin Concerto, sketch for opening theme (HUL 0443/p. [2])

Example 5.6 Sibelius, Violin Concerto: sketch for opening theme (HUL 0443/p. [2])

The next piece in the puzzle, a descending motion to the tonic via the triplet, is added in sketch HUL 0449. The harmony differs from both completed versions, except for the motion in the bass line, which Sibelius adapted for the recapitulation (Ex. 5.4).

Whether the composer had continually been working from the Rapallo sketch while experimenting with different possibilities, or whether he unconsciously invented a melody which had occurred to him earlier, remains unknown. In the sketches that followed, the tonic key is fixed as D minor. In a continuity draft (HUL 0443) the theme begins to take shape in its totality (Ex. 5.5).

Here, Sibelius replaces the triplets of the eleventh bar, which are already evident in Ex. 5.3, with an immediate repetition of the so-called 'dorian melisma'.[13] The asterisk above bar 12 and the question mark in the next bar refer to the melody given as Ex. 5.6, sketched at the bottom of the page.

Example 5.7 Sibelius, Violin Concerto, sketch (HUL 0475/p. [2])

Sibelius's sketches reveal that he was a constructional composer par ex-
cellence, in the sense defined by Aaron Copland:

> . . . in this case the composer really does begin with a musical theme. In
> Beethoven's case there is no doubt about it, for we have the notebooks in
> which he put the themes down. We can see from his notebooks how he
> worked over his themes – how he would not let them be until they were as
> perfect as he could make them. Beethoven was not a spontaneously
> inspired composer in the Schubert sense at all. He was the type that begins
> with a theme; makes it a germinal idea; and upon that constructs a musical
> work, day after day, in painstaking fashion.[14]

From the evidence of his notebooks, sketches and thematic memos, there
is no doubt that Sibelius likewise began with a musical theme. As illustrated above, after making the first thematic memos Sibelius also worked
on his themes in painstaking fashion in order to make them suitable for the
construction of a large-scale musical work.

The themes of the second subject group,[15] however, were not constructed
piece by piece like the first subject. Draft HUL 0459 is of particular interest,
and includes the ending of the so-called mini-cadenza (in the final version
this cadenza begins twenty-two bars before Fig. 2); under the solo violin's
virtuosic figuration, a repetition of the nucleus of the first subject is heard.
The draft ends at this point, after which begins the second-subject group.
At the ending of the draft, Sibelius has drawn a big asterisk (as in Ex. 5.5,
such markings usually refer to another draft or sketch where the music
continues). In addition to the asterisk he also has written 'Aino 5+'.[16]

The Violin Concerto manuscripts also include a draft with the marking
'Aino 5'. In this draft (HUL 0475) there is a theme which appears also in an
early sketch (HUL 0459) as well as on the top of draft HUL 0443, parts of
which were seen in Ex. 5.5 and 5.6. In the latter manuscripts, the purpose of
the melody is not revealed, but the draft marked 'Aino 5' (Ex. 5.7) seems to
show that Sibelius originally intended this theme to introduce the second-
subject group, or even to serve as the second subject itself.

Example 5.8 Sibelius, Violin Concerto, sketch for first movement (HUL 0463/p. [1])

Example 5.9 Sibelius, Violin Concerto, sketch (HUL 1558/p. [2])

Example 5.10 Sibelius, Violin Concerto, sketch (HUL 0446, p. [2])

Example 5.11 Sibelius, Violin Concerto, sketches

However, instead of the Violin Concerto this theme found its way into the *Cassazione*, op. 6. Sibelius's final solution for the beginning of the second-subject group, as realised in the two final versions of the concerto, appears in a few sketches. From the opening of the group (Fig. 2 in the final version), Sibelius builds a series of melodic variations leading to the theme that listeners experience as the second subject itself. In an early sketch, this theme appears in 2/2 instead of 6/4 (Ex. 5.8). However, in another sketch the theme's inherent rhythmic quality begins to emerge in the form of a triplet (see Ex. 5.9).

In the other sketches, this subject appears either in 6/4 or 3/2 time. But if it seems extraordinary to see the familiar second subject in duple metre, it is equally strange to find thematic material for the third subject in triple metre (Ex. 5.10). And before the notes of the first theme in the closing group are finalised, Sibelius tests them in three different configurations (Ex. 5.11).

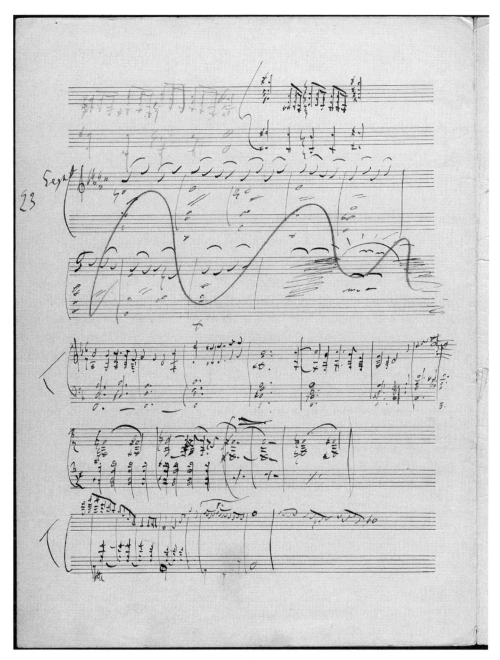

Figure 5.1 Sibelius, Violin Concerto, manuscript draft (HUL)

Whether Sibelius referred to some of these themes when he wrote to Aino that he had 'marvellous themes for a violin concerto' is not known. However, the second theme in the closing group seems to have been composed at Tvärminne. In Sibelius's sketch, the theme opens alongside the sunrise and the slurs in the melody are altered to depict seagulls flying over the sea (see Fig. 5.1).

Example 5.12 Sibelius, Violin Concerto, sketch (HUL 0479, p. [5])

Continuity drafts

In addition to thematic sketches the concerto manuscripts also include material where Sibelius drafted large passages of music. Sibelius used to write such continuity drafts, in some cases even as long as whole movements. Unfortunately, the Violin Concerto's extant continuity drafts are mostly fragmentary: the longest are about three or four pages and were written at different stages of the compositional process. Therefore, it is not possible to show how the complete movements evolved into their final shape. Most continuity drafts deal with the first movement and originate from the composition of both versions. This suggests that the first movement was the most problematic, although, as Timo Virtanen has noted, 'the quantity of sketch material does not in itself indicate that the working process was unusually laborious'.[17]

In the first movement of the original version there are three sections with a developmental character, and drafts have survived for two of these. In place of the traditional sonata-form development Sibelius placed the first cadenza (the original version has two cadenzas, whereas the final version has one). The status of this cadenza is crucial in the revision of the work (a question to which we return below); unfortunately, it is not possible to find out how the cadenza evolved, because hardly any manuscript material has survived for this important section. The second developmental section appears in the transition following the first subject in the recapitulation. In the manuscript HUL 0479 Sibelius drafted the end of this transition leading to the second subject (Ex. 5.12).

This Beethoven-like subject has an important status in the original version. It is introduced in the exposition, first as the orchestra's comment after the solo violin has played the first subject (from bar 37), and later as a codetta for the closing group. According to the sketch material, this subject seems to belong to the work's most original material, and Sibelius seems to have devoted much time to working on it. After this statement of the second subject, the third developmental section begins. In manuscript HUL 0451,

Example 5.13 Sibelius, Violin Concerto, first movement sketch (HUL 0451/p. 12)

Sibelius has drafted this section and the transition to the second cadenza of the movement (Ex. 5.13).

The greatest surprise in the original version is the stylistical diversity of this cadenza. As Minna Lindgren has observed, it strongly resembles the writing in Bach's Chaconne for unaccompanied violin. Lindgren also asserts that the cadenza's material 'differs completely from all other themes of the concerto', although closer examination reveals that the cadenza continues with the subject-matter from the preceding developmental section.[18]

The concerto's revision

Erkki Salmenhaara has suggested that, although most critics acclaimed the first version of the concerto, Sibelius's decision to revise the work was motivated by the devastating criticism of Karl Flodin, the foremost Finnish critic of the time. Flodin wrote that because the violin concerto would always remain a virtuoso work, he did not think it would suit Sibelius's free-flowing inspiration and creative nature. However, to his disappointment Sibelius had 'submitted to this compulsion; as well, he navigated in full sail into the virtuosity's main stream, taking with him all that his predecessors en route had carried as ballast'.[19]

The premiere recording of the original version – by Leonidas Kavakos and the Lahti Symphony Orchestra conducted by Osmo Vänskä in 1991– revealed that the violin part differs very much from that in the final version. The violin has more music to play, and the virtuoso sections are often more demanding than those in the final version. In the polyphonic solo section of the slow movement (beginning at Fig. 2 in the final version of the score), for example, the lower voice has been written as triplets against crotchets in the final version, but in the original version the lower voice has ornate trill-like figuration in demisemiquavers. The runs that follow this section hurry on mostly in hemidemisemiquavers in the original, whereas in the final version they follow in semiquaver triplets (six bars after Fig. 2). Thus, if it is possible to write about the final version that 'the solo part, although of great difficulty, does not sound nearly as impossible as most virtuosi require',[20] the original version is a real virtuoso showcase. No wonder that Burmester wrote to Sibelius enthusiastically, 'all that my 25 years' concert experience, my artistry and insight render possible, will be placed at the service of this work'. According to Flodin, however, 'the result was a technical overload, which not only brought about quite overwhelming difficulties for the soloist but also brought the whole composition down to a mediocre level'.[21] But did Flodin's criticism prompt Sibelius to revise the work? According to Salmenhaara, Flodin's criticism was along the same lines as Sibelius's own thoughts – as demonstrated by the changes Sibelius subsequently made. James Hepokoski, however, does not believe that critics' opinions were of any significance to the composer:

> I think Sibelius's impulse to revise or not to revise came primarily from within. For example, if you look at the Fourth Symphony, its initial performances were not well received at all but he did not revise that work. He knew that was the way he wanted it to be. In the case of the concerto it is quite clear that there are some problematic features in the first version and he realised that as well. The person he had to satisfy was himself, not the critics.[22]

Satisfying Flodin does not seem to have been essential for Sibelius: the critic was also dissatisfied after hearing the revised version, yet Sibelius did not revise the work a second time. On the contrary, he was already very conscious of his work's value. After the aged violin virtuoso Joseph Joachim had disparaged the work following its Berlin premiere, Sibelius wrote to his publisher, 'I am sorry for Joachim, whom I like very much. For his sake, you see. He does not seem to understand the spirit of our time. Old man – irrevocably.'[23]

Tawaststjerna and Salmenhaara have both wondered why Sibelius thought that the revision would take two years, when he actually completed the work in about a month in early summer 1905. The answer is perhaps not the actual amount of work involved, but in the change of conception. If editing alone,[24] that is, correcting or altering certain details, had been sufficient, Sibelius had no need to wait two years. However, the changes he made to the work were so extensive that editing was not enough – he had something new in mind, not a revised version, but a completely new conception of the work.

The changes made in the revision are most extensive in the first movement. Although the difference in actual length is only about fifty bars, in the original version the movement's formal structure differs substantially from that in the revision, and contains whole episodes as well as individual details that do not appear at all in the final version. These differences

Example 5.14 Sibelius, Violin Concerto, first movement sketch (HUL 0455/p. [1])

Example 5.15 Sibelius, Violin Concerto, first movement sketch (HUL 0451/p. 10)

mostly centre on the changes Sibelius made in the recapitulation. Although the return of the first subject remained almost identical, except for some alterations in the orchestral accompaniment, the following developmental transition changed and the section grew larger by more than ten bars in the later version. Most of the revision drafts deal with this section (Ex. 5.14).

In the original version, this transition was based on a Beethoven-like subject, introduced in the exposition (Ex. 5.12). In the final version, however, the theme of the transition is derived from the first subject and also forms the subject of the cadenza/development. In this way, Sibelius replaces the abundant thematic heterogeneity of the original version by increasing the motivic coherence of the movement.

Sibelius made other significant changes in the second-subject group. In the original version, in both the exposition and recapitulation, the solo violin accompanies the initial statement of the second subject with various arpeggios, runs, and embellishments, before its turn comes to play the theme. A charming sequence, which Salmenhaara describes as Mendelssohnian, leads the solo part to the second subject. Surprisingly, in the recapitulation this sequence follows rather than precedes the second subject. Thus, the Mendelssohnian sequence comes later and leads the music on into the new developmental episode (Ex. 5.15).

In the revision Sibelius removed the solo violin's arpeggios, runs, and embellishments, as well as the Mendelssohnian sequence. Instead, in the beginning of the second-subject group in the exposition, the solo violin makes way for the orchestra. Only after the bassoons have played the second subject and the clarinets start to repeat it does the violin join in, playing a countersubject (second bar after Fig. 3 in the exposition), which is thematically related to the closing theme. In the recapitulation, Sibelius uses this countersubject to make a new kind of introduction to the second subject (ten bars before Fig. 10). He also removed the whole development (Ex. 5.13) and the second cadenza of the original version in their totality. In their place, he built a short but effective rise from *stringendo* to *Allegro*, where the closing group begins (starting eighteen bars before Fig. 11).

In addition to these changes, Sibelius made a large number of more detailed adjustments in the solo and orchestral parts, in the melodies, harmonies, dynamics and phrasing as well as orchestration. In the finale, the composer made various changes that do not fundamentally alter the character of the movement. Though the alterations in the slow movement mostly concern details, many of the changes, such as the reduction of the soloist's ornamentation, have a considerable effect in performance.

The case of the first cadenza

In the autograph fair copy of the original version (HUL 0434), the first movement's first cadenza has been cut out and only four bars from the beginning and two from the end have survived. Neither has any such manuscript material relating to the cadenza survived, which would show any draft for the cadenza, original or final version, or how the cadenza evolved or even on which subject material Sibelius was working. However, in the recent recording of the original version there is a first cadenza. How was this possible? When one listens to the cadenza carefully, it is easy to tell that the cadenza is identical to that in the final version. Since the surviving bars of the original cadenza are identical with the final one, for the new recording the assumption was made that the two cadenzas must have been the same. This assumption is not unreasonable: when Sibelius worked on his manuscripts he often used the cut-and-paste method to avoid unnecessary copying. Thus, it seems possible that the two cadenzas were identical, or even that exactly the same piece of paper was pasted into the manuscript of the final version. But there are nevertheless alternative possibilities. In the final version, the subject on which the cadenza is based is introduced in slightly altered form as a codetta of the final-subject group in the exposition; moreover, in the recapitulation Sibelius develops the same subject in the transition after the first subject (Ex. 5.14), whereas in the original version the Beethoven-like subject appears in exactly the same sections (Ex. 5.12). It would therefore seem possible that the cut-off cadenza would also have dealt with the same subject material.

The case of the cadenza is essential to the revision. If the original cadenza was identical to the final one, then one must come to the conclusion that Sibelius has focused his revision around the cadenza. I do not of course mean only concretely; after the second-subject development and the second cadenza have been removed, the first cadenza becomes the true centre of the movement. In the final version the movement's basic dilemma is the tension between the first subject with its modal sonority and the nostalgic, fully romantic second subject. These qualities were not conveyed that clearly in the heterogeneous first version. On the other hand, if the original cadenza was different from the final one, then the recent recording of Sibelius's earlier version is actually an inauthentic reconstruction.

Conclusion

One remaining issue has still not been addressed when considering the re-vised version of the Violin Concerto: Willy Burmester's role in the work's genesis. Erik Tawaststjerna wondered why Sibelius treated his friend so poorly, and supposed that 'the possibility that subconsciously he did not really want Burmester to have the first performance cannot be ruled out. [Burmester's] artistic personality and taste may not have appealed to him though we know he admired his "wonderful bowing arm".'[25] The history of the work's genesis tells a contrary tale: Sibelius was in contact with Burmester during the composition of the concerto; at every stage he made plans for future performances; Sibelius even sent Burmester the first two movements before the whole work was completed; and the newspapers were informed that Sibelius intended to dedicate the work to Burmester. In other words, throughout the early phase of the work's genesis, Sibelius seems to have been composing the work expressly for Willy Burmester and no one else. Burmester's qualities as an artist shed more light on this matter. Accord-ing to Tawaststjerna, Burmester enchanted the audiences with his playing of Paganini and his arrangements of little pieces; yet as an interpreter of classics, he never won universal acclaim. *An Encyclopedia of the Violin*, written during Burmester's life in 1925, states that, 'as a performer on the violin, he is a re-markable interpreter of Bach and Spohr'.[26] This comment rings a bell: what is more surprising in the original version than the second cadenza in the style of Bach? Even if the concerto is stylistically very heterogeneous, the cadenza stands out from the normative context of a romantic concerto. Moreover, the Bachian style of the passage is exceptional among all of Sibelius's works. The initial choice of Burmester as the work's first performer inspired Sibelius to the point of affecting his compositional work.[27]

Burmester's virtuosity gave Sibelius a chance to revive the violinistic dreams of his youth. 'The performer-interpreter was a very essential *persona* in Sibelius, a role of his life: in reality a conductor, in past dreams a violin virtuoso. One can with good reason imagine that while composing the concerto he put his soul into the role of an absorbing, arresting virtuoso who enchants his public.'[28] In the first version we can almost see the composer and virtuoso within Sibelius himself. The stylistic diversity of the first version was the result of his affection for the 'marvellous themes' that the violinist-composer did not want to let go. At the beginning of the century such pluralism was unexpected, but for present listeners the work is revealed in a new light. As Salmenhaara has observed:

> For the listener who knows the definitive version note for note by heart, any deviation from it may sound like an insult of a 'holy text'. On the other hand, a listener in the postmodern age may be more willing to accept the 'unpure aesthetics' of a stylistic diversity than formerly.[29]

Soon after the first performances of the original version, the composer's mind changed. In the revision the subjective violinist-composer was replaced by the objective symphonist, who streamlined the concerto's 'marvellous themes' with a relentless self-critique and unified the work. As James Hepokoski has concluded, 'the versions show a composer extremely careful about what he writes, wanting not to write standard things, demanding the highest originality everywhere'.[30]

6 *Finlandia* awakens

JAMES HEPOKOSKI

For all of its fame, *Finlandia* has not been much examined from an analytical
point of view. Perhaps some commentators have considered this work too
self-evident in its meaning and structure to merit extended study. Perhaps
the piece's primitivist surface has discouraged close attention – its coarse-
grained rhetoric, its thick brush-strokes, its stark primary colours. Or it
may be that Sibelius's most widely known composition, a shopworn concert favourite and a national emblem, has seemed to exist in a space beyond
commentary. And yet there is much of interest to observe about *Finlandia*.
In addition, recent archival work in Finland, uncovering and recording two
early endings for the piece – first presented to the public in 1899 as 'Suomi
herää' (Finland Awakens) – has invited a reconsideration of the music.[1] It
may therefore be appropriate that we ask 'Suomi herää' to awaken into the
world of more sustained reflection. The following discussion will proceed in
two arcs: first, an elementary overview of the music alone; second, a consideration of hermeneutic questions of representation, allusion, and meaning,
questions informed especially by an awareness of its original 1899 context.

The musical shape of the whole

Sibelius channelled *Finlandia* – 'Suomi herää' – into no conventional form.
The piece's initial section (from the *Andante sostenuto* introduction through
the first phrases of the *Allegro moderato*) suggests the preparation for and
onset of a standard generic shape – sonata form – but what follows almost
immediately jettisons this implication to pursue a different, ad hoc musical
process. In other words, once the rapid-tempo part of the work is launched,
the piece seems to 'change its mind' with regard to the form that it intends
to pursue. The main body of the piece, begun with the *Allegro moderato*
in bar 74 (which before long tightens into an *Allegro* at bar 95), shrugs
off sonata norms to create an idiosyncratic shape built around a repeated
rounded-binary form and its consequences. Considered as a whole, this
unusual, blunt-cut structure is doubtless marked by the influence of Liszt's
revolutionary formal ideas of 1855, which were in full resonance among early
modern composers around the turn of the century. Formal innovation was
now the watchword. Far from following standard forms, 'in program music

the returns, alternations, modifications, and modulations of the motive are conditioned by their relationship to a poetic idea. Here one theme does not call forth another by rule of law.' Liszt had urged progressive composers to 'create new forms for new ideas, new skins for new wine', to drive their musical thoughts 'to new and bold, unusual and intricate combinations'.[2]

Most fundamentally, the piece that came to be retitled *Finlandia* illustrates a process of tonic- and structure-building. In purely musical terms, the composition, which begins in a remote corner, on a snarling F♯ minor $^6_4$ chord, is 'about' the eventual production of an unshakeable A♭ major – doubtless construed within the work's implicit programme as a 'Finnish reality' to be attained. Moreover, the emergence of this key is underpinned with decisive thematic statements: as the key becomes solidified, so also do the melodic ideas. (The procedure anticipates 'the crystallisation of ideas from chaos', as Sibelius would later describe the finale of the Third Symphony.)[3] Even though this A♭ assertion first surfaces midway through the piece, it is secured with cadential stability only at the end. As such, in Schenkerian terms the entire composition may be heard as a large auxiliary cadence in A♭. From an only slightly shifted perspective, though, the entire piece suggests the forging of a single, ever-clarifying idea. (I have elsewhere called this procedure teleological genesis, a characteristic concern of Sibelius throughout his career.)[4] *Finlandia*'s A♭ tonic-creation may also recall a similar procedure in the remarkable *Lemminkäinen's Return*, written not too long before. There the expanding musical rotations (ongoing, varied recyclings of source material) had inexorably approached and eventually produced the tonic E♭ major, in this case a tonal analogue of the 'home' to which the Kalevalaic hero is returning.

As it happens, the most opportune place to start this *Finlandia* overview is in the middle, directly at the *Allegro* portion starting at bar 95 (Ex. 6.1). This is the moment at which both the essential architectural structure and the tonic key, A♭ major, begin to coalesce out of the earlier, more fluid promise. Bar 95 is obviously a central point of arrival. It is the first sustained emergence of the goal key – the A♭ major that is now here to stay – and in its fifth bar (bar 99) it launches a decisive, generically recognisable architectural format, in this case, the rounded-binary form (ABA'), which simultaneously signals the abandoning of any prior sonata-form implication. The entire passage is represented in Fig. 6.1, which also indicates a large block of self-repetition, indicated by repeat signs, bb. 99–124. (Thus the ABA' structure is played twice.)

We may characterise briefly each section of the rounded binary. The initial A-zone, bars 99–106 (the beginning is shown in the fifth bar of Ex. 6.1), consists, as is normative, of two similar four-bar modules, the antecedent and consequent of a terse parallel period. We should also observe (see below,

Example 6.1 Sibelius, *Finlandia* (bars 95–100)

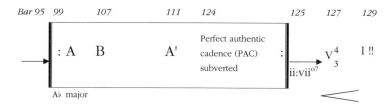

Figure 6.1 Sibelius, *Finlandia* (bars 95–129)

Ex. 6.5b) that the leading idea of the melody in the woodwinds, starting on beat 3 of bar 100, will be recast, pitch by pitch – and in the same register – into the *Finlandia* hymn later in the piece (Ex. 6.5c), a point of thematic transformation that will be revisited later in this essay.

Ex. 6.2 shows the outer voices of the B section, bars 107–10, and the first measure of the return of A′ (the reprise) at bar 111. While B articulates a generically typical dominant-chord prolongation, it also contains a local, fleeting tonicisation of vi of V (C minor) at bar 108, although this tonal colour participates in a larger harmonic motion that, functionally, suggests the clouding, even abandoning, of the normatively clear harmonic inter-ruption at the end of the B section, bar 110. More technically, one might observe that the B section articulates a downward arpeggiation from E♭, through C [minor], thence down (through a passing C♭ and B♭ in the bass in bar 110) to the reprise – A♭ major in bar 111. Within this passage it is worth noticing that the chord setting up the A′ reprise (on the last two beats of bar 110 over the bass B♭), is V$^4_3$ of A♭, a dominant seventh in inversion, rather than the stronger root-position chord that might be expected in this spot. One effect of this, as elsewhere in the piece, is to undermine the sense of a proximate, *fully secured* tonal attainment. Here Sibelius was seeking to weaken dominant–tonic juxtapositions at crucial structural junctures, reserving the strong versions of these things for later in the piece, when he would precipitate the tonic with more resoluteness.

It is on our understanding of the 'frustrated' reprise, A′, beginning in bar 111, that all will hang. As I have maintained in other contexts, the point of any tonal structure or substructure is to call forth or bring into being

Example 6.2 Sibelius, *Finlandia* (bars 107–11)

its tonic as a full reality by means of a *perfect authentic cadence* (PAC) of closure at its end. (A perfect authentic cadence has both the dominant and the tonic in root position – thus producing the typical leap of a fourth or fifth in the bass – and its tonic chord has scale-degree $\hat{1}$ as its highest pitch. The PAC is the archetypal 'full stop' sign making the satisfactory conclusion of a musical phrase, section, or piece.) Earlier perfect authentic cadences within an ongoing structure, however – such as one finds in the consequent of the initial A section, bar 106 – cannot represent this 'ultimate' finality because they are part of merely local, middleground structures subsumed within larger architectural formats. Hence the essential generic task of this spotlighted A′ reprise in *Finlandia* (the final limb of the ABA′ block) is to drive to a conclusive perfect authentic cadence in A♭ major. But in this ex-panded A′ reprise section (bars 111–24), the crucial point is that the final limb of the rounded binary is kept from fulfilling this cadential task and thus completing itself with finality. (See Fig. 6.1.) The drive to the cadence gets subverted, 'turned back'. Sibelius accomplishes this through a slippage to some 'struggling diminished-seventh' music (bars 121, 123) already heard earlier (bars 90, 92), before the onset of the rounded binary. Harmonically we now find a diminished seventh on a♮ (ii:vii°⁷) at bar 121, leading to a $^6_4$ over B♭ in bar 122 – suggesting a local motion further away from the A♭ tonic. A tilt back via the V$^4_3$ of A♭ in bar 124 (just before the repeat sign – notice that, slightly respaced, this is the same 'weak' V$^4_3$ heard earlier in bar 110) recycles us to the beginning of the block. Of course, since we now track through a literal repetition, the same cadential subversion occurs a second time.

Once on the other side of the repeat sign, we encounter a dynamic push through two more diminished-seventh bars (bars 125–6) towards a declared A♭ sonority, as if by sheer force of will. This is executed in bars 127–30 (Ex. 6.3) by a swelling *crescendo molto* from *piano* to *fortissimo*, and it is clearly a moment of asserted A♭ epiphany – the key that the piece wishes to 'make real'. However important this moment may be, it is no perfect authentic cadence (PAC). Instead, the tonic is prepared by the same V$^4_3$ (over a B♭ bass) that we have heard in two differing contexts in the earlier portions of the rounded binary idea.⁵ The structural point is clear: Sibelius

Example 6.3 Sibelius, *Finlandia* (bars 127–30)

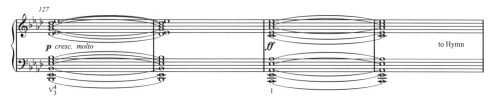

stages the cadence-defining dominant-seventh chord as still 'unable' to right itself into the stronger root position, which would be needed for full closure with a perfect authentic cadence. What we have in bars 127–30, therefore, is a 'weakened' *contrapuntal cadence*, with a $\hat{2}$–$\hat{1}$ motion (not the stronger $\hat{5}$–$\hat{1}$ motion) in the bass, B♭ to A♭. (A contrapuntal cadence, in this sense, is a less emphatic lead-in to the tonic chord in which the dominant or dominant-seventh chord is not in a 'strong' root position. Lacking the leap of a fifth or fourth in the bass, its effect is to make the impression of closure much less certain – if it is to be regarded as any sort of closure at all.) We find this defining $\hat{2}$–$\hat{1}$ motion in the lowest voice, here sounded by the bassoon, tuba, and double basses, while the trumpet sustains a top-voice $\hat{5}$ (e♭²) in both the V_3^4 and the I chords. To be sure, the cadence is fortified by a strong fifth-motion, $\hat{5}$–$\hat{1}$, in the timpani, cellos, and trombones, and also by the jagged $\hat{5}$–$\hat{1}$ leap in first violins. Nevertheless, it is the combination of the lack of decisive root motion in the bass and the persistence of the sustained upper voice $\hat{5}$ in the trumpet that is critical. Because the perfect authentic cadence is withheld, and notwithstanding the sonorous magnificence of the local A♭ epiphany, we are left with uncompleted tonal and architectural business. The A♭ tonic, while made present as a strong sonority, has not yet been secured as a completely disclosed reality. We have had no full conclusion, no cadential point of what I call 'essential structural closure' (ESC) to the attempted rounded binary. There is still work to do.

The suddenly climactic declaration of this A♭ chord in bar 129 is obviously a strong moment. It is to this point of disclosure that the subsequent hymn may be heard as a reaction – the finally possible entrance of something important following the drawing open of dramatic curtains. Still, because the earlier binary structure up to this point is not yet fully closed, the two stanzas of this famous hymn are situated structurally within it as an interpolation, a parenthesis, but also as an expressively crucial, confident response to what has been already attained so forcefully (Fig. 6.2). In part, this sturdy two-stanza hymn, whose opening pitches had been anticipated thematically in the preceding A section, is called upon to demonstrate to the rounded binary from a subordinated position outside the essential structure proper how one may close with cadential clarity, how

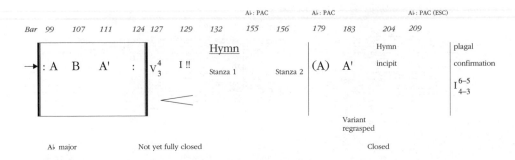

Figure 6.2 Sibelius, *Finlandia* (bars 95–209)

one may attain a secure perfect authentic cadence. In fact, in the hymn we hear not merely one perfect authentic cadence in A♭ major but two, one at the end of each of the two stanzas (in bars 155 and 179).

Neither of the two perfect authentic cadences in the hymn should be understood as providing essential structural closure to the piece as a whole: they are internal cadences produced within a parenthesis that is positionally secondary to the larger, still not fully closed binary structure. (The cadences are best understood as middleground phenomena, not background ones.) Having sounded two stanzas of the parenthetical hymn, we now return to unfinished business with the jump-start of an elided cadence – out of the parenthesis and back into the last limb of the preceding rounded binary, now resumed at bar 179, intending to bring it to full completion with a perfect authentic cadence. The first four measures of this reinvigorated reprise (not a coda) are variants of the original A idea, but once we arrive at the fifth bar, bar 183, the music tracks the original reprise quite closely (bar 183, for instance, is equivalent to bar 111, bar 184 to bar 112, and so on), with only small variants and a few excised bars. In other words, the rounded binary music is now heading for the more secure closure that had eluded it earlier; it is driving toward the moment of essential structural closure, the ESC. What is needed is a perfect authentic cadence in A♭, closing the binary structure and definitively articulating A♭ major as a now-stable reality.

In two pre-publication endings to the piece Sibelius provided two different solutions to the problem of securing that perfect authentic cadence, and we shall revisit them at the end of this essay. For the present we may notice that in the familiar final version the perfect authentic cadence occurs in bar 209, six bars before the end. Producing this cadence is an apotheosis-flourish: a brief thematic identifier of the hymn – now fully integrated into the rounded binary – on the way to its moment of essential structural closure. With its cadence in bar 209 the tonal point of the whole piece, the calling forth of a stable A♭ major, has finally been realised. At the same time the once incomplete rounded binary has finally found its telos of completion.

Example 6.4 Sibelius, *Finlandia*, opening

A plagal confirmation coda ('Amen'), over a tonic pedal, follows by way of affirmation. The entire preceding musical process has been working to construct the right to claim, then ratify, this A♭ major.

At this point we may return to consider the opening of the piece, the slow introduction, *Andante sostenuto*, which had begun far away indeed from this A♭ tonic (Ex. 6.4). The menacing opening sonority is an F♯ minor $^6_4$ chord, decorated locally with its own German sixth. The strenuous initial phrase ends on A major (bar 8); the second, a sequence of the first, ends on a C major abruptly chilled to C minor (bar 17); the third moves to a C major chord also bearing a potential to serve as V of F minor (bars 22–3); and that grim F minor dominates the remainder of the introduction. From the perspective of the introductory F minor shackles, the A♭ major to come is doubtless to be understood as a liberation, as a claiming of F minor's major mediant, III. Conversely, the implication is that one is initially locked in the oppressive, 'unjust' submediant vi, F minor, pleading for emancipation into one's truer self, A♭ major. (This is a characteristically Sibelian use of expressive tonal relations. A similar dialectic of i and III – or vi and I – lies at the core of the First Symphony.)

Within the introductory F minor fetters one finds stirrings of the A♭ major 'true self' within. Some of the F minor phrases in the introduction, for example, pass through their mediants en route to tonic-minor cadences. One such case occurs in the first woodwind phrase, bars 24–9 (Ex. 6.5a). Here the harmonisation of the opening notes of the melody could be heard as in either A♭ major or F minor before the phrase slumps to its F minor cadence. Equally important, the woodwind timbre, pitches, and register forecast the woodwind line of the later rounded binary (Ex. 6.5b), which are themselves to be recast rhythmically into the eventual hymn (Ex. 6.5c). Such features of the introduction may be regarded as prolepses – flashforwards or projections – and they play an important role in the process-orientation of the piece as a whole.

The slow introduction, mostly dominated by F minor, is immediately followed by an impetuously triggered *Allegro moderato*, which seems locally to begin in C minor at bar 74. Such a procedure – slow introduction touching off a stormy *Allegro moderato* – would normally suggest the beginning

Example 6.5 Sibelius, *Finlandia* [excerpts]

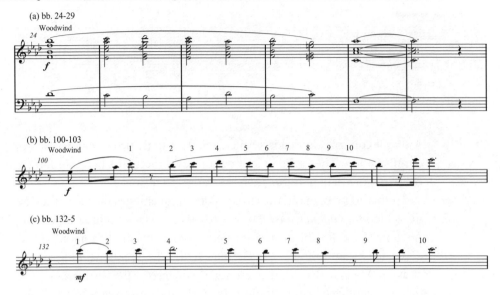

(a) bb. 24-29

(b) bb. 100-103

(c) bb. 132-5

of a sonata form, following, for example, the archetypal struggle-against-resistance models of Beethoven's *Egmont* and Tchaikovsky's *1812* overtures (and dozens of other pieces). But in *Finlandia* – or 'Finland Awakens' – what we learn at once is that this rapid-tempo self-realisation is going to occur on unprecedented, ad hoc terms, not on the 'borrowed' or 'foreign' terms of sonata practice. Instead, the C minor *Allegro moderato* opening is no exposition at all: the potential sonata format is explicitly abandoned. Rather, this is a passage of gradual self-creation, serving primarily as a generative passageway to the 'real' structure-still-to-come. This real structure is the coalescing, out of the preceding motives, of the rounded-binary format on Ab, whose structural cadence is then delayed as I have outlined earlier.

In summary, *Finlandia* provides us with a unique structure that invokes, then immediately casts aside, the sonata tradition, in order to articulate instead a process of ongoing Ab realisation (teleological genesis), and simultaneously with it, the gradual coalescing of a block-like architectural form, here understood primarily in terms of the extended adventures of its rounded binary-based *Allegro* section – adventures that include, most crucially, the important, embedded two-stanza hymn. Within this larger process of increasing clarity, other structural factors are also at work that I shall not expand upon here. Foremost among them are the rotational features of the piece, each of whose major sections takes up and reworks material from its predecessor in the manner of a relay: the *Allegro moderato* elaborates material from the introduction, as if responding directly to it; the binary structure includes the percussive head-motive of the initial *Allegro moderato*;

and the hymn reshapes an important thematic contour first sounded clearly in the binary structure. At this point, however, we might turn to a consideration of the representational intention of this music.

Programmatic implications

Finlandia, of course, was never conceived as a purely abstract structure without extra-musical connotation. On the contrary, it was politically charged from the beginning, initially emerging, as mentioned earlier, as 'Suomi herää' (Finland Awakens) in its first, November 1899 context. It is that original implication that I wish to pursue here, rather than focusing on the national and cultural meaning that the work would take on in the twentieth century. As is well known, 'Suomi herää' was a work conceptually linked with a diachronic sequence of historical *tableaux vivants* presented at the Helsinki Press Celebrations. This is an often-repeated story, and for the present purposes we need only recall that this protest event featured six historical tableaux representing stages of the chronological progress of Finland from primeval to modern times. Most important is the diachronic ordering: each tableau brought us closer to the present. Moreover that present, November 1899, was itself vectored forward: it was poised on the lip of the future, the twentieth century, and it was also poised at a moment of Russian-imposed political repression within Finland itself. Sibelius contributed around thirty-five minutes of music for these six tableaux. The final, seven-minute presentation – the last tableau of the six – was 'Suomi herää', whose ending was eventually revised, at least twice, before being toured separately in 1900 as *Finlandia, Vaterland, La patrie*, and the like, and published as a self-standing work in 1901 as *Finlandia* (a title suggested by Axel Carpelan, perhaps intentionally recalling such symphonic poems as Liszt's *Hungaria*, Balakirev's *Russia*, or Smetana's cycle, *Má Vlast*).[6]

The 'Suomi herää' *tableau vivant* was the capstone of that evening. The key features of the relevant tableau included 'the powers of darkness menacing Finland [at the opening of the nineteenth century]' which nevertheless 'have not succeeded in their terrible threats. Finland awakens.' Viewers also saw a panoply of historical figures who contributed to Finland's sense of self-identity as 'representatives of this period of awakening'. These included Tsar Alexander II, the poet Johan Ludvig Runeberg, Johan Vilhelm Snellman inspiring his students to think of the possibility of Finnish independence, and Elias Lönnrot transcribing the runes of the epic, *Kalevala*. And 'also [present on stage] are: four speakers of the first parliament; an elementary school, and a locomotive'.[7] In sum, this busy tableau proclaimed a linear vision of self-assertion projected into the future – a new, finally awakened

Finland greeting the new century (only two months away) equipped with its own history, with its own poetry and legitimised language, with modern resources (education), and with modern technology (the unstoppable loco-motive in this tableau, an image of industrial progress – a steam-propelled Finland racing, by implication, toward an even more modern form of even-tual self-rule).

Understanding all of this in connection with Sibelius's music is not dif-ficult. Obviously, the musical subsections of 'Suomi herää' articulate the musical process of tonal and formal self-realisation. As a whole, they move chronologically from representations of 'then' (1800) to those of 'now' (1899) – from utter darkness to brilliant light, from instability to stability, from slow to fast, from minor to major, from the cruel, clipped motive of the opening to the broadly unfurled melody of the hymn. It does not take much imagination to propose that the oppressive, minor-mode introduc-tion, *Andante sostenuto*, represents 'the powers of darkness': Finland's dev-astation and futile despair at the opening of the nineteenth century. Nor that the brief, hymnic A♭ melodic and woodwind prolepsis in bars 24–9 (Ex. 6.5a) suggests the cries of the spiritually rooted Finnish people in bondage – the aspiring A♭ major inevitably being drawn back into the chains of F minor.

Similarly, the 'awakening' – the array of nineteenth-century poets, schol-ars, statesmen, educators, along with the drive towards Finnish-language legitimation – is signalled by the very brief *Allegro moderato*, bar 74, initially in a local C minor. This 'false-exposition' moment is faster, more aggres-sive, and dominated by the multiple eruptions of an important rhythm, the rat-a-tat volleys of which are the musical equivalent of the imperative to awaken ('Herää!'). This is surely the *awakening rhythm*, first heard in minor, then more optimistically in major. Moreover, in the initial events of the *Allegro moderato*, this 'awakening' is juxtaposed directly with the 'powers of darkness' motive from the introduction, which are gradually dispelled towards the major – and towards A♭ major at that. And not only towards A♭ major, we recall, but also towards the repeated rounded-binary block in which the modular particles begin to coalesce toward an architectonic solidity. As mentioned earlier, by staging this swerving-away from the ex-pected sonata-form continuation, Sibelius may also have been implying that both he as an early modernist composer and Finland as an emerging cul-ture were proposing to enter the arena on other than merely second-hand, European-imitative terms.

Moving ahead, we arrive at the quickened, A♭ *Allegro* block, bar 95 (Ex. 6.1), gaining kinetic heft and plunging (bar 99) into the rounded binary block, ignited by a more jubilant version of the 'Awaken!' rhythm. Given the images provided to us in the description of the tableau, it seems most likely, as has been suggested elsewhere,[8] that Sibelius composed here a musical analogue to the huffing and puffing of a steam locomotive, its heavy mechanical wheels rotating powerfully through four bars to overcome tons of weighty inertia (in effect, three circular 5/4 bars inlaid into 4/4 notation – see Ex. 6.1) and then setting forth into the binary block, bar 99, with enormous force.

Once again we recall that the upper-voice melody in bars 100–2 (Ex. 6.5b) provides the ten pitches that will soon be refashioned into the two-stanza hymn, presumably representing the voice of the Finnish spirit or people. The presence of that melodic contour, register, and orchestration here suggests that it is the people themselves who are borne forward – vectored toward the present – on that metaphorical locomotive. Similarly, the ostinato, the continued rhythmic exhortations of 'Herää!' ('Awaken!'), the circular repetition of the binary block – each of these things also participates in the central locomotive image. If this supposition is defensible, that would make this section one of the earliest musical depictions of large iron-built industrial machines in the history of music. (Such images would become more commonplace in the 1920s avant-garde.)

Here, it appears, Sibelius was identifying Finland's progress and drive to self-identity with that steam-powered engine. Most important, with the rounded-binary 'locomotive' section 'Suomi herää' has reached a crucial station in its journey. Here it finds its major-key destiny, Ab major, and in that Ab major it will remain fixed – on the rails – for the rest of the work. The message seems clear: 'locomotive' Finland has now found itself, has stabilised; the nation is now unflappably on course. (Sibelius would recreate this fixed-tonic, juggernaut locomotive effect in the remarkably similar, though more radical, finale of the Third Symphony, although there is at present no direct evidence that he had this precise image in mind for that work.) Full closure of that idea, however – the ESC – will be delayed until the perfect authentic cadence at the end of the piece. For the present we are brought to the swelling *fortissimo* point of one important stage of attainment via that huge contrapuntal cadence onto Ab in bar 129 (Ex. 6.3) – the image of a now self-aware Finland pulling with enormous energy into at least one station of 'awakened' arrival.

This powerful epiphany may be understood in a number of ways. One might argue, for instance, that with the swelling contrapuntal cadence onto Ab, Finland's past (in this diachronic review of historical time) culminates in a momentous realisation of Finland's present: 'Here we are!' Past time – represented by the preceding tableaux and the first part of this one – now flows into present time. (Or, at least, the past arrives at a point of fullness within which the 'national spirit of Finland' may be disclosed as an essential, self-assured presence.) Thus it is appropriate that the *fortissimo* climax of grand cultural arrival be followed immediately by the two-stanza

Example 6.6 Emil Genetz, 'Herää, Suomii' (publ. 1882), (bars 36–41)

parenthetical hymn. Even though there is still unfinished cadential business to pursue, at first this hymnic moment seems to function as an
epilogue – a grateful epilogue at rest after a period of stress or struggle (something like the finale of Beethoven's 'Pastoral' Symphony, a hymn of thanks
following the storm – or something like a *Te Deum*, a hymn of thanks after
victory).

As it happens, the multiple connotations of the hymn, even in its
1899 'Suomi herää' context, are worth investigating further. On one level
(Ex. 6.5a–c) it is here that the two earlier prolepses – the pitch-related 'cries
of the Finnish spirit' in the introduction and, even more obviously, the
passengers on the historical locomotive in bars 100–2 – finally mature into
present-time disclosure. On another level it is certainly true, as Sibelius later
insisted, that taken as a whole this hymn was a melody original to him. Nevertheless, as has been pointed out before, it also seems likely that its opening
pitches paraphrased part of a patriotic choral piece from the 1880s, one by
the Finnish composer Emil Genetz. The passage in question stems from an
interior section of Genetz's piece (Ex. 6.6). The linchpin for this connection, of course, lies in the title of Genetz's piece, 'Herää, Suomi!' ('Awaken,
Finland!') – and to the text of the immediate moment alluded to by Sibelius,
which refers to the rising-up of the Finnish lion to overcome the suffering
of the nation. In short, Genetz's imperative, 'Herää, Suomi!', was now answered by Sibelius's ringing declarative, 'Suomi herää' ('Finland Awakens'),
and the link between the pieces was cemented with a fleeting incipit allusion.
By referring to the melody from the Genetz piece, Sibelius was suggesting
that the earlier call to action, 'Awaken', had now been fulfilled. Finally, one
hardly knows what to make of the incipit's additional near-quotation, in
its first four notes, of Schumann's Piano Quartet in E♭ (Ex. 6.7, third bar).
The resemblance might be entirely coincidental, unknown to Sibelius, or it
might have suggested some sort of continued tie to European tradition or
spirit, even as the structure of the work was now veering sharply into the
idiosyncratic or the ad hoc.

Following the two stanzas of parenthetical self-disclosure – the hymn –
Sibelius's piece still had necessary work to accomplish (Fig. 6.2): the securing
of the perfect authentic cadence signalling the full presence and stability of

Example 6.7 Robert Schumann, Piano Quartet in E flat major, op. 47 (bars 11–18)

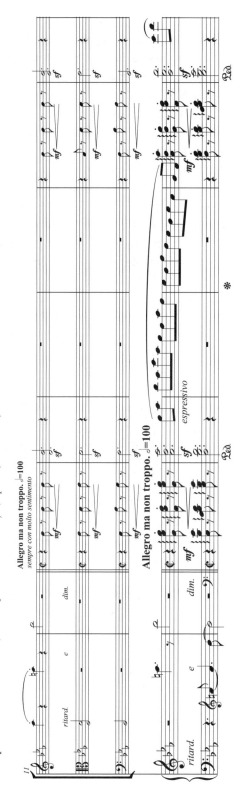

Ab major, its secure arrival. With the forward-rushing elided cadence at bar 179 Sibelius now backs up to regrasp the last limb of the rounded binary, A′, the unstoppable 'locomotive' of progress, in order to drive toward that cadence. In the original, Press Celebrations version, this Ab cadence, the moment of essential structural closure (ESC), was seized and articulated very quickly, and it ushered in at once a celebratory victory-coda. Its original meaning in 1899 – the first version with its 'short' ending, without any further reference to the hymn – could hardly have been more self-evident. Reiterating two building blocks, the repeated victory-shout of 'Awaken!' and the locomotive idea, the now-centred, now-awakened Finland was continuing to steam ahead into the future – into the new century on its own terms, tonally, on its own Ab terms.

In the second version – with the 'long' ending – Sibelius delayed considerably the arrival of the Ab closure, and, most important, he assigned that task to the final moments of a full apotheosis statement of the regrasped hymn (in effect, to a third stanza). Surely after the premiere he had realised the power of that hymn melody and the reaction of the first audience to it, and now he tipped the balance of the whole piece towards this final grand statement. For today's listeners, who know the final version so well, the second version's effect of a *complete* statement of the hymn, mostly over the expectant dominant, provides us with a delicious and unexpected ecstasy of suspension, a prolongation of the great moment. Sibelius also highlighted this 'added' third stanza with an idiosyncratically defiant, neo-primitivist harmonisation, embellished with emphatic and sinuous string-twistings.

The final ending – the one we all know – is a compacted version of the second. Again, it is the hymn, the bearer of self-identity, that provides closure to the binary structure, but that message is carried, in an astonishing demonstration of renunciation, by means of a single phrase only, a brief thematic reference. In a mighty, brass *fortissimo*, that moment fuses the beginning and end of the hymn: it regrasps the hymn's *first* phrase, its melodic incipit, but bends it determinedly at the end toward the perfect authentic cadence of its *final* phrase. Thus the moment of closure is accomplished by a single-phrase, telescoped summary of the complete hymn. And that resolute, supercharged hymn phrase was surely intended as a compressed emblem of self-creation and self-assertion, as a declaration of the identity of tonal and national attainment, and as a launch into the new century of the now-realised spirit of a fully 'awakened' Finland – a Finland coursing, locomotive-like, into what was hoped to be a promising, liberated future.

7 The tone poems: genre, landscape and structural perspective

DANIEL M. GRIMLEY

Categories of genre in nineteenth- and early-twentieth-century music engage with many levels of musical interpretation. Placed in their historical context, generic conventions define our understanding of musical works and serve, above all, to inform our sense of musical meaning.[1] Nevertheless, identifying the precise boundaries between individual genres such as the tone poem and the symphony can be problematic. Despite the hybrid construction of the term 'symphonic poem' (*Synfonische Dichtung*), first coined by Liszt in the 1840s, the tone poem often seems generically opposed, rather than closely related, to the symphony.[2] Throughout the nineteenth century, after Beethoven, the symphony was principally concerned with notions of breadth and monumentality. Regarded as the highest form of absolute music, the symphony aspired to high levels of motivic unity, formal abstraction and goal-directed (teleological) musical form.[3] Symphonies consciously and powerfully engaged in a dialogue with canonical works of the past. Tone poems, by contrast, are concerned at a fundamental level with the evocation of a particular mood or atmosphere, or with the articulation of an extra-musical narrative or programme. In response to such literary or pictorial subject matter, tone poems are characterised by their freer, innovative approach to musical form, particularly the tendency towards structures that telescope the traditional four-movement scheme of a symphony into a single musical span. Such forms often sacrifice dynamic motivic or harmonic development in favour of radically static moments of sonorous or poetic contemplation, intended as musical depictions of the (super-) natural world.[4] Though, as Hugh MacDonald has noted, tone poems arguably succeeded in elevating instrumental programme music to an aesthetic level comparable with that of opera, they were invariably regarded as inferior to symphonies. The perceived difference in status between the two genres remained unchanged, even as programme music flourished at the end of the nineteenth century.

Sibelius's tone poems regularly blur such fixed generic distinctions. Aspects of formal innovation, such as telescoped multi-movement schemes within a single span and other kinds of sonata deformation structures,[5] are as much a feature of his symphonies as of his tone poems. Furthermore, many

of his tone poems are characterised by an intense level of motivic and harmonic unity, and by a demonstrably goal-directed musical structure, more
conventionally associated with abstract symphonic works than with music of an essentially programmatic or descriptive nature. Stretching generic
boundaries was a well-established feature of late nineteenth- and early-
twentieth-century music. Works such as Richard Strauss's *Alpensymphonie*,
for example, fall exactly midway between the generic conventions of the
symphony and the tone poem. As James Hepokoski has observed, however,
Sibelius's tone poems were an integral part of a sustained compositional
project, one that sought to synthesise and transform the conflicting demands of different musical genres into a higher category of 'content-based
forms'.[6] Such organic, intuitively designed musical structures, which bore
less than a passing or secondary resemblance to previous canonical models, were driven by the internal dynamics of their musical material rather
than prescribed notions of musical form and procedure. Recent research has
suggested an even closer level of musical interrelationship between the symphonies and the tone poems. Preliminary ideas for virtually all of Sibelius's
large-scale works from the Fifth Symphony onwards, for example, can be
found in a single sketchbook dated 1914–15,[7] suggesting that, irrespective
of genre, Sibelius's music sprang from essentially the same creative source.
It is a striking indication of the continuing relevance of generic categories,
therefore, that Sibelius ultimately chose to maintain the distinction between different kinds of orchestral works: though the Seventh Symphony
was originally labelled 'Fantasia Sinfonica', it was ultimately published as
a Symphony 'in einem Satze'. *Tapiola*, similarly, for all its motivic rigour
and multi-movement characteristics, appeared in print as a 'Sinfonische
Dichtung'. In Sibelius's mind, at least, the symphony and the tone poem
remained recognisably independent musical forms.

The tone poems span the whole of Sibelius's creative career, from *En saga*
(1892, rev. 1902), to *Tapiola* (1926), his final full-scale orchestral work. The
initial impetus for *En saga* came from Sibelius's older colleague, the Finnish
conductor Robert Kajanus, who asked for a new orchestral work following
the massive critical success of the *Kullervo* Symphony in 1892. Sibelius himself conducted the premiere of the work in Helsinki on 16 February 1893.
Unlike *Kullervo*, based on a passage from the Finnish epic, the *Kalevala*, *En
saga* does not rely on a single specific literary or mythic source. Ever since
the work's premiere, in fact, the tone poem's 'programme' has generated
scholarly speculation. Sibelius's early biographer, Otto Andersson, for example, described the work as 'Ossianic', comparing the mythic atmosphere
of Sibelius's tone poem with the ballad poetry of the fictional Celtic bard.[8]
The German critic Walter Niemann suggested that 'it is rather a question
of a state of mind, the musical atmosphere a saga engenders in the listener,

irrespective of whether it is Icelandic, Swedish or Finnish'. Sibelius himself
may have subconsciously recalled Niemann's comments when he 'confessed'
to his secretary, Santeri Levas, in the 1940s:

> *En saga* is one of my most profound works in psychological meaning. I
> could even say that it contains all my youth. It is the expression of a state of
> mind. I had undergone a number of painful experiences at the time and in
> no other work have I revealed myself so completely. It is for this reason
> that I find all literary explanations quite alien.[9]

Sibelius's comments can be read as a retrospective attempt to distance *En saga*
from the powerfully *Kalevala*-inspired nationalist works of the early 1890s,
as he strove to escape his provincial *Heimatkünstler* image in favour of a
more cosmopolitan international outlook. Critics since have lent considerable weight to the work's supposedly 'autobiographical' content. Veijo
Murtomäki, for example, has argued that, 'if, on one level, *En saga* is situated in Nordic mythological time, on another, deeper level, it has a profoundly autobiographical significance: Sibelius identified himself with his
ancient heroes'.[10] Certainly, images of heroic struggle and transgression
recur in a sufficient number of Sibelius's early works, from *Kullervo* to the
Lemminkäinen Legends and the First Symphony, to suggest the presence of a
narrative archetype, even if the straightforwardly autobiographical interpretation of *En saga* can ultimately seem somewhat reductive. Despite Sibelius's
own claims, *En saga* is a rich and thoroughly characteristic product of his
Karelianist period, when the boundaries between his creative work and his
inner psychological life seem to have been especially close, but the work can
also be located within a wider tragic–heroic tradition, whose subject matter
exerted a particularly powerful fascination over composers at the end of the
nineteenth century.

En saga's material is closely related to the folkloristic style of much of
the music in *Kullervo*, associated particularly with mythic representations
of the Finnish forest. Both works are characterised by the widespread use
of ostinatos and circular, insistently repetitive motivic ideas, usually of a
severely restricted melodic range. Allied to a powerful, craggy orchestral
texture, in which the distinctions between different instrumental groups are
marked by violent rhythmic or dynamic change rather than smooth transitions, this neo-primitivist musical language is the hallmark of Sibelius's
early 'epic' discourse. *En saga* was substantially revised in 1902, ten years
after its premiere. In its reworked streamlined form, the music loses some
of its more exotic instrumental colour. As a consequence, however, the tone
poem's tonal structure is articulated with greater clarity. *En saga* is based on
the interchangeability of the double-tonic complex C minor and E♭ major,
two keys commonly associated with musical representations of the tragic

Romantic hero since Beethoven's 'Eroica' symphony. This tonal complex is ultimately resolved through a process of modal mixture: the Eb minor of the tone poem's epilogue is a gloomy final resting place. According to Erik Tawaststjerna,

> *En saga* belongs formally to the freer sonata pattern evolved by Liszt in his symphonic poems and the sonata and other works. Even in the various subsections of the work, there is a tendency for the material to be subdivided into a miniature exposition, development and reprise, so that the form of the whole is reflected in the structure of the parts.[11]

The structure of the tone poem is based on the broad repetition of varied strophic material, framed by an extended introduction and coda, and may be summarised as follows:

Introduction (invocation) bars 1–95
Strophe 1 (exposition)
   First-subject group, bars 96–201
   Second-subject group, bars 202–75
Strophe 2 (counter-exposition or development)
   First-subject group (closing group only), bars 276–373
   Second-subject group, bars 374–461
Strophe 3 (development and reprise)
   First and second subjects combined, bars 462–555
Interlude and transition, bars 556–601
Strophe 4 (reprise)
   First-subject group, bars 602–99
   Crisis and catastrophe, bars 700–29
Epilogue, bars 730–815

The introduction begins in a remote and desolate-sounding A minor, the *pianissimo* string figuration weaving a mysteriously shifting curtain of sound. The first chromatic alteration in the archaic woodwind passage in bars 9–17 is D♯, the enharmonic equivalent of Eb, the note which plays a central role in the work's modal ambivalence (the constant drift from C major to C minor) and its eventual harmonic goal. Formally, the introduction is concerned with the generation and articulation of a broad epic theme, which, suitably energised, becomes the principal melodic idea of the first-subject group. The main body of the work is divided into two formal statements – an extended exposition and a counter-exposition or development – followed by a third strophe (a dark brooding passage in C minor) that combines elements of development and reprise. Despite its dynamic sense of purpose and forward motion, the introduction's epic theme does not return in its entirety until the end of the reprise, where it ultimately leads to a dramatic climax and catastrophic collapse on an anguished

Tristan chord. Following the work's denouement, the tone poem closes with an extended epilogue in which the clarinet soliloquy intones an icy version of the saga's epic theme from the introduction.

En saga was one of Sibelius's earliest works to attract international attention. His following tone poem, *Spring Song* (*Vårsång*), originated as a very different kind of commission. The work was premiered on 21 June 1894, as part of a grand open-air concert organised by the Finnish Society of Popular Education (*Kansanvalistusseura*). The tone poem was originally titled 'Impromptu', a reference perhaps to its improvisatory melodic structure. Sibelius subsequently revised and retitled the tone poem, transposing the music from D major to F major, a more idyllic pastoral key. The second version was premiered on 13 April 1895, but the tone poem was revised a third time before eventual publication in 1903. The original open-air venue may have prompted a number of the work's characteristic features, notably the affirmatory use of bells in the closing apotheosis, the bold linear approach to orchestration (especially the hymnic quality of the string writing), and the strongly diatonic harmonic language. The subtitle, 'La tristesse du printemps', points towards the sense of melancholy that pervades much of the music in the earlier part of the work, especially the tendency to shift momentarily towards the relative minor rather than attain a perfect close in the tonic major. This pattern of harmonic evasion colours much of Sibelius's work, such as the Sixth Symphony, without disrupting the essentially diatonic character of his music. Tawaststjerna suggests that '*Vårsång* is primarily a work apostrophizing the qualities of the Nordic spring and in particular its quality of light.'[12] Accordingly, the tone poem is not concerned with an extra-musical narrative or programme, so much as the intense contemplation of a radiant orchestral sonority. In terms of subject matter therefore, the tone poem is as 'absolute' as Sibelius's symphonies.

The abstract non-programmatic quality of *Vårsång* and, to a lesser degree, *En saga*, stands in sharp contrast to both *Skogsrået* (The Wood Nymph) and the *Four Lemminkäinen Legends*, which are based upon specific literary sources. Exceptionally among Sibelius's works, *Skogsrået* survives in three different musical forms: an orchestral tone poem, a melodrama for voice and ensemble, and a solo piano piece. The work was based on a poem by the Swedish poet Viktor Rydberg (1828–95), whose work strongly attracted Sibelius with its characteristically *fin-de-siècle* mixture of nature mysticism, inner psychological drama and Nordic myth. Sibelius's other Rydberg works included a number of his most powerful songs, including 'Höstkväll' and 'På veranden vid havet', and a second melodrama, entitled *Snöfrid* (1900). The melodrama version of *Skogsrået* was first performed on 9 March 1895, at a lottery festival arranged by the Finnish theatre in Helsinki. The orchestral tone poem was premiered just over a month later, on 17 April 1895, in a concert of Sibelius's music given at the Great Hall, Helsinki University. The audience was provided with a text of Rydberg's poem on this occasion, underlining the importance of the work's literary programme. The tone poem was performed again on several occasions during the composer's lifetime, but was never published and gradually fell out of the repertoire. The work only received its modern premiere, after it was rediscovered, on 9 February 1996, when it was performed by the Lahti Symphony Orchestra and Osmo Vänskä.

Though *Skogsrået* was positively received at the time of its first performance in 1895, its subsequent reception has proved more equivocal. Tawaststjerna suggests that the music was composed in the shadow of Sibelius's visit to Bayreuth in 1894, when he heard performances of many of Wagner's operas, including *Tristan und Isolde, Die Meistersinger, Die Walküre, Götterdämmerung* and *Parsifal*. Sibelius seems to have experienced a Nietzschean response to Wagner's work: his early enthusiasm was followed by a radical change of heart. In a letter dated 19 July 1894, for example, he wrote to Aino, 'I can't begin to tell you how *Parsifal* has transported me. Everything I do seems so cold and feeble by its side. *That* is really something.' By 19 August, however, his attitude had altered sharply, and he wrote, 'I have found my old self again, musically speaking. Many things are now clear to me: really I am a tone painter and poet. Liszt's view of music is the one to which I am closest. Hence my interest in the symphonic poem.' Tawaststjerna has suggested that:

> *Skogsrået* can be best thought of as an experiment. After his Wagnerian summer Sibelius was still trying to find his feet as a tone-poet using Liszt's example as a starting point. In *Skogsrået* he strictly follows the narrative and allows it to determine the musical shape of the work . . . *Skogsrået* has some fine music in it and could perhaps have been one of Sibelius's most characteristic essays in this form had he perhaps waited a little longer before reworking the material of the melodrama.[13]

Murtomäki, however, has stressed the innovative aspects of *Skogsrået*'s formal structure. For Murtomäki, the late-nineteenth-century orchestral ballad constitutes a specific subgenre of the symphonic poem, and *Skogsrået* exemplifies a number of the distinguishing features of the form, most importantly the articulation of a final 'deviating' or subversive swerve at the end of a goal-directed musical structure.[14] In this case, the effect is heightened by the work's unusual tonal structure: though the tone poem begins breezily in C major, in a mood reminiscent of the overture from Sibelius's recently composed *Karelia* music, the concluding section of *Skogsrået* is a massive funeral march in C♯ minor. As in *En saga*, the absence of clear tonic resolution, and the change of mode, serves to strengthen the work's tragic impact. The most striking music in *Skogsrået*, however, is the episode immediately following the opening presentation of the hero, Björn. Sibelius illustrates Björn's foray into the magical Nordic forest in an extended proto-minimalist passage that generates a tremendous sense of textural and dynamic momentum. In the context of other composers' work from the 1890s, the harmonic stasis and the elevation of texture as a primary structural parameter are among the tone poem's most daring features. The hero's subsequent encounter with the wood-nymph is bathed in an erotic afterglow, but, as Jeffrey Kallberg has observed, the expected moment of musical and narrative consummation is missing. The ballad's final swerve, to borrow Murtomäki's term, is thus a tragic and hollow-sounding one.

The four *Lemminkäinen Legends* were premiered on 13 April 1896. Sibelius revised *The Swan of Tuonela* and *Lemminkäinen's Return* before publication in 1900. The other two tone poems, *Lemminkäinen and the Maidens of the Island* and *Lemminkäinen in Tuonela*, however, were not published until 1935, when they finally appeared also in revised form. The *Lemminkäinen Legends* return to the Finnish mythological source, the *Kalevala*, which had inspired *Kullervo*. Though the two central tone poems, *The Swan of Tuonela* and *Lemminkäinen in Tuonela*, chart the hero's ill-fated voyage to the dark waters of the Finnish underworld, the final movement, *Lemminkäinen's Return*, inverts the tragic trajectory of Sibelius's earlier works to end in a mood of affirmatory triumph. Indeed, *Lemminkäinen's Return* is one of the earliest instances of Sibelius's process of crystallisation, the gradual establishment of melodic, harmonic and textural order through a strongly directed linear growth, in this case the transformation from the C minor motivic fragments of the opening bars to the E♭ major chorale of the conclusion.[15] Allied to the proto-minimalist ostinato textures developed in *En saga* and other works from his 'Karelianist' phase, this device became one of Sibelius's most powerful and characteristic formal procedures, used to particularly successful effect in the finale of the Third Symphony and the first movement of the revised version of the Fifth.

The Swan of Tuonela has become one of Sibelius's most popular and widely performed works, no doubt due to the melancholy beauty of the solo cor anglais melody (Sibelius's most poignant reference to the third act of Wagner's *Tristan*) that dominates the work. The first number of the set, *Lemminkäinen and the Maidens of the Island*, is less well known, but equally evocative. The music is suffused with the same midsummer-night atmosphere as the erotic encounter in *Skogsrået*. The idea of the midsummer night, with its overtones of irrationality and the supernatural, strongly appealed to many Nordic artists in the 1890s, from the landscape paintings of Edvard Munch to the writings of Norwegian novelist Knut Hamsun.[16] The powerful mood of nature mysticism in Hamsun's novels *Pan* (1894) and

Victoria (1896), for example, is paralleled by the opening of Sibelius's tone poem. The work opens with a magical horn call in E♭ major, a particular kind of non-tonic sonority that, according to James Hepokoski, functions as a threshold, 'leading from silence, or near-silence, into sacred space – vast or magical forests or other nature-places, mystical sunrises, and the like'.[17] The echo dynamics, notated pauses and the *allargando* in bars 16 and 27 create a momentary suspension of regular metre, an effect highlighted by the softly undulating entry of the strings and the gentle syncopation of the woodwind's melodic descents. As in the first movement of the Fifth Symphony, the entire introduction is generated from the insistent sounding (or pealing) of this opening horn sonority, through a series of 'misfired' cadences in bars 10–11, 23–4, 25–6 and 32–3. The introduction returns at key moments in the strophic structure of the tone poem, such as at the transition to the second subject (bars 99–119), and at the beginning of the reprise (bars 396–408). Crucially, however, the opening horn call is only resolved at the end of the work (bars 524–32), a super-charged moment delivered with maximum force that becomes the tone poem's ultimate point of structural focus. After the glowing confidence of the tone poem's final bars, the slow unfolding A minor chord at the opening of *The Swan of Tuonela*, rising across a seemingly vast registral space, has a dramatically other-worldly effect. From this transition alone, it is tempting to speculate upon Sibelius's unfulfilled potential as an operatic composer in the light of his ambivalent reception of Wagner's work in the 1890s.

On 5 March 1904, Sibelius conducted the Helsinki Philharmonic in music to accompany a tableau based on Heine's poem *Ein Fichtenbaum steht einsam*. The subject matter had interested him as early as 1897, though whether the music on this occasion bore any relation to an earlier 'Forest Song' he had mentioned to Aino remains unclear. The music comprised an introduction and a waltz for full orchestra. Sibelius sold a piano reduction of the piece to his Finnish publisher Fazer in 1904, but the orchestral version was not published until 1907, by Breitkopf und Härtel, under the title Dance Intermezzo, op. 45/2. In this form, the piece cannot be considered a 'tone poem' in the conventional sense, though the work is one of Sibelius's characteristic miniatures: the kind of music that can easily seem light or superficial alongside his symphonic works without careful attention to its intended context or background. Despite its colourful orchestration and melodic richness, the piece is rarely performed in the concert hall today.

A similar fate has befallen the character piece *Pan and Echo*, which Sibelius composed for the Helsinki Philharmonic at a benefit concert in aid of funds to build a concert hall. The work was premiered on 24 March 1906, and opens with a brief musical sunrise figure (glowing strings and a rising bassoon arpeggio). In the following *commodo* section, the woodwind's pastoral dialogue is increasingly interrupted by wilder outbursts, leading to the work's sudden, almost bestial, conclusion. Unlike Carl Nielsen's pastorale, *Pan and Syrinx* (1918), with its sudden dream-like shifts from a languorous exotic haze to passages of extreme physical excitement, in Sibelius's work the expected return of the opening music never takes place. Rather, the work finishes brusquely in a manner that vividly contrasts with the tone poem's expansive introduction.

Both in terms of tone and subject matter, the *Dance Intermezzo* and *Pan and Echo* illustrate the extent to which, following the Second Symphony's composition in Italy, Sibelius had moved away from the purely Nordic-inspired works of the 1890s. In *Pohjola's Daughter*, however, Sibelius returned decisively, and ostensibly for the final time, to the tragic male-heroic subject matter of the *Kalevala* that had been the catalyst for his earlier works. In this case, the music is based on Canto 8 from the epic, which describes an encounter between the ancient seer Väinämöinen, one of the primal creative figures in the *Kalevala*, and the beautiful daughter of the Northland (Pohjola), who resists his amorous advances and sets him a series of 'impossible' tasks such as tying an egg in invisible knots and constructing a boat from a splinter of her spindle. *Pohjola's Daughter* has conventionally been regarded as the most Straussian of Sibelius's tone poems, both in terms of its colourful orchestral textures and perceived attention to programmatic detail. (This assumption is understandable given the impact that Strauss's new music had made on Sibelius during a visit to Berlin in 1905. In a letter to Aino Sibelius, dated 8 January, Sibelius hurriedly wrote after hearing *Ein Heldenleben* and the *Sinfonia domestica*, 'I was very fascinated . . . I have learnt a lot'.) Timo Virtanen's discussion of the compositional genesis of *Pohjola's Daughter*, however, proposes a more complex and problematic reading of the work.[18] The earliest sketches for the tone poem, for example, date from as early as April 1901, contemporary with Sibelius's work on the Second Symphony. The remaining sketches for the work are numerous, including a twenty-page continuity draft dating from autumn 1905 that may have been intended for a planned performance in Germany that never took place. As Virtanen describes, much of the material used in *Pohjola's Daughter* was originally associated with other projects including two works based on the *Kalevala*: an oratorio entitled 'Marjatta' (the Virgin Mary, who appears in the final Canto of the *Kalevala*) and an orchestral work called *Luonnotar*, after the Finnish creation myth that Sibelius later used in his tone poem for voice and orchestra of 1913. Other material originally associated with the work was eventually transferred to the second movement of the Third Symphony and the second set of *Scènes historiques*. Despite its seemingly specific programmatic content, therefore, the music in *Pohjola's Daughter* drew on a wide range of sources and ideas, and the exact point in

1906 at which Sibelius suddenly shifted his attention from a work entitled *Luonnotar* to one based on Väinämöinen and the daughter of the Northland remains uncertain. In this context, even the work's title can seem ambiguous: the composer suggested 'Väinämöinen', but *Pohjola's Daughter* was the preferred choice of his publisher, who also paraphrased the verses printed at the head of the score. Significantly, given possible narrative readings of the work, for Sibelius the tone poem's true subject matter was the *Kalevala*'s ancient orphic hero.

In a letter to Aino dated 23–4 January 1905, before he had finally decided on *Pohjola's Daughter* as a subject, Sibelius wrote, 'I'm no longer writing a symphony, rather a symphonic fantasy', adding, 'this is my genre!! Here I can move freely without feeling the weight of tradition.'[19] It is tempting, in the light of recent theories of influence, to emphasise Sibelius's anxious sense of the symphonic canon, and underline his generic distinction between the symphony and tone poem. Such comments, however, need to be treated with caution, since any composer's thoughts on their own work are invariably coloured both by their personal circumstances and their particular historical context. Sibelius's statement nevertheless offers an interesting perspective on the formal procedure employed within *Pohjola's Daughter*, as well as on the work's strikingly 'symphonic' contrapuntal density. Tonally, the work hinges on a similar 'tragic' double-tonic complex to that employed in *En saga*, on this occasion pivoting on G minor and B♭ major. As in the earlier tone poem, this tonal duality is reflected in the work's broad outline: the music revolves around two bold cadential utterances (bars 53 and 213), preceded by extended preparatory passages. The function of these two cadential points, articulated by Väinämöinen's heroic fanfare,[20] is to attempt to establish B♭ conclusively as a stable harmonic centre. On the first occasion, the fanfare is immediately deflected by a secondary theme (associated with the Northland's daughter) in F♯ minor (bar 57), a reflection of the conventional nineteenth-century gendering of thematic subject groups as alternatively male and female. In the recapitulation, this initial deflection is temporarily resolved by the modulation from G♭ back to B♭ (bar 221). As Timothy L. Jackson has argued, however, the tonal stability of this second cadential arrival point is also undermined, first by the return of the secondary theme (bar 232), and then by the insistent chromatic presence of G♭ within the diatonic space of the coda.[21] The implications of this second cadential deflection are devastating for the formal and narrative shape of the work. Rather than reaching an affirmatory harmonic close, in the manner of the finale of the Third Symphony, *Pohjola's Daughter* simply drifts away into nothingness. The effect of the coda foreshadows the end of the first movement of the Fourth Symphony, one of Sibelius's bleakest gestures. As Virtanen writes,

> In the last page of the score, Sibelius himself paints a picture which is quite different from the pathetic redemption or transfiguration described in the last strophe of the program text. His conception of the hero – and of himself as a creative man – is darker in tone, more contradictory, almost ironic – and deeper, more human, at the same time.[22]

Though the final four bars provide a measure of harmonic resolution, pointedly rising from G to B♭, the ultimate sense is of desolation rather than fulfilment. The tonic, B♭ major, Väinämöinen's symbol of masculine heroic authority, never receives unequivocal harmonic support. The tone poem's ultimate message is thus one of isolation, contingency and acceptance. Despite the generic concern with the symphonic poem that both Sibelius and Strauss shared, a less confidently Straussian conclusion is hard to imagine.

Taken as a whole, Sibelius's tone poems are perhaps his most diverse musical achievement. Despite their formal and expressive variety, however, the later tone poems, from *Nightride and Sunrise* (1907) onwards, share a common preoccupation with images of nature and landscape. In this sense, they thematicise a single aspect of generic convention, namely the tone poem's long-standing association with musical depictions of the natural world, in a particularly powerful manner. The notion that Sibelius's music could be heard as a sonorous embodiment of Nordic, particularly Finnish, landscape, was one of the earliest and most distinctive aspects of Sibelius reception, and has proved to be a persistent metaphor. The precise nature of Sibelius's musical landscape, however, remains underexamined. Conventional accounts of music and landscape have tended to dwell on nature as a purely external phenomenon.[23] The use of musical landscape figures or *topics* – such as horn calls, the imitation of birdsong such as the woodwind cadenzas in the development of *Pohjola's Daughter*, or the use of folk music – belongs to the domain of what Kofi Agawu has termed *extroversive semiosis*.[24] Sibelius's tone poems are rich in such *invocatory* gestures, musical events primarily concerned with a sense of presence or locale. Many of the tone poems, such as *En saga* and *The Swan of Tuonela*, open with the gradual unfolding of a bleak musical backdrop, often created through the use of an overlapping ostinato texture and a static harmonic 'soundsheet'. The sense of distance is heightened by the articulation of a solitary musical subject, which often represents a programmatic (or autobiographical) hero or tragic figure. Eero Tarasti, for example, has described the opening of the Violin Concerto as 'the impression of a bare landscape without a living soul'.[25] The impression is perhaps rather of the inward, subjective contemplation of an empty landscape, and the entry of the soloist is precisely the element that attempts to humanise the music, adds depth and creates a sense of sonic perspective between musical foreground and background, theme and accompaniment.

Pohjola's Daughter opens with a similar gesture. The low G minor chords with which the work opens, darkly scored for divided cellos, horns and bassoons, create an atmosphere of Nordic gloom (Andersson's 'Ossianic' tone). Tarasti asks perceptively, 'what kind of body speaks in Sibelius's music? Is it a virile, Wagnerian body? Or is it an androgynous one, inclined to Nordic melancholy and Arctic hysteria?'[26] The entry of the solo cello, characterised by its seemingly runic repetitive melodic structure, suggests that Sibelius adopts the heroic presence of Väinämöinen himself. Such performative gestures are a familiar convention in nineteenth-century music, and are used to generate a powerful sense of mythic or supernatural space. Key historical precursors, particularly relevant to aspects of Sibelius's practice, include the opening of Mendelssohn's *Hebrides* overture; Chopin's *Polonaise-Fantasie*; Niels W. Gade's *Ossian* overture; as well as Bruckner's Third Symphony (a work which Sibelius had first heard in Vienna in 1891), all of which evoke the narrative archetype of the tragic hero. The landscape unfolded at the opening of *Pohjola's Daughter*, therefore, has a bleak, fateful presence, foreshadowing the emptiness and loss with which the work ultimately closes.

In the later tone poems, landscape becomes more an aspect of structural process than the description of a physical object. Concurrently, for the listener, landscape is as much a mode of perception as of representation. This underlines the sense in which landscape is far from a neutral, or 'natural' phenomenon. Recent work by critics such as W. J. T. Mitchell has stressed how landscape is an artificial construction: landscape, by definition, requires the presence of an observer or interpreter. As Mitchell argues,

> Landscape is itself a physical and multi-sensory medium (earth, stone, vegetation, water, sky, sound and silence, light and darkness, etc.) in which cultural meanings and values are encoded . . . landscape is already artifice in the moment of its beholding, long before it becomes the subject of pictorial [or musical] representation. Landscape is a medium in the fullest sense of the word. It is a material means like language or paint, embedded in a tradition of cultural signification and communication, a body of symbolic forms capable of being invoked and reshaped to express meanings and values.[27]

Simon Schama similarly has written that 'landscapes are culture before they are nature; constructs of the imagination projected onto wood and water and rock'.[28] Sibelius's later tone poems dwell systematically on landscape as a 'body of symbolic forms', and the meanings and values that they express are often configured through images, such as the ocean or the forest, drawn from Finnish nature and mythology. The subject matter of *Tapiola*, for example, can be understood both as elementally Finnish (the dark pine woods surrounding Sibelius's home), and as part of a more pan-European forest mythos. The image of the forest as both sylvan Arcadia and a site of primeval terror and panic has an extensive historical precedence. The extreme expressive points of this cultural trope, the forest's states of tranquil, ecstatic calm and of storm-lashed anger, define the dynamic and textural range of Sibelius's tone poem.

Closer examination of Sibelius's music suggests that landscape also operates in a more introversive manner. The organisation of musical events in time suggests a structural parallel with the placement of landscape objects in visual space. The temporal perception of the listener is analogous to the visual perception of the viewer. *Nightride and Sunrise* is one of Sibelius's earliest works that consistently employs this spatial–temporal process. *Nightride and Sunrise* was composed in November 1908, but the work did not receive its premiere until January 1909, when it was performed in a notoriously bowdlerised version by Alexander Siloti in St Petersburg. The piece has remained one of Sibelius's most puzzling and least-discussed works: the location of the autograph manuscript, for example, is currently unknown. Furthermore, the tone poem has never managed to attract the same level of attention as other comparably sized orchestral works by Sibelius. This critical neglect might perhaps be attributed to the work's relatively restricted harmonic and melodic range, as well as to the abstract quality of the tone poem's programme. Sibelius commented to Rosa Newmarch that 'the music is concerned . . . with the inner experiences of an average man riding solitary through the forest gloom; sometimes glad to be alone with Nature; occasionally awe-stricken by the stillness or the strange sounds which break it; not filled with undue foreboding, but thankful and rejoicing in the daybreak'.[29]

Landscape motivates the form of the tone poem. The work is divided into two broad halves, articulated more by tempo and timbre than by conventional harmonic or thematic means. Each half of the work is subdivided into two large-scale phrases or cycles, which reconfigure material used in the previous section, so that the tone poem outlines a carefully balanced symmetrical scheme:

'Nightride'
   Prelude, bars 1–11
   Strophe 1 (statement)
      Ostinato, bars 12–230
      'Ride monologue', bars 231–77
   Strophe 2 (counterstatement and development)
      Ostinato, bars 278–359
      'Ride monologue', bars 360–90
   Transition, bars 390–403

'Sunrise'
  Prelude, bars 404–19
  Strophe 1 (statement)
      Preparation, bars 420–6
      Chorale, bars 427–61
  Strophe 2 (counterstatement and apotheosis)
      Preparation, bars 462–73
      Chorale, bars 474–98
  Coda, bars 499–517

Harmonically, the tone poem begins with a misfired tonic cadence that acts as an explosive point of lift-off from which the music subsequently drives towards the affirmative Eb major cadence of the closing bars. The basic structural harmonic progression thus resembles that of *Lemminkäinen's Return*, op. 22/4. Each cycle in *Nightride and Sunrise* represents a different stage in this harmonic journey. The first cycle, for example, moves from an unstable tonic first-inversion chord towards a modal C minor domain, articulated more by reiteration than cadential articulation. The second cycle modulates away towards a parallel modal harmonic domain on G, and the return to the tonic is not accomplished until the transition section (bars 390–420). The harmonic function of the Sunrise cycles is more static than that of the preceding Nightride music. The two formal halves of the work therefore operate in different ways: whereas the energetic figuration of the Nightride emphasises motion and instability, the chorale statements of the Sunrise are concerned with cadential closure.

This shift in structural syntax is supported by other aspects of the tone poem. Each cycle consists of a preparatory or generative episode and a more stable melodic statement. The purpose of the extended first stage of the Nightride music (bars 11–230) is both harmonic and textural: a reconfiguration of the process of 'the crystallisation of ideas from chaos' that Sibelius had developed in the finale of his Third Symphony (1907).[30] The ostinato fragments left behind by the explosive opening gesture slowly coalesce to form a stable accompanimental background. At this point, the ostinato fragments of the opening pass into the musical background, and the foreground is occupied by a new melodic phrase that, following Sibelius's description according to Newmarch, could be heard as a 'Ride monologue'. After the liquidation of the first statement of the monologue, the ostinato picks up again at a point corresponding to bar 65 in the initial statement. The second preparatory statement is a highly compressed and intensified version of the first. The music continues as before until bar 294, where it breaks off and veers into a developmental episode based on thematic and textural material derived from the opening prelude. Whereas the first preparatory statement was dominated by the string ostinato, the scoring from bar 294 onwards is more varied, as the strings, woodwind and brass exchange increasingly jagged thematic fragments. The phrase rhythm also becomes more uneven, so that the return of the Ride monologue in bar 360 has a local recapitulatory function, temporarily resolving the textural and rhythmic tension of the preceding bars.

Set alongside this pattern of constant exposition, reiteration and development is a process of continual thematic evolution. The chorale theme of the second half emerges slowly from the ostinato material of the Nightride section. The gradual effect is of an increasingly sharp sense of focus, of successive musical boundaries or frames being crossed towards a point of arrival or goal. The tone poem, however, is not simply concerned with the final arrival point, or with a single musical gesture or motive, but rather with the levels of relationship between musical events across the work as a whole. Higher levels of relationship create a large-scale structural counterpoint, or perspective, that allows the listener to experience the work as simultaneously both a complete entity and a series of individual moments. The listener's perception of the work corresponds to the changes of perspective in a landscape painting that direct the viewer's gaze through successive frames or visual levels towards a distant vanishing point.

The lines of structural perspective in *Nightride and Sunrise* converge at the end of the second statement of the chorale. The clarinet swirl in bar 502 suggests the unveiling of some distant prospect or vista. What follows, however, is a process of abstraction rather than a straightforward apotheosis. The clear dominant chord in the brass is echoed by an other-worldly sonority in the upper strings, a functionally unrelated sound that appears out of nowhere and grows to *fortissimo* as the brass chord dies away. Indeed, the sound suggests the inner voices that occupied Sibelius's thoughts in his next work, the string quartet *Voces intimae*. Much of the material in this passage derives from the opening prelude, and the II^7–I cadence in bars 510–11 pointedly resolves the misfired harmonic progression that launched the work. But the music is better regarded as a point of reduction rather than resolution. Sibelius pares the tone poem down to archaic blocks of sound, just at the moment where the listener might have expected a sudden flowering of the generative cycles that have driven the work. The gesture is all the more breathtaking given the generic significance of the work's title. The second half of the tone poem depicts a dawn sequence,[31] much like the opening of Wagner's *Das Rheingold*, or the 'Morgendämmerung' interlude in *Götterdämmerung* Act 2. In *Nightride and Sunrise*, however, daybreak is followed swiftly by closure. Just for an instant, the listener loses all sense of musical time and direction. At the single most important point of orientation in the work, the tone poem steps outside its own sense of dynamic, generative present, into a static, abstracted musical past. In a moment of intense stillness, the passage at the end of *Nightride and Sunrise* represents the interpenetration of different temporal processes that runs through the whole piece.

Sibelius's next tone poem, *The Dryad*, is the relative exception among his late series of tone poems, in that landscape remains a background rather than foreground feature of the work. The work was premiered alongside Sibelius's Mahlerian funeral march, *In memoriam*, in Christiania (Oslo), on 8 October 1910. Structurally, the sense of large-scale formal perspective developed in *Nightride and Sunrise* is here subordinate to the work's abbreviated ternary design. A sylph-like waltz, seemingly never heard in its entirety but with strangely Spanish colouring through Sibelius's use of castanets and *saltato* strings, is framed by a wistful introduction and coda. Robert Layton has commented on the work's stylistic proximity to the formal and expressive terseness of the Fourth Symphony, particularly in the almost weightless feel of the opening bars. According to Tawaststjerna, however, the tone poem reflects the influence of Debussy, whose *Nocturnes* Sibelius had heard for the first time in London in 1909. Certainly, the tone poem dates from a period when Sibelius was beginning to feel increasingly alienated from, as well as simultaneously attracted by, avant-garde developments in music on the Continent. A diary entry dated 13 May 1910, for example, reveals Sibelius's deeply ambiguous attitude to notions of stylistic progress and the reception of his music:

> Don't let all these 'novelties', triads without thirds and so on, take you away from your work. Not everyone can be an innovating genius. As a personality and 'eine Erscheinung aus den Wäldern' [a spirit from the woods] you will have your modest place. Here at home you are a past number in the eyes of the general public! Just soldier on! Nous verrons![32]

From our current critical perspective, it seems strange that Sibelius should apparently disclaim the innovative quality of his work, especially at the time of the composition of his Fourth Symphony. But Sibelius's comment constitutes a powerful response to a sense of marginalisation from a perceived musical mainstream. The increasingly intense recourse to images of landscape and nature, and Sibelius's perceived creative isolation as a 'spirit from the woods', whether real or imagined, can be understood as an attempt to reposition himself within the contemporary European musical marketplace. Sibelius's use of landscape is therefore a means of marking cultural and musical difference, and of defining an individual musical voice.

The sense of inward withdrawal that colours *The Dryad* is even more powerful in *The Bard*, among his most elliptical and aphoristic works. The tone poem was begun in spring 1913, as Sibelius was toying with the idea of a short orchestral piece, provisionally titled *The Knight and the Naiads*, based on Ernst Josephson's poem 'Hertig Magnus' (Duke Magnus).[33] After the premiere in Helsinki on 27 March, Sibelius decided to revise the work as a two-part fantasy or 'Intrada and Allegro'. His plans to expand the work were abandoned, however, and the revised version of the work in its final highly compressed form was premiered on 9 January 1916. Sibelius later denied that *The Bard* was in any way connected with Runeberg's eponymous poem, but the portrait of the ancient Nordic figure must have seemed especially appropriate at a point when he was reassessing his own fundamental compositional principles.

The schematic two-movement structure that Sibelius considered after the premiere of *The Bard* is still evident in the final version, which falls into two short halves: a static, contemplative *Lento assai*, which takes the form of a dialogue between harp and orchestra, and a more dynamic *Largamente*, which brings the work to a brief, epiphanal climax before fading away in an abbreviated reprise of the opening. As in *Nightride and Sunrise, The Bard* opens with a misfired cadential gesture, a rising cadential figure in the woodwind harmonised by the harp so that it cadences on the subdominant (iv^7) rather than the tonic. After this initial introductory gesture, the music proceeds through a series of short musical sentences: a set of verses and a repeated refrain (bars 3–11, reconfigured in bars 34–41), followed by a brief contrasting passage (bars 42–52, Fig. D) defined principally by textural change (the string tremolando). The material of this contrasting episode forms the springboard for the *largamente* section, which generates a sense of momentum through the timpani and bass ostinato, the harp's glissando flourishes and the rising melodic sequences in the woodwind. The music's energy is directed towards the dramatic emergence of the rising trombone and trumpet figures in bars 97–100 (*a tempo* before Fig. L). Sibelius referred to this event as resembling the sound of lurs, the ancient Bronze Age brass instruments uncovered in burial mounds in southern Scandinavia at the turn of the nineteenth century. But the event can also be understood as a form of *elementalisation*: the reduction of music to its simplest constituent parts, in this case perfect fourths and fifths.[34] The ultimate goal of the work is revealed as the deliberate attempt to present music in its purest, natural state, and the climax at Fig. L is followed by a simple cadential close. Just as the landscape processes in *Nightride and Sunrise* converge on an infinitely distant vanishing point, the varied strophic structure of *The Bard* is directed towards a basic and essentialised form of musical expression.

The most striking and obvious difference between *Luonnotar* and Sibelius's other tone poems is the presence of a vocal text, based on the first Canto of the *Kalevala*. The work was specifically written for the leading Finnish soprano, Aino Ackté, and premiered at the Shire Hall in Gloucester on 10 September 1913, as part of the Three Choirs Festival. After the first performance, *The Musical Times* complained that 'the orchestral undercurrent seemed more interesting than the vocal part', a comment perhaps on the stark angularity of the melodic line. The reviewer nevertheless conceded that, 'as with most of this composer's works, one has to exert faith that there is more in the music than is apparent on one hearing'.[35] In this sense, at least, *The Musical Times* was perceptive, since *Luonnotar* is one of Sibelius's most powerful and intense works. The text describes the creation of the world in Finnish mythology, from the pieces of a gull's egg fallen from the knee of the (female) nature spirit, the 'Luonnotar' of the work's title, floating amid the waves of an archaean ocean. At one level, the tone poem's subject matter is an explicitly literary–mythic narrative. James Hepokoski has argued, however, that *Luonnotar* also invites deeper readings that engage with issues of gender, nature and human creativity.[36] Whereas works such as the Sixth and Seventh Symphonies, Hepokoski suggests, are primarily concerned with the uncovering of being, 'the Kalevala creation myth in *Luonnotar* takes up the problem quite literally from the perspective of the gestational *production* of being'.[37] In other words, the subject of *Luonnotar* is the act of creativity itself, and the birth pangs of the nature spirit illustrated in the music up to the powerful moment of release in bars 149–60 offer a complex and ambivalent metaphor for Sibelius's own compositional work.

As the *Musical Times* perhaps realised, texture and harmony operate together as the primary structural parameters in *Luonnotar* to an even greater extent than in *Nightride and Sunrise* and *The Bard.* The tone poem begins with a characteristic string ostinato, a rhythmic gesture that, according to Hepokoski, powerfully suggests 'a forward vector, an urge towards resolution, action, and potential'.[38] Indeed, the seeds of the tone poem's eventual climax are contained within the intervallic contour of the ostinato figuration in the opening bars. This contrasts sharply with the first entry of the voice, accompanied by wind instruments. Despite the almost static, recitative-like setting, the vocal line's gradual registral expansion towards C major, a distant tritone away from the tonic F sharp minor, creates a dynamic tonal polarisation. This initial exchange of ostinato and vocal recitative is repeated, to establish the generative process of circular variation that drives the work, before the first contrasting episode, the *Tranquillo assai* in Bb minor (bar 54). At this point, the energetic ostinato of the opening is replaced by a weirdly dissonant accompanimental figure, seemingly half lullaby and half cortège, over which the vocal line ascends in largely trochaic steps. In the intensified second strophe, this contrasting episode is omitted, replaced by the wild cries of the gull as it flies around seeking a place to lay its egg (Fig. G, bars 120–30). Significantly, as the music surges to its climax in the third strophe, the vocal line drops out, submerged by the weight of the full orchestra. The narration of the world's creation itself is left to the reprise of the contrasting episode from the first strophe, marked *visionarico*. This passage is among Sibelius's most haunting and remarkable achievements, and the slow rocking of the ostinato figuration has an unearthly quality. Despite the ethereal brightness of the final chord, over which the vocal line ascends to describe the creation of the stars in the night sky, the dissonant fifth continues to echo, leaving the work's tonal structure unresolved.[39] As the musical illustration of a cold new world, the final bars invite comparison with the desolate closing pages of Vaughan Williams's Sixth Symphony, which likewise finish with a long oscillating 'fade-out'. Conventionally, ostinato patterns serve to generate a sense of momentum or relative stability. Here, however, the ostinato ending seems deeply ambivalent. At the close of both *Luonnotar* and Vaughan Williams's symphony, the future is faced with a sense of mystery and unease.

In 1914, Sibelius travelled to the United States at the invitation of businessman Carl Stoeckel, to conduct the premiere of *The Oceanides* at the Norfolk festival, Connecticut, on 4 June. Sibelius's American visit was in many senses the most successful professional event of his career. After visiting New York and Niagara Falls, which evidently made a deep impression, Sibelius received an honorary doctorate from Yale University, before returning to Europe on 18 June. The subsequent outbreak of war prevented the composer from consolidating his success across the Atlantic, and inevitably reinforced Sibelius's sense of isolation as a peripheralised figure in contemporary European music. In this sense perhaps, the dramatic climax of *The Oceanides* with its suggestion of dark, unstoppable forces moving beneath the musical surface, as with the ending of *Luonnotar*, has a strange fateful prescience. Sibelius sketched *The Oceanides* in Berlin, and the tone poem was substantially revised before it reached its definitive form. Several commentators have made a comparison between the work and Debussy's *La mer*, in terms not purely of subject matter but also of musical material. Tawaststjerna's analysis points to Sibelius's use of whole-tone and other modal scales in *The Oceanides* as analogous to Debussy's use of non-diatonic pitch collections in *La mer* and other works.[40] The implication, however, that Sibelius's music is in some way less 'progressive' than Debussy's, because his use of such material is less extensive or systematic, is challengeable. In the broader European musical context, the relative diatonicism of *The Oceanides* is striking. The convincing manner in which Sibelius was able to reconfigure familiar diatonic figures as part of the large-scale structural design of *The Oceanides* is in many senses the music's most progressive feature.

Tawaststjerna comments cryptically that 'the overall shape of *The Oceanides* seems to mirror nature itself'.[41] Cycles, arches and wave shapes dominate the music, from the rocking string accompaniment of the opening bars which begins to branch and overlap as the tone poem opens. At the broadest level, the work proceeds through a series of three generative, wave-like cycles, alternating the woodwind's playful dialogue with a yearning second-subject group (first heard at bar 29, six bars after Fig. C). The second cycle modulates from the tonic D major towards F, and the third begins with an eerie sense of harmonic and textural instability but builds swiftly in power and intensity towards the climax at bar 132 (*Tempo I*, two bars before Fig. R). The sense of structural perspective in *The Oceanides* is radically different, however, from that in *The Bard* or *Nightride and Sunrise*. Whereas in the earlier works, the music is directed inwards towards a seemingly distant vanishing point, *The Oceanides* is concerned with a gradual widening and deepening outwards towards a point of textural, dynamic and chromatic saturation. As Tawaststjerna describes, 'the final vision that the coda brings before the listener is the immutability and vastness of the ocean waters into which the Oceanides themselves do not venture'.[42]

Sibelius's final tone poem, *Tapiola*, unfolds a similar sense of perspective. Like *The Oceanides*, the structure of the tone poem can be understood as a series of varied cycles (or 'rotations'), ultimately focused on two statements of an elemental cadential figure (bars 356 and 569). The musical material of *Tapiola*, however, is even more minimal than that of *Nightride and Sunrise* or *The Bard*: the entire work is based upon various modal (whole-tone) and chromatic extensions of a simple B minor scale.[43] As Tim Howell has demonstrated, texture and phrase rhythm operate as primary structural parameters.[44] The transition from the end of the first cycle to the beginning of the second (bars 69 to 106, Figs. B to C) illustrates how this process works. The first cycle consists of three independent layers of music moving simultaneously but at markedly different rates: the virtually static bass ostinato, a slow wave-like accompaniment in the cellos and bassoons, and the moderately paced melodic statements in the divided violas. The entry of violins and trumpets in bar 89 introduces a very gradual brightening of the timbre. Texturally, the accompaniment figure begins to shift from the background into the foreground as it rises in pitch and dynamic level. At the same time, the incantatory viola statements slowly fade, and, eventually, even the static bass ostinato begins to move, before it drops out altogether at the beginning of the second cycle. Here, Sibelius introduces two entirely different timbral layers: a luminous oscillating violin ostinato, and a new series of melodic statements in the upper woodwind. Just as the texture changes, the phrase rhythm also contracts, from a spacious four-bar pattern to a more urgent three-bar metre. The overall effect of the transition is cinematic: a gradual shift in screen or focus from one texture to another. Such smooth, almost imperceptible changes are a characteristic feature of much of Sibelius's later tone poems, in sharp contrast to the rough-hewn epic blocks of his earlier works, but in *Tapiola* they are raised to the highest level of structural importance.

The long-range sense of perspective in *Tapiola* is also dependent upon a sense of harmonic resolution. Like *The Oceanides, Tapiola* begins arrestingly with an auxiliary cadence that initially tends towards the submediant rather than the tonic. The opening chord, a second-inversion subdominant seventh chord, is resolved modally rather than diatonically.[45] The tone poem only attains the tonic after the sudden octatonic outburst in bar 21, a powerful premonition of the concluding storm passage, and a 'corrective jolt' that initiates the chorale-like theme that dominates the first half of the work. The repercussions of this opening sonority echo throughout the tone poem, and second-inversion seventh chords, similar to that in the first bar, dominate much of the musical surface. Harmonic stability is only achieved in the final bars, where the initial subdominant sonority is resolved to a serene root-position tonic chord.

All tonal music premised on the resolution of large-scale harmonic disso- nance demands both prospective and retrospective listening. What makes the idea of landscape of fundamental structural importance in Sibelius's tone poems, however, is the way in which such cumulative cycles create a strong sense of directed motion towards a musical horizon. These mo- ments of structural convergence are relatively common in early-twentieth- century music. In the work of Elgar, Mahler and Nielsen, they often assume an epiphanal character, as a transcendent 'breakthrough' or apotheosis. In much of Sibelius's music, such structural high points are commonly artic- ulated as sudden moments of clear cadential articulation, often coincident with a large-scale thematic return or synthesis. In *Tapiola*, the storm se- quence (bars 513–77) has similarly massive closural impact. The passage begins with little sense of measured time beyond the rustling string figura- tion, but as the music proceeds the sense of two-bar phrase rhythm becomes stronger. The storm swiftly reaches a point of massive chromatic, dynamic and textural saturation, at the point where the entry of the brass brings the return of the elemental cadential figure from bar 356. Jackson has de- scribed the storm sequence as a 'dramatic cadenza', implying, perhaps, that the episode lies outside the main body of the work.[46] In reality, however, the passage functions as the tone poem's single focal point. After the cli- max, the music's textural and harmonic energy has been exhausted, and the work swiftly draws to a close. The storm sequence is simultaneously an epiphany, a breakthrough, and a cataclysm. The means by which the storm is brought about are deeply symphonic, the culmination of an almost over-determined motivic rigour that generates every single musical idea in *Tapiola*. But as a local event, the storm seems terrifyingly unmotivated, and in terms of large-scale form its implications are shattering: little seems left resolved, even as the music dies away. As Arnold Whittall has suggested, the work thus conceals an inner contradiction between form and genre. 'The

hysteria in *Tapiola* is that of the suicide', he suggests; 'logically, it is Sibelius's
eighth Symphony, his last word on symphonic form: a musical death wish of
formidable effectiveness'.[47] After *Tapiola*, Sibelius composed his incidental
music for a production of Shakespeare's *The Tempest* at the Royal Theatre
in Copenhagen, and it is ironic to imagine the finished piece as the drawing
together of two great 'late works'. Whereas in Shakespeare's play, however,
the storm is a dramatic opening gesture that subsides to reveal Prospero's
magic isle, in *Tapiola* the tempest is followed only by silence as the forest
closes in.

A preoccupation with the destructive elemental forces of nature and
the corresponding fragility of human subjectivity is a recurrent feature of
Sibelius's tone poems. According to James Hepokoski, 'Sibelius accepted
the notion of "pure nature" as a given, but then attempted through the processes of music to work his way back into the earth, water and sky to unlock
the essential animating forces believed to lie therein.'[48] In an age of growing environmental awareness and eco-criticism, such an interpretation is
both compelling and relevant to our contemporary context. Sibelius's tone
poems, to a greater extent than any of his other works, are explicitly engaged with such processes at various structural levels. Furthermore, the way
in which they articulate and attempt to resolve the tension between their
dynamic, temporal unfolding and static, contemplative circularity adds a
peculiarly modernist poignancy to the music. It is precisely this tension, and
the silence that it ultimately engenders, that is the distinguishing characteristic of Sibelius's musical landscape vision.

8 Finnish modern: love, sex and style in Sibelius's songs

JEFFREY KALLBERG

Sibelius's songs, a trove of lyrical and dramatic gems, refract his compositional, aesthetic, and cultural outlooks in myriad ways. Sibelius proved as adept at framing a brief lyrical mood, or an intense dramatic outburst, as at staging a mighty orchestral climax. His distinctive musical interpretations of poetic texts lend themselves to all manner of critical explorations, but we might best introduce the attractions of his hundred or so songs by focusing on a representative sample of them.[1] Examining a selection of Sibelius's songs on the subjects of love and sex serves our purposes particularly well, as they reveal the multiplicity of musical styles that he brought to bear on his texts, and the modernist outlook around which these sundry styles coalesced.

Transient love

Josef Julius Wecksell's poem 'Var det en dröm?' reflects on the impermanence of a lover's happiness, its titular question repeatedly calling into doubt the reality of memories of a past affair of the heart:

Was it a dream that sweetly one time
I was your heart's friend? –
I remember it like a silent song,
when the string still trembles.

I remember a thorn rose given by you,
a look so shy and tender;
I remember a parting tear, which glistened –
Was it all, was it all a dream?

A dream like the life of a windflower so short
out in a spring-green meadow,
whose beauty quickly fades away
before new flowers' multitude.

But many a night I hear a voice
on bitter tears' stream:
hide deeply its memory in your breast,
it was your best dream.

> *Var det en dröm att ljuvt engång*
> *jag var ditt hjärtas vän? –*
> *Jag minns det som en tystnad sång,*
> *då strängen darrar än.*
>
> *Jag minns en törnros av dig skänkt,*
> *en blick så blyg och öm;*
> *jag minns en avskedstår, som blänkt. –*
> *Var allt, var allt en dröm?*
>
> *En dröm lik sippans liv så kort*
> *uti en vårgrön ängd,*
> *vars fägring hastigt vissnar bort*
> *för nya blommors mängd.*
>
> *Men mången natt jag hör en röst*
> *vid bittra tårars ström:*
> *göm djupt dess minne i ditt bröst,*
> *det var din bästa dröm.*

The same phrase, 'I remember' (*Jag minns*), introduces a short catalogue of retrospection: of the love affair itself, now reverberating like the silence just after a song, of a gift from the lover, of their farewell moment. From the tearful perspective of the present, though, all these recollections take on the hazy, indeterminate status of a dream. The last stanza poignantly reverses the conceit of memory (*minne*), which the narrator embraces as dream in order to preserve the happiness of the past.

Wecksell, a Finland-Swedish romantic nationalist (Sibelius in his songs gravitated most often to texts in Swedish, his native tongue), locates these memories in a Nordic landscape of spring-green meadows, thorn roses, and windflowers, but Sibelius's setting (op. 37/4, 1902) ignores this invitation to national sentiment. Indeed, he pays little attention to Wecksell's individual words and phrases (the music does reinforce the proper syllabic and syntactic stresses of the text), and only glancing reference to the stanzaic structure. Instead, Sibelius fastens onto the central poetic conceit, the consistent textual repetition around ideas of memory, and focuses the majority of his song on its musical expression. Over a continuous accompaniment in the piano (cross-rhythms and appoggiaturas bubbling away contentedly in a crystalline B major) the melodic line builds a rising trajectory of emotion that peaks initially in the third line of the second stanza (Ex. 8.1). After a short break for a shivering evocation of the poignant brevity of the windflower's life (the third stanza, the only one in the poem not to evoke directly the idea of memory) – a glimpse at the netherworld of dreams staged in a harmonically contrasting, faintly dissonant realm – the opening melody and accompaniment resumes for the climactic fourth verse. The vocal high points in

Example 8.1 Sibelius, 'Var det en dröm?' (bars 10–19)

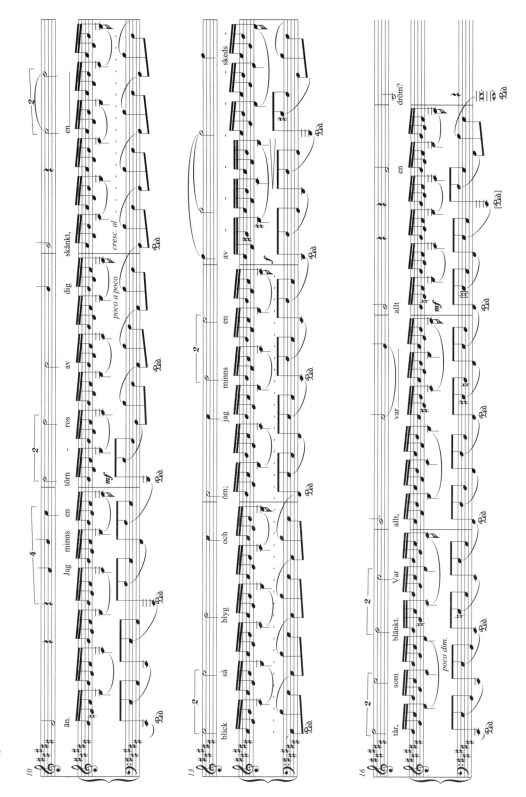

the second and fourth stanzas fall on the words 'parting tear' (*avskedstår*) and 'deeply' (*djupt*), but Sibelius plainly does not intend us to meditate on the sense of these particular moments. Rather the climaxes fit into the general emotional climate announced already in the first several bars of the song. When we hear the poetic reversal of the last stanza, the words merely confirm what the music established at the very beginning of the song: the memory of lost love taps the narrator's deepest vein of happiness.

Johan Ludvig Runeberg, Finland's national poet and thus its most renowned proponent of romantic nationalism, employs some of these same poetic images in 'Flickan kom ifrån sin älsklings möte' (The Girl Came from Meeting her Darling). Betrayal in love, roses, and thorns all figure in Runeberg's poem as they did in 'Var det en dröm?', only now a girl tells the tale of loss in response to a series of questions from her mother. Just as did Wecksell, Runeberg imbued 'Flickan kom ifrån sin älsklings möte' with recurring images, principally the colour red as it shades hands, lips, blood, and raspberries ('From what did your hands redden, girl'; 'From what did your lips redden, girl?' [*Varav rodna dina händer, flicka?*; *Varav rodna dina läppar, flicka?*]; 'I have plucked roses, / And have pricked my hands on the thorns'; 'I have eaten raspberries, / And painted my lips with the juice' [*jag har plockat rosor, / Och på törnen stungit mina händer; jag har ätit hallon, / Och med saften målat mina läppar*]). Secondarily, too, we read repeatedly of the absence of colour in the 'pale cheeks' (*bleka kinder*) of the betrayed girl. Runeberg's poem unfolds as a stark question-and-answer among nameless characters (mother, girl, lover), one whose tawdry images take place among the sights and smells of a Finnish summer (berries and flowers).

The feeling of grandeur established by the mellifluent, syncopated Db major chords and ardent opening melody of 'Flickan kom ifrån sin älsklings möte' (op. 37/5, 1901) holds sway for the majority of the song (Ex. 8.2). As in 'Var det en dröm?', Sibelius briefly digresses from the principal style of the song to prepare a climactic, and stunningly dramatic, return to the opening material. The shift into a recitational manner to accompany the mother's observation of her daughter's pale hands, and the girl's response that her mother should prepare her grave, only readies an exultant return to the main theme of the song. An exchange of parts between the voice and piano (the vocalist sings what the piano first played, and vice versa) adds to the fervour for the culminating explanation of the girl's deceit and betrayal ('Once she came home with red hands' [*En gång kom hon hem med röda händer*]).

As other commentators have noted, the passionate principal tune of 'Flickan kom ifrån sin älsklings möte' bears a distinct similarity to the music of Tchaikovsky.[2] (The key of the song suggests a comparison with the opening of his First Piano Concerto.) But more important than the fact of the allusion is the expressive purpose to which Sibelius puts it. The stunning

Example 8.2 Sibelius, 'Flickan kom ifrån sin älsklings möte' (bars 1–6)

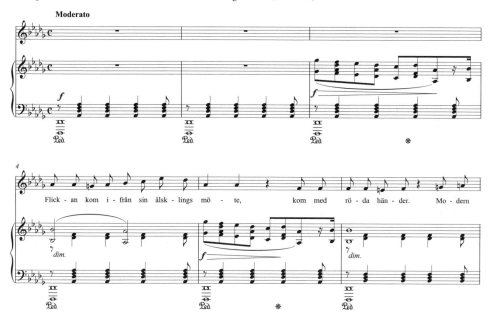

contrast between the lushly triumphant style of the music and the anonymity of the stark narrative serves to focus attention intently on the nameless girl's mortification. The details of the poem's narrative matter relatively little (though Sibelius does draw attention to the lies the girl tells to her mother ['and have pricked my hands on thorns'; 'and painted my lips with their juice'] through a gentle chromatic slide into Neapolitan harmonies, and also shifts to the minor mode for the final revelation of the lover's betrayal ('for they had paled from the lover's infidelity' [*ty de bleknat genom älskarns otro*] – see Ex. 8.3a and b). Instead Sibelius's setting trumpets out from its very outset what it considers the fundamental, broad message of the poem: the dire consequences of immoral behaviour.[3]

Songs without words?

In both 'Var det en dröm?' and 'Flickan kom ifrån sin älsklings möte', Sibelius abjures piano postludes. Indeed, he avoids them in the majority of his songs, and the reason for this is clear. As we have seen, Sibelius customarily seizes the lyrical or dramatic essence of a poem through a single, broadly profiled musical gesture, swerving from this central interpretative slant only in order to give new life to the atmosphere established at the beginning of the song. As a song evolves, it may heighten its expressive purview, but rarely will it transform it. In the Sibelian world of song, then, postludes would inevitably

Example 8.3a Sibelius, 'Flickan kom ifrån sin älsklings möte' (bars 11–14)

Example 8.3b Sibelius, 'Flickan kom ifrån sin älsklings möte' (bars 48–50)

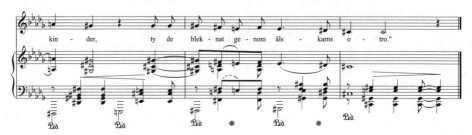

sound redundant or extraneous. With no interpretative work left to do, his songs generally end when the words cease.

This fundamental quality of Sibelius's songs provides the necessary context for understanding the composer's seemingly quirky pronouncements on the relationship between words and music in his songs and projected dramatic works:

> My songs can also be sung without words. They are not so dependent on words as the songs of many other composers.[4]

> Doubts regarding the text. 'The words' are always a burden to my art.[5]

> I see plainly that this opera that I will write must not have words. Only architectonic coulisses and songs, which will be sung on 'a' [i.e., the vowel]; above all no words. The whole will work fine, song and colours, music and accompanying gestures. No intrigue?! Ja, ja ihr Herren.[6]

Words troubled Sibelius, but even he recognised that he could not do without them in his vocal music (of course he never completed the wordless opera). In remarking that his songs lacked a dependence on words, he meant that his musical renderings of poems focus on total, unified impressions of the texts, and that a listener would gain more from meditating on the expressive values of the principal musical gestures than on the nuances of individual words and phrases. Though not unprecedented in the history of art song

(Schumann in particular tended to dilate on a single musical gesture in many of his lieder), Sibelius's insistently reiterative style does produce a rather idiosyncratic stance with respect to this vaunted tradition. His practice in the songs probably arose as a consequence of his tendency in larger orchestral works to favour the epic, obsessive repetition of motives. In these works, as James Hepokoski has noted, the insistence on a single motive draws attention to what Sibelius conceived as an essential, almost primitive truth in sonority.[7] Just as obsessive repetition in the orchestral works tends to defamiliarise sound, so too Sibelius's relentless concentration on the musical evocation of a single poetic conceit in his songs alters the customary status of text in song, shifting attention away from discrete words and towards overall meaning.[8]

Heady rapture

Even when Sibelius significantly varied the affective topology of his songs (something that tends to occur mostly in earlier works), we can still perceive the strong imprint of a guiding musical idea. The sixth number of the *Seven Songs with Texts by Johan Ludvig Runeberg*, op. 13 (the first publication with Sibelius's name on the title page; 1892), 'Till Frigga', contains four contrasting themes organised around a mobile set of tonal centres. (B♭ major/minor, D major/minor, and G minor function as tonics at different times: while the song sounds most stable when focused around B♭ or D, it unpredictably and unsteadily closes on G minor.) The first of the themes prepares the way for much of what happens later in the song. The opening stanza sounds more like an incantation than a lyrical song, with the melody set in the singer's low register and the accompaniment sounding a mysterious series of syncopated, (mostly) root-position chords that commence on B♭ minor and finish on D major (Ex. 8.4). The resultant hint of modality underscores the exotic allure of the addressee of the poem (Frederika 'Frigga' Juvelius, an early love of Runeberg, was the inspiration for much of his erotic poetry;[9] the name 'Frigga' can also more generally conjure images of the Norse goddess of marriage and sexuality):

> Your treasure does not entice me, Africa's golden river!
> Nor have I sought your pearls, sparkling Ocean!
> Frigga's heart entices me,
> revealed in teary eye's dew.
>
> *Mig ej lockar din skatt, Afrikas gyllne flod!*
> *Ej din pärla jag sökt, strålande Ocean!*
> *Friggas hjärta mig lockar,*
> *Röjt i tårade ögats dagg.*

Example 8.4 Sibelius, 'Till Frigga' (bars 1–8)

This archaic style gives way, surprisingly (at first) to a more lyrical, quasi-oriental vocal line ('oriental' by virtue of its mixture of major and minor modes and the decorative shake on the word *ringa*) set over a simple, detached, waltz-like accompaniment (Ex. 8.5). An 'orientalised' melody could powerfully communicate erotic sentiments to late-nineteenth-century ears, and particularly when set in the context of waltz-like music. From the onset of its popularity in the later eighteenth century as an urban dance, and throughout the nineteenth century, the waltz could convey meanings ranging from the pleasantly amorous to the licentious.[10] In 'Till Frigga', the waltz introduces the stanza that speaks of the narrator's erotic coupling with Frigga:

> Oh, how small a boundless world would be for me,
> with its suns of gold, with its diamonds' shine,
> compared to the world I with her
> rapturously hide in the closed embrace.

> *O, hur ringa för mig vore en gränslös värld*
> *med dess solar av guld, med dess demanters sken,*
> *mot den värld, jag med henne*
> *hänryckt gömmer i sluten famn.*

That the last two lines of this stanza slide smoothly back to the syncopated chordal accompaniment of the opening provides the first clue to the

Example 8.5 Sibelius, 'Till Frigga' (bars 10–18)

significance of this opening gesture: it acts as a sort of waltz *manqué*, a sign whose absent downbeat prepares later culminating moments where the downbeats sound forthrightly.

Sibelius stages these climaxes carefully. The first of them emerges suddenly out of a repetition of the detached waltz motive, and accompanies the narrator's account of the quasi-orgasmic daze into which he falls during his embrace with Frigga (Ex. 8.6):

> Mind and sight reel when I look into her gaze,
> as if I looked down into an immeasurable depth,
> until I start from the trance
> at a kiss from her purple mouth.
>
> *Tanke svindlar och syn, när i dess blick jag ser,*
> *liksom såge jag ned i ett omätligt djup,*
> *tills jag spritter ur dvalan*
> *vid en kyss av dess purpurmun.*

The suddenness of the outburst deliciously conveys the delirium felt by the narrator in the presence of his lover. But the shock of the last climactic ejaculation of the narrator is even greater, as it bursts out midway through what had seemed an orthodox return to the opening theme (Ex. 8.7):

Example 8.6 Sibelius, 'Till Frigga' (bars 27–36)

Example 8.7 Sibelius, 'Till Frigga' (bars 47–52)

If the path sometimes clouds over, if a thorn sticks out,
if the spirit once sighs, oppressed by its shackle's yoke,
oh, how blessed to speed
then into the lover's arms!

Mulnar banan ibland, skjuter ett törne fram,
suckar anden en gång, tryckt av sin bojas ok,
o, hur saligt att ila
i den älskades armar då!

The musical representation of this fulfilled desire falls largely on the impression created by the last measures of the excerpt, where finally the implied waltz gains its necessary downbeats. The final stanza of the song ('The earth fondles my foot, sweet as a spring breeze there'[*Jorden smeker min fot ljuv som en vårvind där*]) eases gradually back through the detached waltz figure to a final sounding of the waltz *manqué*: a lovely musical evocation of a post-coital afterglow. Thus the waltz, actual and implied, looms as a controlling presence in this highly innovative song by the young composer.

Modern cravings

Through this unabashed engagement with the representation of sex, Sibelius revealed his modernist inclinations. (And the frequency with which sexual topics animate many of his other larger works – among others, *Skogsrået*

[The Wood Nymph], *Lemminkäinen and the Maidens of the Island, Kullervo and his Sister*, and, most inscrutably, *Luonnotar* – only strengthens this impression.) A relatively new notion, sexuality figured centrally in *fin-de-siècle* visions of 'modernity', attendant notions of 'the individual', and new versions of subjectivity. Although just when this concept emerged is a matter of contention among scholars, by the second half of the nineteenth century the modern phenomenon of sexuality was widely established, its presence most readily perceptible in the nascent discipline of sexology, the quasi-Darwinian science that comprehensively mapped sexual persons and forms of desires. It is not by chance, then, that Sibelius's forthright engagement with sex should be contemporaneous with the rise of sexology: both activities form part of the same impulse to survey the conceptual possibilities of this newly conceived building block of identity and to inscribe them in various cultural forms.[11]

As Sibelius continued to explore nuances of sexuality in his songs, the subject matter grew ever more frank. In the summer of 1906, Sibelius fulfilled a commission from the Berlin publisher Robert Lienau for a set of songs (published as op. 50) to texts by contemporary German poets, an effort on the part of both publisher and composer to tap into the rich central European market for lieder. One of the poets that Sibelius and Lienau settled on for the collection, Richard Dehmel, often featured explicit sexual themes in his poetry. In 'Aus banger Brust' (From a Fearful Heart, the fourth number of the set), the narrator, lying in the dewy grass at midnight, has just awoken and restlessly rues the absence of his (just-departed?) lover. The third stanza of the poem captures the feverish tone of the whole (Ex. 8.8):

> So I never knew before,
> as often I embraced your neck
> and enjoyed your innermost essence,
> why you, from a fearful heart,
> moaned when I overflowed.

> *So hab ich es noch nie gewußt,*
> *so oft ich deinen Hals umschloß*
> *und blind dein Innerstes genoß,*
> *warum du so aus banger Brust*
> *aufstöhntest, wenn ich überfloß.*

Again Sibelius establishes the emotional climate of the work from the very start, and does not digress from it. The expressive consistency of the song derives from the accompanimental figuration that, in rustling single-mindedly from beginning to end, at once conveys the intensity of the narrator's sexual desire and the image of its illicit 'overflowing'. In addition to the unceasing

Example 8.8 Sibelius, 'Aus banger Brust' (bars 33–45)

semiquaver motion (arrested only in the last four bars of the song), the harmonic structure contributes strongly to the sense of incontinent excitement that permeates the piece. The song imaginatively varies a basic strophic design: each of the last two stanzas explores new melodic material when it starts, but returns to the closing phrase of the principal theme when it ends. But in a tonally estranging gesture, the end of each stanza tilts a tritone away from the key established at the beginning. Moreover, an added lower third to the basic triad obscures the definition of the tonic: the D pedals suggest the primacy of D minor, but the presence of a B♭ introduces an element of doubt (indeed, the end of the song leans more toward B♭ major than D minor). The move to G♯ minor escapes similar contamination until the end of the third stanza, where the addition of the lower third likewise throws its identity into question. With the implied cadence on *überfloß* thus undermined, the music implies that the completion of the sexual act has done nothing to staunch the narrator's desire.

Lingering desire also characterises the conclusion of the vocal part, which, by pitting its g♯′ against the D in the piano, both recalls the principal tonal poles of the song, and also leaves decidedly unfulfilled its musical trajectories (Ex. 8.9). The gesture of avoiding vocal closure finds amplification in the concluding blurred harmonies in the piano (B♭ major or D minor?). (It is telling that, although Sibelius gave over the final seven bars of the song to the piano, the rare postlude does nothing to alter the central message of the song.) 'The roses are still radiant' (*Die Rosen leuchten immer noch*) are the final words intoned by the singer, but in the unsettling end of 'Aus banger Brust', rather than radiance, we hear the shiver of sexual craving.

The most astonishing of Sibelius's lyrical explorations of raw sexual desire came two years later, in his setting of Bertel Gripenberg's 'Teodora' (op. 35/2, 1908). A lustful lover's sensuous description of the nocturnal arrival of the Byzantine empress Theodora, 'Teodora' lays bare Gripenberg's aesthetic sympathies with the Decadent movement as embodied by such authors as Verlaine, Huysmans, and Wilde. Sibelius's initial musical encounter with Gripenberg's frothy verses came in 1903 (the year of the publication of the poem), when he improvised a piano accompaniment to a recitation of them by the great Norwegian actress Johanne Dybwad.[12] (In the late nineteenth and early twentieth centuries, melodrama remained a significant feature of musical life in Scandinavian musical culture in general, and for Sibelius in particular. He composed half a dozen pieces for recitation and accompaniment, the most striking of which are 'Skogsrået' [to Viktor Rydberg's poem, a condensed version of the orchestral tone poem of the same name] from 1895 and 'Ett ensamt skidspår' [A Lonely Ski-trail, poem by Gripenberg] from

Example 8.9 Sibelius, 'Aus banger Brust' (bars 57–68)

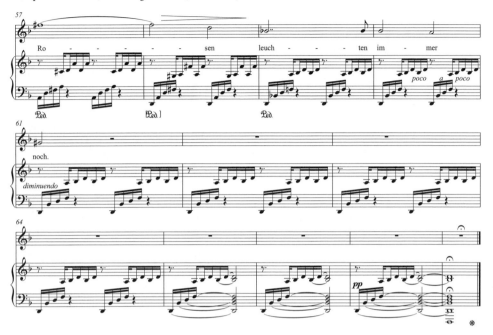

1925.) Whether Sibelius really 'had in mind' this particular improvisation when he came to compose the song five years later cannot be known on the evidence presently available.[13] Nonetheless, the composed song does project an improvisational quality both in its vocal line and its accompaniment. As one might expect to encounter in an improvisation, each part grows out of its own very small fund of motives. The outer verses feature one basic melodic phrase, which Sibelius allows to expand slightly at the conclusion to each verse, and two versions of a chromatic growl, one in shorter note values than the other, deep in the bass of the piano (Exx. 8.10a and b). The central verse introduces another melodic phrase, higher in register, and some spooky diminished-seventh and chromatic-scalar riffs in the piano (Ex. 8.11).

The importance of this quasi-impromptu style lies less in what it might tell us of the origins of the song than in what it contributes to Sibelius's published musical interpretation of Gripenberg's poem. As in several of the songs examined here, the limited repertory of musical gestures responds to aspects of the structure of the poem (especially the sixfold repetition in the last verse of the words 'I want' [*Jag vill*] – the ultimate distillation of the narrator's desire) and in so doing creates a remarkably concentrated reading of the unbridled lust that infuses the poem:

Example 8.10a Sibelius, 'Teodora' (bars 76–84)

Example 8.10b Sibelius, 'Teodora' (bars 103–16)

Example 8.11 Sibelius, 'Teodora' (bars 59–71)

> Theodora, I want to kiss your lips, which command
> and kiss and smile in the same second,
> Empress, I want to kiss your coldly mocking
> and thirstily hot, treacherous mouth –
> I want to drink your gazes, which force and suck,
> I want to fondle your flaming red fragrant hair.
> Theodora, I want to believe your oaths, which lie,
> I want to forget the ruin that follows in your wake!
>
> *Teodora, jag vill kyssa dina läppar, som befalla*
> *och kyssa och smila i samma sekund,*
> *kejsarinna, jag vill kyssa din hånande, kalla*
> *och törstande heta, förrädiska mun –*
> *jag vill dricka dina blickar, som tvinga och suga,*
> *jag vill smeka ditt eldröda, doftande hår.*
> *Teodora, jag vill tro dina eder, som ljuga,*
> *jag vill glömma fördärvet, som följer ditt spår!*

Much of the sense of threatening desire derives from the blurry noise that emanates from the piano in the first and third stanzas. Like the bizarre, 'unknowable sound' (in the felicitous phrase of Carolyn Abbate) that emerges from Strauss's orchestra while Salome listens to Jokanaan's murder, and perhaps even deriving from it, Sibelius's rumbling bass resists aural definition.[14] Although visually it appears to be centred on the pitch of D♯, the ear strains to perceive this because of the ways that Sibelius saturates the chromatic space around the D♯. The seven pitches in the motive as it sounds at the beginning of the first and last verses, for example, fill in every semitone between B and D♯. (That Sibelius instructs the pianist to lift the pedal just before each final D♯ in the demisemiquaver version of the bass figure only barely mitigates the tonal shadows cast by the ten pedalled notes that precede it.) When to this piano part that hovers in the interstices between tonality and atonality is added a vocal line that, following the key signature, sounds rather more like G♯ minor than D♯ minor (though it stresses d♯ at the end of each phrase), the result is a pair of outer sections in which the weakness of gravitational tonality brings Sibelius close to the expressionist styles being explored by Schoenberg and others in Austria and Germany.[15]

The consciousness of style

Sibelius's modernist leanings surface not only in the amorous and erotic subjects of these songs, and not only in the dissonant, tonally blurring strategies essayed in 'Aus banger Brust' and 'Teodora', but also in the very range of their compositional styles. Only a span of sixteen years separates the dates of composition of 'Till Frigga' and 'Teodora', yet the songs we have examined from this period display a remarkable diversity in their musical means. From a later vantage point, it seems scarcely possible to negotiate, in the figure of a single composer, the aesthetic distances between the incantational modality of 'Till Frigga', the radiant late Romanticism of 'Flickan kom ifrån sin älsklings möte' and the Decadent dissonance of 'Teodora', but such contrasts must have seemed a matter of course in the musical world of the time (think *Elektra* and *Der Rosenkavalier*, or, for that matter, Sibelius's Second and Fourth Symphonies). Indeed, our appreciation for the stylistic diversity of Sibelius's songs would only grow stronger were we to expand our discussion to include works that explore topics outside the realm of love and sex: for example, the sternly dramatic, quasi-Wagnerian recitative of 'Höstkväll' (Autumn Evening, op. 38/1, 1903), the almost Schubertian bonhomie of 'Blåsippan' (The Blue Windflower, op. 88/1, 1917), or the sonorous, ritualistically repetitive 'Norden' (The North, op. 90/1, 1917) – this last offering the analogue in song of the innovations that the master symphonist brought to the world of orchestral sound.

The mark of the modern lies in the fact not simply that Sibelius deployed a variety of styles in the service of expression, but that he appears to have done so wilfully. Culminating a development of several generations, 'style' by the last decade of the nineteenth century had emerged as an attribute that composers felt they might consciously choose, as opposed to a quality that they possessed innately. The complexities of this historical phenomenon cannot be explored here, but in the form of it that affected Sibelius (and others of his generation), composers no longer permitted themselves the luxury of writing unreflectively (as if naturally). Doubtless in response to the new sonic possibilities presented by such composers as Debussy, Schoenberg, Stravinsky, and Bartók, a composer's style could become a fraught posture, one capable of being deployed or heard in the service of larger ideologies, such as beliefs in Hegelian progress or anti-modernism. Though earlier examples of a composer donning a different style as a carnivalesque sort of gesture (Schumann masquerading as Chopin in *Carnaval*) might seem similar to the situation around the turn of the twentieth century, something different is happening with the idea of style for Sibelius and his contemporaries. Around 1900, the shift of a composer into a different style was not likely to connote a masking of identity. Rather it was likely to help constitute that identity.[16]

For Sibelius, the consciousness of style reached an acute phase between 1909 and 1914, when, as James Hepokoski has convincingly argued, he struggled intensely with the challenges to the relevance of his own music posed by such avant-garde figures as Schoenberg and Stravinsky.[17] In his diary, Sibelius at various times expressed worries about his musical style:

Must go home. It's not possible to work here any longer. A style change?

(Berlin, 21 May 1909)[18]

Whatever you, glorious Ego, still write – do not sacrifice that
heat-radiating, life-giving, living that is your music's innermost essence.
You, glorious, will not become 'bigger' through outdoing – seeking to
outdo – your contemporaries in revolutionary *Ansichten* [opinions]. So
then no 'racing manners'!

(5 June 1912)[19]

Now we have to not lose our courage; and – above all – not our head. They
think – at least the world's foremost musicians – that I am a dead man. But
nous verrons [we will see]. Is this now the end of Jean Sibelius as composer?

(20 February 1913)[20]

As Hepokoski notes, this consciousness of style brought about feelings of
disillusionment in Sibelius (and in contemporaries like Strauss and Elgar)
as they sensed various avant-garde initiatives overtaking their position as
leading modernists. They all struggled to find some ethical mode of em-
bracing a modernist agenda while turning away from the avant-garde, 'new
music' forms of modernism.

But an awareness of the possibility and desirability of frequent stylistic
change plainly also formed part of the very texture of Sibelius's compositional identity well before the years of crisis around 1910. From the evidence
of the songs, mutability of style comprised a significant element in his basic
compositional arsenal, a tool to further his expressive goals just like form and
orchestration (to name only two). This suggests, simply, that the question of
Sibelius's relationship to notions of musical 'progress' should be understood
within the larger context of his established penchant for stylistic change. It
is no more the case that his resistance to (or fear of) the musical avant-
garde in the second decade of the twentieth century marked a regressive
move somehow 'outside of history', than that his explorations in dissonant
Decadence in the first decade of the century marked a progressive move 'in
advance of history'. To be conscious of one's mode of artistic expression, and
to be willing significantly to change it in response to all manner of impulses
(personal, political, cultural), lay at the heart of the definition of the modern
creator. Sibelius's songs, in their marvellous and moving stylistic multiplicity, thus remind us of the range of expressive possibilities embraced in the
concept of musical modernism.

9 Sibelius and the miniature

VEIJO MURTOMÄKI

There are few great composers whose miniatures seem so problematic as those of Sibelius. Grieg, Paderewski, Rakhmaninov, Chabrier, Debussy and Ravel have all at some point been criticised for their preference for working in smaller genres, but Sibelius is a rather different case. His achievements in large-scale symphonic forms are widely recognised, but his miniatures have often been neglected or misunderstood and demand critical re-evaluation. The majority of Sibelius's smaller works were written for the piano, and his piano music has been the object of particular critical scorn.[1] According to the English critic Cecil Gray, who held a lofty opinion of Sibelius as a symphonist, it was strange that Sibelius wrote so many pieces for an instrument that he did not understand and that he reputedly disliked. Gray stated that Sibelius's piano works were 'for the most part completely undistinguished in conception and musical substance', and concluded that 'they are also singularly ineffective from the point of view of the instrument'. Gray also felt that Sibelius's piano music suffered by comparison with his other works, and that, 'so far from there being any discernible process of development from the early [piano pieces] to the late, the contrary rather is the truth . . . and the latest volumes are definitely the weakest'.[2]

Generations of writers after Gray have willingly followed his assessment of Sibelius's piano miniatures. Eric Blom, for example, noted that 'there are about 120 of them, a great many nothing more than suavely lyrical things [and] a large number of them may be said to be potboilers'.[3] Robert Layton states that 'all but the fanatic would concede that he seemed unable to draw from the piano sounds that do justice to its genius or to his'.[4] In the most recent English biography, by Guy Rickards, Sibelius is described as 'an abstract symphonist of imposing classical severity yet the perpetrator of light music pot-boilers of embarrassing vacuity'.[5] For Rickards, 'the future composer never grew to like the piano, nor did he write any successful major pieces for it', with the apparent result that 'an embarrassing emptiness of a large section of his output is often held to have diluted the value of the whole of it'.[6] Nor are such sentiments limited to the English reception of Sibelius's work. A similar response can be found in a new French dictionary of piano music, where Guy Sacre writes that 'his compositions for the piano are mediocre and sometimes of alarming quality'.[7] One of the very few writers who understood Sibelius's output as a whole was the German Ernst Tanzberger, who, partly for political reasons following the war, was able to place Sibelius's piano music in a wider context. 'Sibelius wrote piano music in times of relaxation as a breathing space between the larger-scale works', Tanzberger observed, and added, 'the controversial quality of his piano music causes no harm to his artistic reputation; we have to take it as it is: as entertainment music in the best sense of the word!'[8]

Sibelius himself was not entirely innocent in the reception of his piano miniatures, but his comments were perhaps intended only as a confidential exchange of thoughts between close friends. This perhaps explains his reported conversation with Bengt von Törne, in which Sibelius said half jokingly that, 'I write piano pieces in my free moments', before concluding seriously, 'as a matter of fact the piano does not interest me; it cannot sing'.[9] Much the same might be true in the case of Walter Legge, to whom Sibelius again 'confessed' that 'I do not care for the piano – it is an unsatisfying, ungrateful instrument, which only one composer, Chopin, has fully succeeded in mastering, and two others, Debussy and Schumann, have come on intimate terms'.[10]

Doubts concerning Sibelius's piano works can be divided into two categories: those questioning his ability to write for the instrument, and those contesting the quality or substance of the music. The latter must be discussed in a wider cultural and aesthetic context, whereas the former is more easily answered. Many of those who criticise Sibelius's perceived inability to write for the piano are music historians, critics or journalists, guided more by aesthetic prejudice than practical pianistic expertise. In contrast, pianists themselves are often positive and understanding, even enthusiastic. Glenn Gould, for example, maintained that 'Sibelius never wrote against the grain of the keyboard . . . in Sibelius's piano music, everything works, everything sounds – but on its own terms, not in lieu of other, presumably more sumptuous, musical experiences'.[11] The Finnish composer-pianist Ilmari Hannikainen, a pupil of Liszt's disciple, Alexander Siloti, described Sibelius's F major Sonata as 'a brilliant work, new, fresh and full of life'.[12] Erik Tawaststjerna, the eminent Finnish Sibelius scholar and pianist who studied under the legendary Alfred Cortot and often performed Sibelius's piano music, sometimes even in the presence of the composer, challenged Cecil Gray directly:

> Many of Sibelius's compositions for piano are noteworthy both in conception and in musical substance, and are characterised by a personal piano style well suited to the nature of the instrument. Viewed as a whole they reveal the same general curve of development, as do his large-scale works.[13]

Tawaststjerna's son, the Finnish pianist Erik T. Tawaststjerna, who has recorded Sibelius's complete piano works for the Swedish BIS label, defends Sibelius against those who accuse him of having composed his 'bread-and-butter' pieces just for the sake of money, since 'most of the world's great composers have also created out of financial necessity – it might even be claimed that only amateurs are motivated by pure "artistic inspiration"'.[14] Another Finnish pianist, Eero Heinonen, goes further in attacking this kind of attitude towards composition: 'If we think that a composer's work is less valuable when he does it for money, we would have to denounce all of Bach's cantatas. Or is commissioning in general a suspect activity?' Heinonen concludes that 'behind all this lurks the bourgeois attitude of seeing the artist as a hero whose poverty motivates him to ever higher selfless achievements'.[15] It could equally well be claimed that 'accusing a professional composer of writing music to earn money for living is at least absurd'.[16]

The criticism of Sibelius's miniaturism, especially the idea that a great composer could not, at the same time, write both large-scale and small-scale pieces with equal success, is an illuminating problem in Sibelius reception. A composer who wrote miniatures at the turn of the twentieth century seemed suspicious, especially if he/she still employed the techniques of the Romantic era and could thus be placed in a conservative, rather than modernist, stylistic category. The phenomenon is part of an increasingly common trend in twentieth-century music, which has led to the situation where 'concert pianists' repertoires today very seldom contain any small-scale pieces'.[17] As Heinonen notes, 'music making at home, an activity for which miniatures are supremely appropriate, has been declining throughout the twentieth century', so that consequently, 'as concert halls have grown larger, miniatures have been branded minor or occasional works'.[18]

Two aspects, the relative compositional complexity of small pieces and the musical genre they represent, are crucial factors in evaluating Sibelius's miniatures. The notion of genre was of crucial importance for the composer, publisher and audience in the nineteenth century, having a mediating function between the concert hall and publishing institutions. Genre was not immediately linked with the idea of musical value. The idea was rather to determine the use and function of different kinds of musical works, and, especially, to determine the connections and interactions between them.[19] However, as instrumental music and conceptions of absolute music became an aesthetic ideal, theories of musical genre (*Gattungstheorie*) were increasingly understood as implying a fixed hierarchy of musical forms. The result was that individual genres were identified with different aesthetic values and expectations.[20] Throughout the nineteenth century, large-scale forms such as the sonata, string quartet and especially the symphony enjoyed the highest status in art music.[21] Their prestige increased as the century progressed, supported by conservative textbooks on composition and musical form (*Kompositionslehre* and *Formenlehre*) used in the leading German conservatories of Berlin and Leipzig, as well as numerous booklets and reviews. Ferdinand Hand, for example, wrote, 'in the same way that poetry strives through its course of development towards drama, instrumental music strives towards its point of culmination, the symphony'.[22]

In addition to this process, music with a specific utilitarian function was regarded as being of intrinsically less musical value than abstract or autonomous works, and the smaller forms, especially piano miniatures, were in danger of losing their aesthetic value and seeming trivial.[23] According to Dahlhaus, the Romantic song, character piece and symphonic poem became refined from inferior and 'lower' traditions, and could maintain their 'high' place in the hierarchy only by fulfilling specific aesthetic requirements.[24] Hence, the lyrical piano piece, an ennobled form of the older eighteenth-century character piece, could become a genuine and profound representative of Romantic art, bound by the idea of aesthetic contemplation. If 'lower' genres and styles during the eighteenth century (such as the divertimento) were, according to Dahlhaus, aesthetically neutral, 'in the nineteenth century, a composer who wrote music in the "lower" style and genres belonging to it was exposed to the danger of being held in contempt [*verachtet zu werden*], even if nobody doubted his or her talent or mastery of compositional technique'.[25]

It is also significant, as Dahlhaus suggests, that 'the aesthetic doctrine of genre was more rigid in Northern Germany than in Southern Germany, Austria and Switzerland'.[26] In Vienna, a broad range of music was tolerated, from dances, especially the waltz, and marches, to operettas, operas and symphonies. Due to the variety of musical styles, Vienna was among the most attractive musical centres in Europe, and numerous composers studied in Vienna or made their career there. By comparison, Berlin as a musical town appeared much less lively.

When Sibelius wrote miniatures, does it necessarily follow that he was risking his reputation as a composer of high art music? It would appear so, given that patterns of German musical thinking and the doctrine of autonomous instrumental music were willingly accepted in other countries as well. According to post-colonialist theory, Germans assumed a dominant role in musical culture, while neighbouring countries assumed that of the colonised.[27] This colonialised imagination is characterised by an internalised awareness, in which the colonised adopt the 'higher' knowledge of the dominant group, and act as if they had invented it themselves. Thus, Sibelius's critics outside Germany are merely following a rigid, yet widespread, Germanic musical thought, based on the hegemony of a strikingly narrow aesthetic doctrine.

The dichotomy between high art music and music 'lacking substance' resulted in a number of new categories for music that was not perceived to be sufficiently demanding: salon music, trivial music, entertainment music, domestic music, light music, popular music, musical *Kitsch*, and even *Musik als Nicht-Kunst* (music as non-art). Character pieces, not only the 'lyric piece' subgenre, and surprisingly, programmatic pieces, were generally held in slightly higher esteem due to their poetic content, and were furnished with descriptive titles which reflected particular states of mind (*seelische Befindlichkeiten*).[28] Throughout the nineteenth century, there was a place for genuine character or lyric pieces that were able to satisfy this mysterious aesthetic requirement. Though it took a long time for composers such as Schubert, Chopin or Brahms, all now highly respected miniaturists, to establish a representative position, a canon of valuable miniatures was gradually formed. The places where the miniatures were played, however, also began to determine their musical value. 'Salon music' was initially a neutral term, and referred simply to the drawing rooms of the aristocracy and upper-middle-class bourgeoisie, in which virtuoso pianists such as Chopin, Liszt and Thalberg performed. During the latter half of the nineteenth century, almost any kind of small-scale piece could be called 'salon music', and, at the same time, the term gained its pejorative meaning.[29] Criticisms of salon music were not solely based on musical factors. In Germany, Parisian salons were officially disapproved of for their alleged 'moral corruption and lack of healthy naturalness', whereas domestic music-making (*Hausmusik*) was regarded as a genuine, sound and mentally constructive activity.[30] (The political attitude to *Hausmusik* changed radically, of course, once it became part of the National Socialist ideology.) Anything that referred to entertainment, amusement or relaxation was regarded as belonging outside the realm of true music. Any music aimed at gaining popular appeal or commercial success was indefensible in the eyes of certain learned critical authorities. The wider the gap between art and entertainment music became, the more critics strove to preserve the level of high art music 'as the only legitimate representative of music'.[31]

Evaluating music purely in terms of aesthetic content, however, not only ignores music's function as a form of cultural practice,[32] but fails to recognise the fact that all such aesthetic categories are historically contingent. French composers, for example, rejected certain German musical genres and techniques (consider Debussy's sarcastic comment on hearing the development section of a Beethoven symphony, for example), in favour of a marked inclination towards smaller forms and a more salon-like, elegant and precise expression. As a question of musical taste, value judgements depend on a great many factors. It is instructive to read Debussy's article entitled 'On musical taste',[33] where he argues that professional musicians are in error when they blame the public for loving only light music (bad music). He adds, 'in reality, any music becomes always "difficult", when it is not living; seriousness is a camouflage to conceal its poverty'.[34] It is perhaps not surprising that Sibelius's initially strong German orientation changed during his career, and that he even began to resent Berlin's musical atmosphere, whereas Paris symbolised for him everything that was fresh and vigorous in contemporary music.[35]

Perhaps Sibelius's 'mistake', from the point of view of his critics, was that he did not compose more large-scale works, such as a piano concerto, 'to prove his musical-masculine virility at the piano', whereas he wrote dozens of 'pensées de piano lyrique' instead.[36] He should have used his time and energy to compose more symphonies, because writing miniatures prevented him from giving us an Eighth and Ninth Symphony, as Eric Blom believed.[37] Since, as Jeffrey Kallberg has convincingly argued, the piano was closely associated with women and domestic music-making in the nineteenth century, miniature genres such as the nocturne were invariably regarded as effeminate by comparison with 'masculine heroic' sonatas and symphonies.[38] A few of Sibelius's miniatures have been accepted as significant by association, where they seem to have some similarity with larger-scale pieces or share material with a symphony. But though this association can be of interest in shedding light on compositional process or the composer's working methods, it cannot guarantee the quality of an individual piece.

The nearly two hundred small-scale miniatures composed by Sibelius for piano, piano and violin, and piano and cello, form a heterogeneous group of pieces. They contain some real masterpieces and, equally, some charming occasional pieces, intended chiefly for domestic or didactic use. Every piece deserves to be taken on its own terms. There are many pieces of excellent quality belonging to the genre of character or lyric piece with a powerful sense of poetic feeling and atmosphere. Some of them are small scenes with a dramatic or programmatic narrative. Then there are proper salon-music pieces, which can be either elegant and charming, or demanding showpieces with virtuosic passages, suitable as encores. The miniatures also contain a variety of dances, some of them genuinely intended for dancing (especially the earliest ones), whereas most of them are stylised pastiches or, at best, lyrical, meditative or ironic pieces with some private reference to the composer's inner life at certain key moments. There are two sets of pieces with an obvious didactic purpose, children's music similar to that of Schumann and Tchaikovsky. Then there are enigmatic bagatelles, comparable with those of Beethoven. The six folk-tune arrangements for the piano are a special case, being original in concept, demonstrating Sibelius's modal compositional techniques and belonging to the best of his miniatures.

As Erik Tawaststjerna has argued, the miniatures broadly follow the general stylistic development of Sibelius's music. Sibelius's early piano and chamber music was written for himself to play (violin), or for family ensembles (duos, trios and quartets) with his brother Christian (violoncello), sister Linda (piano) and close friends, at musical soirees and at social gatherings in Hämeenlinna and during the summer. The pieces from Sibelius's childhood (up to 1885) and student days in Helsinki, Berlin and Vienna (1885–1891) are mostly standard house or salon music, but among them are already some memorable and remarkable achievements. The earliest dated piano piece, *Con moto*, 'Keepsake from J. S. 1885', with its combined mazurka, waltz and scherzo characteristics, is pianistically adventurous, a rewarding piece with a brilliant Lisztian written-out fermata. Three piano pieces from the summer of 1887, an *Andante* in E♭ major, an *[Aubade]* in A♭ major and *Au crépuscule*, demonstrate how Sibelius's improvisations possibly became written pieces; they are small and colourful fantasies. The fourth piece from the same summer, *Trånaden* (Yearning) for piano and reciter in five movements, is actually one of his largest piano works, lasting almost twenty minutes, with an impressive storm scene and some interesting anticipations of his mature style. *Valse 'à Betsy Lerché'* in A♭ major (1889) is an exciting piece in several sections, and was written as a gift for his girlfriend at the time, Betsy Lerché. The sections carry descriptions from the stages of a love affair: after 'Introduction' come sections entitled 'douce', 'avec force', 'à la Betsy', 'avec passion' and 'adieu!' In *Florestan* (1889), a Schumann-influenced piece in four movements, the pianistic writing varies from easy to demanding; the music is imaginative with its prevailing Romanticism and glimpses of Sibelian originality.

Sibelius began writing violin pieces soon after starting formal violin lessons (autumn 1881). He had already been playing the instrument for some time, and his free improvisations were apparently well known. In addition to sonata movements and suites, he was able to compose some beautiful melodies, as in the *Andante grazioso* (1884–5), the *Andante molto* from his [Five Pieces] of 1886–7, and the *Andante cantabile* (1887). The *Andantino* from the Suite in D minor (1887–8) is a small, yet inspired composition. The virtuosity in his violin writing increases markedly in the fast runs and pizzicatos of the breathtaking [Étude] in D major (1886) and the *Quasi Presto* finale of the Suite in D minor. The distance from the Romance in B minor op. 2/1 (1888, rev. 1911) to the slow movement of the Violin Concerto is not as far as one might imagine. Of Sibelius's early music for cello, three pieces must especially be mentioned: the *Andante molto* in F minor (1887) for the equality of its piano and cello parts and its virtuosic cadenza; the tiny *Lulu Waltz* in F♯ minor (1889) because of its melancholy mood, caused perhaps by an undocumented affair, and finally the Theme and Variations for solo cello (c. 1887), a stunning piece lasting more than ten minutes and employing a variety of styles and cello techniques from Bach to Popper.

During the earliest phase of his professional career (1891–1902), Sibelius concentrated on learning to master large-scale symphonic forms, which might account for the relatively small number of miniatures from this time. Yet he composed the Six Impromptus for piano (1890–1893), in which he tried to create a new 'Karelian' piano style, inspired, at least partially, by the *kantele* melodies and dances he had heard in eastern Finland.[39] The Impromptus have often been criticised for being unpianistic. Other critics, however, have praised the music's 'freedom from the clichés and trivial virtuosity of the period after Liszt'.[40] One contemporary recalls that, after the Impromptus had been published (1893), 'he [Sibelius] played the *dolcissimo* middle section of the third Impromptu again and again. Sibelius was extremely satisfied with that passage; we too were very fond of it and never tired of listening to it.'[41] The second Impromptu is a wild Karelian *trépak* dance, whereas the fifth has been compared to Liszt's famous *Les jeux d'eau à la Villa d'Este*, because of its harp or *kantele*-like arpeggiation.[42] For Blom, however, it was 'tiresome beyond words'.[43]

The Ten Pieces for piano op. 24 (1894–1903) are among Sibelius's most popular miniatures, with good reason. Although Sibelius did not develop his 'Karelian style', but rather fused it with a more Romantic idiom, the result is often exciting and unique. The first two pieces, 'Impromptu' in G minor and 'Romance' in A major, are evocative, half-dramatic scenes, close to the sinister mood of the second half of the tone poem *Skogsrået* (The Wood Nymph). The popularity of the crisp 'Caprice' in E minor (no. 3), the Chopin-like E major Waltz (no. 5) with its interesting 2/4 accompaniment, and the eloquent, pianistically rewarding 'Romance' in D♭ major (no. 9) may easily persuade pianists to forget the merits of the more delicate pieces, such as the 'Idyll' (no. 6), with its demanding violin-inspired writing for the right hand, the simple beauty of the 'Andantino' (no. 7), and the profound 'Nocturno' (no. 8).

The *Malinconia* op. 20 (1900) for cello and piano is one of the few large-scale pieces for cello. Scott Goddard thinks that 'as a whole the work lacks that distinction which is now associated with Sibelius's name'.[44] Although the juxtaposition of the cello and piano passages may at the beginning seem strange and the piano arpeggiations are perhaps excessive and mechanical, the piece with its noble melodic content and chromaticism anticipates the slow movement of the Violin Concerto and even the symphonies of the 1910s, and can make a startling impression with its deep expression of grief and full-bodied *grandioso* sound.

The *Six Finnish Folksongs* for piano (1903) are the most fascinating demonstration of how Sibelius's compositional technique derived from his

Example 9.1 Sibelius, 'Minun Kultani' (My Beloved) (bars 16–28)

experiences with folk music. Anyone who wishes to become familiar with Sibelius's very individual modal tonality and ways of constructing textures (*Satz*) should study these arrangements carefully. The basic textural elements are line, pedal point and ostinato.[45] Without an awareness of these parameters, Sibelius's music remains incomprehensible. Sibelius discussed the basics of his technique in his famous academic trial lecture from 1896: his way of harmonising melodies, consisting usually of a minor pentachord, based, according to him, on another pentachord a fifth lower, results in taking the ninth chord as the basic harmony.[46]

In the first arrangement 'Minun kultani' (My Beloved), the B-oriented melody lies almost through the piece upon the pedal E and, consequently, on an E major ninth chord. In the second half of the piece, the melody is doubled in octaves (Ex. 9.1). The contrapuntal middle voice is doubled in thirds or fourths, and the harmony, consisting mainly of parallel motions of sixth or seventh chords, is a result of these components, complicated further by some polymodal inflections. The three sharp accidentals at the outset of the piece refer to a B aeolian–ionian (or minor–major) scale. Here a new musical language in connection with a freshly genuine pianistic way of handling the instrument has been introduced.

Sibelius's new vein continues in *Kyllikki*, three lyrical pieces for piano op. 41 (1904), which is perhaps Sibelius's pianistically most advanced and demanding solo work. Though based on episodes from the *Kalevala*, it is not so much programme music as a triptych based on the three successive states of mind of its female protagonist – although the very aggressive and masculine character of the opening movement may refer also to Lemminkäinen.[47] The Sibelian *Satz* technique, described above and in relation to Exx. 9.3 and 4 below, is used everywhere, and it is at its most apparent at the beginning and end of the second movement, *Andantino*, where the melody is doubled in tenths and tonic and dominant pedal notes are used simultaneously.

The Ten Pieces of op. 58 (1909) are arguably Sibelius's most individual and satisfying set of piano miniatures, yet Layton's verdict is merciless: 'they are at best undistinguished'.[48] If *Kyllikki* combines features of Sibelius's Romantic period (the dark Romantic colouring of the first and second movements) with a more classical orientation (the playfulness of the dance-like closing movement), in the Ten Pieces we are in the midst of his modernist phase. Although traditional features appear now and then, the music strives towards a more polyphonic and linear mode of writing, characterised by sparse textures, concise and concentrated expression, and experimental harmony with dissonant clashes. The movements are no longer conventional late Romantic character pieces, which could be characterised as inferior salon or domestic music.[49] They are altogether more individual, and challenge both the fingers and mind of the pianist. Sibelius himself was aware of the progress, and noted in his diary that he 'thought the op. 58 pieces an improvement technically on his earlier piano writing'.[50]

The very first number, 'Rêverie', is strikingly modern. The texture is mostly in two parts, and the seeming independence of the left hand from the vague rhythmic and tonal ambivalence of the right hand creates an enigmatic atmosphere. Although the middle section and the strongly varied return of the opening contain more traditional elements and are texturally thicker, the piece satisfies both intellectual and musical curiosity. The 'Scherzino' (no. 2) makes a strong impression with its slight bimodality and liveliness, and has 'something of the character of Benvenuto Cellini about it'.[51] The 'Air varié' (no. 3) is a remarkable achievement with its tonal adventurousness and Bachian two-part-Invention textures. 'The Shepherd' (no. 4) charms with its pastoralism, and the clash between the 2/4 accompaniment figure and the prevailing 3/4 metre. The E♭ minor 'Tempo di Minuetto' (no. 7) is filled with 'melancholy of the old times'. The way in which Sibelius juxtaposes the gloomy main section with the music-box-like textures of the contrasting episodes is ingenious and lends the piece an estranged character, reflecting perhaps the thoughts of the composer at a certain nostalgic moment. The same sense of estrangement can be heard in the restless and 'disturbing' right-hand trills of the 'Ständchen' (no. 9).

The products of Sibelius's deepening classicism, the Three Sonatinas op. 67 (1912) and the Two Rondinos op. 68 (1912) for piano, as well as the Sonatina in E major op. 80 (1915) and the Rondino op. 81/2 (1917) for violin and piano, have won more universal recognition. They were the first examples of Sibelius's creative spring offering 'pure water' instead of the 'many-coloured cocktails of his contemporaries'. New classicism was in the air, and similar Sonatinas were composed also by Ravel (1903–5), Reger

Example 9.2 Sibelius, Piano Sonatina in B♭ minor, op. 67/3. Thematic correspondences

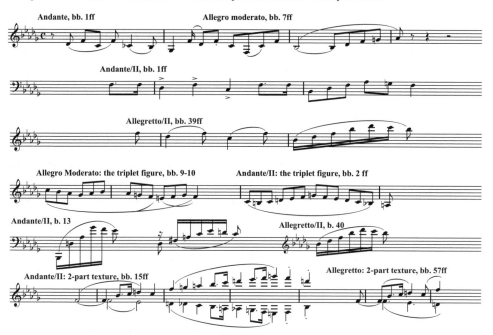

(1905–8), Busoni (1910–21) and Roussel (1912). Sibelius's pieces, however, were in many respects more retrospective than those of his contemporaries. Sibelius's new kind of classicism was far removed from Neoclassicism, even though the Rondino in C♯ minor for piano (op. 68/2), with its cheerful polka rhythms and spicy minor second dissonances, resembles aspects of the music of Poulenc or Prokofiev. The G♯ minor Rondino (op. 68/1) is like the opening of an unknown *Valse oubliée* by Liszt.

The Sonatinas for piano are important also for their formal characteristics, especially the third in B♭ minor, whose cyclical form points towards Sibelius's preoccupation with fusing the separate movements of a multi-movement form into a single entity. After the initial attempts in the first and second movements of the string quartet, *Voces intimae*, and the finale of the Third Symphony, the B♭ minor Sonatina prefigures the solution adopted in the opening double-movement of the Fifth Symphony. As in the Seventh Symphony, the three hypothetical movements are thematically unified. The first movement's *Allegro moderato* opening motive with its characteristic skips (F–D♭, F–C, F–B♭), anticipated in the *Andante* introduction, acts as the principal motive throughout the Sonatina. The work offers perfect proof of Sibelius's masterly control of musical form (Ex. 9.2).

It would be easy to pass over the next two sets of miniatures, the Ten Bagatelles op. 34, and the ten *Pensées lyriques* op. 40, which were written around the time of the First World War and have been characterised as 'unworthy'.[52] Guy Sacre, however, counts them 'among the best of Sibelius; they form together a kind of *Jugend-Album* agreeable both to the fingers and mind of the young sight-reader (and to the less young too!)'.[53] Though not among Sibelius's greatest works, they are nevertheless imaginative and humorous pieces. Among them are pastiches: a gavotte ('Tanzweise', op. 34/2), and a minuet ('Minuetto', op. 40/4). There are genuine dances: the Mazurka op. 34/3, and the Polonaise op. 40/4. The 'Rondoletto' op. 40/7 and the 'Scherzando' op. 40/8 are polkas with surprising chordal progressions. The 'Pensée mélodique' op. 40/6 is tonally vagrant, and only finds the tonic (C major) at the end of the piece. Some of the pieces are homages to Chopin, Schumann, Liszt or Tchaikovsky, and in other passages a slight affinity with Prokofiev can be discerned.

Sibelius almost wrote 'too many' sets of miniatures during the 1910s, in the sense that opp. 74, 75, 76, 85, 94, 97, and 99 (all composed between 1911 and 1922) have often been bundled together with little awareness of their individual strengths and characteristics. The *Lyric Pieces* for piano op. 74 (1914), for example, are perhaps one of his best sets. The pureness of the 'Ekloge' (no. 1) and Debussyan spirit of the 'Soft West Wind' (no. 2) are disarming. The five 'Tree' pieces of op. 75 (1914), of which 'The Spruce' (no. 5) is unquestionably the most popular, powerfully convey Sibelius's pantheism, and the parallel 'Flower' suite of five pieces op. 85 (1916–17) is refined and attractive in character. The other works mentioned above include a number of exquisite pieces, such as the Lisztian 'Arabesque' op. 76/9, the fragile 'Linnaea' op. 76/11, the tonally ambigious 'Capriccietto' op. 76/12, and the 'Harlequinade' op. 76/13, which invites comparison with some of Debussy's shorter preludes such as 'Minstrels'. The capricious 'Nouvellette' op. 94/2 reminds us of Beethoven's Bagatelles. The Lullyan 'Gavotte' op. 94/6, the Schumann-like 'Humorous March' op. 97/4, the burlesque 'Humoresque II' op. 97/6, and the 'Petite marche' op. 99/8, with its oriental flavour and hints of the Seventh Symphony, are also worth mentioning.

With the exception of the Violin Concerto, Sibelius seems to have 'abandoned' his own instrument after his early chamber-music period. During his most intense period of economical difficulties, however, he 'rediscovered' it, resulting in twenty-nine pieces for violin and piano (1914–29), and ten pieces for violin (or cello) and orchestra (or piano). The solo violin pieces divide, according to Melinda Scott, into several categories: 'lyrical' (graceful melodies within a slow tempo), 'folk-influenced' (with strict metre and measure, clear and regular phrases), 'pictorial' (impressions of subjects inspired by nature), 'classical con fantasia' (Rondino op. 81/2), 'virtuosic dances' (pyrotechnic bravura), and 'florid' (figurative, in *Allegro* tempos).[54]

The neglect of Sibelius's violin pieces seems particularly strange, as the violin was after all his own instrument, and violinists have generally loved pieces that have a salon flavour, such as those of Wieniawski, Sarasate, and Kreisler. One possible reason for their neglect could be the fact that the music has been usually difficult to find, mostly being out of print for a considerable time. Although some violinists from the older generation, such as Emil Telmányi, performed Sibelius's violin pieces, modern players do not seem to have discovered this repertoire, which is a pity, since there is much more to enjoy than the popular 'Romance' in F major op. 78/2 (1915). Why should the violinist fond of this Romance not seize the 'Impromptu' (no. 1) from the same opus, which displays in characteristically Sibelian manner the proximity of the C major and A minor keys, spiced with the tritone/dorian sixth of the F♯, or enjoy the 'Religioso' (no. 3), in the style of Vitali, or the Wieniawski-like 'Rigaudon' (no. 4), as all the romantic virtuosi (Sarasate, Kreisler etc.) wrote these kind of cheerful pastiches?

It would be an error to think that the violin pieces are all alike. On the contrary, most of them are based on individual ideas and are both musically and instrumentally demanding. The 'Souvenir' (no. 1), 'Tempo di Minuetto' (no. 2), and 'Danse caractéristique' (no. 3) from op. 79 (1915–17), for example, challenge the violinist in many ways, not least with their original virtuosity and intelligent attitude towards exploiting traditional dance forms, much in the same way as Rakhmaninov did. The Mazurka op. 81/1 (1915) might be Sibelius's best salon or show piece, with its chromatic passages, double stops and chords, wide skips and pizzicato. Sibelius sometimes plays with the audience's expectations, as in the Menuetto op. 81/5 (1918), which is more music about the ancient dance form than a paraphrase or invocation of it. Much the same is true of the exciting Danse champêtre no. 2, *Alla polacca*, from op. 106 (1924), which is like a neoclassical deconstruction of the genre; if not in the way Stravinsky handled traditional forms, yet at least in the vein Sibelius composed his *Wedding March* (1911).

The next two piano collections, *Cinq morceaux romantiques/lyriques* op. 101 (1923–1924), and *Five Characteristic Impressions* op. 103 (1924) are at the threshold of Sibelius's late style. In the place of the earlier thin and linear textures 'a more massive, more full-toned handling of piano' prevails, and the pieces are 'conceived directly in terms of the resources of the piano'.[55] According to Sibelius, op. 101 'can be played as a suite',[56] and it possibly reflects his youthful memories. The 'Romance' (no. 1), however, is harmonically bolder than his early Romances. 'Scène lyrique' (no. 3) and 'Humoresque' (no. 4) reveal their closeness to the Sixth Symphony. All three works have common virtuosic elements that refer back to Sibelius's rejected plan for a second violin concerto. The 'Scène romantique' (no. 5) resembles Schumann's *Novellette* in E major, though the harmonies are at times more reminiscent of Fauré, and the piece as a whole 'is one of the brightest jewels in Sibelius's piano output'.[57]

The penultimate set of piano pieces, op. 103, prefigure the Seventh Symphony. The first piece, 'The Village Church', sounds familiar as it is based on the then unpublished and hardly known *Andante festivo* for string quartet (1922). At the same time, it also looks towards the grandiose final symphony, all three works being in C major. The possibly programmatic 'The Oarsman' (no. 3) also shares some material with the Seventh Symphony, whereas 'The Tempest' (no. 4) is perhaps connected with Sibelius's music, yet to be composed, for Shakespeare's play. 'In Mournful Mood' (no. 5) is surprisingly Mahlerian sounding.

Sibelius's swansong in the field of piano music, the *Five Esquisses* op. 114 (1929), was not published until 1973, which might be the reason for its critical neglect. However, the *Esquisses* are the key to Sibelius's late style and modal techniques. They are musically fascinating, although they contain, unfortunately, several misprints caused by the hasty and careless editing and publishing process.[58] Joseph Kon has described how these pieces contain 'elements of tonal and harmonic innovation' that 'reveal a trend in the composer's thinking . . . which unexpectedly draws Sibelius close to Scriabin and even Bartók'. The use of the tritone, according to Yuri Holopov's theory of tritone substitution, 'allows at least two tonics, corresponding to the two possible resolutions of a tritone as augmented fourth or (enharmonically) as diminished fifth'.[59] In 'The Forest Lake' (no. 3), a column of thirds, having B as its lowest note and D as the tonic, forming a ninth, eleventh, or even in some places a thirteenth chord, functions as the principal harmony: almost half of the piece is based on modal improvisation upon this chord (Ex. 9.3).

These two Sibelian techniques – interpreting and resolving intervals, in this case the tritone, in an unorthodox way (B and F as B and E♯, or C♭ and F, resolving to A♯/A♮ and F♯, or B♭/B♭♭ and G♭), and the column technique – opened up entirely new methods of composition and could have offered Sibelius new creative ideas and possibilities during the final twenty years or so of his life. For instance, the fourth piece of op. 114, *Song in the Forest*, is based on the column of B–D♯–F–A–C/C𝄪, i.e. on a major-ninth chord with diminished fifth and two possible ninths. Alternating the different notes of a column generates a huge number of potential chords.

This modal–tonal ambiguity is Sibelius's major contribution to the compositional thinking and methods of the first half of the twentieth century. Joseph Kon is right to say that 'Sibelius's interest in the potentials of unstable tonal formations characterises him as a composer reacting to modern tendencies',[60] except in one point: Sibelius was not simply a reactionary. The difference is that he explored modal material with chromatic influences, and

Example 9.3 Sibelius, 'The Forest Lake', op. 114/2 (bars 1–13)

never rejected the idea of tonal centres, whereas the inheritors and developers of Wagnerian chromaticism were not interested in tonal centres and perhaps regarded music containing modal/tonal elements as old fashioned. In doing that, they did not see the possibility that music could go in a different direction from their own.

Sibelius's two last violin works, opp. 115 and 116 (1929), are again products of his experimental late style. The 'Ballade' op. 115/2 displays a series of exciting appoggiaturas, resolving into other dissonances; the 'Humoresque' (no. 3) is a weird piece with its apparent simplicity, and 'The Bells' (no. 4) offers an enigmatic riddle, difficult to decipher (Ex. 9.4). 'The Bells' is characterised by an almost minimalist saltarello motion and is based on changing tonal centres. E initially seems to be the tonal centre, despite the intrusion of F×; the music is also coloured by a combination of major and minor scale fragments. Later, the music seems to be active around F♯ (bars 41–55), then around C (57–65), and the piece looks as though it will be based on a column of fourths. It would be more logical, in the context of Sibelius's modal language, to interpret the column of thirds, with their alterations, as the basis of the piece: C♯–E/E♯–G/G♯–B/B♯–D/D♯–F♯/F×–A/A♯–C, using all the twelve tones of the chromatic scale. The C♯ appears finally to be the tonic, the F× being a tritone relation to it, and the tonic is reached by the emphatic *Dies irae* motive in the bass (bars 97ff.), at the moment at which C♯ aeolian mode seems to prevail. However, in order to

Example 9.4a Sibelius, 'Die Glocken', 'The Bells), op. 115/4 (bars 1–15)

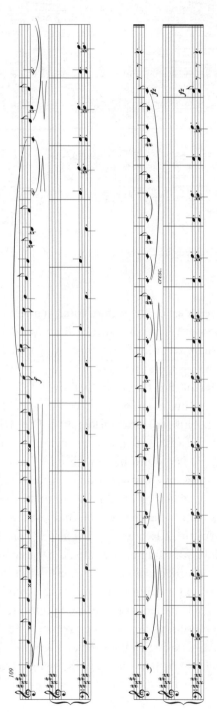

Example 9.4b Sibelius, 'Die Glocken', 'The Bells), op. 115/4 (bars 110–28)

Hypothetical tonic column on C♯

avoid an easy solution, the ending of the piece hints towards F♯, and the music uses C♯ phrygian and melodic minor materials.

The final violin work is enigmatic too. 'Scène de danse' (no. 1) is based on parallel-seventh chords with diminished fifth/augmented fourth and sounds strangely distant and obscure. The 'Danse caractéristique' (no. 2) is centred on C, but has a B♭–G ostinato in the bass as an independent element. As the tritone F♯ is again very striking in the bass, the piece can be understood as being based on the acoustic scale and the column of thirds (C–E/E♭–G–B♭–D–F♯), E♭ functioning as a temporary tonic in the middle section.

We do not have much music composed by Sibelius after 1931. The 'Funeral Music' op. 111/2 (1931) for organ was written for the death of his old friend, the symbolist painter Akseli Gallén-Kallela, and was perhaps taken from the partially finished music for the Eighth Symphony. This was later confirmed by Aino Sibelius, when asked by Joonas Kokkonen after Sibelius's death. It seems plausible, given that Sibelius had only a few days to compose the piece for the funeral.[61] With its merciless dissonances and open intervals, the music sounds as though it is coming from another planet. In the light of this highly original music, it would have been remarkable to hear the rest of the symphony too.

In conclusion, large parts of Sibelius's music are still waiting to be found. And this process of discovery will surely happen in the near future. There will be many more interesting pieces, which will shed new light on Sibelius's original techniques and methods of composition. In this sense, Sibelius is in good company, as most of the piano works by Weber, Mendelssohn, Schumann and Liszt still lie in oblivion.

Santeri Levas, Sibelius's secretary from 1938 onwards, tells us that:

> up to now very little had been made of the piano pieces, but that could not convince the composer that they were unimportant. On the contrary, their limited popularity aroused in him an aggressiveness that was rarely evident. 'I know that they have a future,' he said, 'even though they are almost forgotten today.' We had been talking about Robert Schumann, and Sibelius added that one day his piano pieces would perhaps be just as popular as those of Schumann.[62]

PART THREE

Influence and reception

10 *Sub umbra Sibelii*: Sibelius and his successors

ILKKA ORAMO

It is difficult to establish who was the first to mention 'Sibelius's shadow'. The idea pops up in the 1920s at the latest. In an essay on 'the youngest Finnish music' from 1928, the composer Ernest Pingoud (1887–1942) refers to the 'reappraisal of certain values' during the First World War, notably to the 'bankruptcy of Romanticism' in the field of aesthetics.

> Sibelius's output, cherished and tended by reverent hands, did not lose a tad of its value; on the contrary, it secured an officially-sanctioned eternal value and still flourishes in all its beauty. A new phenomenon, nevertheless, showed up: the mountainous overall shape of Sibelius's output came to be seen in a new light, or perhaps from a different perspective, and where its shadow had once fallen, new curious searchlights began to play their games. The consequences did not fail to reveal themselves, and new life emerged: new Finnish music, more or less independent from Sibelius, was born.[1]

Pingoud was of Russian origin and had emigrated to Finland from St Petersburg in 1918, in the aftermath of the Russian Revolution. Although well integrated into the society of his *patrie choisie* ten years later, he remained an outsider in one important respect. Nationalism, the fundamental generating force in Finnish culture at the turn of the century, was none of his concern. He sympathised with it from the outside, as revealed in an article on Sibelius from 1909 in which he described the tone poem *Finlandia*, 'the most national of Sibelius's works', as 'radiating a deep sorrow for his enslaved fatherland'.[2] But in principle he was against national art since, according to him, it belonged to a nation's infancy and, in fact, represented only the infancy of art. In an essay on national music from 1922 he used the word *Heimatkunst* – first applied to Sibelius's music by the German music historian Walter Niemann in 1906[3] – to denote an art for which it is enough simply to satisfy the needs of the artist's own nation; this kind of art has a strange attraction to others as well, but its appeal is superficial, as is its impact on the recipient.[4]

The composers of the new Finnish music that Pingoud had in mind were Yrjö Kilpinen (1892–1959) on the one hand, and Väinö Raitio (1891–1945), Aarre Merikanto (1893–1958) and Uuno Klami (1900–61) on the other. Kilpinen was a composer of lieder, of which he wrote more than seven hundred. He has been characterised as a Finnish Hugo Wolf, and, according to Seppo Nummi (1932–81), a composer of lieder himself, he was the most coherent neo-classicist in Finnish music.[5] Raitio, Merikanto and Klami, along with Pingoud, were the main representatives of what is known as the '1920s modernism' in the history of Finnish music; and, as Pingoud remarked, they tended to be regarded as a group.

Who, then, were the composers overshadowed by Sibelius? Pingoud does not mention any names. Obviously he had the whole generation between Sibelius and the modernists in mind, composers who actually formed the core of national Romanticism in Finnish music: Oskar Merikanto (1868–1924), Armas Järnefelt (1869–1958), Erkki Melartin (1875–1937), Selim Palmgren (1878–1951), Toivo Kuula (1883–1918), and Leevi Madetoja (1887–1947), to mention the most important of them. Robert Kajanus (1856–1933), whose symphonic poem *Aino* (1885) opened Sibelius's eyes to the musical possibilities of the Finnish national epic *Kalevala*, practically abandoned the composition of large-scale orchestral works because of Sibelius and became the most ardent protagonist of his compatriot's music instead.[6]

Sibelius's fame – and his shadow – began to grow in 1892 with the first performance of the *Kullervo* Symphony. In this work he offered a solution to a problem that had occupied Finnish artists, painters in the first place, for some time: how to create a work of art which is at the same time both national and universal?[7] The national element of the *Kullervo* Symphony consists in the Kullervo legend of the *Kalevala*, and in the world of the ancient modal runes originally associated with its poetry. But the Kullervo legend also has something of the universality of a myth. A tragic hero, like King Oedipus, Kullervo commits an act of violence against a person whose identity as a close relative only becomes uncovered afterwards, and then punishes himself by taking his own life. Musically, as well as dramatically, the particular is combined with the general: the modal world of runes with tonal harmony, and the *Kalevala* world of mythical structures with the forms and genres characteristic of the western musical tradition, such as the symphony, the symphonic poem, the oratorio and the operatic *scena*. The *Kullervo* Symphony is a rough work, far from the technical perfection of, say, the contemporary tone poems of Richard Strauss, but its sheer originality and the vigour of the artistic vision that lies behind it were something unheard-of in Finnish music at the time of its creation.

The *Kullervo* Symphony was followed by a series of symphonic poems, notably the *Lemminkäinen Legends*, in which Sibelius penetrated even deeper into the soul of the *Kalevala* by means of purely instrumental music.

Selim Palmgren, at that time a student at the Helsinki Music Institute, described the impact of these works upon his contemporaries in his auto-biography:

> Those who had an opportunity to listen and to see Jean Sibelius himself conduct his *Kalevala*-poems at that time – in the years 1895–99 – will most certainly never forget these experiences. 'My dear Palmgren,' I said to myself, 'you have nothing to do on the field of *Kalevala*, just let Sibba [Sibelius] take care of it and try to find out something else!' And I tried.[8]

This overwhelming impact, the intensity of which a modern listener can hardly imagine, seems to have had two different causes. This music was *modern*, not only in the context of the musical life of a small country on the fringes of Europe, but also in its wider international context. It was different from, but by no means less modern than, Strauss's *Don Juan*, Mahler's First Symphony or Debussy's *Prélude à l'après-midi d'un faune*. The other factor was that it was received as something belonging to the Finnish people, because its composer was Finnish and because its inspiration came from Finnish poetry and Finnish nature. Sibelius's music thus offered his compatriots an object of self-identification, which contributed in their minds to the definition of 'who we are'. The delight was not quite unanimous, however, since by choosing a text in Finnish (instead of Swedish) Sibelius took sides with the 'Young Finns', who wanted to strengthen the position of the Finnish language in a society in which the language of the upper class was still Swedish. Supporters of the 'Swedish Party', including his former teacher Martin Wegelius, strongly disapproved of his choice.[9]

From 1809 Finland's national status was a form of semi-independence. Having been a Swedish province for centuries, it had become an autonomous grand duchy of the Russian Empire with most of the institutions of an independent state, such as its own legislature, army, customs, money, mail and national symbols (coat of arms, flag, national anthem). The supreme power, however, was in St Petersburg, and towards the end of the century the Russian authorities began to tighten their grip on the annoyingly separatist grand duchy. Their aim was to remove some of Finland's constitutional privileges, granted during the reign of Tsar Alexander II (1855–81), and to harmonise its legislation with the rest of the country; in brief, to make Finland a Russian province like many others. This policy culminated in the so-called February Manifesto of 1899.[10] There was a strong reaction in Finland, in which both painters and musicians protested against this perceived act of despotism and injustice. Sibelius wrote his *Atenarnes sång* (Song of the Athenians) and performed it in a concert of his works on 26 April 1899. The reception of this simple march song, a setting of Viktor

Rydberg's adaptation of the battle song of Tyrtaeus, was so enthusiastic that it overshadowed the premiere of the First Symphony, given in the same concert.

If the *Kullervo* Symphony and the *Lemminkäinen Legends* had contributed to the development of national identity among the Finnish people by making its Finno-Ugrian past newly accessible, *Atenarnes sång* made Sibelius a hero, who stood up for the nation in time of need. During the 'frost years' or 'time of oppression', as this period (from 1899 to 1905) in Finnish history is known, Sibelius wrote a considerable number of works with a more or less overt political message, including the cantatas *Islossningen i Uleå älf* (The Breaking of Ice on the Oulu River, to a libretto by Z. Topelius, 1899) and *Tulen synty* (The Origin of Fire, *Kalevala*, 1902), the orchestral work *Suomi herää* (Finland awakens), the revised version of which is known as *Finlandia* (1899/1900), and several songs for male-voice choir, notably *Isänmaalle* (To the Fatherland, Paavo Cajander, 1900), *Veljeni vierailla mailla* (My Brothers in Foreign Lands, Juhani Aho, 1904) and *Har du mod?* (Have you Courage? J. J. Wecksell, 1904). Some contemporaries even regarded works like the First and Second Symphonies (1899, 1902) as having a hidden patriotic programme, although it is likely that such a programme was read into them by people with more imagination and nationalistic fervour than critical judgement. There is nothing to indicate that their heroic *topoi* should refer to local politics rather than the vocabulary of the generic traditions that lie behind them. The patriotic interpretation of these two works, nevertheless, does continue to find support among more recent scholarship.[11]

It is clear, though, that by writing patriotic pieces that could be interpreted as subversive, Sibelius showed considerable civilian courage. Many Finnish intellectuals were expelled to Siberia or forced to flee to Sweden due to their political opinions (this is what the song *My Brothers in Foreign Lands* is all about), and Sibelius could easily have been one of them. He had now become, before his fortieth birthday, one of the nation's spiritual leaders. In his obituary of Sibelius in a Helsinki newspaper, the composer Joonas Kokkonen (1921–96) emphasised the uniqueness of his feat: 'Jean Sibelius's position in the thoughts of the Finnish people has been very special for decades already: there are probably only a few even remotely similar cases in the history of western culture, in which an artist becomes almost a legend during his lifetime and is so unequivocally counted among the nation's great men.'[12] A modern commentator has referred to Sibelius as a 'cultural icon', by which he means 'persons or phenomena that have attained the status of "concepts" inasmuch as they have assumed a permanent place and significance in people's everyday thinking'.[13]

The Romantics

How, then, did Sibelius's contemporaries cope with the living legend? Palmgren's 'try to find out something else' was a typical reaction. Palmgren turned to the piano, took Schumann and Chopin as starting points, and proved rather successful as a composer of Romantic character pieces and piano concertos, reminiscent of Grieg and Rakhmaninov. Järnefelt, Sibelius's brother-in-law, wrote a couple of symphonic works in the 1890s (*Korsholma*, 1894; *Symphonic Fantasy*, 1895), but then left this field to Sibelius and found a more suitable idiom in lyric songs and instrumental pieces, of which the atmospheric *Berceuse* (1904) is the most well known. Oskar Merikanto became a songwriter and his music, popular in style and manner, spread in much wider circles on home ground than Sibelius's, which was often harsh, gloomy and difficult to understand. So it seems that there was plenty of room in Finnish musical life for composers who did not try to step on Sibelius's toes; and nothing, except prejudice against the unfamiliar, would have prevented their success abroad, had they been of sufficient interest. Palmgren actually made some progress both in Germany and especially in the USA, where he became professor of composition at the Eastman School of Music in the early 1920s. Järnefelt's and Merikanto's music was of a more *Heimatkunst* character that did not travel well outside its home country.

Another way to cope with Sibelius was to try to learn from him. Sibelius's most talented students were Kuula and Madetoja, whom he agreed to see once in a while in 1908–9. They soon realised that they could not expect composition lessons from him in the ordinary sense. He might take a casual look at their exercises and scores and make a few general remarks such as 'no futile notes', but the rest of the lesson consisted of a spirited discussion of musical and aesthetic issues.[14] In autumn 1909, Kuula left for Paris to continue his studies with Marcel Labey. When Madetoja started to plan his continuing studies abroad in January 1910, he asked Kuula for advice. 'Sibelius has been my teacher. From your own experience you know that his guidance is not very detailed.' Kuula answered that he had not learnt anything in Finland, except from Järnefelt, and advised his younger colleague to head for Paris as well.[15]

If Kuula and Madetoja did not learn much by way of craftsmanship from lessons with Sibelius, they certainly learnt from his scores. Surface-level stylistic influences are not very obvious, nor could they be, because of the utmost simplicity of the means that define Sibelius's style. Take, for example, the C minor theme at Fig. H in *En saga* (1892/1902), which – instead of using alternating tonic and dominant chords – is sustained by the mediant pedal note, E♭. The composer Einar Englund (1916–99) describes the effect as follows: 'Suddenly a miracle happens. Poetry enters into the music, which, owing to this simple idea, assumes a melancholy tone.'[16] A large part of Sibelius's style, to put it broadly, is based on conventional elements that behave in an unconventional way, and this makes it impossible to imitate him without immediately sounding like him. His fellow composers in Finland were, of course, aware of this, and it seems as if they took special care to avoid being trapped by the smallest amount of 'Sibelianism'.

Sibelius may have influenced them by his example, instead. His work opened up new paths in the virgin lands of modern solo song and choral music to Swedish and Finnish texts. The songs and choral works (initially for male-voice choir) of Järnefelt, Kuula, Madetoja, Palmgren and others would be hard to imagine without the model of Sibelius's early Runeberg, Josephson, Wecksell, Fröding and Rydberg settings (opp. 13, 17, 36, 37 and 38) and his radical choral pieces from the 1890s (op. 18 and others without opus number), which broke decisively away from the petty-bourgeois Biedermeier style of the previous decades. The extensive repertory of vocal music that flourished in his footsteps continued to construct the Finnish national self-image and, at the same time, reflected the characteristics of those parts of the country from which the composers came. It was principally music for local use, and most of it was of somewhat limited appeal because it required an understanding both of the poetry, and of its local context; but it was nevertheless an essential part of Finnish national Romanticism and contributed to the prevailing spirit of national determination.

Some of Sibelius's songs and choral works may be unique works of art. But so are some of the songs and choral works of Kuula and Madetoja. When it comes to this repertory, there is no aesthetic or artistic reason why their works should have fallen under Sibelius's shadow. There are true masterpieces among them. Nevertheless, if Sibelius's songs and choral works are considered to be of greater interest, it is only because they are the work of a composer who was undoubtedly superior to any of his Finnish contemporaries in another repertory, usually regarded as a higher level of achievement: symphonic orchestral music. Even the minor works of a major composer were of more interest to the public than the major works of a lesser composer and, in this sense, the origin of Sibelius's shadow actually lies in patterns of popular reception rather than in the intrinsic value, beauty or importance of the works of art themselves.

There is also another reason why the vocal music of Sibelius's contemporaries did not (and does not) suffer from his shadow. In the early twentieth century there was an enduring social need for new vocal repertory. Choral singing had become a popular movement and a vehicle for nationalist ideas in the latter part of the nineteenth century, but the number of choirs only increased after the turn of the century when mixed choirs became as fashionable as the traditional male-voice choirs. No single composer could possibly satisfy the demand for new pieces, and everything that was written came to be performed. Solo songs were required just as urgently. In Finland there were a number of internationally renowned singers (Aino Ackté, Ida Ekman, and others), who constantly needed new music for their recitals. An additional explanation for the increasing interest in vocal repertory was the simultaneous emancipation of poetry written in Finnish, which had only recently become a true literary language.

When speaking of the 'mountainous shape of Sibelius's output', Pingoud probably had his symphonic music in mind, since the hard core of his output undoubtedly consists of his seven symphonies, thirteen symphonic or tone poems, and the Violin Concerto. As fine as some of his other works are, they are hardly mentioned in general discussions of late-nineteenth- and early-twentieth-century music.[17] In view of this orchestral repertory, contemporary Finnish composers were, indeed, doomed to a gloomy existence in Sibelius's shadow. The most productive among them was Erkki Melartin, who wrote six symphonies (1902, 1904, 1907, 1912/16, 1916, 1924), a couple of symphonic poems, and a violin concerto (1913/30). The symphonies, although competently written, could not secure a place in the repertory, not even in Finland, because of their eclecticism. The Violin Concerto has recently been dug out of oblivion and recorded, but – despite its merits as a virtuoso showpiece – it has failed to establish a permanent place in the repertory.

More personal are Madetoja's three symphonies (1916, 1918, 1926). In the first two, contemporary critics discerned some formal and structural features that can be compared with Sibelius, if not necessarily explained as his 'influence'.[18] Such observations are of interest since they show that no symphonic music written by Sibelius's younger colleagues could escape comparison with his works; they had become an inevitable point of reference, in relation to which everything else was measured and evaluated. Not even modern scholars can avoid this comparison. Erkki Salmenhaara, author of Madetoja's biography, writes:

> While Madetoja's first two symphonies are stylistically related to Sibelius's early symphonies and suffer by comparison with them in terms of thematic originality, strangely enough the closest reference point to Madetoja's Third Symphony is similarly Sibelius's Third. Madetoja does not perhaps quite attain the majesty of this symphony's first movement, but as a whole the works are fully on level pegging.

The relationship between these two works, however, is not based on the stylistic similarity, but rather on the similarity of mood. Stylistically, the French connections in Madetoja's Third are so evident that a French commentator has nicknamed it the 'Sinfonia Gallica'.[19] Why, then, compare it to Sibelius's Third? The idea is that Madetoja's Third Symphony relates to his Second in the same way that Sibelius's Third relates to his Second: a dramatic, large-scale symphony full of conflict is followed by another which is serene and harmonious in style and expression. When Madetoja's Third was performed in Stockholm in 1946, one of the leading daily newspapers reckoned him among the Finnish composers unjustly fallen '*sub umbra Sibelii*'.[20] Perhaps his style, as Salmenhaara supposes, is still so close to Sibelius's landscape that it is difficult to perceive its individual merits.[21] Madetoja's musical voice only comes into its own in a field practically untrodden by Sibelius, that of opera. As an artistic breakthrough, Madetoja's *Pohjalaisia* (1923) is as significant to the Finns as *Peter Grimes* to the British.

A general reason for the virtual disappearance of Melartin's and Madetoja's symphonies (Kuula did not write any) was that the historical life of the symphony as a genre had, for the time being, arrived at its final phase. Mahler was its last major representative in Central Europe, Nielsen and Sibelius in the 'Nordic Countries'. The First World War had put an end to national Romanticism, or, at least, to its soft, idealised aspects, and, as a consequence, music that still cherished its values appeared anachronistic.

The modernists

Pingoud and the creators of the 'new Finnish music, more or less independent from Sibelius' still wrote 'symphonies', but these works often attest to the decline of the genre. Pingoud's First Symphony (1920) is in one movement, like Sibelius's Seventh (1924), and has the character and disposition of a symphonic fantasy since it does not obey any conventions of the genre. The two others (1924, 1927) display a more traditional appearance in their four-movement design, but they are saturated with the same whimsical spirit that characterises the composer's symphonic poems. Merikanto's first two symphonies (1916, 1918) and Raitio's single one (1919) are works of young composers still in search of their own voice, whereas Klami's two symphonies (1938, 1945) are less successful works of a mature composer. According to Kalevi Aho, co-author of Klami's biography and a symphonist himself, the symphonic form 'somehow seemed to shackle Klami's creative imagination'. The constraint at work here was probably the shadow of Sibelius, as Aho discreetly suggests.[22]

While the symphony was in decline in post-Sibelian Finland, the symphonic poem flourished in the 1920s and 1930s. The fact that Merikanto worked on a third symphony but finally decided to entitle it *Fantasy* (1923) is indicative of this shift of emphasis.[23] He thus did the opposite of Sibelius, who was working on a 'Fantasia sinfonica' but ended up calling it 'Symphony No. 7'. In a letter of 2 December 1922 Merikanto explained himself: 'It was all planned out, but maybe certain forms are no longer satisfying, and hence it makes no sense to call the composition a symphony.'[24] The *Fantasy* was the boldest music written in Finland so far. For the composer it became a personal disappointment, since it remained unperformed for almost three decades. Tauno Hannikainen and the Helsinki Philharmonic Orchestra gave the first performance in November 1952. The fate of his *Symphonic Study* (1928), an even bolder work than its predecessor, was worse still. Interviewed on the radio in 1957, Merikanto recounted:

> The *Symphonic Study* for orchestra, composed in 1928, is my most radical work. A pretty large work! It has never been played, and hopefully it never will be played. It can never be played, in fact, because last summer I cut five or six pages from here and there out of it with scissors – since I had promised my wife that I would not burn it. I spoke of this work to Pingoud, who was the manager of the Philharmonic Orchestra at the time, and he said 'Give it to me and I will pass it on to Professor Kajanus.' Professor Kajanus got it, invited me in to see him, and said: 'Mr Merikanto, you are so talented, but you really must retreat from this.'[25]

The work's musical language and form, which do not obey any textbook rules, were apparently incomprehensible to Kajanus's eyes. Fortunately, the composer Paavo Heininen, who studied with Merikanto for a while in 1958, understood them better and reconstructed the mutilated score, thus saving the *Symphonic Study* for posterity.[26] Worst was that Merikanto destroyed his Third Violin Concerto (1931) beyond recovery and that his masterpiece, the opera *Juha* (1922), only received its first performance on the radio in December 1958, a couple of months after the composer's death, and was not staged until 1963.

The lack of understanding that greeted Merikanto's most advanced music in the 1920s led to the tragic fact that he lost faith in his own work and began to write in a more conventional style in the 1930s. And yet, according to Heininen, 'what critics, conductors and the musical authorities of Merikanto's own time condemned as extreme radicalism seems to us today merely a blend of impressionism and expressionism that never entirely severed its links with late Romanticism and folk music'.[27] The problem was that Finland's musical climate at that time did not favour music that was too different from the familiar and the well-tried. Even though the 'modernists' had turned their back on national Romanticism, the 'musical authorities' (and the audience) had not. No fundamental change had taken place in their attitudes since before the First World War, when Sibelius's Fourth Symphony had been a daunting prospect for any audience.[28] Its performance, however, could not have been prevented, because, although incomprehensible, it was the work of a living legend. Merikanto had no such status. He tried to prove himself with works that moved decisively away from worn-out ideals of beauty, but failed to convince the 'musical authorities' upon whom he was ultimately dependent. The shadow, in this case, was not that of Sibelius. Rather, it was the shadow cast by a traditionally agrarian society over the evolving urban culture represented by composers like Pingoud, Raitio and Merikanto. They had grown more interested in ancient myth[29] and in symbolist or urban subjects[30] than national history and folklore, and they often expressed themselves in an ecstatic musical language more reminiscent of Skryabin than anything else.

Klami, whom Pingoud placed in the same group as Raitio and Merikanto, was a different case. Influenced by Stravinsky, Ravel and contemporary Spanish music, he distanced himself from German modernism (Strauss, Reger) and the Skryabin brand of the Russian legacy that had influenced the other members of the 'group'. His independence from Sibelius, as well as from Finnish national Romanticism, is shown by the fact that he could tackle subjects from the *Kalevala* and other Finnish literature from a new angle.[31] In *The Adventures of Lemminkäinen on the Island* (1935) he even has the boldness and wit to quote the opening melodic cells from Sibelius's *Lemminkäinen's Return* (Ex. 10.1). He did not face rejection by the Finnish 'musical authorities' or suffer uncomplimentary reviews the way Merikanto did, and his works were generally well received. In his case, Sibelius's shadow is only apparent in the manner that it affects all Finnish composers: if Sibelius had not existed, their works would possibly have found an easier access into the programmes of Finnish orchestras.

This was Einar Englund's point, when he took the 'shadow of Sibelius' as part of the title of his autobiography. The essence of his complaint reads as follows:

> In his own lifetime, Sibelius had already attained a strong position in Finland's musical life. His immense power overshadowed all the composers of that time to such an extent that the music of many of them has only experienced a late rebirth today. Who could have predicted in his wildest dreams that the shadow cast by Sibelius would extend so far, up to the present day, suffocating the music of our time as well? One only has to take a look at the symphony orchestras' concert catalogues in order to notice how crushing the dominance of Sibelius's work over the work of all other, still-living composers remains. There is a complete consensus that no alternatives shall be accepted.[32]

An author of seven symphonies himself, Englund (1916–99) had every reason to make a plea for more variety in planning concert programmes. Similar

Example 10.1 Uuno Klami, *The Adventures of Lemminkäinen on the Island* [excerpt] views are addressed to the 'musical authorities' every now and then by other composers as well. It might not, however, be quite correct to blame the dominance of Sibelius entirely for this situation. One could perhaps speak of an excessive weight of nineteenth- and early-twentieth-century music in the orchestral repertory in general. This phenomenon, which is not unique to Finland, is connected to the increasing tendency (or necessity?) to obey market laws in cultural activities as well as in other areas of life.

In addition to the shadow cast by Sibelius's music over other composers via the decisions of administrators and concert programmers, there is also a Sibelian legacy that has a direct impact on the minds of other composers, many of whom did or do not feel overshadowed by Sibelius. As Sibelius's influence on recent music is covered in detail in chapter 13 of the present book, I shall point out just one strain of influence that is worth mentioning, because it is different from any previous reception of his music. In an essay on the symphonies of Joonas Kokkonen, Edward Jurkowski argues that 'Kokkonen's significant achievement within the line of twentieth-century Finnish music is his role in extending Sibelius's ideals of large-scale organic logic while, at the same time, avoiding folk-music influences or the "nationalistic" surfaces of Sibelius's compositions.'[33] The observation that Kokkonen was attached to this feature in Sibelius's symphonic thinking, which James Hepokoski has called 'the principle of teleological genesis', is absolutely relevant.[34] According to Hepokoski, Sibelius creates this feeling of goal-direction by 'varied recyclings of the thematic pattern established in the piece's first rotation' (hence the term 'rotational form'). Kokkonen did the same thing with twelve-tone rows. This goal-oriented thinking, with its roots in Sibelius's late work, continues to flourish in Magnus Lindberg's recent orchestral music, based on recycling a set of harmonies in combination with a number of 'models', a model being a pattern or a situation defined in relation to several parameters. The results of this technique are, as I have pointed out in another context, 'a sense of continuity and direction, an ultimate aim, that controls a work's development from beginning to end according to a carefully designed plan'.[35] It is interesting to compare Lindberg's monolithic *Fresco* (1998) with Sibelius's Seventh Symphony (1924), in order to recognise how far the emphasis of Sibelius's influence has shifted from surface-level characteristics to basic structural principles.

11 Sibelius and Germany: *Wahrhaftigkeit* beyond *Allnatur*

TOMI MÄKELÄ

Celebrating the music and musician

In 1921, the Academy of Fine Arts in Berlin elected Jean Sibelius as an honorary fellow. Even if, as a foreigner, he could not become a full member, it was a great honour for a Finnish composer. In a letter to the composer dated 21 July 1921, the committee chairman, conservative composer Friedrich E. Koch, cited the exceptional 'truthfulness' (*Wahrhaftigkeit*) of Sibelius's music as the basis for their decision.[1] Ironically, the concept of *Wahrhaftigkeit* in Sibelius's work has subsequently been one of the most problematic areas of his critical reception: the notion of 'musical truth' had very different connotations for the theorists of the Frankfurt School such as Adorno. Yet at the time, the accolade was a sign of deep appreciation, based on Sibelius's output as far as his Fifth Symphony. By the time the distinguished Regia Accademia di Santa Cecilia in Rome had asked him to join the Comitato Internazionale d'Onore in 1916, Sibelius had been widely acknowledged as a leading representative of the last Romantic generation in European music. In Santa Cecilia he joined a host of other musical celebrities, including Guido Adler, Arrigo Boito, Max Bruch, Claude Debussy, Edward Elgar, Alexander Glazunov, Carl Goldmark, Engelbert Humperdinck, Vincent d'Indy, Giacomo Puccini, Camille Saint-Saëns, Max Reger, Alexander Skryabin, Charles V. Stanford and Richard Strauss.[2] This was, by any standards, an impressive range of great turn-of-the-century European musicians, even exceeding the Bertin Academy, and eloquently attests to the international reputation that Sibelius's music already enjoyed.

Sibelius himself had always sought success in Germany. He visited Berlin at least thirty-six times during his lifetime (approximately once a year between 1890 and 1931, excluding the war years), and gave many performances of his music. In 1902 he conducted the revised version of *En saga* (originally composed in 1892), and in 1904 Ferdinand Neisser presented *Finlandia* in Berlin for the first time. The following year, Sibelius conducted his Second Symphony, and Richard Strauss gave the world premiere of the final version of the Violin Concerto with Karel Halíř as soloist. In 1906, Neisser conducted popular masterpieces such as *Spring Song* and *Valse triste* and Traugott Ochs performed *Pelleas et Mélisande*. In 1907, the Violin Concerto was given by

Max Lewinger, and in 1908 Busoni conducted *Pohjola's Daughter*. In 1909, meanwhile, the Violin Concerto was played once again by Franz von Vecsey (to whom the composition had been dedicated). Even the Fourth Symphony, a demanding modernist piece that only received its first live Austrian per-formance in Vienna in 1970,[3] was performed by the Berlin Philharmonic Orchestra under Oskar Fried as early as 1916. The Fifth Symphony was given by Ferruccio Busoni in 1921, just two years after the world premiere of the final (1919) version in Helsinki.

Sibelius was supported in Germany by local publishers. Both Robert Lienau (Schlesinger) in Berlin and Breitkopf & Härtel in Leipzig were keen to secure performances of his music. Among Lienau's favourites were the Violin Concerto and the string quartet *Voces intimae*, first performed in Berlin in January 1911 (nine months after the world premiere in Helsinki).[4] Besides these, Lienau also published a volume of German songs (op. 50), settings of Arthur Fitger and Emil Rudolf Weiss alongside the fashionable Richard Dehmel, as well as the underrated Third Symphony. Breitkopf & Härtel published the First and Second Symphonies as well as the Fourth. Their favourites were *Valse triste* and *Finlandia*. German publishers continued to promote Sibelius's work, even after Sibelius sold his Fifth Symphony to the Danish firm Wilhelm Hansen in 1921, when the value of German currency was almost at its lowest. Only after the composition of the Seventh Symphony could Breitkopf & Härtel persuade Sibelius back to Germany, but then solely for *Tapiola* and the 1954 edition of the two *Lemminkäinen Legends*, op. 22 that had not originally been published alongside *The Swan of Tuonela* and *Lemminkäinen's Return* in 1901. Wilhelm Hansen published the inci-dental music for *The Tempest* (1929), and Sibelius also promised them his Eighth Symphony,[5] though the work, of course, never actually appeared.

Berlin remained the principal foreign venue for Sibelius's professional activities throughout his life, whereas his occasional visits to Italy and Paris were for inspiration and enjoyment. Sibelius was a member of the German performing rights society GEMA (1915–33 and from 1947), as well as STAGMA (the equivalent between 1933 and 1947), and he was the client of a tax syndicate in Berlin. Even his very last voyage abroad in 1931 brought him to Berlin. The foundations for his Berlin connections were laid in 1889, when Sibelius went there to study with Albert Becker. At that time, Berlin was about to emerge as the main foreign centre for Nordic modernism: Henrik Ibsen, Edvard Munch, and August Strindberg all spent time in the city. The city had also become Germany's capital of the performing arts, introducing important musical events almost daily. After a year, Sibelius moved to study with Robert Fuchs and Carl Goldmark[6] in Vienna – a city which had a profound impact on his artistic and personal development, but which he would visit on only one further occasion, for some secret reason, on his return from Italy in 1901.[7] The Vienna-based Universal Edition, one of the main publishers of modern music on the continent, published only two minor sets of Sibelius's chamber music, the two Rondinos for piano, op. 68, and two early violin pieces (op. 2, rev. 1911).

Sibelius's close acquaintances in Germany created a deep personal attachment to the country and its culture. One of his oldest friends was Ferruccio Busoni, with whom he had performed the Schumann Piano Quintet op. 44 in March 1889. These two composers spent many long evenings together in the Finnish capital's best restaurants while Busoni was teaching at Martin Wegelius's new Music Institute (today the Sibelius Academy). Less well known is Sibelius's long-lasting friendship with another famous pianist, Wilhelm Kempff. As late as August 1956, Kempff wrote to Sibelius from Italy:

> I played your Sonatina in the Basilica Constantini. For me it was a very special experience. That small piece has grown into my heart in a special way. It made a profound impression. I felt as if the Nordic spirit could conquer eternal Rome, but in a peaceful way . . . The first movement made the usually complacent Romans sit up and listen, during the second movement there was an attentive serenity, whereas the third – for me one of the most genius-like movements in the whole piano literature – was less accessible for the audience . . . This is where Sibelius belongs, at the point where the Homeric landscape becomes music.[8]

At Ainola, Aino Sibelius christened Kempff 'Willy the Brave', since Sibelius demanded that he should play the 'Hammerklavier' Sonata several times a day.[9] Kempff visited *Ainola* from 1922 on,[10] and he was one of the contemporaries who understood Sibelius's music spontaneously. Writing about *Scaramouche* in 1923, Kempff thought, 'This is all so strange and yet natural, it has to be that way.'[11] Sibelius often discussed his own music in a similarly laconic and yet powerful manner. In 1932, Kempff dedicated his Violin Concerto to Sibelius.

Political confusion

The rise of National Socialism in the 1930s did not cause Sibelius any immediate trouble but it gave the reception of his music a totalitarian shape. As a Nordic composer, Sibelius strongly appealed to the National Socialists' distorted cultural imagination, and as a Finn he was valuable in terms of the war. In 1942, Hitler gave an order to treat the Finns with 'Samthandschuhen' (velvet gloves) (Order 35, 23 July 1942),[12] a few weeks after having visited Finland himself. As a national artist, Sibelius was regarded (from both sides) as a symbol for all Finns. Sibelius's own attitude to National

Socialism was at least ambivalent. From his short and often fragmentary diary entries it is hard to reconstruct the exact context of his ideas. In a late diary entry from 1943, however, Sibelius discussed the general problem of the race legislation in Germany with some disdain.[13] In contrast to many of his fellow countrymen and artists in Finland, who composed political songs and marches, Sibelius had no substantial contacts with the Nazi government and never composed anything for its celebration. At the same time, he was approached by senior representatives of the Hitler government. His music received much appreciation in Germany during that time (as in Britain and the United States), but he did not seize the opportunity to become the great Northern star in the Third Reich which he could easily have done. He answered German letters politely and self-confidently, and was obviously advised by the Finnish Foreign Office and politically informed family members (his sons-in-law in particular), but he carefully maintained a proper distance. This must be emphasised, since Sibelius faced a serious conflict of interest. From the beginning of his professional career, he had strongly desired to be heard in Germany, and he valued the German musical tradition highly. He also spoke and wrote idiomatic German (less so French and English), so that interaction with Germany was particularly natural for him. Not only his publishers but Sibelius himself felt obliged to get his music performed in Germany – even under National Socialist rule.

A good example of Sibelius's communication with the Germans is a draft letter to the German ambassador in Helsinki, Wilpert von Blüchner, dated 12 December 1940. The ambassador had sent a birthday address, to which Sibelius replied:

> Excellency, your great kindness in sending greetings on the occasion of my seventy-fifth birthday has given me much pleasure, for which I cannot fail to thank you. [It would please me deeply if my music succeeded in bringing my homeland closer to the German people.][14]

Someone else had typed the first version of the letter, but Sibelius himself then toned the original enthusiasm down by omitting the last lines. The person in question was presumably his secretary Santeri Levas (responsible for his correspondence from 1938, and simultaneously a member of staff at the Kansallis-Osake bank that was managed by one of Sibelius's sons-in-law). Sibelius was not, perhaps, willing to support the opportunistic anti-Soviet pro-Nazi habits of many Finns in the 1940s.

From an early stage, Sibelius had composed music for the Finnish independence movement. Alongside such famous pieces as *Finlandia* and the *Karelia* Suite (both originally parts of the patriotic *tableaux vivants* of 1893 and 1899, the latter also known as *Scènes historiques*), he composed a march song for a secret Finnish *Jägerbattalion*. This unit had been trained by the German Imperial Military to fight against the Russians during the First World War and was active in the Finnish War of Independence in 1918, and later became an important bond between the independent Finnish Army and the *Wehrmacht*. Sibelius also wrote music for the Boy Scouts and the Freemasons, but nothing at all for any movement politically oriented towards the socialist Left. Even the *March of the Working People* (*Työkansan marssi*, 1896), is closer to Tolstoy's political idealism than to Marx or Lenin. It is easy to locate Sibelius ideologically thus far. The intensity and inner ambivalence of his national conservative spirit, however, remains an open question. A telling piece of evidence is provided by a frequently cited press photo that shows Sibelius seated among an extreme right-wing assembly in the summer of 1930.[15] He sits at the front of the stage, demonstratively facing the audience beside his wife Aino, whose posture clearly shows her support for the public speaker. By contrast, Sibelius's head has drooped in a position that suggests either a serious lack of interest or even that he had fallen asleep. It is easy to conclude that Sibelius's political convictions were far less certain than those of his wife and other relatives, but that he was not at all interested in articulating his ambivalent views in public.

'Poeta laureatus (!)' of the North

Sibelius once described himself as a 'Poeta laureatus (!)'.[16] Elsewhere – in England no less than in New England and Germany – he was widely thought to represent the nature and people of the North. Instead of being regarded as an individual artist on his own terms, Sibelius attracted superficial nationalist headlines from an early stage. As in the well-known writings of American critic Olin Downes,[17] German Sibelius reception emphasised the link between Sibelius and Finnishness as a fundamental expression of the pure Nordic spirit. In Germany, the ideological context for such a conception was initially the *Heimat* (homeland) movement, regional and rural patriotism opposed to the Wilhelminian centralism of Berlin and the cosmopolitanism as well as the industrialism of the years around 1900. This movement was powerful in Schleswig and Holstein, an area close to the Danish border and encompassing the north part of Germany around Hamburg and Kiel together with eastern Prussia (Königsberg). One of its magazines, *Der Kunstwart* (since 1887 the official journal of the Society of Garden Cities and Environmental Awareness), published several articles on Sibelius. In 1908, Georg Göhler heavily emphasised the link between the world-views of the typical *Der Kunstwart* subscriber and Sibelius's style. The importance

of the regional roots for all valuable human expression and an awareness of
local particularities was stressed by the modest claim that only a Finn can
properly understand Sibelius. Or, at the very least, that a knowledge of the
Finnish soul (the *Volksseele*) was necessary for a genuine understanding of
his work. 'The music of Sibelius rises out of the habits of thought and feeling
among the Finns,' Göhler wrote in 1908.[18] Another author, Richard Batka
(mainly active in Prague), had put it in a similar way in 1907: 'Whom ever
desires to understand the tone poet must go to his land. It is not difficult to
see the link between Sibelius's music and the land of a thousand lakes with
its terrible winters and incomparable Spring, its wonderful clear nights full
of stars.'[19]

The most theoretically sophisticated of the authors within this once
progressive context was Walter Niemann. He was a native of Hamburg and
did not feel comfortable in the southern regions of Germany.[20] Niemann's
work is still widely regarded as old-fashioned and reactionary, even though
the importance of landscape has recently received wider scholarly attention.
In the context of Sibelius research, it is particularly difficult to read Niemann
without prejudice, since it is well known that Sibelius himself did not like his
book of 1917. However, the idea that Sibelius's music was closely connected
with Finnish landscape and nature was also common among the composer's
closest friends. Axel Carpelan, for example, wrote in a long letter in January
1914 to Sibelius, that refers to Niemann's early essays on Sibelius and perhaps
his *Die Musik Skandinaviens* of 1906: 'If Niemann and others had known
Finnish history and nature properly, they would have understood your style
and some specific details more clearly.'[21] Similarly, another local friend,
Eliel Aspelin-Haapkylä, wrote in December 1915: 'Please let me thank you
for the beautiful world which you have composed out of the Finnish nature
and soul of the people.'[22]

Carpelan's criticism is important, since it underlines the fact that foreign
authors did not know Finland properly from the inside, even though they
tried to draw significant similarities between Finland and Sibelius's music.
Those, of course, could only remain superficial. For Carpelan, this meant
that the *Heimat* movement's initial premise was correct, but that its specific
application in Sibelius's case was wrong. Indeed, the idea of Finland as the
pure and original North is already ridiculous – at least to the Finns who see
Helsinki as essentially a nineteenth-century cultural centre (located close
enough to St Petersburg, one of the most powerful and dynamic capitals
of the period). In the case against Niemann, it is more useful to point out
how cosmopolitan Sibelius was as an individual. He often visited major
European capitals, not only Berlin but also Rome, London and Paris, in
periods of intense composition, even though his music invariably sounds
Finnish rather than Parisian or Berlinesque.

The common disparity between Sibelius's reception on the one hand, and his actual 'essence' as an artist on the other, is a vital and reglected part of Theodor W. Adorno's famous attack. Adorno's criticism – even though written in exile – has often been regarded as typical of the German perception of Sibelius. Despite Adorno's influential work in critical theory, however, his Sibelius criticism needs to be understood in the context of his promotion of the Schoenbergian model of atonal modernism and Gustav Mahler's music. This does not reflect the German reception of Sibelius as a whole. A telling piece of evidence is Ernst Tanzberger's study of 1962. The author does not mention Adorno even once, whereas several authors, more famous in the 1930s and 1940s, are quoted. Either Tanzberger chose to ignore Adorno's earlier writings on Sibelius (the concise 'Fußnote' on Hamsun and Sibelius of 1937 and the more famous 'Glosse' of 1938), or he did not know them.[23] Adorno's *Introductory Lectures on the Sociology of Music*, which includes an important chapter on 'Nation' and a fascinating Sibelius–Ernest Newman anecdote,[24] was only published in 1962, too, so it could easily have been missed by Tanzberger. Other shorter comments on Sibelius, like that in *Aesthetic Theory* (published posthumously), where Sibelius is listed alongside Hans Pfitzner, Hans Carossa and Hans Thoma, are hardly known even today,[25] whereas the widely read *Philosophy of New Music* (1949) does not include anything on Sibelius.

It is not surprising that after the Second World War German musicology was deeply interested in Schoenberg and other modernist composers who had been banned by the Nazis. Adorno in general was widely read by the younger generation that gradually assumed positions of critical authority in many important universities and institutions in the late 1960s and 1970s, though his work was less well received by his slightly older post-war professional colleagues. It is most likely the more general interest in the Second Viennese School that has (with all its consequences) presented the greatest obstacles to recent Sibelius scholarship and appreciation in Germany, however, rather than an unconditional acceptance of Adorno's ideas.[26]

In common with the patterns of Sibelius reception in most other countries, the tendency to emphasise the Nordic elements, Finnish nature and the character of the Finnish people as a source of inspiration for Sibelius's music is much more typical for Germany than Adorno's critique. Tanzberger's 1962 study did not present an alternative. Nevertheless, Tanzberger's authority seemed to come from Sibelius himself. In March 1943, Sibelius wrote Tanzberger a letter that could be read as an authorisation of the doctoral thesis that Tanzberger had defended in Jena. In his enthusiastic response to Sibelius's politeness, and as yet unaware of the composer's often less congenial manner of expression, Tanzberger wrote, 'Your opinion of my thesis makes me deeply happy. That is the most beautiful reward and it will give me the power to work further for your music.'[27] In January, Sibelius added some critical lines that Tanzberger wanted to consider in the second edition of his book, but which never appeared.

1950s and beyond

In August 1946, Tanzberger started to think about a new study, and not simply a revised edition. It would be important, he wrote, to emphasise that Sibelius's symphonies were not *Programm-Musik*. By February 1948, Tanzberger had studied Walter Legge's article in *Hufvudstadtbladet* (1934), which quoted Sibelius's extended explanation of his personal attitude towards abstraction and the programmatic in instrumental music. Tanzberger's project proceeded only slowly, and in 1949 his former academic supervisor, Otto C. A. zur Nedden, supplied an enthusiastic letter of recommendation: 'The publication of Dr Tanzberger's book, written in an exceptionally clear and precise style, is of the greatest urgency!'[28] Meanwhile, Tanzberger's communication with Sibelius continued throughout the 1950s. As late as August 1957, Tanzberger wrote to Sibelius from Hanover where he was active as a high-school music teacher, and sent him a chapter on the Third Symphony in order to ascertain whether he was on the right path. In his book, Tanzberger proudly mentions the fact that he received an answer written just the day before Sibelius died, on 19 September 1957.[29] The Sibelius Museum owns an undated draft of that letter, written by Jussi Jalas, in response to Tanzberger. Jalas wrote, on the composer's behalf, that Sibelius was pleased to know that Tanzberger's interest in his music had not diminished, and that the book would address issues of musical structure. He was particularly happy that Tanzberger would emphasise Sibelius's classical approach to musical form, instead of repeating strange nature associations and folklore allusions (as Tanzberger himself had done). Since Sibelius's own view of his music was inevitably subjective ('synthetic'), he would leave the precise details of the analytical discussion to Tanzberger.

The idea of publishing a new Sibelius biography was discussed between the composer and Helmuth von Hase, the director of Breitkopf & Härtel, as early as 1942 in Helsinki. Tanzberger's name was not mentioned, but Herbert Gerigk and Günter Haußwald[30] were proposed instead. Gerigk was famous as the editor of the *Lexikon der Juden in der Musik*, and intended even to fly to Helsinki in order to discuss the project with Sibelius himself. According to von Hase, Sibelius was extremely critical about the idea of someone writing about him without being in Finland. Even in the 1940s, Sibelius still remembered Niemann.[31] Consequently, the publisher agreed that even a minor biography should only be written by someone familiar

with Finland. Since these plans were never realised, however, Tanzberger's
1943 study became the main source of reference in German Sibelius criticism
for years.[32]

Tanzberger's 1943 dissertation, 'Die symphonischen Dichtungen von
Jean Sibelius. Eine inhalts- und formanalytische Studie', was published in
the *Musik und Nation* series, edited by Nedden. The Preface was signed by
Heinz Drewes, at one time director of the Music Department in the German
Ministry of Propaganda, and from 1942 till the end of the war the President
of the German Sibelius Society. The publication was not intended to appeal
solely to a scholarly readership, and made its political links obvious from
the very beginning. Drewes sent his greetings 'to our Finnish friends and
fellow warriors across the sea'.[33] Even though the book responded to certain
'requirements of German music literature', it focused (like Niemann in 1917)
on the symphonic poems rather than the more complex symphonies.

In his preface, Nedden reported upon performances of Sibelius's music in
the Weimar-Jena region where Tanzberger had studied. Here, as elsewhere,
pieces such as *The Swan of Tuonela* and *Finlandia*, the first two symphonies
and the Violin Concerto provided the first impulses for Sibelius scholarship. Even though Nedden follows a populist line of argument, he had in
fact engaged himself with Sibelius's music in a scholarly capacity for years,
in addition to advising Tanzberger in his academic work. Even after the war,
Nedden did not forget Sibelius. He wrote to him from Duisburg (Federal
Republic) in December 1949 and thanked him for the photograph that
Sibelius had sent him. He also proudly mentioned his former student
Tanzberger, as well as describing his own early impressions of Sibelius's
music through the Violin Concerto and *Finlandia*, concluding, 'in your
works of art, I see the final fulfilment of Western symphonic music – in your
personality, the greatest living composer of our day'.[34] Though Sibelius may
have been somewhat irritated by Nedden's use of the word 'living', he must
nevertheless have been happy to receive such words in German.

At the very beginning of his book, Tanzberger makes direct reference to
Heinz Drewes.[35] Drewes provides a breezy description of the Finnish people
and their relationship with the Germanic world. After an introduction to
Finnish mythology and folklore (*Kalevala*), which he suggests shows clear
parallels with the Scandinavian *Edda*, Drewes discusses the secretly beautiful landscape of Finland as the source of Sibelius's music, and describes the
symphonic poem as his most noble expression. Tanzberger's next authority
is Alfred Rosenberg, in particular a speech that Rosenberg gave to a National
Socialist party assembly in Nuremberg, the *Parteitag der Freiheit*, in 1935.
Rosenberg was indeed a true Sibelian. In 1940, the German celebrations
for Sibelius's seventy-fifth birthday were postponed for a whole month
to allow Rosenberg to participate.[36] The event subsequently took place in

January 1941. Tanzberger quoted Rosenberg's notion of the fundamental *Landschaftlichkeit* of all great art, and applied them to Sibelius. For his part, Sibelius seems to have had no problems in accepting such abstract ideas in this context. In Tanzberger's later book (1962), Rosenberg's name is missing, but the argumentation at the beginning is exactly the same: *Landschaft, Volksseele, Nährboden, Natur, Geschichte, Kulturgüter* – the list of the categories is identical to that in his doctoral dissertation of 1943.[37] By comparison, Niemann's work seems quite progressive for his time, whereas in his 1962 volume, Tanzberger still seems wedded to ideas from twenty years before.

Tanzberger's argument is hardly helped by his quoting authorities from the 1910s like Ferruccio Busoni, without a clear sense of historical context. In March 1916, Busoni published an essay in the *Zürcher Theater-, Konzert- und Fremdenblatt* in which he wrote how 'Sibelius developed himself swiftly on the soil of Finnish folk music, a soil which he never left behind – even as he was drawn along on the crest of a Tchaikovskian wave.'[38] Though Busoni's argument was modern and relevant in 1916, as he fought against post-Wagnerian forms of academic musical style, the context and the meaning of such ideas was quite different in 1962. By then, Tanzberger was writing for an audience which regarded the more recent developments in musical modernism with scepticism and which certainly did not read Adorno.

Adorno and the great Pan

The most valuable section in Tanzberger's book is the interview with René Leibowitz, whose short essay *Sibelius, le plus mauvais compositeur du monde* of 1955 is frequently mentioned beside Adorno's. The interview took place in 1961, and it not only gives a deeper insight into the way of thinking among modernist circles, but also provides important information about the context of the 1955 essay.[39] Leibowitz claimed:

> I never said that Sibelius's music was worthless . . . The expression that
> Sibelius was the worst composer in the world was a joke. In France we had
> a questionnaire about who was the best composer in the world. Sibelius
> was mentioned. I reacted to this over-exaggeration by saying that he was
> the very worst . . . I only know the Fifth Symphony and the Violin
> Concerto well; those works I have conducted. I have also heard other
> symphonies, such as the Fourth and the First.

In Adorno's case, it is important to recognise that his work was primarily concerned with a critical analysis of modern culture in Western society, and that Sibelius's music was significant enough to be taken seriously in such an environment. This aspect is most obvious in Adorno's 'Fußnote' on Sibelius, which develops Leo Löwenthal's critical study of the work of the Norwegian author Knut Hamsun in the *Zeitschrift für Sozialforschung* with interesting parallels to Sibelius.[40] The categories that Adorno applies to their work are negative in his theoretical context, but would have seemed progressive in the context of late-nineteenth-century symbolism. For Adorno, it was irrelevant whether there had been any genuine personal contact between Hamsun and Sibelius. In Sibelius scholarship, this question has never really been answered, but it can be resolved with reference to the Swedish writer Ernst Malmberg's correspondence. Malmberg wrote several letters to Sibelius in 1948–56, mentioning the 'joyful trip' from Stockholm to Hecinki and the meeting of Sibelius, Hamsun, Albert Engström, Calle Cederström and Malmberg in summer 1899.[41] Erik Tawaststjerna presumed that Hamsun and Sibelius had met just briefly during 1898–9, but published an enthusiastic note from Hamsun to Sibelius, dated Constantinople, 30 September 1899, which includes quite private allusions.[42] It is also known that Sibelius read at least the first volume of Hamsun's monumental novel *Landstrykaren* immediately after its publication in 1927.[43]

Adorno did not believe in the true *Allnatur* in Sibelius music or in any other modern art. For him, Sibelius's musical style was 'a reinvention of the conventions of traditional bourgeois art'.[44] In more recent studies of symbolism, elements of salon art have been analysed in a different context.[45] Hans H. Hofstätter points out that much late-nineteenth-century art was a reaction against the aesthetics of the industrialised mass production of the previous decades,[46] even though symbolism had much in common, seemingly, with the art that it critiqued: the inclination towards 'literary content and non-logical treatment of realistic and naturalistic means of expression'. Symbolism can justifiably be regarded as a progressive movement after realism and impressionism. For Adorno, Sibelius did not possess a 'protesting subjectivity', typical of symbolism. Therefore, the characteristic darkness of his music was a 'product of technical deficiency', which only pretended to be 'deep'. In contrast, for Odilon Redon darkness was *la lumière de la spiritualité*.[47] Symbolism had great critical potential in the 1890s as a response to the cultural mainstream of industrialism and cosmopolitanism. How close this movement was to Adorno's basic concepts has recently been discussed in Wolfgang Welsch's work on post-modernism.[48] Indeed, many of the technical details which Adorno attacked in Sibelius's music (the perceived lack of real development, over-emphasis on 'colouristic' effects, trivial motivic material, and lack of musical syntax) appear more vigorously in post-modernism.

More important than Adorno's text is the fact that similarly negative arguments can easily be reconfigured elsewhere on a less sophisticated level.

In the case of Niemann, whose work has been compared with Adorno by Tawaststjerna,[49] such criticism has to be read in the context of the *Heimat* movement that makes his seemingly negative, dialectical notions positive and appreciative. Whereas Niemann's world-view and aesthetics built a solid framework for his biographical and hermeneutic music criticism, for Adorno, Sibelius's music was an example, or rather a symptom, of the decline of Western civilisation. In the 'Glosse', unlike the 'Footnote' the emphasis is not on Sibelius's music but on his reception. This distinction has not always been perceived.[50] The following passage, for example, includes some technical details at first, and then proceeds to a short phenomenology of Sibelius's reception:

> The false triad: Stravinsky has composed it. Through hitherto wrong notes, he has demonstrated how wrong the right ones have become. In Sibelius, they simply sound wrong. He is the antithesis of a Stravinsky. But he has less talent . . . His followers do not realise this. Their song hinges on the refrain: 'it is all Nature, it is all Nature'. The great Pan, yearning for 'blood and soil', swiftly presents itself. The trivial passes for the elemental, the unarticulated for the sound of unconscious creation.[51]

The mighty Pan, a figure associated with the 'Blood and Soil' ideology of the 1930s, and the myth of originality are presented as the conceits of an over-enthusiastic and ideologically obscure Sibelius cult. The focal point of Adorno's criticism is the pretentious anti-intellectualism of much of the adulatory writing on Sibelius that emerged especially in the late 1930s. As to the first section of the cited passage, it is fascinating that Adorno recognises the parallels with Stravinsky that can be seen already in *Kullervo* (1892). The problem with Sibelius's use of triadic harmony is of more central importance. A quick comparison between Bruckner's early symphonies and Sibelius's early orchestral music reveals that Bruckner almost always uses passing dissonant notes in his ostinato accompaniments, whereas Sibelius hardly ever does. To post-Romantic ears of the Viennese school, tired even of new kinds of triadic harmony, Sibelius's music may very well have sounded less appealing than a more chromatic (post-Wagnerian) style. In the 1890s, however, dissonant harmony was not at all new, whereas the modal foundation of the harmonies in Sibelius's *Kullervo* became common only decades later.

Once we realise that Adorno's 'Glosse' was a reaction to naive English and American Sibelius reception during the 1930s, directed particularly at Bengt de Törne's *Sibelius: A Close-Up* (1937), it becomes difficult to see how his argument could ever have been read as a technical analysis rather than a brief study in reception sociology. Adorno rightly saw de Törne's book as an extreme symptomatic expression of the one-dimensional Sibelius cult

that sought to elevate the Nordic composer at the expense of other contemporary figures. For de Törne, Gustav Mahler, to name just one, was the
most 'pathetic case' in the whole history of music: 'intellectually interesting'
at best, but ultimately just another 'uninspired' Austro-German symphonist. In comparison with Mahler, composers such as Schubert, Berlioz and
Tchaikovsky offered hope for the future,[52] but only Beethoven was the equal
of Sibelius, 'the greatest composer now living' and the 'meridian of contemporary music'.[53] Nothing in de Törne's argument is fair or professional. It is
all the more remarkable that Sibelius scholarship has not drawn attention
to the problematic aspects of de Törne's book, even though this principal
target of Adorno's 'Glosse' has been well known. In retrospect, it is quite
clear that Adorno was far more prescient than de Törne, particularly given
Mahler's recent reception history.

   The fact that de Törne gave the impression of quoting Sibelius reliably
and being his favourite student certainly made the case more piquant in
Adorno's eyes. He could hardly know that Sibelius himself was unhappy
about the book and did not have 'students'. Sibelius's German-Danish friend,
Georg Boldemann, had good reason to write to the composer in February
1940 in privacy: 'I very much regret your student's memory. I've known you
for almost fifty years now and have often heard you speak about Wagner,
for example, so I cannot understand how that man could get such wrong
ideas.'[54]

12 Sibelius in Britain

PETER FRANKLIN

It must have been in 1968 that I found myself sitting with a group of fellow undergraduates in Professor Wilfrid Mellers' first-floor study in the music department of the new University of York. At that time the department was in two elegant former town houses in the centre of the medieval city. It was spring or early summer and shadow-patterns of leaves moved across the walnut-coloured grand piano by the window as Mellers played and talked his way through *Tapiola*, weaving his own magic spells with words about ecstasy, terror and infinity and echoing with cryptic grandeur the concluding sentence of his piece on Sibelius in *Man and his Music*: 'Perhaps we have to "go through" *Tapiola* in order to live again.'[1] At the end we listened to the whole piece on record, the mood of enthralled absorption disturbed only by a colleague's insistence that Sibelius should have ended it in B minor. But Mellers had persuaded us that we were listening to an unequivocally 'great' work which he had once, he told us, learned to score-read all the way through at the piano.

We were, of course, being introduced to *Tapiola* little more than ten years after Sibelius's death in 1957 – a point emphasised by the uncorrected tense in Mellers's *Man and his Music* (first published in 1962): 'in the thirty years that have elapsed since he wrote *Tapiola* he seems to have created no music of consequence'.[2] Mellers had clearly devoted himself to the study of *Tapiola* during the composer's later, silent years, when Sibelius's reputation in Britain was still unshaken by the critical implications of a more contemporary 'new music' and the pending inrush of American and continental avant-garde experimentation. Devotees of such experimentation in the 1960s would find in Mellers one of their most significant educational gurus, but his pioneering music course at York was defined by its stylistic and historical diversity. Only the Wagnerian parts of the nineteenth century were effectively neglected, but Schoenberg and the Second Viennese School, followed closely by Boulez and Stockhausen, tended to dominate the twentieth-century part of the course and might have left little room for a 'conservative' like Sibelius, as he seemed in those days. Mellers's eagerness to celebrate and make us hear *Tapiola* as an apparently unmediated revelation of spiritual insight, in and yet somehow against an encroaching world of industrial, economic and technological modernity and the emotional desolation it could inspire, resonated both with the tradition of European Romanticism at whose end *Tapiola* stood, and also with the peculiar British and perhaps specifically English response to Sibelius, whose tone and character were fully formed by the period in which Mellers's own musical and literary education were being completed in Oxford and Leavisite Cambridge.

Sibelius's pre-1914 visits to England

Sir Granville Bantock – one of Sibelius's key personal friends in Britain, who had first invited him to conduct here in 1905 – articulated that response in a revealing, if avuncular, manner when introducing recordings of Sibelius on BBC Radio in 1941[3] (the emphasis is his; unclear or actually inaudible words are indicated in square brackets):

> It is no easy matter to make a short and limited selection from records of the works of *Sibelius* that will satisfy everybody. As you all know, or ought to know, he is the great Finnish composer – I might almost say the greatest living composer in the world [today], and happily alive, active and *well*. We are so used to the idea of Mohammed going to the mountain that it is the more gratifying to realise that in this rare instance the mountain [of men] of its own free will has moved to Mohammed. Sibelius has always held aloof in supreme isolation from the [? inaudible] and has always been quite unconcerned as to what was written, said or thought by others of his music. As a creative artist he stands alone on a mountain summit high above and far removed from all rivalry and idle slander of the multitude. His thoughts are with the eternal mysteries of nature and the hero-legends of his race; he is like a sensitive microphone making new and strangely original records of the musical impressions as they germinate and develop in his mind. His music brings its own message to all who are willing to learn and are hoping to unravel some of the hidden secrets of nature in the soul of man.

Bantock, too, seems to have equated high artistic achievement with the aspirations of a spiritual and even philosophical quest for insight into the 'hidden secrets of nature'. As an English Wagnerian who completed his training at the Royal Academy of Music in the early 1890s, he had inherited Romantic idealism almost at first hand from Liszt and Wagner, while expressing it in various forms of exoticism and fancy-dress orientalism that make his own music seem now so much a symptom of late-Victorian Imperial dreaming that we forget how enterprising and, in his day, how cosmopolitan a musician he was. His friend and secretary, Howard Orsmond Anderton, in his 1915 monograph on him, nevertheless felt inclined to stress the gentlemanly (if non-conformist) restraint and good sense of Bantock as compared to Elgar's 'peculiar nervous excitement, which seems to arise from a somewhat feverishly neurotic temperament':

> With Bantock all is different. His outlook is rationalistic and largely
> Eastern . . . Instead of Imperial or Coronation marches, he gives us a
> *Labour March*. His music shows none of that nervous excitement of which I
> have spoken. So far from the devotionalism of the Catholic Church, we
> find in him not infrequently that note of arraignment of the very nature of
> things, that defiance of Providence, which is so strong in Shelley.[4]

Aesthetic, political and temperamental affinities seem to have played their part in cementing the friendship between Sibelius and Bantock, who was able to converse with the non-English-speaking Finn in French. But other factors may also have been involved: on Sibelius's side an attraction to the aristocratic 'old culture'[5] of England and the rather grand houses and formal lifestyle into which Bantock was able to introduce him; on Bantock's a fascination for a fellow patrician seeker after ancient and 'authentic' poetic inspiration (Bantock would often address Sibelius by the *Kalevala* name of Väinämöinen) who also had what Constant Lambert would later praise as a willingness to 'come down to earth' and write popular or 'commonplace' music like *Finlandia* or the *Valse triste*.[6]

The period in which Bantock seems first or most productively to have encountered Sibelius's music was between 1897 and 1900, when he was establishing a name for himself as conductor of the military band and dance orchestra of the Tower pleasure gardens at New Brighton, near Liverpool. So efficient was he with the outdoor military band that the management permitted him to extend the remit of the dance orchestra to include symphony concerts. These began with Beethoven, Wagner and Tchaikovsky but turned into a series devoted for the most part to living British composers like Parry, Elgar, Corder, Hamish McCunn and Joseph Holbrooke. These concerts established Bantock's reputation as a conductor, impressed the young Ernest Newman (who wrote most of the programme notes for concerts in that part of the country, while working in a bank in Liverpool) and established Bantock's position as a conductor of other orchestras and musical societies, including the Liverpool Philharmonic. All of which would lead to his appointment, with Elgar's support, as Principal of the Midland Institute School of Music in Birmingham in 1900. It was, however, during his time at the Tower pleasure gardens that Bantock began to perform Sibelius, helping to confirm the opinion of both Newman and Sir Henry Wood (who at some point heard Bantock conduct *En saga* in Liverpool and had himself introduced the First Symphony at a London Prom in 1903)[7] that there was more than fashionable Celtic twilight to Sibelius's music.

During the first visit that Sibelius made to England at Bantock's invitation in the winter of 1905, Sibelius stayed at his orientalia-filled house in Birmingham, but conducted his First Symphony and *Finlandia* in Liverpool at a 'Ladies' Concert' of the Orchestral Society.[8] The symphony inspired a review from Newman that highlights the escapist elements required of new music by the more advanced and outward-tending English critics of the day, on the lookout for poetic visions from the plush seats of bourgeois concert halls. He wrote of it:

> I have never listened to any music that took me away so completely from our usual Western life, and transported me into a quite new civilization. Every page of it breathes of another manner of thought, another way of living, even another landscape and seascape to our own.[9]

Other influential conductors, like Wood in London and Hans Richter in Manchester, would play their part in establishing Sibelius on the British concert platform, but it was in Liverpool that his British reputation was formally inaugurated. While the 1905 visit had started inauspiciously, with Sibelius being apprehended and fined by Dover Customs for smuggling in cigars,[10] it concluded with him having secured an important circle of supporters. These included someone who would be no less significant a British ally and personal friend than Bantock: the cosmopolitan writer on music and devotee of Russian and Scandinavian culture, Rosa Newmarch, who found in Sibelius 'nothing of the *naiveté* or rusticity of a man brought up in a small country'.[11] Although Tawaststjerna has Bantock introducing her to Sibelius after the concert, Bantock claimed that he enlisted her linguistic expertise earlier in the visit, and Newmarch herself recalled staying at the Bantocks' with Sibelius and attending the Liverpool concert.[12] She referred to the concert at the beginning of her London lecture on Sibelius to the Concert-Goers' Club in February 1906 which formed the basis of her thirty-two-page pamphlet *Jean Sibelius. Ein finnländischer Komponist*, published in a German translation by Ludmille Kirschbaum in Leipzig later that year.[13] Bantock, Ernest Newman, Henry Wood and Rosa Newmarch would henceforth form the core of Sibelius's British circle. Having thoroughly enjoyed himself and taken to England, he seems readily to have accepted the more prestigious invitation from the Royal Philharmonic Society to conduct his Third Symphony in London in 1907, although financial difficulties and delays over completing the symphony (which was premiered that year in Helsinki) eventually led to the trip being postponed until February 1909.

This time Sibelius's visit began rather more auspiciously, with him meeting Bantock for lunch in an Oxford Circus restaurant where the musicians chanced to strike up with the *Valse triste*. In fact that event might have been taken as a darker omen: a reminder that already European critics were tending to categorise Sibelius as a folkloric nationalist, a tone poet and populist rather than a genuine symphonist. The London audience and critics received Sibelius's debut conducting performance with warmth, but greeted the Third Symphony itself (dedicated to Bantock) with a degree of well-meaning incomprehension, marked by an assumption that his themes were taken from 'folk' sources.[14] The concert did him no harm, however, and led to a follow-up invitation to conduct at the Queen's Hall in February 1909. This time he offered the sure-fire successes *En saga* and *Finlandia* for an afternoon concert at which he wore a fashionable morning-dress outfit, seemed to overcome his usual nerves and was, as he put it to Aino, 'sober for once'.[15] Wood, Bantock and Rosa Newmarch made much of him, and his further explorations of London and its sights convinced him that it might be pleasurable to stay and work there.

In fact one or two minor dissonances coloured Sibelius's experience of the otherwise harmonious cultural and social events of that extended visit. He began to worry about his throat in the London smog and his long-term financial troubles led Rosa Newmarch to seek advice on his behalf.[16] His appearance at a dedicated formal session of the London Music Club was awkward – a fact attested to later by Arnold Bax, who had found Sibelius taciturn and severe and his chamber music and songs, performed at the same event, rather second-rate (he would later describe the occasion rather surprisingly as 'lamentable . . . a serious setback to the acceptance in England of Sibelius's best work').[17] On another occasion Sibelius himself decided for some obscure reason that Delius ('that snake')[18] was against him and, for reasons that are a little more comprehensible, that his relations with Bantock were starting to cool. It was almost certainly Sibelius's fault if they were, linked perhaps to a hint of jealousy with regard to Bantock's more secure personal circumstances. In a letter to Aino following the Queen's Hall concert he had commented a little ruefully on his friend's latest 'important position': 'University professor. Everyone else gets positions; only I compose and live in my moods and dreams.'[19] Following Elgar's resignation in 1908 from the Richard Peyton Chair of Music at Birmingham (which he had held since 1904), Bantock had indeed been appointed. He clearly took the post very seriously, in spite of holding it simultaneously with that at the School of Music, but the financial security Bantock's efforts secured him, and the spacious rented house (Broad Meadow) in which Sibelius would stay in 1912, must inevitably have aroused more envy in Sibelius than did Bantock's rather thickly post-Wagnerian music (Sibelius heard the second part of *Omar Khayyám* during the 1909 trip).[20] Other, more positive musical encounters during that trip included a meeting with Debussy, following a Queen's Hall concert at which the French composer had conducted poorly before a nevertheless supportive audience (Debussy too suffered guest-night treatment at the Music Club, with no greater pleasure than Sibelius).[21]

Whatever shadows may latterly have darkened that visit, they seemed largely to have been dispelled when Sibelius returned in 1912 for his last pre-war visit to Britain. He conducted the Fourth Symphony, following Elgar's *The Music Makers* (conducted by the composer) in a concert that formed part of Bantock's Birmingham Festival. Rosa Newmarch had again been in attendance, taking him on a Shakespearean trip to Stratford-upon-Avon and finding him in an improved psychological state from that in which she had encountered him in Paris the previous year (she had also stayed in Finland with Sibelius for three weeks in 1910).[22] Bantock and Sir Henry Wood (the festival's main conductor) had assisted at the rehearsals, which began in London and were attended also by Delius, who was clearly impressed by the Fourth Symphony, as were most of the critics.[23] Ernest Newman seems to have found in it confirmation of his inclusion of Sibelius amongst the modern composers he had featured, at the time of the composer's previous visit, in a lecture series at Birmingham University (presumably at the invitation of Bantock, who had been the first to give him a musical post, as a teacher at the Midland Institute School of Music in 1903–4).[24] Indeed, Newman played his part in clarifying the reading of the Fourth as a work of severe and concentrated modernity that bore relevant and flattering comparison with the less successfully communicative Schoenberg.

A request to write a sacred choral work for the 1913 Three Choirs Festival in Gloucester represented a single incongruous counterpoint to the demands of eager autograph hunters that he sign photographs of himself that they had left for his attention. Sibelius left England on 30 October 1912 almost as an honorary member of its musical avant-garde. He did not produce a choral work for Gloucester in 1913; instead the festival got the one British premiere there was to be of a significant Sibelius work (in his absence): *Luonnotar*, sung by Aino Ackté, in a concert that included the closing scene of Strauss's *Salome*. It was accordingly not presented in the cathedral.[25] Sibelius would make only one subsequent visit (in 1921), but his position as a leading 'British' modern would hold firm against contestation for nearly thirty years.

The final visit

Sibelius was clearly attracted to Britain not only as a source of income and esteem – he found both in other European countries – but also for the cities and aristocratic homes that afforded him a stage on which to indulge his decidedly bourgeois aspirations to worldly elegance and comfort. While his closer British friends saw the mass of contradictions and vulnerabilities that shrouded his deeper creative aims and preoccupations, those who knew him only through second-hand gossip and mythology may have grasped, however crudely, something of the image that his art often constructed: the Romantic ideal that would find its most eloquent definition in Bantock's 1941 image of the artist standing 'alone on a mountain summit' thinking of the 'eternal mysteries of nature', or Mellers's sense that in *Tapiola* 'the human personality seems to dissolve away in Nature's infinities of time and space'.[26] That image of Sibelius found characteristic, if rough-hewn expression in the brief portrait of Sibelius that was included by J. Cuthbert Hadden in the chapter 'Some modern Continentals' of his 1913 *Modern Musicians. A Book for Players, Singers and Listeners*:

> Not much is known about Sibelius, for he lives in far-away Helsingfors and shrinks from all forms of publicity . . . He receives a pension from the Government to enable him to work in peace, and he lives in patriarchal simplicity with his wife and five children, in a house surrounded by a network of lakes, rivers and forests. He revels in the wild, and the pinewoods bring to him literally 'thoughts that do almost lie too deep for tears'. His relaxations are boating and fishing, tramping through the storm, wrestling with Nature in her savage moods, basking in her beauty, driving about the moorland in his trap, or lying on the hills dreaming and brooding. One of his daughters is reported as 'of a strange, wild, elfin type' who has composed tales and songs from early childhood.[27]

What is curious, of course, is that that image of Sibelius should have been thus further popularised at a time when his best known works remained the rabble-rousing *Finlandia* and the restaurant-friendly *Valse triste*, which Beecham included in a 1915 Prom programme that had ended, presumably with political intent, with Saint-Saëns's arrangement of *La Marseillaise*.[28] It was left at that time to the earlier devotees to persevere in fostering the symphonic works which might more convincingly have resonated with Hadden's romantic image of Sibelius 'wrestling with Nature in her savage moods', which had certainly communicated itself to Rosa Newmarch (who intrepidly visited Sibelius in Finland in 1915, on her way to Russia). On her initial hearing of the First Symphony, she was struck by the '*plein-air* style of this music. Sibelius's oneness with Nature and that variety of poetic pantheism which is the birthright of his people, are encountered on every page of this symphony.'[29] Also in 1915, Bantock would send Sibelius an account of his performance of the first two movements of the Third Symphony with his Birmingham students (who could not manage the Finale), going on to note the wartime concentration 'upon maintaining a place in the world where we can live and work . . . without being dominated by an alien and brutal ideal'.[30] When Sibelius returned to Britain for his last visit in 1921, it came as one of a series of experiences of reconnection with external culture after the nightmare of the war and its losses. It had been a period in which Sibelius had completed the first version of the Fifth Symphony, turned fifty and suffered in his own way the traumatic experience of the Russian Revolution and the ensuing civil war that had caused him to move his family into Helsinki for a time in 1918. Certainly for his British friends and, apparently, the immigration officer who on this occasion recognised the Finn, his return was interpreted as marking Sibelius's emergence from wartime 'isolation'. It must have felt like that when he found himself once more among old friends like Rosa Newmarch, Bantock and Sir Henry Wood, along with younger admirers like Eric Blom and, briefly, the composer Ralph Vaughan Williams.[31]

During February 1921 Sibelius attended a number of receptions in his honour in London, Birmingham and Oxford (where he dined with Hugh Allen at high table in the still all-male New College, leaving Rosa Newmarch to eat alone in Allen's rooms). He conducted a series of high-profile concerts, beginning with the Fifth Symphony at the Queen's Hall on 12 February and continuing with a performance of *En saga* with students at the Royal College of Music and the Third Symphony in Bournemouth and Birmingham (along with other works and the inevitable *Valse triste*).[32] It was a taxingly busy tour, in effect, with the symphonies having the greatest effect upon the orchestral musicians and Sibelius's established admirers – as on the occasion of a shared 26 February Queen's Hall concert with his old friend and drinking partner Busoni, at which Sibelius had conducted the Fourth Symphony, to the delight of Busoni more than the audience and critics, some of whom responded with little more than polite interest.[33]

More dinners and concerts followed (with another *Valse triste* and *Finlandia* in Manchester) before his farewell performance in London at the beginning of March 1921, which included *The Swan of Tuonela*, 'Festivo' from *Scènes historiques* suite no. 1, op. 25, and *Finlandia* (encored). Rosa Newmarch fussed over him, wrote letters for him and exhorted him not to accept the invitation to teach at the Eastman School in New York, while watching a little nervously over his developing acquaintance with the pianist Harriet Cohen. Finally, on 10 March 1921 it was over, and Sibelius set sail from Newcastle for Bergen, leaving his friends and admirers to hope that their anticipated wider triumph for his music in Britain would eventually come.[34]

British writing on Sibelius

It came, in fact, as much in writing as in sympathetic performances – although these certainly increased under the batons of Wood, Beecham and then younger conductors like Adrian Boult (who had met Sibelius at the end of the 1921 visit). One or two articles appeared in the mid-1920s, but the main flow of British Sibelius criticism of the 1930s and 1940s began, in a way, with Eric Blom's essay on him in the third edition of *Grove's Dictionary of Music and Musicians* in 1928. For all its factual errors, it represented a serious attempt at a balanced account, whose critical assumptions are interesting. Sibelius the 'nature' mystic is fully reinscribed in the account of the symphonies, in which the Fourth is credited with 'mystical and almost primitive nature worship', but also with 'complete maturity in the way of adjusting matter and manner'.[35] The cultural character of that maturity is clarified in Blom's earlier characterisation of what one might call the Romantic–modernist aspect of the mentality revealed in the symphonies: 'unrestrained by historical precedent and uncomplicated by aesthetic preconceptions'.

Here, of course, we are approaching a 'canonic' reading and evaluation of the symphonies' uncompromising form of lucidity, whose 'elliptical manner may disconcert the hearer who expects a certain amount of relaxation into decorative or transitional passages in a symphonic movement':

> To him Sibelius may seem almost brutally abrupt and cursory, but familiarity with this compact and pithy style makes it appear immensely satisfying to those who can accustom themselves to understand the general statement of a syllogism without the adduction of minor premises and conclusions.

The insistence on the 'compact and pithy', philosophically abstract style is matched by a judicious expression of distaste at the more accessible side of Sibelius:

> There is no need to deal at length with the popular aspects of Sibelius's work. Such things as 'Finlandia' and 'Valse Triste' . . . have become so familiar that they are liable to obscure the larger and profounder works.

And along with the popular goes the 'national' aspect of Sibelius's achievement, here reduced simply to a rootedness 'in the soil of his native country' which nevertheless 'becomes individualised in its growth by contact with the composer's experience of life, which is never impeded by aesthetic prepossessions'. Thus grounding the authentically *sui generis* in specific native soil, Blom sets up the matrices of his own fundamentally conservative aesthetic preconceptions of the period. The particular is transcended by an authentically personal vision of what is universally natural – yet inaccessible to the popular audience.

It is for this reason, perhaps, that Blom had earlier come close to theorising Sibelius's best qualities as according with the virtues of a British sensibility marked more or less by the proverbial stiff upper lip and a suppressed melancholy (and note the 'almost' in the first sentence):

> The predominant traits of his most representative works are an almost passionate adoration of nature, a patriotism that is never vainglorious, and a resoluteness tempered at times by a deep and genuine tenderness free from sentimental ostentation. All this is almost incessantly accompanied by a ground bass that plays up and down the gamut of a fundamental sorrow varying between dreamy sadness and utter despair.

The point had still more nearly been made when Blom earlier characterised the way Sibelius was regarded 'by his compatriots with the veneration which only so highly cultured, united and sanely democratic a people, and perhaps only a small people, can accord to a creative artist of their own race'. We are surely close here to what Laura Gray has described as 'important reasons for the "Sibelius cult" in England', some of which, she nevertheless oddly suggests, 'have little to do with music'.[36] The way in which they often match or mirror the later Sibelius's own evident aesthetic aspirations with regard to his public image as a composer emphasises just how much these matters *might* have 'to do with music'.

They certainly have a good deal to do with the first real book-length study of the composer in English by Cecil Gray, the iconoclastic critic who had also been an early supporter of Bartók, along with his friends Philip Heseltine and Bernard van Dieren. Gray's *Sibelius* (1931) theoretically extends Blom's characterisation of the symphonies as set nobly apart from the more colourfully popular works, into their transandence of 'a weakness that reflects adversely on his work as a whole'.[37] But Gray's purpose, in this influential study, is actually to resolve the apparent tension between 'what is detestably called "classical" music on the one hand and "popular" music on the other'.[38] That he does not altogether succeed is made clear by his embarrassment over aspects of the Fifth Symphony, whose second-movement theme 'might have occurred to any tenth-rate composer, and . . . been dismissed by him without a second thought as altogether too banal and commonplace':

> Similarly the broad, swinging theme in the last movement . . . is almost note for note identical with a popular music-hall song of some ten years ago, but in Sibelius's hands it is endowed with a grandeur and a dignity that banish entirely from our minds its dubious associations.[39]

Gray's attempt to resolve this problem comes in his final chapter, 'The music considered as a whole'. He concludes that the 'popular' side of Sibelius's output should be reinterpreted as a positive virtue, like his immense fertility, and one of the signs of his true greatness:

Most of the ills, indeed, to which modern music is subject are the outcome
of over-sophistication, the self-conscious fear of the banal and the
commonplace, the inability to relax and be spontaneous, simple,
unaffected, straightforward, unpretentious. Even many of those who are
sufficiently intelligent to be well aware of this are unable to escape from
their inhibitions.[40]

Gray's suggestion is that Sibelius answers the questions as to whether the
artist should

create for himself like Flaubert, for an ideal audience of the 'happy few' as
urged by Stendhal, primarily for his own countrymen in accordance with
the doctrines of the nationalists, for Mr Newman's hypothetical 'average
intelligent music-lover', or for the ordinary man in the street or simple
peasant as Tolstoy would have him do; and he has solved the problem by
writing music for all of them, of each kind, at different times, in different
works.[41]

By building on Blom's isolation of the contradictory elements in Sibelius's
output, Gray's study represented a more consistent attempt to unify the
disparate aspects of his subject in a way that might better facilitate the
categorisation of Sibelius as a 'great' composer; it also offered an important
tool to the next major British critic to engage seriously with Sibelius.

While Constant Lambert's famous 1934 *Music Ho! A Study of Music in
Decline* was in no sense primarily about Sibelius, it is the Finn who comes
out on top, as it were, in the peroration with which Lambert concludes his
diatribe about the rather passé nature of post-war 'modern music' ('it is
my melancholy duty to point out that all the bomb throwing and guillo-
tining has already taken place').[42] Proposing that every great composer of
the past has eventually established 'contact with his audience . . . in spite
of initial prejudice', his concluding three sections ('Sibelius and the integration of form', 'The symphonic problem' and 'Sibelius and the music of
the future') present a serious case for Sibelius as an ally of the sensible and
sensitive against the excesses of European modernism, including Stravinsky,
Hindemith's *Gebrauchsmusik* and the Second Viennese School 'atonalists'.
Moving on from the enthusiasts' project of establishing Sibelius's creden-
tials as a master, Lambert contextualises and, in a sense, politicises Sibelius's
supposed solitariness and conservatism as the misunderstood signs of what
was actually, along with the music of Schoenberg, 'most interesting and
stimulating to the post-war generation', in spite of his belonging to the era
of Strauss and Elgar.[43] Perhaps he might have said 'post-war *British* generation', since it is difficult to avoid the sense that Lambert's Sibelius is, in
effect, being appropriated as a British composer in all but name.

For Lambert, the stylistic contradictions in Sibelius suggest something more than Gray's masterly comprehensiveness, although he echoes Gray's suspicion of the self-consciousness and over-sophistication of much newer music. Lambert explicitly praises Sibelius's ability to 'come down to earth' in pieces like *Finlandia*, but laments the way in which, as a result, his reputation has hampered the understanding of his best works, regarded as too popular by the snobs but too enigmatically intellectual for the ordinary listener. The Fourth Symphony is again celebrated as 'in every way as remarkable and challenging a work as the famous "spot" pieces of Debussy, Stravinsky and Schönberg that were studied in the first chapter of this book',[44] in spite of its neglected and misunderstood character. Not surprisingly, although the Seventh Symphony was clearly gaining ground, *Tapiola* is celebrated as a kind of *ne plus ultra*: 'There is nothing to perplex the ordinary listener, yet to the technician it is a never-ending source of wonder.'[45] Its climax is presented as a 'symbol of Sibelius's art as a whole': an overwhelming effect created with the simplest means: 'In a sudden moment of intense vision he has, like a Newton or an Einstein, revealed the electrifying possibilities that are latent in the apparently commonplace.'[46]

The scientific allusions and reference to electrifying possibilities might conveniently remind us that while Lambert was reconfiguring Sibelius as a kind of honorary British anti-atonalist, the new media of recording, radio and film were themselves appropriating Sibelius in new ways. More academically orientated popularisers like pioneering analyst Donald Francis Tovey were doing something similar. Tovey's first Sibelius analyses (on the Third and Fifth Symphonies) appeared in 1935,[47] the year in which Cecil Gray's *Sibelius: The Symphonies* came out and in which the March *Musical Times* carried an important piece by Walter Legge entitled 'Conversations with Sibelius' – which reminds us, amongst other things, that Arnold Bax, as well as Vaughan Williams a decade later, dedicated his Fifth Symphony to the Finn.[48] It is a subsequent Tovey analysis, of the Seventh Symphony, that chances to remind us of Sibelius's appropriation by the new media when he recalls how, in spite of musicians' objection to the use of their art as a 'background to talking and eating',

> I confess I was thrilled when, in its New Year review of 1933, the British Broadcasting Corporation used a gramophone record of parts of Sibelius's Seventh Symphony as 'slow music' during the recital of the flight over Mount Everest. Let this sentence do duty for all further efforts to describe in words the austere beauty and rare atmosphere of Sibelius's mature style.[49]

While confirming the long-ingrained tradition of associating Sibelius with wild and unpeopled nature, Tovey's recollection is a testament to the absorption of Sibelius into the lingua franca of background music for certain kinds of film, occasionally even mainstream British films like the 1936 feature *A Stolen Life*. It had a score by William Walton, whose friend, the conductor and Sibelius enthusiast Hyam Greenbaum, had assisted him in meeting his deadline by suggesting that he utilise parts of Sibelius's music for *The Tempest*, which few would have been likely to know.[50]

The mid-1930s through to the late 1940s saw a real turn in the tide of wider British Sibelius appreciation, with increasing concert and radio performances, and a continuing series of articles and books on him. The English translation of Ekman's biography appeared in 1936, followed by Rosa Newmarch's account of her friendship with Sibelius, published in America in 1939 and in Britain in 1944, towards the end of the Second World War. Gerald Abraham's 1947 collection *Sibelius. A Symposium* marked a further significant stage in the academic adoption of Sibelius, the first contemporary composer to be included in this new, although actually short-lived, series. The tradition of British Sibelius scholarship would later be nobly continued by Robert Layton, whose invaluable dedication to the editing and translation of Tawaststjerna's *Sibelius* has contributed so much.[51]

The 1940s nevertheless bring us back to Bantock's introduction to the BBC Sibelius programme, in which he reformulated the then standard picture of Sibelius as an isolated composer, standing 'alone on a mountain summit' – while adopting a modern image when likening his old friend to 'a sensitive microphone making new and strangely original records of the musical impressions . . . in his mind'. But Bantock's was already a voice from the past, and although this may have been precisely the period in which Wilfrid Mellers was first studying *Tapiola*, post-war Britain saw the Sibelius cult eclipsed by creative preoccupations of the new European and American avant-garde movements. By 1941 Benjamin Britten, for example, had publicly coupled Sibelius and Brahms as 'heavy-handed late romantics'.[52] His generation's allegiances were often to those same 'anarchists' of the inter-war period that Lambert had regarded as being trumped by the visionary severities of Sibelius, whose relevance to Blom's implicitly Anglo-Finnish 'cultured, united and sanely democratic . . . people' might best have been figured in his other image of the tender patriot, given privately to 'dreamy sorrow' while avoiding 'sentimental ostentation'.

Other signs of the passing of the heyday of the British Sibelius might have been glimpsed even in the early 1930s: Elgar offering retrospective comfort to the ailing Delius by taking him recordings of the Fifth Symphony, *Tapiola* and *Pohjola's Daughter* in 1933,[53] for example, or perhaps Basil Cameron and the Royal Philharmonic Society waiting through the mysterious Järvenpää 'silence' for the promised Eighth Symphony that would never come. Yet if the Sibelius of English gentility and Romanticism was on the wane (a British

Sibelius Society is nevertheless still in existence), a popular Sibelius, whose works could be heard on the radio and bought as recordings of Beecham and others, was now coming into his own. The reception of *that* Sibelius was not, however, altogether 'British' – in either the literal or the figurative sense – although from Beecham and Anthony Collins, through Barbirolli and Charles Groves to Simon Rattle, the contribution of British conductors to the Sibelius performance tradition, both on record and on the concert platform, has certainly remained significant.

13 Sibelius and contemporary music

JULIAN ANDERSON

France in the 1970s

The influence of Sibelius on contemporary music is now so substantial and lasting that one can speak of him as a key figure in the shaping of current musical thought. Yet, given the disdain with which his music was treated by members of the European avant-garde following the Second World War, the growing interest in Sibelius's work amongst a younger generation of composers has been one of the least expected developments in music during the past thirty years. The presence in France of musicologists Marc Vignal, Patrick Szerznowizc and Harry Halbreich is significant here. Initially a composition student of Messiaen at the Paris Conservatoire between 1955 and 1958, Halbreich abandoned composition to become one of the most unusual and influential impresarios of the 1970s and 1980s, notably as Artistic Director of the Royan Festival in France between 1973 and 1977. His full range of enthusiasms extends to such neglected areas (in Central European terms) as the music of Vaughan Williams and Tippett. We are concerned here mainly with the manner in which he provided the crucial link for a whole generation of avant-garde composers to Sibelius, considerably altering their musical style in the process. The main French composers involved directly or indirectly include Hugues Dufourt, Tristan Murail, Pascal Dusapin, Alain Banquart and, to a lesser extent, Gérard Grisey.

Born between 1940 and 1952, these composers grew up in a musical culture dominated by the influence of Pierre Boulez and the concerts of the *Domaine musicale*, which placed the music of figures such as Sibelius, Janáček or Nielsen at the furthest possible remove of consequence. Even when Boulez started to show any interest in music prior to Schoenberg and Stravinsky, it was primarily Debussy and Mahler who were the centre of attention, the latter both as progenitor of the Second Viennese School and because of the daring modernity of his juxtapositions of different types of music. These were seen as powerful alibis for the experiments of the 1960s, the most overt instance of this being the Mahler-based collage in the third movement of Luciano Berio's *Sinfonia*. It is only very recently that Boulez himself has shown any interest in other figures of the period.[1]

Boulez's dramatic strike against the French musical establishment in 1966 led to his departure from France for a period of ten years. These years saw the emergence of this new generation of composers. Alternative figures such as Iannis Xenakis, Henri Dutilleux and Maurice Ohana, hitherto kept out of the limelight and marginalised or ignored altogether at the *Domaine musicale*, received more serious and consistent attention during these ten years of Boulez's absence. With the notable exceptions of Phillipe Manoury and Michael Jarrell, the majority of prominent younger composers in both France and Germany deliberately turned away from Boulez and serialism generally as primary sources of inspiration. In this they seem to have been encouraged at least in part by Messiaen, with whom most of them studied. Despite his brief but enthusiastic participation in the serialist experiment, Messiaen became increasingly and openly critical of serial music from the late 1960s onwards.[2]

What became known as spectral music emerged at this time as a viable alternative aesthetic to serialism in France, Germany and elsewhere. Primarily initiated by Grisey and Murail, this music took as its starting point the acoustic structure of sounds and the psycho-acoustics of human perception over time – precisely those factors deemed to have been neglected by the serialists.[3] The first fruits of this tendency – Grisey's *Périodes* and *Partiels* (1974 and 1975 respectively) and Murail's *Sables* and *Mémoire/Érosion* (1974 and 1976 respectively) – were characterised by an avoidance of sudden contrasts and abrupt juxtapositions in favour of gradually evolving processes of greater continuity and carefully measured changes of texture. They mark a sharp move away from the parametric thinking of the Darmstadt school in favour of the study of continuity and change.

This is precisely the area in which Sibelius was to prove a useful catalyst. Repeatedly in Sibelius's music, we encounter a bold and experimental attitude towards time, timbre, musical texture and form which transcends the late Romanticism of his origins and places him amongst the most innovative composers of the early twentieth century. This is especially true of the Symphonies nos. 5, 6 and 7 as well as of *Tapiola* and the incidental music from *The Tempest*. The Prelude to *The Tempest* consists of violent oscillations up and down a single whole-tone mode, together with occasional shifts to the adjacent mode a half-step higher. No resolution is provided by the conclusion of the piece, which consists of an augmented triad repeatedly built up note by note on sustained brass and tremolo strings – a kind of inharmonic spectrum,[4] like the sound of a receding surf, examined partial by partial, shimmering statically.

Tapiola features a similarly extreme storm passage near its conclusion. This latter piece has many other instances of what Hepokoski has termed 'sound sheets',[5] many of them distinctly unconventional in spacing and sonority by the orchestration habits of the time. The oddest such passage is perhaps the complex eighteen-part string texture built up between Fig. D

Example 13.1 Sibelius, *Tapiola*, string texture built up between Figs D and F.

(strings)

and Fig. F, consisting of a single major second octave-doubled through every register including the lowest (see Ex. 13.1). The presence here of the lowest three octaves produces very noticeable beats in performance due to the closeness of the adjacent frequencies and the relatively high dynamic indicated. The resultant sonority, which functions as a dense screen through which the woodwinds' chromatic compression of the piece's main motive can only intermittently be perceived, has a startling, almost electronic quality. Sibelius's readiness to produce deep acoustic throbbing, through the cultivation of crushed spacing in the bass register, is found in many places in mature (not just late) Sibelius, and places him at the opposite extreme from the Franco-Russian school of orchestral resonance. It is a tendency which can crop up in the most unexpected places, such as the inexplicable, shocking surge of bass dissonances found at the start of the middle section (Fig. L) in the last movement of the Fifth Symphony. There is little doubt that Sibelius connected such passages with the study of natural sonorities.[6]

The other factor in Sibelius that attracted the spectral composers was his strangely distended timing. The passage from *Tapiola* cited in Ex. 13.1 lasts an abnormally long time – nearly a whole minute. The rotating chromatic storm near the end of the same work lasts even longer. The *Tempest* prelude lasts over three minutes. During all such textures, any clear sense of harmonic direction is virtually suspended in a manner not found in any other music prior to 1960. Furthermore, Sibelius's habit, even in supposedly developmental sections, of simply letting a melodic-rhythmic cell grow progressively by gradual changes – bypassing the dialectical tension of developing variation – also results in a sense of organic transformation through large areas of time. Whilst not static (unlike the 'sound sheets'), these passages convey to the listener a keen sense of time being stretched out as the transformations take on a life of their own, heedless of traditional symphonic rhetoric. Such passages are found very frequently in the last three symphonies and *Tapiola* (which, in any case, reduces all melodic activity to the curvilinear oscillation stated at its opening).

Halbreich had attempted briefly to persuade his contemporaries in the Messiaen class of the importance of Sibelius – to no avail, unsurprisingly.[7]

He had more luck with the next generation of composers. Hugues Dufourt (b. 1943) was one of the most persistently influenced in this regard. He emerged as a major figure suddenly at the Royan Festival in 1977, as the author of several generally large-scale pieces such as the vast percussion symphony *Erewhon* (1972–6) and the shorter *La Tempesta* (after Giorgione, 1976–7) for mixed ensemble. His key pieces, which postdate his study of Sibelius, are *Saturne* for wind, brass, percussion and live electronics (1979) and the orchestral piece *Surgir* (1980–4). Both of these are ambitious structures – lasting about forty-five minutes, in the case of the former – and they attempt a highly original fusion of several different musical and acoustical phenomena.

Saturne remains a key work of the Parisian group *L'Itinéraire*, whose composers were many of the chief protagonists in spectral composition.[8] It is also one of the most expressively convincing fusions of instrumental and electronic sonorities to this day. The scoring was deliberately set up to provide the composer with the widest acoustical range of sonorities, from pure sine tones (provided by several live electronic instruments including synthesisers and *ondes martenot*), through instruments with various filterings of harmonic spectra (the wind and brass) to white noise (provided by percussion, electric guitars and other electronic instruments). Every grading in between is also thoroughly exploited through the careful deployment of orchestration and mixing of instrumental layers. Dufourt makes a particular feature of the lowest wind instruments such as bass flute, cor anglais and baritone oboe, contrabass clarinet and contrabassoon – all of them rich in overtones and susceptible, in combination, to the production of complex, ambivalent sonorities. The influence of Sibelius is felt on the levels of both form and sonority. Sibelius's late works often feature rich, low wind textures – his oboe writing is often notoriously low (he had a particular fondness for pairs of low oboes in parallel thirds), and the woodwind scoring in *Tapiola*, especially, is often biased towards exposed combinations in the lowest registers for long periods (such as the remarkable passage starting at letter F, combining low clarinets, bass clarinet, bassoon, contrabassoon and timpani).

Dufourt's *Saturne* extends and develops this tendency to an extreme degree. The form of *Saturne* is ambivalent: there are three sections (labelled 'A', 'B' and 'C') but the first is loosely ternary in structure, and the second, which occupies nearly two thirds of the whole work, is deliberately obscure formally, a series of passages which build up and transform over large stretches of time. In his programme note for the piece, the composer remarks that he sought to create 'a new syntax of tensions and transitions'.[9] Sibelius proved particularly helpful in this regard, given the tendencies delineated above, and the composer has admitted that his example proved important in helping him to dare to make the transitions the main substance of the piece.[10]

The longest such passage is exclusively for the electronic and percussion instruments, starting at around 31′ in the commercial recording, and continuing for several minutes thereafter. The percussion writing in *Saturne* might superficially remind one of Varèse (another favourite composer of Dufourt) – but close listening reveals quite readily that it consists of detailed, quasi-canonic figures which are nearer in their sequential, propulsive effect to a Sibelius string tremolo texture. The harmonic substance of the music – on the electronic instruments – is crammed into the extreme treble and bass without any secure middle-range writing. Here the electronic instruments create a mixture of harmony and timbre which is strongly reminiscent of the dense screen of sound from *Tapiola* in Ex. 13.1.[11]

Such slowly transforming aural screens are common in the works of other *Itinéraire* composers, notably Grisey, who was also interested in Sibelius at this period.[12] This can clearly be detected in the second section of *Partiels* (1975, starting at Fig. 12), which forms a very gradual transition from the extreme bass instruments of the ensemble (low cor anglais and clarinets, contrabass clarinet, low horn and trombone) to octave Es in the middle and high register, dominated by string harmonics (another *Tapiola* texture). The parallel second section in Grisey's orchestral work *Transitoires*[13] (1981) is even more radically dark in spacing and scoring, and its timing still more distended. Sibelius helped to de-gallicise the sound world of the spectralists, opening their ears to a rougher kind of orchestration (not, one imagines, covered in their Conservatoire training) as well as pointing away from the established habits of thinking in isolated *blocs sonores* prevalent in Messiaen and Boulez.

Murail's orchestral work *Gondwana* (1980) even incorporates a substantial passage directly modelled upon a Sibelius piece.[14] The work in question is, oddly, not a late one but the relatively little played tone poem *Lemminkäinen in Tuonela* from the *Four Lemminkäinen Legends* op. 22 (1896). The principal texture of the piece consists of wave-like ascending string tremolos answered by circuitously descending woodwind lines, the two meeting in a culminating brass and bass drum chord in the middle register; this sequence is repeated many times with variations in the duration of each part as the piece works up to a main climax. This procedure was borrowed, with obvious differences in harmonic and orchestrational syntax, for the central development section of *Gondwana*, starting at bar 50, pp. 27–30 (which leads to the climax of that work). Murail took both the wave-patterning and the orchestration from Sibelius's piece and recreated them in his own terms; the complex harmony is derived from the sum and difference tones of frequency modulation, incorporating quarter-tones, and the rhythmic language is more irregular and fluid in its details. The effect, however, is clearly analogous, whilst not superficially Sibelian to the innocent ear. It's a fascinating example of the way French composers found Sibelius a suggestive formal influence rather than an inhibiting stylistic model.

Significantly, for the French premiere in December 1980, Murail selected a major Sibelius work as a companion piece in the concert – the single-movement Seventh Symphony.[15] Halbreich's review in *La Croix* noted the new-found 'power and breath' of *Gondwana*, partly attributable in his view to the links with Sibelius. The co-programming with the Seventh, 'hewn in a single enormous bloc', proved 'highly revelatory': 'beyond the obvious differences of language, one notices astonishing parallels – [in particular] a feeling of gradual growth and transformation very close to a sort of cellular multiplication. It is a sign of the times', he added, 'that composers as different as Dufourt, Dusapin and Murail should be turning towards Sibelius . . . Sibelius has henceforth taken the place of Mahler' [as the chief influence on young composers].[16]

The music of Alain Banquart and Pascal Dusapin reflects their interest in Sibelius in a more indirect manner. Banquart is a singular figure in recent French music in that he is the only major composer there since the 1950s to have embarked on a cycle of symphonies (there are six to date). This is all the odder for someone who has devoted his mature output to an exploration of microtonality. Banquart was never a member of *L'Itinéraire*, and although he, Murail and Dufourt founded the short-lived *Collectif de Recherche Instrumentale et de Synthèse Sonore*, he remained a strongly independent figure. His First Symphony (1980) was the first work to receive widespread attention,[17] and is representative of his personal synthesis of the French symphonic tradition with Bruckner, Sibelius and more recent harmonic innovations. The rough, decidedly austere orchestral palette is completely lacking in stereotypically French colouristic devices (no tuned or exotic percussion, just tuned and untuned drums) and avoids blending in favour of stark choruses of instruments.

Casual listening would indeed suggest a Northern or German symphonist. Given the ubiquity of quarter-tone intonation, unison doubling is generally avoided, although some of the violins are tuned down a quarter-tone, greatly facilitating the performance of accurate, even unison, microtones. The three-movement plan suggests immediate parallels with Sibelius's Fifth, and there are some signs that this work does indeed lie in the background to Banquart's piece. For instance, Banquart's central movement, like that of Sibelius, offers a point of harmonic contrast through simplicity relative to its companions: scored for strings alone, it uses a select microtonal modality with a distinct flavour of pentatonicism, even diatonicism, which is largely avoided elsewhere in the piece. Banquart's first movement, however, is closer to a normal sonata structure than that of the Fifth, with clear first and second thematic groups. The first is a bold succession of dense harmonies

derived, like *Gondwana,* from sum and difference tones (and by the composer's admission, directly influenced by Murail in this regard, although it
sounds very different).[18] The second group is for horns and winds alone.
Both are subjected to extensive alteration and combination in the development and reprise, using large-scale time-structuring and transformation
processes that are reminiscent of Sibelius's first movement. Banquart's finale
uses a new type of orchestral extreme bass timbre by substituting two bass
guitars for the double-bass section: their deep, Sibelian pedal tones, spaced
in narrow intervals such as seconds and thirds, proceed regardless of the
other instruments throughout. The rest of the orchestra is engaged in two
opposite tendencies: one constructive, consisting of increasing segments of
a fast toccata on wind and higher strings; the other, predominantly destructive, is a series of extremely loud sharp chords for percussion and brass,
separated by silences, which attempt to halt the progress of the music with
increasing frequency. These inevitably recall the sequence of *tutti* chords
which end Sibelius's Fifth, but Banquart deliberately denies Sibelius's sense
of harmonic resolution: the three elements in this finale never coalesce, and
the final sequence of chords leaves Banquart's symphony open-ended and
ambivalent.

It is difficult to point to an exact passage in the output of Pascal Dusapin
as evincing the influence of Sibelius. In a glowing tribute,[19] Dusapin has
acknowledged the strong effect of the Fourth Symphony on his work as a
whole, admiring its density, its radical attitude towards form and time, and
its masterly orchestration in spite of the fact, Dusapin feels, that Sibelius was
not really interested in decorativeness of musical surface for its own sake.
Unlike Banquart, Dusapin has never written symphonies; his numerous
large orchestral works bear little trace of traditional forms, each tracing its
own path through the allotted time span with a general avoidance of repetition or thematic statement. Dusapin's orchestral palette is marked, like that
of Banquart, by a lack of the resonant percussion instruments so prominent
in the Boulez school (no vibraphones or crotales), timpani usually being the
only percussion present. Beyond this general sobriety of orchestral texture,
and other less important tendencies such as a habit of supporting swelling
brass crescendos with timpani and a fondness similar to that of Dufourt
for low wind instruments, Sibelius must be understood as playing a more
distant and metaphorical role in Dusapin's musical thought than in that of
his confrères. His style has undergone considerable change in the last two
decades, moving from the Xenakis-like sound masses of his early orchestral
pieces *La Rivière* and *Timée* to the limpid modality of *Apex* and *Extenso.*
However, the stripped-down plainness of the simpler diatonic passages in
these two latter pieces is not dissimilar in effect to the opening of Sibelius's
Sixth or the C major modality of some parts of the Seventh, and it may be

that Sibelius's example gave Dusapin the courage to simplify his surface in these later pieces without in any way diluting his substance of thought. This use of overt diatonicism is almost unique amongst Dusapin's compatriots, and deeply unfashionable; indeed, Dusapin's stubborn independence from the faction-fighting of contemporary French music is also not without parallels in the stance of the Finnish composer from 1915 onwards in relation to the modern music of his day.

Scandinavian and Nordic composers

In 1954, Sibelius received a long and detailed letter[20] from the then youngest prominent Danish composer, Per Nørgård (b. 1932) in which Nørgård claimed that Sibelius's later works had made a more lasting and continuing impression on him recently than those of several more contemporary figures such as Stravinsky and Bartók. Specifically, Nørgård cited his interest in the 'metamorphic' school of composition, as practised by his teacher Vagn Holmboe in his mature works, most obviously the *Sinfonia Boreale* (no. 8). This means of linking distinct thematic areas by continuous metamorphosis between them was much used by a number of Holmboe's pupils, in particular Nørgård himself (his *Constellations* for strings is a fine example).

Following his study of the Holmboe *Sinfonia Boreale*, Nørgård has stated repeatedly that he felt the sudden and inexplicable need to study Sibelius (inexplicable because Holmboe 'never mentioned Sibelius', says Nørgård).[21] He was extremely surprised to find the metamorphosis technique clearly present in later Sibelius, composed over thirty years before. Indeed, his letter continues, he is increasingly aware of the fact that Sibelius's music is virtually limitless in its depth and novel implications, in contrast to the work of other more recent composers. 'You may imagine, against this background, my feelings on discovering this new, genuinely symphonic principle fully blossoming in works normally labelled under the heading of an earlier historical period of music! . . . It's very possible that you have known about what I'm trying to say for a long time – and understood that it was the way it should be.' Sibelius himself was taken aback, as his reply states, 'by how deeply you had penetrated into my music . . . Only rarely have I received a letter which showed such understanding of my work.' The exceptionally warm tone of his reply – the majority of Sibelius's later letters quoted in print are more formal – would indicate that Sibelius was particularly delighted to see the start of a revival in the study and influence of his music amongst younger composers.

In Nørgård's case, the interest in Sibelius was to continue and augment to the present day – it is clear that Nielsen's music has affected him

Example 13.2 Sibelius, Symphony no. 5, III (bars 117–35)

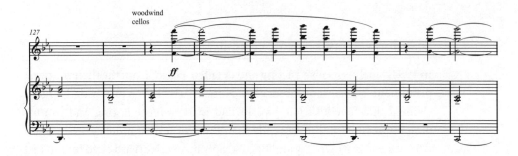

comparatively little. Sibelius was to play a crucial role in the generation of Nørgård's most famous technical discovery, the so-called 'infinity row'. Both Nørgård himself and his pupil Hans Gefors[22] have cited a passage from the last movement of Sibelius's Fifth Symphony as a direct precedent for Nørgård's row, especially its properties of 'interference' – a term Nørgård uses to describe the crossing and simultaneous interaction of different speeds, metres and frequencies. The passage is the famous 'swan hymn', as Axel Carpelan called it,[23] in which a theme heard in the horns is accompanied by itself at a third of the speed in the bass (see Ex. 13.2). As Gefors comments,[24] the superimposition of the two speeds results in an interference of metric stresses between the fast triple metre of the horns, cycling in metres of 3/2, and the slower triple metre of the bass-line, cycling in metres of 9/2.

Nørgård's infinity row produces such self-reproductions at slower speeds and metres automatically. A detailed technical description of the row's generation is out of place here.[25] The following example (Ex. 13.3) shows on five staves one form of the resultant row – the two-tone chromatic form used throughout Nørgård's Second Symphony (1970). The original row is shown on the top stave in quavers; the following staves show successively its inversion at half-speed, its transposition up a half-tone also at half-speed (on the off-beats), the original row at a quarter of the original speed, and the original row at a sixteenth of the original speed. Astonishingly, all of these speeds are unison doublings of pitches from the original row on the top stave, as careful comparison of any of the lower staves with the top stave reveals. In fact, the row contains itself or its inversion at an infinite

Example 13.3 Per Nørgård's infinity row (two-tone chromatic version)

(All lower staves show slower speeds of the same melody, all of them occurring in unison with the original melody on the top stave.)

number of speeds, all of them in pitch unison with the original. Nørgård discovered this phenomenon almost by accident in 1959.[26] It was not until 1968 that he began to focus exclusively on it, in the second movement of *Voyage into the Golden Screen* and the aforementioned Second Symphony, the latter consisting of the first five thousand pitches of the row played very much as illustrated in Ex. 13.3. Orchestral doublings, hairpins and a variety of dynamic accents are employed to bring out each layer of the row and distinguish it from its neighbours, allowing the ear to drift from layer to layer and from speed to speed, whilst never losing sight of the original melody moving steadily in quavers for most of the work. The result is like a gigantic elaboration of Sibelius's polymetric discovery in the Fifth Symphony, a melodic kaleidoscope that seems to change perpetually and yet stay remarkably consistent as it very slowly expands in range and intensity.

Nørgård's Third Symphony, completed in 1975, employs infinite rows in the realms of harmony and rhythmic stratification, as well as melodically. Nørgård discovered that the harmonic spectrum was self-reflexive in an exactly parallel manner to the melodic infinity row: each partial in a harmonic spectrum has its own harmonics present in the whole spectrum. Thus a harmonic spectrum on a low G contains harmonic spectra on each successive partial of its spectrum, just as the infinity row contains itself at an infinite variety of slower speeds. In the domain of rhythm, Nørgård discovered the same properties in the Golden Section via the Fibonacci series: since each successive number in such a series is the sum of its two immediate predecessors, it too contains its own proportions at an infinite number of slower speeds. If, as in Nørgård's works, the numbers are translated into rhythmic proportions, it is possible to play each speed of the melodic infinity row starting on a different partial of a harmonic spectrum, with each speed moving in Fibonacci-derived rhythmical layering. Music composed in this way sounds at once familiar and elusive, replete with consonances each time the melodic strands converge, but novel in its harmonic progressions and in its rhythmic transitions from periodic metre to complete aperiodicity.

The use of consonance via harmonic spectra in this period of Nørgård's work, together with other areas of technical and textural overlap – such as the interest in transformations away from and back to periodicity, clearly bears some resemblances to the contemporary works of spectral composers mentioned above,[27] which makes the common interest in Sibelius of all these composers all the more significant. Interestingly, neither party had any knowledge of the other's work at the time. Nørgård abandoned his literal use of the infinity row in 1979, but has since returned to it, and has continued to explore and discover other means of generating interference in pitch and rhythmic layers, such as his complex tone-lakes. Thus the influence of Sibelius ran extremely deep in his output, to the point of being a fundamental starting point for all his most characteristic work. Since Nørgård has also had considerable influence as a teacher of many younger composers (aside from Gefors, Karl-Aage Rasmussen, Hans Abrahamsen and Bent Sørensen should be mentioned), Sibelius has decisively re-emerged as a major force in Scandinavian music, not through any slavish imitation but through a deep study of his music's technical implications from a contemporary standpoint.

Amongst the Sibelius-influenced Nordic contemporary composers under consideration here, Magnus Lindberg (b. 1958) is a special case in that not only is he Finnish, but he is by far the most prominent Finnish composer to have emerged onto the international scene since Sibelius's death. Therefore the anxiety of influence must weigh on him particularly heavily. Unsurprisingly, his earliest published works are at the farthest possible remove from Sibelius, showing instead an absorption with dense chromaticism, extended instrumental techniques and formal discontinuity, much influenced by Vinko Globokar, with whom he studied. His first large-scale piece, *Kraft* (1983–5, for seven instrumental soloists and orchestra), has a deliberately unsymphonic, anarchic form – a sequence of episodes which follow each other either by means of block juxtaposition or through smooth transformation. The division into two movements is thus almost arbitrary: the arrival of the second movement brings no major change of pace or texture.

Kraft is important not merely in its own right but as a reminder of just how far from his compatriot's music Lindberg's own work began. His music underwent a change starting in 1988 with the piano piece *Twine* and the orchestral *Kinetics* (1988–9), which evince a much greater interest in resonant harmony and a move away from abrasive surfaces. Lindberg studied in the early 1980s with Gérard Grisey and he has attributed his rediscovery of Sibelius directly to the then widespread fascination amongst the spectralists for such pieces as the Seventh Symphony and *Tapiola*. Their idiosyncratic view of his work helped Lindberg to see the radical aspects of Sibelius afresh, stripped of nationalist trappings. Lindberg's eloquent statements regarding this change of mind, given in interview in 1993, are worth quoting in full, as they reflect many of the views of contemporary composers on the subject:

> I have often said that it is a pity that Sibelius was Finnish! His music has been deeply misunderstood. While his language was far from modern, his thinking, as far as form and the treatment of materials is concerned, was ahead of its time. While Varèse is credited with opening the way for new sonorities, Sibelius has himself pursued a profound reassessment of the formal and structural problems of composition. I do not think it is fair that he has been considered as a conservative . . . His harmonies have a resonant, almost spectral quality. You find an attention to sonority in Sibelius works which is actually not so far removed from that which would appear long after in the work of Grisey or Murail . . . For me, the crucial aspect of his work remains his conception of *continuity*. In *Tapiola*, above all, the way genuine *processes* are created using very limited materials is pretty exceptional.[28]

Lindberg's harmonic thinking is a combination of his interest in combinatorial serial techniques with aspects derived from spectral theory. This enables him to fuse a logical syntax of dissonant aggregates and purely consonant harmonic spectra: with the help of computer software, Lindberg can analyse any chord, no matter how dissonant, as the upper harmonics of a low fundamental.[29] This means that the bass line has a structural importance in his music that is rare in composition today. In *Kinetics*, *Marea* and *Joy*, he used a chaconne-like recurring sequence of chords, dissonant in themselves but consonant when reharmonised with low fundamentals. The first section of *Joy* builds gradually towards the emergence of the bass fundamentals as a structural point of focus, and it is precisely at the moment of the bass notes' emergence (bar 51ff.) that the orchestration and sonorities of later Sibelius are most in evidence. At such points *Joy* has a harsh brilliance, a textural depth and roundness of sound which results from 'the music itself supporting its own acoustics',[30] bringing to mind the stark clarity of the Fourth Symphony's opening, as well as the moments from *Tapiola* already mentioned. This is unsurprising, given Lindberg's statement quoted above, in which he draws attention to Sibelius's advanced sense of sonority, a factor often perceived as irrelevant by more traditional writers about the music (such as Robert Simpson). At half an hour, *Joy* is more or less the same length as *Kraft*, but by contrast with the earlier piece's wilful discontinuity, *Joy* is composed in long, continuous paragraphs which evince a similar sense of growth and change to that discerned by Halbreich as the influence of Sibelius in Murail's *Gondwana*.

This greater musical breadth enabled Lindberg to break out of single-movement forms into a full-blown four-movement structure lasting forty minutes in his largest work to date, *Aura* (1994) for orchestra. The composer's note on this work is revealingly ambivalent about its form:

> The overall form of *Aura* would make it appropriate to call the piece a symphony. Yet it is not a symphony. The piece could more easily be called a concerto for orchestra, but it isn't that either. Instruments and instrumental groups are often treated in a very virtuosic way, but this is more the result of a certain treatment of the material than an instrumental approach.[31]

Lindberg's evident reluctance to call a large orchestral work 'symphony' is, I believe, partly attributable to the negative side of his Finnish inheritance. It is indeed inconceivable that a composer of his mentality would wish to be associated with the outputs of eclectic traditionalists such as Sallinen or Kalevi Aho, the two most prominent symphonists in recent Finnish history.

At the same time, sound musical reasons also lie behind Lindberg's argument. *Aura* is primarily about texture and harmony. There are musical types – such as the sombre chorale which opens the second movement, or the more hectic scurrying figures which pervade areas of the third – but *Aura* avoids clear thematic groups, let alone obvious melodic statement and development typical of traditional symphonic thought. True to his modernist stance, such things are eschewed in favour of large harmonic evolution and dramatic orchestral colouration. Lindberg's second point, regarding the approach to instrumental writing in *Aura*, is curiously reminiscent of Dusapin's assertion that Sibelius's orchestration was almost beside the point: Lindberg seems here to be implying that the essence of the piece lies in the transformation of musical material, rather than its instrumentation per se. Perhaps it might be more accurate to assert that both are on an equal footing, since at any moment in *Aura* it is hard to think of another set of instruments being substituted for those assigned the material. Ex. 13.4, taken from the third movement, illustrates this vividly: a rapidly converging string texture, strongly reminiscent of a similarly lengthy passage for strings in the second movement of Sibelius's Sixth, articulates the harmonic progression in rapid waves, which towards the end of the extract spread to the woodwind. This is not pastiche Sibelius, however, and the distinctive intervallic content of the music – derived from Lindberg's complementary hexachordal system – is all his own.

Another remarkable feature of *Aura* is the repeated long-range harmonic drive towards cadential consonances – often open fifths (as at the end of the

Example 13.4 Magnus Lindberg, *Aura*, III [extract]

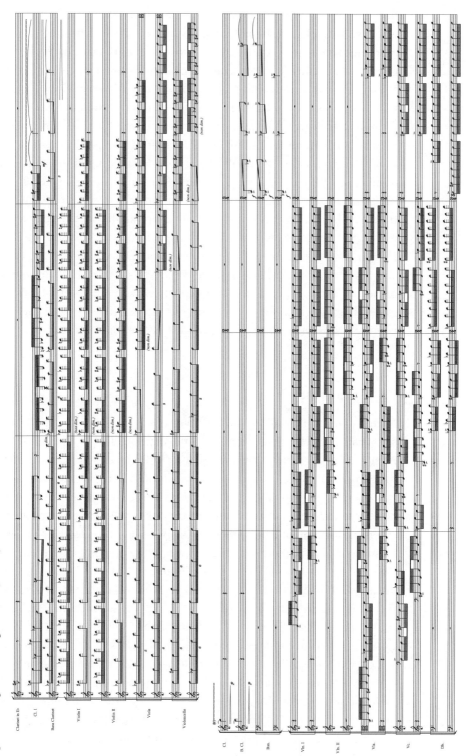

first movement) or overtone string harmonics (as at the conclusion of the work as a whole): these do not feel like sudden intrusions from a previously harmonic language – there is no return to tonal habits. Instead, Lindberg has managed to create a fresh syntax in which they feature strongly and logically as long-term outcomes. This is an important formal tool in his work, and it is here that his debt to the irresistible forward propulsion of Sibelius's late forms is at its clearest. The calm, unassertively inevitable cadence onto D and its harmonics at the conclusion of *Aura* has an understated rhetoric which, to my ears at least, is the result of a real understanding of the conclusion of Sibelius's Seventh. As we now know from published sketches, a draft full score of that work had originally proposed a conclusion of blazing triumphalism.[32] Sibelius's choice of the more lightly scored final version is a highly deliberate move away from late Romantic rhetoric towards a more unassertive manner, already evident in the conclusions to the Fourth and Sixth Symphonies, emphasising modal process rather than excessive orchestral garb. In its similar preoccupation with sheer musical matter, rather than showiness for its own sake, Lindberg's *Aura* is perhaps the truest heir to these works, as its beautifully poised conclusion proves.

Britain and the USA

As in Finland and Scandinavia, British musical culture was somewhat slow in certain areas to emerge from the immediate shadow of Sibelius. A large number of mid-century British symphonists reflected too vividly the imme-diate impact of Sibelius's mannerisms, without always having the merit of understanding the full consequences of his musical language. E. J. Moeran's nonetheless charming Symphony in G minor (1930–7) is perhaps the best of a mixed and often tepid bunch. Many passages of the work ape Sibelian harmony and textures: the bluff plainness of the opening movement, long passages in the slow second of modal B minor woodwind scales in thirds, much use of Sibelius-style modality generally (especially the so-called acous-tic scale), and most blatantly of all, a *Tapiola*-like storm in the finale, and the sequence of abrupt concluding chords clearly but for no evident formal reason adapted from the end of the Fifth. The work is a fine and personal one despite these failings, but it illustrates clearly the problem Sibelius posed to composers of his time. Influence of this sort was not leading anywhere.

The only major product of immediate post-Sibelius symphonism, Robert Simpson (1926–97), has been widely discussed elsewhere and a lengthy list-ing of all his many and profound absorptions of the essence of Sibelian thought is out of place in an article devoted primarily to contemporary composers. He may be thought of not as the last of a great line (as some of his supporters have claimed) but as a unique figure who stood at a juncture in British musical history. He fashioned a remarkably consistent and sturdy output out of his own deep knowledge of the classics and the then wholly unfashionable Sibelius and Nielsen. The conflict between the main trends of his day and these deep loves informs the stern persistence of the music strongly, almost as if it were created out of active defiance of his immediate musical surroundings (which was surely true, at least in part). His most substantial achievement, the masterly single-movement Ninth Symphony, offers a personal twist on the Sibelian trick of underpinning long arcs of music with relatedly pulsed tempi: here the structural devices employed in the first movement of Sibelius's Fifth were extended massively over some fifty-five minutes. Remarkably, Simpson is able to fill out his enormous time spans with substantial musical thought that holds the attention. The Ninth remains an isolated case of Sibelius-influenced uninterrupted transformation extended to previously unheard-of lengths within a relatively traditional harmonic and orchestral idiom. As such it is an undervalued and underplayed masterpiece by a lone figure in British music.

The anti-Sibelius reaction that supposedly set in with the 1960s and the influx of continental European serialism has been much written about. But aside from the apparent reluctance of the BBC to allow Hans Rosbaud to conduct Sibelius with the BBC Symphony Orchestra, I have found surprisingly little concrete evidence of it. Neither Sargent nor Barbirolli dropped their persistent advocacy of the symphonies, and recording companies continued to issue complete cycles of them. True, the London Promenade Concerts reflected Sibelius's achievement less consistently, but these years also marked great discovery of the achievements of other major and hitherto underrated masters such as Nielsen, Schmidt and Janáček – all much promoted by the BBC Third Programme at this time.[33] Nevertheless, it seems clear that younger composers, at any rate, were no longer interested in Sibelius: Anthony Payne has testified that it was 'not cool to allude to the likes of Vaughan Williams or Sibelius'[34] in London's new-music circles in the 1960s, which is perfectly understandable given their hitherto extreme prominence.

The sudden mention of Sibelius as a major influence on the leading iconoclastic composer of the 1960s, Peter Maxwell Davies, came as a shock to many of his admirers. Davies has cited his enthusiastic attendance at Barbirolli's legendary Sibelius performances as a boy, particularly his exceptional enthusiasm for the Seventh Symphony – 'my hair stood on end! . . . Sheer awe of this extraordinary piece.'[35] But his 1962 conversation with R. Murray Schaefer[36] makes no mention of this (nor indeed of his lasting passion for Beethoven), leading one to suppose that either a reaction had set in or that Davies realised the mention of such music would simply cause bafflement. Mahler was clearly an influence on the *Second Taverner Fantasia,* as was widely mentioned at the time, and remained a cited model for the elements of parody and stylistic allusion in Davies's expressionist phase, running approximately from *Revelation and Fall* (1966) to *Miss Donnithorne's Maggot* (1974).

Sibelius came to the surface for the first time in print in connection with Davies's Symphony (1976, later numbered 1). Whereas the *Second Taverner Fantasia* had been called by more than one critic 'a symphony in all but name',[37] this time Davies had produced the genuine four-movement article, as Stephen Pruslin observed with some wonderment.[38] The extent of the influence of Sibelius on this piece is complicated by the fact that the composer himself cited a whole group of composers as having bolstered his conception of the work, including not only Sibelius but Schumann's Second Symphony, and most puzzling of all, Boulez's *Don*, which served as a formal model for Davies's finale.[39] The second movement of the Symphony, a slow movement which transforms step by step into a scherzo, was modelled on the form of the first movement of Sibelius's Fifth. Sibelius arrived at this solution by knocking two movements together into a continuous whole. Davies states, similarly, that he first composed 'a moderately long single movement' which he withdrew, then 'compressed to become a short slow movement, that changes into a kind of "scherzo"'.

Davies clarifies the parallel between his movement and the Sibelius by his treatment of thematic material across its changing tempi. After an initial slow alto-flute paraphrase of the *Ave Maris Stella* plainsong, followed by an accelerating transition, the main thematic substance of the slow movement is presented as a broad, lyrical melodic statement for high cellos (three bars after Fig. 54 in the full score), surely one of Davies's finest and most sustained inventions. At the parallel formal point in the scherzo section of the movement (three bars after Fig. 69), this theme and its accompanying harmony are themselves paraphrased and recycled at a swifter speed, as if in fast-forward playback, propelling the music onwards to its hasty conclusion. Sibelius's reworking in the first movement of the Fifth of his opening ideas, speeding them up and paraphrasing them to form the basis of its scherzo second half, is the evident and audible model for Davies here, without the model being stylistically or harmonically obtrusive. Such transforming movements – *Lentos* steadily transforming into fast movements – feature prominently in several of Davies's other symphonies, although without the more explicitly Sibelian features evident in this example.

Aside from that, the sole evident and acknowledged influence from Sibelius is the 'adaptation', as the composer puts it, of the abrupt chordal conclusion of the Fifth in the 'stabbing, offbeat chords' which conclude Davies's own Symphony. This gesture has some parallels with the conclusion of Banquart's (later) First Symphony cited above. Just as Banquart (who may not, however, have been *consciously* alluding to the Sibelius) deprived his Symphony of any sense of Sibelian affirmation or conclusiveness, so here Davies states explicitly that he 'did not want the concluding gesture to sound "final" in a rhetorical way'. For this reason he placed these final chords 'a fifth above their harmonically "logical" position', according to his personal harmonic system in the work. Whilst the audibility of this latter harmonic subtlety to all but the very initiated may be a matter of conjecture given the complexity of the pitch-content immediately preceding the final page of this Symphony, it remains a suitably and explicitly offhand conclusion, its abruptness aptly mirroring the composer's intention that it should be heard to 'put a brake on the generation-transformation processes, no more'.

Davies's later symphonies include a number of occasional parallels with Sibelius. His persisting admiration for Sibelius's single-movement Seventh resurfaces in his own one-movement, multi-sectional Fifth Symphony, which takes Sibelius's 'many movements in one' idea to even further extremes. The piece consists of innumerable short sections, some arrived at by jump-cutting, others by transitions which frequently complicate matters by turning into whole sections themselves. Like Sibelius, Davies nevertheless maintains clear overall direction of purpose beneath the seeming diversity on the surface, but his conclusion offers a new twist to its single-movement model. Here, avoiding even the tentative affirmation of Sibelius's final C major, Davies ends with an intensely focused single line in even crotchets, traversing the entire range of the string orchestra unaccompanied and unharmonised, ending the work still more interrogatively than the offhand chords of his First Symphony.

Still, it would be erroneous to regard Davies's symphonism as wholly Sibelian. Davies's assignation of key centres in his works from the *Ave Maris Stella* onwards remains controversial. It is especially hard to perceive such 'tonics' in the dense chromaticism of the earlier symphonies which, to complicate things, have dominants frequently not at the distance of a fifth but rather a tritone or some other interval. This renders at least one important aspect of Davies's formal intentions extremely difficult to grasp in certain symphonies. Another distinctly un-Sibelian feature of the first three symphonies is the plethora of tuned percussion instruments, often given multiple thematic and polyrhythmic material over and above the busy musical argument in the rest of the orchestra. And it is hard to think of the composer of *Tapiola* or the later symphonies subscribing to Davies's statement about his First Symphony, that 'as in my previous works, there is no "orchestration" as such – the instrumentation functions simply to make the musical argument clear' – an attitude about which Davies soon changed his mind in any case. Davies, then, is no slave to his model: he is prepared to differ, even on fundamentals, being interested not in mere imitation but in absorbing the lessons of Sibelius at any level which can be of use, and then moving on to create his own utterly distinctive symphonic language.

British composers of younger generations have remained fascinated by Sibelius, albeit more indirectly than Davies. George Benjamin (b. 1960) and Oliver Knussen (b. 1952), for example, are Sibelius enthusiasts without this being readily obvious from listening to their music. Knussen points to Sibelius's powerful and resonant bass writing[40] – particularly the tendency for bass lines to wander independently from their harmonic surroundings, as in *Tapiola* and the Fifth and Seventh Symphonies – as a major source of interest, and something that is reflected in his own work. This type of bass writing can be found in many places in Knussen's music: the ground bass which drifts repeatedly through his Horn Concerto (1994) in many transpositions against slower-moving upper harmonies is perhaps the clearest instance – entering at bar 94 and continuing with several interruptions through much of the rest of the score. Knussen has also pointed to other momentary examples of Sibelian influence in terms of texture, such as the transition passage starting at Fig. 33 of his Third Symphony's second movement.[41] Here the passacaglia-like sequence of revolving string chords which forms the basis of the movement dissolves in a haze of string tremolos and shimmering textures which suddenly come quite close in effect to a Sibelius transition passage, without any element of stylistic anomaly. The moment is a brief one in Knussen's piece, but structurally important as here the passacaglia chord-sequence disappears from the immediate foreground structure. Throughout the passage that follows (Fig. 34) the tremolos continue in the extreme bass – in double basses and pairs of timpani – underpinning a high trio of clarinets, with no harmony in the central register (aside from a couple of brief horn interventions). This focusing on registral extremes of treble and bass with a removal of harmonic centre is also typical of later Sibelius, and certainly it makes an analogous effect here.

George Benjamin's *At First Light* (1982) for chamber orchestra of fourteen players reflects his own enthusiasm for Sibelius's bass writing by making reference to *Tapiola* at the violent opening of his own work's second movement. The passage being referred to here is just before the brief Mendelssohnian scherzo of the work, at Fig. F in *Tapiola*, a slow, chromatically winding progression scored for low clarinets, bass clarinet, bassoons, contrabassoons and timpani. These extremely dark chords are magnified in Benjamin's piece (from bar 3 of the second movement to three bars before Fig. B) into a series of crushed, harsh progressions for bass clarinet, bassoon, low horn, trombone, cello and double bass emphasising similar intervals to the Sibelius – low tritones, fourths and fifths. The chord progressions between these are similarly a semitone apart, here emphasised by numerous glissandi between them, and at one point they almost quote the lower voice progressions of the passage in *Tapiola*. The effect is an exaggeration of the Sibelius, bringing it closer to the world of Varèse and, indeed, electro-acoustic music. Not coincidentally, *At First Light* also marks the closest Benjamin has ever come to writing spectral music.

Benjamin is equally enthusiastic about the evolving form of the Fifth Symphony's first movement, 'which seems to invent itself as it proceeds'.[42] This model of seemingly spontaneous form building influenced Benjamin's *Sudden Time*, in which the whole compositional process was built upon the premise that musical form could be radically altered by slight changes in patterns or textures. Small alterations repeatedly multiply into major and unexpected swerves in the form of the work, so that it seems to be in a state of constant self-renewal. Whilst Benjamin disclaims any cult of Sibelius, he admits that the Fifth was often in his mind as he tried to build a continuously unfolding structure which, whilst quixotic and malleable, maintained coherence and a strong directionality.

Morton Feldman (1926–87) is more often associated with Cage and the American experimentalists. This misleading impression conceals the fact that he was a highly knowledgeable and cultured musician whose tastes extended to deep affection for Skryabin, Busoni, and both Stravinsky and Schoenberg, as well as Sibelius, whose music would have been virtually ubiquitous in the America of Feldman's youth. With deliberate provocation in his Darmstadt lecture of 1984,[43] Feldman spoke up for both Stravinsky and Sibelius, blaming Adorno's influence for the ignorance of young composers with regard to the former.[44] He might well have blamed him for the ignorance of Sibelius, as well, for he recounts, 'I remember a graduate student of mine, I'm raving about the Fourth Symphony of Sibelius and he says, "You really like that?".' According to Feldman, Toru Takemitsu shared his fondness. At a dinner organised by Takemitsu's French publisher, the radio was playing the Fourth Symphony and the publisher rose to turn it off: 'Takemitsu and I jumped up, "Leave it on! leave it on!" He looked at us [in amazement], it was Sibelius.' Feldman raises this anecdote to support his important remark that 'The people who you think are radicals might really be conservatives. The people who you think are conservative might really be radical.'

Feldman raised Sibelius in connection with one specific work of his own, the orchestral piece *Coptic Light* (1985). His programme note explains that 'An important aspect of the composition was prompted by Sibelius's observation that the orchestra differs mainly from the piano in that it has no pedal.[45] With this in mind, I set to work to create an orchestral pedal continually varying in nuance.'[46]

Coptic Light is perhaps the ultimate Sibelian 'sound sheet', a continuously changing orchestral texture whose form is entirely governed by changes to the many small quasi-repetitive patterns that make it up. The orchestral pedal effect is achieved by the accumulation of these patterns across the entire range of the orchestra from beginning to end: the piece is a permanent *tutti*. Unlike the examples by Knussen and Benjamin cited above, here the extreme bass is not a sustained resonance but a gentle pulsation given by the harps – the double basses provide a middle-range backdrop of chords in harmonics.

Each page of the score consists of eight bars of 8/8 (until the coda, where additive time signatures suddenly appear). Changes are applied to the patterns each time a new page is reached (i.e. every eight bars), although the density of the material renders the metre difficult, although not impossible, to perceive. Feldman does not change a whole texture at once: the evolution is carefully measured by degrees, some patterns maintaining across many pages, others altering or disappearing altogether after a single eight-bar stretch. As the piece nears its close, the first violins' falling perfect-fifth A–E returns, along with some other elements from the opening texture. The net result is not an exact return to the opening harmony, but establishes enough similarity to make such a return clearly implicit. Thus the whole form of *Coptic Light* could be seen as an illustration of Hepokoski's definition of rotational forms in Sibelius as a set of varied restatements around a central material, the last of which links up with the harmonic area of the opening. At once static and continuously evolving, *Coptic Light* is an unexpected instance of Sibelius's effect on one of the most unusual and innovative recent works composed for orchestra in the last two decades.

All told, this survey – albeit far from complete – shows that a surprisingly large number of seemingly contradictory composers have drawn upon Sibelius as a source of inspiration in a musical world whose current plurality and lack of direction is often confusing. There is general agreement amongst contemporary composers that beneath the obviously traditional elements of his harmonic syntax, Sibelius addressed some of the most essential problems of composition in innovative and utterly original ways that are of continuing relevance to the newest music. Delighted and surprised as he was by Nørgård's 1954 letter, Sibelius could never have guessed at how prescient it was. For there is virtually no major composer working today who has not been directly affected by the work of Jean Sibelius. He is indeed definitive proof of Feldman's assertion that 'the people who you think are conservative might really be radical'.[47]

PART FOUR

Interpreting Sibelius

14 Different kinds of fidelity: interpreting Sibelius on record

BETHANY LOWE

Recording Sibelius

'Few composers have benefited as much from the invention of the phono-graph as has Sibelius,' claimed Harold Johnson in 1959.[1] Appreciating the role of recording technology in shaping our view of Sibelius's music is vital, whether we are studying his historical importance or his musical style. There is useful information to be extracted from any part of the recording tradi-tion we choose to examine: the emergence of the earliest recordings, the flourishing of different performing styles, and his continued popularity on record today each tell a story.

With the wealth of recorded material available on CD and other accurate, easily accessible formats at the beginning of the twenty-first century, it is hard to imagine how different life must have been for a music student, enthusiast, or scholar before the advent of musical recording. Favourite pieces, stan-dard repertoire, and new works could be encountered only through close study of the score, by playing them oneself (in piano solo or piano duet versions for orchestral or other large works), or in occasional, treasured performances. The study of complex, large-scale, or musically innovative works was greatly facilitated once listeners could obtain a reliable way of hearing them repeatedly. The major wave of popularity for Sibelius in the 1930s was caused by many factors, including a political and aesthetic re-sistance to the German avant-garde and a desire for symphonic works as a comprehensible alternative;[2] however, another significant factor was the new process of electrical recording which allowed relatively faithful repro-duction of the complex sounds of a symphony orchestra. An article by Scott Goddard, appearing in 1931, claimed that 'one of the most significant signs of the past year is the considerable increase of interest in the music of Sibelius in this country', a development which he attributes to the pioneering 'Columbia gramophone record of the Second Symphony, which meant that one could play the work daily and at last get close to the music'.[3] The com-bination of twentieth-century musical style with the formal complexities of symphonic writing, together with a fragmentary orchestral manner, meant that Sibelius's music, along with other contemporary styles, could be more widely understood and appreciated when recorded. And the music repaid this favour to the technology: in 1941 the editor of *Gramophone* magazine claimed that the music of Sibelius was 'the greatest contribution that the gramophone had made to culture'.[4]

As a composer of the late nineteenth and early twentieth centuries, Sibelius occupies an interesting position: the earliest recordings of his music were made during his lifetime, yet often many years after the completion of the works in question, and even after he had ceased to compose actively. Historically, he could be compared with near-contemporary symphonists Elgar (born eight years earlier) and Mahler (born five years earlier) in that early recordings of his works offer us a glimpse into a distant musical past that is still close enough to the time of the composer to tempt us to look for signs of an 'authentic' performing practice. Like Mahler – and in contrast to Elgar and, for instance, Stravinsky – Sibelius did not leave a recorded legacy that would enable future generations to hear his own performing intentions directly.[5] Nonetheless, there are early recordings that have some particular connection with Sibelius and which we can consider partially representative of his expectations. These recordings suggest two case studies: the songs, and the symphonies, and provide a useful place to start exploring the vast collection of recordings, which include a variety of interpretative, stylistic, structural and ideological approaches.

The songs

One of the earliest recordings of Sibelius's music is the Finnish soprano Ida Ekman's performance of the song 'Svarta rosor' (Black Roses, op. 36/1), in 1906 (Scandia SLP541). Several songs from the opp. 36, 37 and 38 sets were written for or dedicated to Ekman, including 'Flickan kom ifrån sin älsklings möte' (The Tryst, op. 37/5) and 'Vår det en dröm?' (Was it a Dream?, op. 37/4), and her son, Karl, who was later to compile a colourful biography of Sibelius,[6] accompanied her on this recording. For these reasons, as Matti Huttunen has pointed out, 'it is difficult to avoid giving this interpretation the glory of an authentic performance'.[7] However, Ekman's self-imposed dotted rhythms, long pauses on high notes, and sobbing timbre in the most emotive phrases – not to mention her pianist's habit of waiting for her on the bottom note of each rippling arpeggio – may surprise those expecting a straightforward realisation of the score. Understanding this performance entails placing it in a historical context: 'Svarta rosor' dates from 1899, the same year as *Finlandia* and the First Symphony, and a time when the Finnish people's striving for independence was being strongly opposed by the Russian government. The increasing

suffering in the text of the song would have been easily interpreted by contemporary audiences as a nationalist (rather than, for instance, romantic)
sentiment:

> A rose tree is growing in my heart
> Which will never leave me in peace,
> Thorn upon thorn grows on its stems
> Causing me perpetual pain and rancour;
> For sorrow has night-black roses.

(verse 2)

The unique mix of 'artistic aims, national desires, social engagement and
entertainment' which Huttunen identifies as the motivation in such recordings gives us an insight into the heartfelt expression and drama with which
Ida Ekman performs this song.

Later recordings of 'Svarta rosor' demonstrate different approaches to
Sibelius's songs. The more literal reading in Aulikki Rautavaara's performance (with Jussi Jalas, piano, on the recording Finnlevy SFLP8570 from
1949) throws more emphasis onto the tonal drama, which moves from C
major through E major and abruptly to C♯ minor for the refrain, all structured around a pivot note of E – an approach which Huttunen links to the
composer's contemporaneous reception as a leading formalist in Britain
and America.[8] Anne Sofie von Otter (with Bengt Forsberg on BIS CD-457,
1990) creates a carefully planned melodrama by clearly portraying the opening dialogue between two different characters, and by building the tension
throughout the song. The apparent contrast of moods between the verse,
the climax, and the refrain is one of the reasons for the song's popularity
with singers – as is the range of interpretative possibilities overall: whilst
Ekman sounds overwrought in her sorrow, Rautavaara is grave and digni-
fied; Karita Mattila (with Ilmo Ranta on ODE 856–2, 1996) is mournful
and despondent, whilst von Otter's snatched phrase-endings and overall
crescendo portray a personal fury at her fate.

Von Otter's dark tone and intense dramatic expressivity, together with
her close attention to the detail of the lyrics, have made her a notable interpreter of the Scandinavian song repertory. With her fellow mezzo-soprano
Monica Groop she has produced an extensive collection of Sibelius's songs
on CD.[9] Amongst male singers, the Finn Tom Krause (with Pentti Koskimies
on Decca LXT 6046 and LXT 6314) and his compatriot Kim Borg (with Erik
Werba on DGG LPEM 19113) are outstanding: Robert Layton claims that
'Kim Borg's performances are the epitome of style in that one never questions whether it is even possible to sing these songs in any other way.'[10]
Borg is a versatile musician who has also written about these songs; he

encourages non-Scandinavian singers to explore them with confidence since the wide range of Swedish dialects mean that minor mispronunciations go unnoticed![11]

Sibelius agreed to make orchestral version of his songs only under duress, and in general was opposed to the process.[12] Criticisms of the heavy texture of the original piano parts,[13] and mention of Sibelius's apparent lack of sympathy for the piano,[14] by early British writers in particular, have been met with indignation by recent Scandinavian writers who are keen to retain the original scoring in a bid for greater 'authenticity'. But the orchestrations which Sibelius agreed to make, as well as those done by other hands, show the dark miniatures transformed into effusive colourful gems, some of which would serve as effective companion pieces to *Luonnotar*, the composer's extended vocal tone poem. Hearing these orchestral realisations permanently changes the listener's perception of Sibelius's piano scoring, and also reveals kinships with unlikely composers and genres, as is evident from Kirsten Flagstad's influential and noteworthy collection of selected Sibelius songs with the London Symphony Orchestra and Øivin Fjeldstad from 1958 (Decca SDD 248). The passionate accompaniment underneath the girl's lying words in 'Flickan kom ifrån sin älsklings möte' (op. 37/5), which blossoms into the vocal line in the final verse when she admits truthfully that she has been meeting her lover, reveals its origin in Wagnerian orchestral *Leitmotif* technique through the rich string octaves of Pingoud's orchestration. The 'Diamond on the March Snow' ('Demanten på Marssnön', op. 36/6) glitters uncharacteristically brightly in Sibelius's own orchestration, with the harp in this recording providing just the right degree of crispness, whilst the simple pattern of the melody treated to such a lush accompaniment puts one in mind of the folk-song settings made by Canteloube in *Songs of the Auvergne* (1923–30). Sibelius's opening wind-band scoring for 'Se'n har jag ej frågat mera' ('Since then I have questioned no further', op. 17/1) similarly enhances the modal qualities of this music which hint at aspects of Bartók's style. Flagstad sings throughout with unfailingly clear, rich and expressive tone, and shows interpretative subtlety where needed: for instance, she is not deceived by the ostensibly joyous exterior of the opening of 'Svarta rosor' into making a pronounced contrast between this and the sorrowful refrain, but remains impressively sombre throughout, picking up the underlying mood of the song's main character (and in this she is helped by Pingoud's orchestration which remains on the dark side of Sibelius's neutral piano arpeggios, using heavy low brass and thumping timpani in the climaxes). Though these recordings hail from the late 1950s, they remain a benchmark and a challenge to those who would prefer to hear the songs performed only with piano.

Symphonies: the early recordings

The Columbia company's pioneering recordings of the Second and First Symphonies (LX50–4 and LX65–9), sponsored by the Finnish government, were both released in 1931, and used Robert Kajanus (1856–1933) as the conductor of an unnamed 'symphony orchestra' formed from London-based players. The premiere recordings of the Fifth and Third Symphonies (HMV DB1739–42 and DB1980–3) appeared in 1932 and 1934 respectively, with the London Symphony Orchestra also conducted by Kajanus.[15] The importance of these early recordings cannot be overestimated, since Kajanus was not only a prominent figure in Finnish musical life, but also a close friend (and regular drinking partner) of Sibelius. His performances were intended to be as faithful as possible to the composer: Kajanus was once discovered hiding in the gallery of the concert hall where Sibelius was rehearsing in order to study his conducting, despite the fact that Sibelius had forbidden any spectators to be in the building.[16]

Kajanus's musical insights were appreciated by Sibelius who (according to the latter's biographer Bengt de Törne) praised his colleague's 'acquaintance with the score . . . which went far beyond even the most accurate knowledge of all his notes'.[17] This appraisal provides a clue to unlocking the secrets of the performance: Kajanus's performing style, in common with many other conductors of the early part of the century, is not a literalistic rendering of the notes but an attempt to convey the inner structure or impact of the music. Many old recordings may initially impress us with their greater degrees of rhythmic freedom and flexibility of tempo, even to the point of seeming slapdash and uncontrolled – as Robert Philip has pointed out – although this is to judge them from a more recent perspective which has come to prize accuracy more highly.[18] These observations are certainly pertinent to Kajanus's recordings, which Guy Thomas has called 'a frustrating mixture of the memorable and the untidy and sloppy'.[19]

General observations from Kajanus's performances might include the high amount of tempo fluctuation (so-called *rubato*) used[20] and their fast speed compared to later performances, in the first movements of the Second and Fifth Symphonies in particular. Comparing Kajanus's performances of Sibelius (and indeed those of any of his immediate successors) to those from the 1960s onwards confirms José Bowen's observations that 'early recordings . . . tend to contain large numbers of small tempo fluctuations', compared to later recordings of the same music, whose tempo profiles tend to be 'simply flat'.[21] Bowen also speculates that whilst performances of baroque music have become faster throughout the century, late Romantic music such as Tchaikovsky's seems to have been performed more slowly in recent years.[22] Certainly Kajanus's pioneering performance of the Fifth Symphony's first movement is one of the fastest on record, at least in its early stages: the opening portion maintains an average speed of between 60 and 70 beats per minute, whilst many later performers average about 50 beats per minute throughout this section.

Kajanus's performance of the first movement of the Fifth Symphony skilfully blends the contrasts, dramas, and gradually quickening tempo (in the second part of the movement) into a single unified experience, though not without some eventful moments: he pulls the tempo right back at the *Largamente* in bar 92 in order to quicken it again, and marks the change of key and recurrence of opening material at bar 106 with a surge in tempo. The next conductors to release recordings of this piece mostly follow this pattern: Koussevitzky, the second to go on record, produces a related pattern of ebb and flow, as do Leinsdorf, Tuxen, and Collins.[23] However Koussevitzky introduces a strikingly fast passage (during bars 69–91) that is unique amongst conductors – apart, that is, from a recording by Bernstein, his erstwhile student.[24] Bernstein was proud of his connection with Koussevitzky and frequently referred to him as 'my teacher and great friend',[25] and his interpretation of this passage shows that more than a flamboyant manner was conveyed from teacher to pupil. Other noteworthy early recordings of the Fifth include that by Gibson, whose first attempt with the London Symphony Orchestra (RCA RB16184, 1960) aroused controversy: the *Stereo Record Guide* dubbed it 'a little premature . . . This reading does not show an intellectual grasp of the symphony as a whole,'[26] whilst *Gramophone* endorsed it, calling it 'marvellously paced and splendidly controlled'.[27] In his later recordings of this work[28] Gibson ensured greater variety in the first movement by using a generous amount of tempo fluctuation in the first, exploratory, part of the movement (bars 1–105), and a more level approach in the second, scherzo-like, portion of the movement (bars 106–586). The Fifth Symphony, due to the wide range of possible contrasts within it, can thus be taken as a case study for identifying distinctive performance patterns on the large scale.

Symphonies: some later traditions

With the recordings of Herbert von Karajan, beginning in the early 1950s, a new approach entered the tradition of recordings of the Sibelius symphonies. Karajan was known for his strict orchestral discipline and longing to make (and publicise) the 'perfect' recording; thus spontaneity of interpretation was subjugated to close control of tempo, quality of tone, and impeccable ensemble.[29] This control shows in his Sibelius recordings, where Karajan has replaced faithfulness to the composer's interpretative style with faithfulness to the markings in the score – a different kind of fidelity. The resulting change of style and focus within the Sibelian tradition is typical of a wider change in interpretative fashion taking place at this time: Richard Taruskin has documented the widespread change from 'vital' to 'geometric' performance styles during the mid-twentieth century, and the positivist tendency that lies behind it.[30]

One of the most distinctive features of Karajan's Sibelius recordings, along with the increased glossiness of sound, is his use of transition between periods of stasis. For this reason Thomas considers his second reading of the Seventh Symphony 'the best of all in creating a truly seamless musical continuum'.[31] In the Fifth Symphony this takes the form of a pronounced tempo transition between the first, *molto moderato*, portion of the movement and the second part with its perpetual stretto – forming another sharp contrast with the earlier, integrated approach of Kajanus and his successors.[32] The new pattern spreads through the recorded tradition into the performances of conductors as disparate as Prêtre, Colin Davis, Ashkenazy, Salonen, and Blomstedt[33] and becomes exaggerated further, with conductors frequently doubling their speeds in as little as thirty bars. There are many possible reasons for this change in interpretative approach: the wide distribution of Karajan's recordings, the new 'geometric' fashion in performance style, the virtuosic opportunity to make a striking tempo increase, the desire to create contrast in this long and complex movement, and/or the increasing tendency to construe this passage of music as two movements, rather than one movement, could be responsible in any combination.[34] Neither the old nor the new approach is better than the other, though a desire to create contrast between the two sections can lead to some dismally slow openings to the movement, as in Colin Davis's performance with the Boston Symphony Orchestra (Philips 420 013–1, 1975): his speed of 37 beats per minute just before beginning the stretto is not within striking distance of the composer's suggested 63 beats per minute.[35]

Further examination of these recordings shows that nationality, influence, fashion, and individual temperament all have a role in shaping interpretation of Sibelius, and furthermore that the richness of his symphonic structures means that they lend themselves to many imaginable performances. One distinct school of interpretation comprises the Russian conductors, Kondrashin, Rozhdestvensky, and Horenstein, who eschew gradual tempo transition of the types found above in favour of step-like tempo levels.[36] More individualistic interpretations can be found in recordings by Celibidache, whose slow tempos and unfocused tone colours give Sibelian textures a dream-like quality,[37] and Berglund, who admirably combines structural awareness and an attractive orchestral sound with the insights gained through close study of editions.[38]

String Quartet in D minor, *Voces intimae*

Sibelius's D minor String Quartet is an outstanding example of his chamber music in terms of its maturity and critical acceptance, and as such is better represented on record than any other work within this genre. Its title *Voces intimae* ('intimate voices') was supplied by the words that Sibelius pencilled over the three *ppp* chords at bar 21 of the slow third movement. For this reason, this moment at the heart of the work needs especially careful rendering in performance. The New Helsinki Quartet, recorded in 1997 (Finlandia 3984214452), produce an ethereal and almost 'fluffy' tone at this point, the weak timbre strengthening slightly towards the end of the passage – a highly expressive interpretation. At the F major passage before Fig. 2 in the same movement, Sibelius's careful marking of *p* for the cello tune and *mp* for the syncopated violin figuration (in fact derived motivically from the preceding music) is ignored by nearly all quartets, in favour of bringing out the 'melody' more strongly in the cello; here the New Helsinki Quartet provide a reasonable compromise by balancing both parts at an approximately equal dynamic, once again revealing their sensitivity to the needs of the music. These performers are exemplary throughout the work, revealing each movement to be authentically part of the Sibelian canon: the grim quality of the fourth movement makes more sense of the marking *Allegretto (ma pesante)* than its usual rendering as a folk *Ländler*, whilst the steadiness of the finale gives it the solidity and sense of narrative it deserves.

A more surprising interpretation comes from the Voces Intimae quartet (BIS CD-10, 1974). The over-solemn tempo of the *Andante* opening of the first movement persists into the *Allegro molto moderato* at the expense of any forward motion, whilst the tenuto markings over the E^9 and C^9 chords around Fig. 2 are extended into a whole bar's *rallentando* beforehand and a pause the length of a bar, catapulting us into a weighty Elgarian sound world from which the music struggles to re-emerge. In contrast, the excessive lightness of the finale gives the impression of a continuous development section with little content. Unfortunately such performances are more common than those which show a penetrating grasp of all the work's issues, perhaps contributing to the neglect of Sibelius's chamber music compared to his symphonic works.

Representative of the early recorded tradition of this work is the Budapest String Quartet, recorded in 1933 (SH 285). They provide a brisk opening and a fast *Allegro*, with a light spiccato in the violins' figuration at bar 17, both of which allow the cello melody underneath to sound sincere and discursive rather than ponderous. The tenutos are well handled with a slight hiatus at the end of the preceding phrase, and then are gently stressed before moving off again. In general the Budapest Quartet are more literal in their approach than later interpreters – an interesting contrast to the pattern of interpretative behaviour in the song and symphonic traditions.

Other genres: Sibelius on record today

At the beginning of the twenty-first century, Sibelius still shows a healthy presence in the recording catalogues. The Violin Concerto regularly appears in the top five such pieces, as Maarti Haapakoski has pointed out: in 1990 only the Mendelssohn, Beethoven, Tchaikovsky and Bruch violin concertos had more different recordings available,[39] whereas by 1996 Brahms had displaced Bruch but Sibelius remained at number five, outshining, by more than twice the number of recordings, all comparable twentieth-century violin concertos such as those by Bartók, Prokofiev, Berg and Nielsen.[40] Currently, the situation is still impressive, with Sibelius's concerto ahead of the hugely popular Bruch G minor by eighty-one recordings to seventy-seven, and not far behind the Beethoven at 110 recordings.[41] Whilst there are good reasons for this piece's overwhelming popularity, including its institutionalisation within the quinquennial Sibelius Violin Competition in Helsinki and its consequently obligatory status for most young violinists, Sibelius compares well in other orchestral genres too: *Finlandia* shows eighty-six different recordings currently available (reasonable comparisons might be the *1812* overture which has seventy-four, or the *Egmont* with ninety), and the most-recorded Symphonies, the Second and Fifth, have fifty-six and forty-nine recordings available respectively, slightly more than most of Bruckner's symphonies and more than twice the number of any of Elgar's, Vaughan Williams's, or Nielsen's symphonies. Numbers do not tell the whole story, of course, but they do reveal that Sibelius's music remains popular with recording companies and with artists looking to sell records.

Perhaps more importantly, one can now obtain lesser-known works such as the many early chamber pieces on disc, enabling listeners to enjoy or critique these works according to temperament.[42] A notable contribution to the dissemination of Sibelius's choral music has been made by the Helsinki University Chorus (or 'YL' in Finnish), who produced a recording of *The Origin of Fire*, op. 32, in 1953 and the world premiere recording of the *Kullervo* Symphony in 1970, as well as collections of the smaller part-songs.[43] And it has been fascinating to hear Sibelius's earlier, rejected versions of the Violin Concerto and the Fifth Symphony in recorded performances by Osmo Vänskä and the Lahti Symphony Orchestra.[44]

In conclusion, the study of recordings can only reveal part of the picture, since those performances captured on record form a tiny percentage of those that take place. Nonetheless, there is much to be learnt from Sibelius recordings, which have glimpses of personal, national, and historical narratives woven into the notes. In addition, they teach us that issues of taste, fidelity, and interpretative 'accuracy' are subject to the changes of fashion, and give us an insight into the practices of a musical past which is nearly contemporary with Sibelius's compositional practice. Approaching each recording by asking 'What is it trying to achieve?', and 'What can it tell us?' rather than just 'Is it any good?' – although issues of quality and preference inevitably arise – one can better appreciate the rich resource that is Sibelius on record.[45]

15 Performing Sibelius

SIR COLIN DAVIS AND OSMO VÄNSKÄ IN
CONVERSATION WITH DANIEL M. GRIMLEY

Though Sibelius conducted the premieres of the vast majority of his major symphonic works himself, he committed none of them to record.[1] As Bethany Lowe points out in the preceding chapter, unlike with Elgar, we do not have a recorded legacy of Sibelius's interpretative view of his own music. During his lifetime, however, Sibelius enjoyed the support of a wide range of leading interpreters, from Robert Kajanus in Finland, to Sir Thomas Beecham in England and Herbert von Karajan in Germany, many of whom committed their work to recording on gramophone. The contrast with the relative lack of international interest in music of Sibelius's Danish contemporary, Carl Nielsen, is both striking and significant: the recorded reception history of the two great Nordic composers could hardly be more different.[2] Even during the period, following his death, when Sibelius's music seems to have occupied a less prominent place in the concert repertory, new recordings of his work continued to appear, and recent years have witnessed a remarkable number of new interpretations issued on compact disc.

The relationship between performance and academic criticism has sometimes seemed rather a distant and ambivalent one. The final chapter is an attempt to bridge the divide and find common ground, by examining aspects of Sibelius interpretation from the perspectives of two authoritative interpreters of his work, Sir Colin Davis and Osmo Vänskä. The two conductors were chosen not simply for their pre-eminence, but also because their work is the product of very different interpretative contexts. Davis's performances are among the most powerful and original in the Anglo-American Sibelius tradition, while Vänskä leads a younger generation of Finnish interpreters. Though their views sometimes collide, or flatly contradict each other, their thoughts reveal a shared preoccupation with issues of tempo, articulation, texture, balance and closure in the performance of Sibelius's music, and reflect their deep knowledge and appreciation of Sibelius's work.

Sir Colin Davis

Sir Colin Davis is arguably the foremost interpreter of Sibelius's music outside Finland. His outstanding symphony cycles, with the Boston and

London Symphony Orchestras, are widely regarded as landmark accounts of Sibelius's works, and Davis has also recorded many of the tone poems. At the time of the interview, Davis is shortly to begin recording a new cycle of the symphonies from live performances. Davis's interpretative view of Sibelius appears to have changed in recent years. The taut, nervous excitement of his earlier Boston and London recordings has shifted towards a more spacious reading of Sibelius's music. Davis's focus on texture, and on the sub-motivic accompanimental figuration characteristic of Sibelius's orchestral work in particular, has become increasingly intense. His recent account of *Tapiola*, for example, is one of the broadest on record, yet there is nevertheless a tremendous underlying sense of structural momentum that underpins his reading. Paradoxically, in drawing our attention so close to the surface of the music, Davis appears to have uncovered even deeper layers of Sibelius's structural imagination.

The interview takes place at the Royal Academy of Music, London, on 15 May 2002, in between Davis's conducting masterclasses on Sibelius's First Symphony. There is a sense perhaps that Davis is happier to discuss Sibelius through his performances rather than in conversation with a musicologist. By the end of the interview, however, the dialogue has become more fluent and seems to be touching on new areas of interpretation and musical meaning, tantalisingly left unexplored by the start of Davis's next masterclass.

Have you conducted much of Sibelius's music in Germany and the Mediterranean?
Only in Germany, and I shall be conducting his work there again in the autumn.

How do you find that audiences react to his music in those countries?
Not very well at all. The orchestra was very resistant to Sibelius's music. They play more Mahler, Bruckner and Brahms.

What was your first encounter with Sibelius's music? Was Sibelius being played a lot in Britain when you were training as a conductor?
I remember it was my brothers who were interested in Sibelius when I was a very small boy, aged seven or eight. They had some recordings – of the Third and Seventh Symphonies, conducted by Koussevitzky with the BBC Symphony Orchestra and Kajanus with the Helsinki Philharmonic.

Did that mean you had any sense of a Sibelius performing tradition?
No, because I was a very small boy! I simply liked the noises. Later on, I didn't like Sibelius at all. It's really old man's music.

What was the breakthrough work?
Maybe it was being made to do the Second Symphony by the London Symphony Orchestra in the Sheldonian Theatre in Oxford. I said I didn't

want to do it at first, but they insisted. It was a very dry acoustic, as I remember.

Did you find it difficult when you started conducting Sibelius in Boston?
No, they had a long tradition of playing Sibelius there because of Koussevitzky. And by that time I was completely hooked on it.

Why do you think it is 'old man's music'?
By that, I don't mean that only old men can like it! It's not really frivolously attractive music, though, is it?

It can be, bits of the Violin Concerto are, but most of the Fourth Symphony isn't.
That's true, but the texture is often very low. Sibelius's piccolo writing, for instance, is often in the bottom register of the instrument, where it's hardly audible, and in *Nightride and Sunrise* it often only doubles the bass clarinet. In my recording, we put it up an octave so that it can be heard.

I also wanted to ask you about your choice of tempo in Nightride and Sunrise, *especially towards the conclusion.*
It's such a wonderful moment. It's really slow music. It needs a lot of space, just as it needs an appropriate acoustic. You have to listen to the music, and try and find out what the pulse of it is. Sibelius's instructions were vague in any case.

Is there a tension between his tendency to qualify tempo directions, and his broad designations, such as the Allegro moderato *in* Tapiola, *which runs through the whole piece?*
Yes, but there are 105 different tempos in *Tapiola*! Tempo is never a straitjacket in Sibelius's music, it can't be.

I'm very interested by your idea of 'space'; does that refer to texture and balance as well as to tempo?
What I mean, I suppose, is that the spirit of the music seems to inhabit large spaces, even when it's travelling very fast. Sibelius creates that sense partly by using incredibly long pedal points, where it is as though you stay in a single place for a long time and stand and view the landscape and the flora and fauna. If you don't do that, what is the use of the pedal point?

How do you pace the finale of a work such as the Third Symphony?
It depends on what effect you are trying to achieve, but you have to try to create the sense that the music is inevitable. On the way, I might find that I am disobeying some of the things in the score, but I can't help that. I don't think that matters, because many composers don't fully realise what they've done. I'm not sure that Benjamin Britten, for example, ever really understood what a ferocious piece *Peter Grimes* was. That doesn't mean that

they become bad conductors, rather that there are different ways of hearing and performing things.

What sort of things do you 'disobey'?
At the beginning of the C major chorale in the finale of the Third Symphony [bar 246], for example, Sibelius writes *forte* on the first note, but only *poco forte* on the second. I can't make anything of that: Sibelius is such a strong, male spirit, it is hard not to play it in a heroic way. Perhaps he is trying to hold it back, so that it can flower more fully later in the movement, or maybe he is even slightly alarmed at what he himself has written.

Do you think the same about the closing bars of the Fourth Symphony, where Sibelius marks absolutely nothing? Is that how it should be played?
The music is absolutely indifferent. It should be played exactly straight, at least, that's always what I do, I think that's absolutely right. It is such a peculiar movement. That is his genius: everything starts off beautifully, nature is smiling, but after a few minutes the most appalling things happen, and it is all mangled up. The carnage is appalling, and he buries the lot and smooths it over under the A minor chords. It's like patting the earth on a grave.

Isn't there always that ambivalence about Sibelius's endings, even when the music seems outwardly optimistic?
Yes. The finale of the Third Symphony is especially interesting, because the music is a hunt. I have a suspicion that it is a hunt to get the F♯ out of the way. The other interesting detail, in those final pages, is that there is no B♭: there is no attempt to bring up the subdominant. He uses an A♭, of course, but there is no flattened seventh, which would have been the usual classical means of signalling closure.

That reminds me of the ending of the Seventh Symphony too, where he pointedly resolves the B♮ to the C. How would you describe the quality of those endings in Sibelius? Is it a sense of hyper-sharp consonance, as though the subdominant clouds the clarity of the tonic in some way? Or does it have a darker undertone?
Well, the end of the Seventh Symphony is a very bleak affair. After the hurricane, the wind screeching through the music, Sibelius finally begins to pray, but the undertakers are already there. The last bar is like closing the coffin lid. But then think what happens to the C major trombone tune: it gets smashed to pieces during the piece. It's as though all human ideas are doomed to the most appalling failure.

That would also provide a suitable context for the allusion to Valse triste *on the final page.*
Yes, but the way the symphony begins is so tragic as well. A simple C major scale, that hits A♭ minor. And then he gropes through all the twelve tones save one, before he finally reaches the light of the subdominant.

What's remarkable about Sibelius's music, in that sense, is that he is able to create so much out of such straightforward material. I've always been puzzled by the Sixth Symphony, which is based on very simple dorian harmony with various chromatic and whole-tone inflections, yet the way he puts things together in that work seems so complex and problematic.

In the first movement, for example, we reach a Neapolitan on E♭, but the brass intone a C major chord, in order to deny the resolution. Yet, perversely, very near the beginning there is a VII^7 chord with a C♯, which gives rise to the beginning of the second movement.

What strikes me especially about that link is the way that, metrically, the second movement effectively begins in the duple time of the preceding Allegro before moving into a regular triple time, without ever actually changing metre.

It's madness, nobody knows what to do with it. And the ending of that movement is very strange also.

Do you feel as though nature is a mocking presence rather than a contemplative one at that moment?

It's always transient, something which cannot be captured. Did he actually see anything in the woods, or was it an apparition? The forest is, after all, an alarming place. To be alone, to wander off and get lost in the forest, is terrifying. Wherever you look, it all looks the same. The opening of the Sixth Symphony, for example, is a vast expanse of sky, with blues, greys and violets. I suppose what we take from the music is a sense of our own insignificance.

Not simply a Finnish landscape, but a global or cosmic one?

Yes, but it is also a landscape of the soul.

Such nature gestures seem especially prominent in Sibelius's later music. What role do you think they play in earlier works such as Nightride and Sunrise?

Nightride and Sunrise is probably the most obsessive piece that has ever been written. It's infernally difficult for the strings to play the ride rhythm quietly but accurately. But the effort is worth it, because when the rhythm finally stops, when we finally break out of this manic, Kafka-like space, it's like opening a window into another world. The storm conjured up by the three spirits in *The Oceanides* is terrifying, but it's pent-up sexual frustration.

How difficult is it to get the balance right in Sibelius's music?

It is hard, because there has to be an element of mystery and weirdness about it. You don't want to look at all of the detail under a microscope.

Does that mean that some things are half heard?

Yes, and that doesn't matter. You have to play some passages without any effort as though they are of no interest at all, and then they sound wonderful. Those are the kind of textures in the first movement of the Fifth Symphony.

The music begins in bright sunshine, but when the strings enter, a mist rises, and unmentionable things appear peeping through the gloom.

Does that colour the way we hear the end of the work? The final chords almost seem as much a negation as a moment of transcendence or summation.
We don't know what they are. He mangles the tune harmonically. Those chords seem to punctuate the absence of the tune. There's an entry in Sibelius's diary where he goes for a walk in autumn and writes 'scent of decay – muted *fortissimo*', and that seems to capture the mood at the end of the Fifth Symphony.

Is there a similar feeling at the end of Elgar's later works? Both composers share an intense awareness of nature and of the transience of things.
I love Elgar's music, especially the Second Symphony, but Sibelius is a more rugged and original composer. And he does things that no other person has done, because of this quality of unquiet and disruption. And that quality is there in works as early as the *Kullervo* Symphony. I think the girl's lament in the third movement is one of the most beautiful things he ever wrote. The method is incredibly primitive in some senses: but the effect of space and loneliness created by the vocal line over the woodwind ostinato is incredibly moving.

I'd like to ask you about the First Symphony. How do you pace the opening of the Allegro?
It's like much of his music. The opening is made up of scraps of melody that appear all over the place. He composes more like Mozart than Beethoven (except in the *Missa solemnis*): all of the melodies are sufficiently alike, and yet different: everything is related, but it cannot be proved. Where I think Sibelius is especially clever is the way he overlaps layers. In the slow movement of the Fifth Symphony, there are almost two different thought processes going on side by side.

Yes, in Tapiola *that effect of superimposed layers can seem jagged or painful. Could you ever imagine conducting Sibelius with a chamber orchestra, as Paavo Berglund has done?*
No, because you need that weight of sound, for instance at the apotheosis of the string tune at the end of the slow movement of the Fourth Symphony. It's not loudness so much as a body of sound.

What quality or weight does the end of the Seventh Symphony have?
It has to be dark, almost mahogany-coloured. It's hair-raising. The violin pizzicato D [bar 521] is the end of the world. In the final chord, Sibelius writes the strings *fortissimo*, and then the brass *fortissimo* but *diminuendo*, but that doesn't seem to work. It withdraws support, and no amount of

strings can compensate for the loss of the brass at that point. I alter the final chord slightly, by not allowing the brass to fade away too far. They drop down so that the strings can be heard, but then come back up again. It sounds more final that way.

Osmo Vänskä

Among the remarkably gifted younger generation of Finnish conductors, including Leif Segerstam, Esa-Pekka Salonen, Jukka-Pekka Saraste, and Sakari Oramo, Osmo Vänskä's commitment to performing and recording Sibelius's music is outstanding. His interpretations, with the Lahti Symphony Orchestra and the BBC Scottish Symphony Orchestra, have won widespread critical acclaim for their intense, high-octane energy. Vänskä has made a major commitment, through the complete cycle of Sibelius's music on the BIS label, to recording newly discovered or hitherto unknown works by Sibelius. The first commercially released performances of the first versions of the Fifth Symphony and the Violin Concerto, for example, have given scholars a unique insight into Sibelius's compositional process, and Vänskä's account of the complete incidental music for *The Tempest* has added immeasurably to our appreciation of Sibelius's mysterious late work. At the same time, Vänskä's recordings of the symphonies have often offered new interpretative perspectives on seemingly familiar music. In the most positive sense, Vänskä's interpretations challenge our received view of Sibelius, and continue to provoke new questions about the meaning of Sibelius's music.

The interview is held, somewhat incongruously, in the foyer of the Hyatt hotel in Birmingham, on 22 March 2002, as Vänskä is preparing to conduct a concert featuring Sibelius's work in Symphony Hall. Despite the surroundings, the conversation quickly shifts to a detailed discussion of technical aspects of Sibelius's music, many of which are reflected in the following dialogue. Vänskä brings with him a score of the Seventh Symphony, and the interview lasts well over an hour and a half – significantly longer than scheduled. The discussion is brought to a close only reluctantly, Vänskä looking forward to a well-earned Easter vacation in Lapland with his family.

Do you think there is an authentic way of playing Sibelius? Is there a definitive interpretation which comes from the score and the composer?
As far as I know, that is not the Finnish tradition at all; it is doing something other than what is written in the score. Someone once described the tradition as a collection of common mistakes, and without wishing to be too cynical, I think that probably is the case. The tradition partly consists of exaggeration, so that every *pocchissimo ritenuto* or *diminuendo* becomes *moltissimo*. That

doesn't come from the score at all. It is the same with some of Sibelius's rhythms. They may be hard to play, but conductors tend to follow what they think they know, rather than what Sibelius has actually written.

If we remember what musical life was like in Helsinki at the end of the nineteenth century, there was only a single orchestra, Kajanus's Helsinki Philharmonic Society, and they gave most (though not all) of Sibelius's premieres. That gives us an idea of how limited Sibelius's resources were at this time: only one orchestra, those players, and I think he knew the players individually. For instance, we know that Sibelius never wrote anything for the tuba after the Second Symphony, when the tuba player came in drunk one night and destroyed the whole thing: played wrong notes, came in at the wrong points. During the rehearsal, Sibelius understood that it was better to write a certain way than to get angry with the musicians and cause trouble for the next premiere. And then when another conductor came to conduct the same piece later on, the orchestra could say: but this is how the composer wanted it. It is difficult to be certain, but they probably conceived of the music in big lines, rather than concentrating on all the details in the way that we do now. But then he has written all these things in his score.

Yes, Sibelius is the master of the tiniest nuance. His scores are full of incredibly precise directions such as pocchissimo largamente. *And then he seems to be almost obsessive about their accuracy: I'm thinking particularly of the way that he uses directions such as* Andante mosso quasi allegretto, *for instance. When you go about preparing a complex score such as the Seventh Symphony, do you feel that you have to get these things exactly right?*
Yes, I try to get them all fixed in advance, and I use a lot of metronome markings. In particular, I try to get the correct relation between two different tempos. Of course, Sibelius himself didn't use many metronome marks, except very occasionally such as in the First Symphony, and when they are there I try to follow them exactly. But otherwise I spend a lot of time playing or singing through the music and fixing my own metronome markings in advance. I have also referred to Sibelius's own manuscripts a lot in my recordings.

How important are the manuscripts for your work?
You can trust them totally. There are never any wrong notes in his manuscripts, even when his handwriting is unclear. For example, the way that he indicates a *diminuendo* or an accent: very often, they are meant to be both. That was entirely new for me. He sometimes uses an accent that is a little longer than usual, but not a *diminuendo*. And when we think about what this kind of accent actually means, you have to play with a heavier start and then a lighter release.

So it's more a matter of weight than of volume?
Yes, that's right. Not a sharp attack, but something more gradual. And that's just one single example.

Accents are a particular problem in the Seventh Symphony. It's not always clear from the printed score how he wanted them played, especially in the strings.
In the printed score the copyist marked them as *diminuendos*, and there are a lot of similar mistakes. In the manuscript it is very clear what he wanted, but it is often difficult to print such things exactly as they are written in the score. Sometimes the mark is just a few millimetres either side of a note, but it is always obvious what he means.

Do you think there is one basic tempo that underlies pieces such as the Seventh Symphony or Tapiola? *Your performance of* Tapiola *is one of the fastest on record, but there is a compelling sense of coherence, so that everything within the piece relates to everything else.*
There are only three real tempos in *Tapiola*. There is the tempo at the opening [*Largamente*], then comes an *Allegro moderato*, and then nothing. Usually people slow down, but it should be exactly the same as before. Then comes an *Allegro*, and then *Allegro moderato* again, followed by the storm, so there are really only these three tempos in the whole piece. For me, that works. Balance is also very important. When the strings start to play their ostinato [at Fig. C] and the woodwind enter, most conductors add an extra *diminuendo* in the strings to allow more space for the woodwind. But that is not marked. I try to imagine what it is like in a forest, as the wind starts to rise and becomes stronger and stronger. The woodwind do not need to be so clear at first, they are meant to be within this string texture. So there are a lot of good reasons to trust what Sibelius wrote, and if I can do exactly what the manuscript says, there is no need to change anything.

Do you think landscape is a very important element in Sibelius's music?
[Laughs] Foreign people always ask that!

That's why I'm asking about it! For British people, Sibelius is often perceived as a great landscape composer. Is that something, as a Finnish conductor, you feel impatient with?
Maybe I am too used to it! I don't think that so much. But the forest is certainly an underlying presence in his music. For example, we have sometimes played Sibelius in Lahti when the timpanist has been ill, and it changes dramatically when the timpani are not there. Everything seems so dry, the music loses its feeling of echo. It might be frustrating for the player to play ten minutes of *pianissimo*, but if you take it away, everything is changed. And I think Sibelius deliberately wrote this kind of 'pedal noise' that you hear in the forest.

It's almost a kind of rustling, or a feeling of something moving.
Yes, you don't recognise it when it is there, but you sense when it isn't.

Is the same true for tempos in the Seventh Symphony?
Again, there are not as many tempos as people often think. The beginning is *Adagio* until four bars before Fig. F. Then he marks *un pocchettino meno adagio*, less and less slow, then in the manuscript he very clearly marks *a tempo* (and not *primo tempo*) one bar before G. So this is a place where we have to play a little bit slower, and the strings are marked *tenuto*. But this *a tempo* doesn't negate the previous *meno adagio*. Sibelius marks *poco a poco affrettando* after Fig. I, which I think is always a local effect, intended to ensure that the general accelerando is still going towards *vivacissimo*. Paavo Berglund told me that *vivacissimo* means just what it says: faster than *vivace*. Personally, I find it difficult to do, but he's right, and I've just taken a metronome marking for myself that seems to fit. The next event is a return to an *Adagio* [Fig. L] that should be exactly the same as the opening (for the second appearance of the trombone theme). Then *poco a poco meno lento* [two bars after Fig. M], which allows us to set the next marking, *Allegro molto moderato* [at bar 258]. This is always difficult for the orchestra because they have to play both faster and softer, and that seems unnatural. Then *un pocchetino affrettando* to *allegro moderato* [bar 285], followed by Sibelius's longest accelerando apart from the Fifth Symphony (first movement), from *Vivace* [bar 409] to *Presto* [bar 449] and a final return to *Adagio* [bar 476].

That is the section I particularly wanted to ask you about, because it seems to be the hardest change of gear in the whole work.
Exactly. The trombone theme is like Sarastro in *The Magic Flute*, it is always the same. One typical mistake, which I have made myself, is at bar 463, where it says *subito piano* in the first and second violins and *mezzo forte* in the violas and cellos. Usually, people bring everything down here, but that is not what is actually written. At the start of the *Presto*, the repeated notes are all *pianississimo*, and the moving notes *piano*. When the *Poco a poco rallentando* starts, I begin to play the moving notes longer, so that they become gradually heavier and heavier until they stop.

Another important detail is the change from *fortississimo* to *forte* in bar 500. It is as if the strings are screaming at Fig. Z, but by the fifth bar they are only crying to themselves. That is very typical for Sibelius: when there are a lot of tears, they are much more sad and introverted. For the Seventh Symphony, the *Adagio* is central, and everything comes from that. In *Tapiola*, it is the *Allegro moderato* tempo. Sibelius said to Jussi Jalas that the tempo changes indicated in his scores should be so slight that people are hardly aware of them. The finale of the Fifth Symphony is another good example. The tradition is to play the *pocchettino largamente* [Fig. N, bars 407ff.] very broad and loud, but it is only *mezzo forte* and the tempo change is 'un pocchettino'. That was a turning point for me. The triplets in the original version have to go smoothly together with the new tempo. So why do we do so much in the final version? And then I realised it said 'pocchettino', and I wondered why everything in the Finnish tradition is so extreme. In my opinion, we should make much less of the differences, and follow what the composer wrote more closely.

Was this Finnish interpretative tradition something you learnt as a student at the Sibelius Academy in Jorma Panula's conducting class?
No, it was earlier. Panula was not so much a Sibelius conductor, but I think he was the first to conduct a complete Mahler cycle in Finland. People listened to Jussi Jalas very carefully because he had the family connections with Sibelius, and we know that he had a lot of discussions with Sibelius about certain things. Since then, the most important conductor has been Paavo Berglund. We know something about Kajanus, and it's funny, people tell me that my performance of the First Symphony is very close to his. I listened to it ten years ago or so, but the parallel is not something I deliberately tried to create, it's just coincidence and what I have learnt from the score. When I was young, I remember going to a concert with my parents in Kotka when Leif Segerstam, who must have been about eighteen or nineteen, conducted a youth orchestra and they played the Fifth Symphony. I didn't know anything about the Finnish tradition at the time, it just seemed the Finnish way of doing it.

What has it been like conducting the original versions of some pieces? Did you encounter a lot of opposition?
Not really. A lot of people have asked why when there are the other versions, but I think they've understood in the end. It is partly because of the record company, BIS: they are recording a complete cycle, and they want to include every single note that Sibelius wrote. That was the reason why it first came to the table, and of course I had to think about it very carefully. The whole intention of those recordings was not to create a scandal, but to give people an opportunity to follow a little of the creative process through which Sibelius worked. Another important thing for me is the question of how he could find energy to revise and rewrite these works. After all, the first version of the Violin Concerto is not a bad piece, it's just different!

A lot of people in the Lahti Orchestra prefer the original version of *En saga*, as did Aino Sibelius. My own theory is that, when he was accused by one German critic of writing 'local Nordic music', Sibelius tried to find out what was so Nordic about his music so that he could take it out. As a result, he cut all of the links with the *Kullervo* Symphony out of *En saga*, and that was why he revised the work.

Is that why he also withdrew The Wood Nymph?

Actually, he didn't. He wanted to rework it. It's always been in the University Library, but people such as Erik Tawaststjerna have always felt that it wasn't such a strong work. The manuscript is full of crossings out, it's very difficult to read, so I used the parts they prepared for the last performance in the 1930s to help to know where to go. It's a tremendous piece. He never managed to revise it, but nothing is wrong with the music. Sibelius never forbade performance of *The Wood Nymph*.

One of the things you've done especially well, I feel, is put his incidental music back in its rightful place as among his most important music. When I listen to your recording of the complete Karelia *music, for instance, I'm struck by the thought that he left all the best music out of the concert suite.*

I totally agree. He was very good at incidental music, and had a genuine understanding for drama. And he was extremely good at writing short pieces of music, especially in *The Tempest*. He knew exactly what to do.

How do you perform the Tempest *music in concert?*

We have done it several times using a narrator for Prospero's monologues. *Everyman* and *Belshazzar's Feast* also work very well in concert. I think they could be done in the theatre with a good director, but the music has lasted much longer than the original productions, and the audience can always use their imagination in the concert hall. I've always wondered why he left one single number out of the *Pelleas* suite. It has a very beautiful solo for cor anglais, and we have often used it as an encore. But it is virtually the only piece left out of the suite, and he included some much less important music.

I also wanted to ask you about the Sixth Symphony, and in particular about the final bars, because that work seems to have caused a good deal of controversy. What do you think the Sixth Symphony is about, and what does the ending mean? Is it a positive or negative conclusion?

Both! I have my own thoughts on the work, based on my own experience of the symphony and what I know about Sibelius's family circumstances when he wrote it. He was sixty when he wrote the piece, and for me the whole symphony is a kind of confession. I think it is an open summary of his life. He felt that his composing was getting slower, and he was old and honest enough to understand that he would not realise all of his ambitions or ideals. He couldn't be a marvellous husband or who knows what else. The ending is both positive and negative, because life continues. For instance, if someone very close to you becomes ill, you have to accept it and go on. This is a very common feeling in Sibelius's music. When I last conducted the Fifth Symphony in Birmingham, I was crying for the last two minutes. Everyone describes it as a triumphant work, but I don't think so. There is always this element of ambivalence in Sibelius's music, as though the music sounds 'through the tears'. There is always this kind of shadow. Maybe it's a Finnish thing, I don't know.

Do you feel that about the Fifth Symphony because you've conducted the original version?
Yes, that's a good question. Actually, it immediately reminds me of the ending of the first movement in the original version. It's often said that there is a great leap from the Fourth Symphony to the Fifth, but if you listen to the original version it is not such a big step, especially if you consider the use of dissonance at the end of the first movement and in the finale. When we rehearsed that for the first time, the players were quite shocked, because it sounds so dramatic. There is always an element present in Sibelius's music that lies on the other side of happiness; there are no happy moments without that counterpoint.

That's especially true of the Sixth Symphony, I think, which seems so precariously balanced.
It's classical; you cannot take a single note away from it. Incidentally, I can never do a *ritenuto* at the end of the Sixth Symphony. It's not notated, but a lot of people do it when the string chorale starts [bar 224]. The same thing at the end of the Fourth Symphony. Again, I would like to say to young conductors: trust what he wrote. It is too easy to try and change things if they don't work first time round, but I think that is a big mistake.

So, do you think that young conductors should go out into the forest if they want to understand the 'screaming' and the 'tears'?
I think that's a good idea. If we compare this music with Haydn and Mozart, the same elements are there, but there are many more details. If you don't know what happens to the theme, for instance, it's very hard to get the right balance. You need to find out from the score what the most important things are, if you are to understand the large-scale form.

Does that mean you have a fixed idea of what the background and foreground of the music are before you start?
Not so much from the outside, but I need to know where the important events are if I am going to understand why something is marked *forte* and something else is marked *piano*. For example in the Second Symphony, second movement, when the strings start to play *pianississimo* in F♯ major, Jalas reports that Sibelius wrote 'Christus' in the manuscript. And where the trombone theme first enters in the Seventh Symphony, he wrote 'this must be played as though in front of the face of God'. And it is so obvious how you have to play the music. Those kind of things tell us so much. So perhaps that's why I cry so much at the end of the Fifth Symphony!

Might it also be to do with the silences between the chords at the end of the Fifth Symphony? Everything has become so final that it cannot be entirely triumphant.

It could be. There are no fermatas, everything is printed in tempo. It's unbelievably well written. I try and count the beats in concert now. I think he knew exactly what he wrote.

Does that explain your tempos in the First Symphony?

Yes. The first movement is written ♩ = 104, but no one takes it that fast apart from Kajanus. I think Sibelius lived long enough to change the marking, if he felt it was wrong. The second movement is 52, exactly half the basic tempo of the first movement, which also gives the feeling of a genuine *Andante*, not *Adagio*. I conducted the first movement many times with a slower tempo, but one day I took my metronome and realised the music was totally different. Before that work he had written the *Kullervo* Symphony and the *Lemminkäinen* suite, but this was still his first symphony, and I think that was a kind of milestone. He was about thirty-four years old, and we know what a wild character he had as a young man – not so typically Finnish! So his tempo marking, *Allegro energico*, is young man's music! And I believe this faster tempo must be correct: he wanted it to be wild as well. People have told me that, once they have heard this faster version, they cannot listen to the music any slower. Often, when we think about Sibelius's music, we have the photos of him as an old man in our mind, but he was a young hero when he wrote that symphony. This has been such a great discovery for me, there's a sense that the door has opened a little for me to see through.

Notes

Introduction

1. 'The Silence', *Granta* 76: *Music* (Winter 2001), pp. 137–47.
2. Erik Tawaststjerna, *Sibelius. Vol. III: 1914–1957*, trans. Robert Layton (London: Faber, 1997).
3. *Farewell, My Youth* (London: Longman, 1943), p. 61.
4. James Hepokoski, 'Sibelius, Jean (Julius Christian)', *The New Grove Dictionary of Music and Musicians*, second edn, ed. Stanley Sadie and John Tyrrell (London: Macmillan, 2001), vol. XXIII, pp. 319–47.
5. Balilla Pratella, 'Manifesto of Futurist Musicians 1910', in Umbro Apollonio (ed.), *Futurist Manifestos* (London: Thames and Hudson, 1973), p. 33 (first published in *Musica futurista per orchestra riduzione per pianoforte*, Bologna, 1912).
6. James Hepokoski, *Sibelius: Symphony no. 5* (Cambridge: Cambridge University Press, 1993).

1 The national composer and the idea of Finnishness

1. Both Carl Dahlhaus and James Hepokoski have used the term modernist to describe the music of a generation of composers born around 1860 (see Dahlhaus, *Nineteenth-Century Music*, trans. J. Bradford Robinson [Berkeley: University of California Press, 1998], pp. 332–7, and Hepokoski, *Sibelius: Symphony no. 5* [Cambridge: Cambridge University Press, 1993], pp. 3–4), for whom Wagner was a crucial precursor.
2. See the discussion in Hepokoski's monograph, *Sibelius: Symphony no. 5*, especially pp. 1–18.
3. On the concept of national originality, see Carl Dahlhaus, 'Einleitung', *Neues Handbuch der Musikwissenschaft, vol. 5: Die Musik des 18. Jahrhunderts*, ed. Carl Dahlhaus with Ludwig Finscher (Laaber: Laaber Verlag, 1985), p. 19; Ilkka Oramo, 'Beyond Nationalism', in Tomi Mäkelä (ed.), *Music and Nationalism in Twentieth-Century Great Britain and Finland* (Hamburg: von Boeckel, 1997), pp. 35–43.
4. See Otto Andersson, *John Josef Pippingskiöld och musiklivet i Åbo 1808–1827* (Helsinki: Åbo Akademi, 1921).

5. On Kajanus's *Aino* see Matti Vainio, *'Nouskaa aatteet!' Robert Kajanus: Elämä ja taide* (Helsinki: WSOY, 2002), pp. 194ff.
6. Erkki Salmenhaara, *Suomen musiikin historia II: Kansallis-romantiikan valtavirta 1885–1918* (Porvoo: Werner Soderström, 1998), pp. 65–8.
7. Erik Tawaststjerna, *Sibelius. Vol. I, 1865–1905*, trans. Robert Layton (London: Faber, 1976), pp. 141–61.
8. Ibid., p. 143.
9. See Matti Huttunen, 'Sibeliuksen nuoruudenkriisin sosiaalihistoriallinen ulottuvuus', in Irma Vierimaa, Kari Kilpeläinen and Anne Sivuoja-Gunaratnam (eds.), *Siltoja ja synteesejä: Esseitä semiotiikasta, kulttuurista ja taiteesta* (Helsinki: Gaudeamus, 1998).
10. Tibor Kneif, 'Der Gegenstand musiksoziologischen Erkenntnis', *Archiv für Musikwissenschaft* 23 (1966); Dahlhaus, 'Zur Theorie der musikalischen Gattungen', *Systematische Musikwissenschaft*, ed. Carl Dahlhaus and Helga de la Motte-Haber (Laaber: Laaber Verlag, 1982).
11. Kotilainen, *Mestarin muokattavana* (Aulos, 1925).
12. The episode is described in Tawaststjerna/Layton, *Sibelius. Vol. I*, pp. 190–8.
13. See William Weber's studies in reception history, *Music and the Middle Class: The Social Structure of Concert Life in London, Paris and Vienna* (London: Croom Helm, 1975), and *The Rise of Musical Classics in Eighteenth-Century England: A Study in Canon, Ritual, and Ideology* (Oxford: Clarendon, 1992).
14. *Uusi Suometar*, 24 May 1891.
15. Karl Flodin, *Die Musik in Finnland* (Helsinki: 1900). The Helsinki Philharmonic Society's European tour in 1900 comprised Sweden, Norway and Germany, and culminated in concerts that were given at the Paris World Exhibition. Kajanus conducted the orchestra, which was specially enlarged for the tour, and Sibelius's First Symphony received its foreign premiere in Stockholm. Sibelius accompanied the orchestra as an assistant conductor, but as far as we know did not conduct any concerts.
16. Furuhjelm, *Jean Sibelius: hans tondiktning och drag ur hans liv* (Borgå: Holder Schildts Forlag, 1916).

17. Haapanen, *Suomen säveltaide* (Helsinki: Otava, 1940).
18. See Fabian Dahlström, 'Otto Andersson och Jean Sibelius', in Vierimaa, Kilpeläinen and Sivuoja-Gunaratnam (eds.), *Siltoja ja synteesejä*.
19. Haapanen, *Suomen säveltaide*, p. 99.
20. Cecil Gray, *Sibelius* (London: Oxford University Press, 1931 [1934]).
21. See, for example, the discussions in Erik Tawaststjerna, *Sibelius, Vol. III, 1914–1957*, trans. Robert Layton (London: Faber, 1997), pp. 290–304, and Kari Kilpeläinen, 'Sibelius Eight. What happened to it?', *Finnish Musical Quarterly* (1995), pp. 30–5.

2 Vienna and the genesis of *Kullervo*

1. A German-language version of this article entitled 'Wien und die Entstehung von *Kullervo*' was presented at the Vienna symposium 'Jean Sibelius: Begründer der nordischen Moderne', in conjunction with the first performance of the complete cycle of Sibelius symphonies in Vienna by Jukka-Pekka Saraste and Finland's Radio Symphony Orchestra, 10–13 April 2002.
2. With the preparation for the first publication of a critical edition of *Kullervo*, investigating these experiences has become fundamentally important. The symphony will appear in the *Jean Sibelius Works* edition, vol. I/1.1–3, 1a (Wiesbaden: Breitkopf und Härtel, in press), ed. Glenda Dawn Goss. Discussion of the work's genre designation together with other relevant issues, including the importance of the early brass-septet writing, will appear in those volumes.
3. The letters to Aino Järnefelt, as well as those to Martin Wegelius, are preserved in Finland's National Archives and, together with other primary sources described in this chapter, furnished the basis for the present study. Unless otherwise indicated, all translations are the author's. For secondary studies on the intellectual atmosphere in Vienna during the time Sibelius studied there, see Peter Berner, Emil Brix and Wolfgang Mantl (eds.), *Wien um 1900: Aufbruch in die Moderne* (Munich: R. Oldenbourg Verlag, 1986); William A. Johnston, *The Austrian Mind: An Intellectual and Social History 1848–1938* (Berkeley: University of California Press, 1972); Alfred Schick, 'The Vienna of Sigmund Freud', *Psychoanalytic Review* 55/4 (1968–9), pp. 530–51; and Carl E. Schorske, *Fin-de-siècle Vienna: Politics and Culture* (New York: Alfred A. Knopf, 1980).
4. 'Jag har trott mig vara melankolisk men nu tror jag att Gud skapte mig för glädjen.' Sibelius, autograph letter signed (hereafter ALS) to Wegelius, 25 October 1890. Sibelius's nineteen

original letters to Martin Wegelius, the whereabouts of which were unknown for many years, were deposited at the National Archives only in 2001. My special thanks to Gita Henning, who assisted in the transcription and interpretation of the most difficult passages in these documents.
5. 'Tänk nu t[il] ex[emple] Wien i eftermiddags sol och värme, ett bref från Aino och rekommendationer samt penningar från Dig.' ALS to Wegelius, 19 November 1890.
6. Mark Twain, 'Stirring Times in Austria', *Harper's, A New Monthly Magazine* (1898), p. 532.
7. 'I synnerhet efter nederlag blir jag som stål numera.' ALS to Wegelius, 11 January 1891.
8. Johnston writes a thought-provoking chapter entitled 'Fascination with death' in *The Austrian Mind*, pp. 165–80.
9. Wolfgang Amadeus Mozart, 4 April 1787; quoted from *The Letters of Mozart and His Family, Chronologically Arranged*, ed. and trans. Emily Anderson (London: 1938), vol. III, 1351.
10. 'Hvar månne nu Sibelius finnas? Jag tycker numera alltid att en person är bakom mig. Månne det vara döden som är på lur?' ALS to Wegelius, 21 November 1890.
11. Helsinki University Library manuscript 0419 [p. 78].
12. Johnston, *The Austrian Mind*, p. 249.
13. Helsinki University Library ms 0419, [pp. 141–2].
14. Freud entered the University of Vienna in 1873 and, with the exception of some weeks in Paris during 1885, carried out his studies in that city until his departure for London in 1939.
15. See especially Erik Tawaststjerna, *Sibelius. Vol. I, 1865–1905*, trans. Robert Layton (London: Faber, 1976), pp. 69–95; Peter Revers, 'Jean Sibelius and Vienna', in *The Sibelius Companion*, ed. Glenda Dawn Goss (Westport: Greenwood, 1996), pp. 13–34, and the recent symposium '*Jean Sibelius und Wien*, ed. Hartmut Krones (Vienna: Böhlam, 2003).
16. Sibelius communicated this important piece of information to Wegelius in a previously ignored passage of a November letter that reads, 'Gevaerts' Instr. [sic] lära har jag erhållit, har genomgått den redan'. ALS to Wegelius, 13 November 1890. The composer's copy of the treatise is preserved today in the Helsinki University Library's Sibelius Collection 206.99. The flyleaf bears the stamp of the Vienna bookshop Musikalien-Handlung Emil Bertie & Cie. Wien, 1 Kärtnerring Nr. 6. Receipts from the same shop preserved in the Sibelius Family Archive (National Archives, Helsinki) show that Sibelius also purchased there the Prelude to

Wagner's *Die Meistersinger von Nürnberg*,
Goldmark's overture *Im Frühling*, a Bruckner
symphony, Ries's Op. 27, Vieuxtemps' Opp. 10
and 37, and Saint-Saëns' Op. 20.
17. *Neue Instrumenten-Lehre von F. A. Gevaert.*
Ins deutsche übersetzt von Dr. Hugo Riemann
(Paris and Brussels: Lemoine & Fils, 1887);
German edition, Leipzig, Breitkopf und Härtel.
18. 'Der Grundzug ihres Wesens ist
Offenherzigkeit: kein Instrument drückt mit so
überzeugender Wahrheit aus, was es überhaupt
auszudrücken vermag.' Gevaert,
Instrumenten-Lehre, p. 144.
19. 'Du skall få se att mitt nya opus gör furore
hos Dig, engel. Det är allt sant der.' ALS to Aino
Järnefelt, 29 February 1892.
20. 'Dieses rein rhythmische Instrument ist
sozusagen autochthon spanisch.' Gevaert,
Instrumenten-Lehre, p. 343.
21. 'I går var jag hos en cello virtuos, en bulgar
Diminico. Jag skref åtskilliga melodier åt
honom, alla finska folkmelodier eller baserade
på dem. Han var mycket anslagen af dem, tyckte
de voro så originala och melodiosa.' ALS to Aino
Järnefelt, 24 December 1890.
22. ALS to Aino Järnefelt, 12 March 1891.
23. For a lucid discussion of this phenomenon
vis-à-vis Sibelius, see William A. Wilson,
'Sibelius, the *Kalevala*, and Karelianism', in
Goss (ed.), *The Sibelius Companion*, pp. 43–60.
24. 'I hans digter finner jag det mesta verkliga af
allt hvad hag hittals läst.' ALS to Aino Järnefelt,
2 November 1890.
25. 'Jag tänker taga saken mycket mera
"verkligt" än förut. I verkligheten är äfven
mycket musik.' ALS to Aino Järnefelt, 24
December 1890.
26. 'Die Moderne', *Moderne Dichtung*, 1 January
1890, p. 15. The English translation is quoted
from *Vienna 1890–1920*, ed. Robert
Waissenberger (London: Alpine Fine Arts
Collection, 1984), p. 244.
27. See, for example, the discussion in George
C. Schoolfield (ed.), *A History of Finland's*
Literature (Lincoln, NE, and London: University
of Nebraska Press, 1998), pp. 83–99. Further
examination of both the literary and the artistic
context for the *Kullervo* Symphony will appear
in conjunction with the author's forthcoming
Kullervo edition.
28. 'Har Du läst förut något af Zolá? Det är min
man.' ALS to Aino Järnefelt, 9 April 1891.
29. 'Skada att jag ej mera läst dylik
skönlitteratur utan hållit mig till Zola et
consortes.' ALS to Wegelius, 4 May 1891.
30. See George Holden's introduction to *Nana*
(Harmondsworth: Penguin, 1982), p. 11. Zola
had planned the novel as part of a saga to study
the effects of heredity and environment on

members of a single family in order to trace the
passage of madness and disease.
31. ALS to Wegelius, 9 April 1891; ALS to Aino,
29 February 1892.
32. See Helmi Krohn, *Suomalaisen oopperan*
ensimäinen tähti: Emmy Achtén elämä ja työ
(Helsinki: Otava, 1927), p. 118.
33. For an evaluation of *Yksin*, see Irma
Rantavaara, 'A Nation in Search of Identity,
Finnish Literature 1830–1917', in *The Modern*
World II. Realities, ed. David Daiches and
Anthony Thorlby (London: Aldus Books, 1972),
p. 344. As Irma Rantavaara observes of Aho at
this moment, 'the rightness of combining
realism and Romanticism became clear to him
and formed the literary credo to which he was to
remain faithful'.
34. 'Det der ur Kalevala (Soitto on murehista
tehty–) är storartadt. Kalevala är enligt mitt
tycke alldeles modernt. Jag tycker den är endast
musik, tema med variationer.' ALS to Aino
Järnefelt, 26 December 1890.
35. 'I går lästa jag för tror jag tionde gånge
"Yksin".' ALS to Aino Järnefelt, 25 February
189[1].

3 Pautoralidylls, erctic anxieties
1. Erik Tawaststjerna, *Sibelius. Vol. I,*
1865–1905, trans. Robert Layton (London:
Faber, 1976), p. 170.
2. For further discussion see Daniel M. Grimley,
'*Lemminkäinen and the Maidens of Saari,*
op. 22/1: acculturation, Italy and the
midsummer night', in Veijo Murtomäki, Kari
Kilpeläinen and Risto Väisänen (eds.), *Sibelius*
Forum (Helsinki: Sibelius Academy, 1998),
pp. 197–207. Veijo Murtomäki describes the
dialogue between cello and high woodwind in
this theme as an 'amorous duet'; 'Sibelius's
symphonic ballad *Skogsrået*: biographical and
programmatic aspects of his early orchestral
music', in Timothy Jackson and Veijo
Murtomäki (eds.), *Sibelius Studies* (Cambridge:
Cambridge University Press, 2001), p. 132.
According to Murtomäki many of these early
erotically charged works may be heard as
'confessional' of Sibelius's 'bohemian excesses'
and 'bacchic indulgences' (pp. 98–9).
3. Tawaststjerna/Layton, *Sibelius. Vol. I*, p. 170.
In 1890 Sibelius had heard *Tannhäuser* in Berlin
and in 1894 studied the score in detail. This was
part of a profound and complex engagement
that Sibelius had with Wagner's music during
that decade. According to Eero Tarasti 'these
Wagnerian encounters' led to an 'inner crisis'
involving 'inferiority' and 'antagonism', which
demanded from the composer an heroic
response; Eero Tarasti, 'Sibelius and Wagner', in
Glenda Dawn Goss (ed.), *The Sibelius*

Companion (Westport: Greenwood, 1996), p. 64. For Tim Howell *Lemminkäinen* is 'an attempt at combining Wagnerian pacing with symphonic form' and 'marks a turning point in the processing of Wagnerian influence towards symphonic ends'; *Jean Sibelius: Progressive Techniques in the Symphonies and Tone Poems* (New York and London: Garland, 1989), p. 25.

4. Timothy Jackson, 'Observations on crystallization and entropy in the music of Sibelius and other composers', in Jackson and Murtomäki (eds.), *Sibelius Studies*, pp. 176–9.

5. James Hepokoski, 'Sibelius', in D. Kern Holoman (ed.), *The Nineteenth-Century Symphony* (New York: Schirmer, 1997), p. 421.

6. Tawaststjerna/Layton, *Sibelius. Vol. I*, pp. 201, 209.

7. Howell, *Jean Sibelius*, p. 7.

8. Lionel Pike, *Beethoven, Sibelius and the 'Profound Logic'* (London: Athlone Press, 1978), pp. 5, 170.

9. Tawaststjerna/Layton, *Sibelius. Vol. I*, p. 211.

10. Timothy Jackson, *Tchaikovsky: Symphony no. 6 'Pathétique'* (Cambridge: Cambridge University Press, 1999).

11. Joseph Kraus, 'The "Russian" influence in the First Symphony of Jean Sibelius: chance intersection or profound integration?', in Murtomäki, Kilpeläinen and Väisänen (eds.), *Sibelius Forum*, pp. 142–52.

12. Veijo Murtomäki, *Symphonic Unity: The Development of Formal Thinking in the Symphonies of Sibelius*, trans. Henry Bacon (Helsinki: University of Helsinki, 1993), p. 39.

13. Hepokoski, 'Sibelius', p. 427.

14. Ibid., p. 422.

15. Tarasti, 'Sibelius and Wagner', p. 70.

16. Tarasti, *Myth and Music* (The Hague: Mouton, 1979 [1978]), p. 83.

17. For a brief discussion of these competing formal readings see Irina Baranova, 'Sibelius's musical form as process and result', in Murtomäki, Kilpeläinen and Väisänen (eds.), *Sibelius Forum*, pp. 185–9.

18. Murtomäki, *Symphonic Unity*, p. 36.

19. On the *nega* – a chromatic melodic topos of the orientalized female Other – see Richard Taruskin, *Defining Russia Musically* (Princeton: Princeton University Press, 1997), pp. 165–85. Murtomäki identifies *nega* variants in several of Sibelius's works, including *Lemminkäinen and the Maidens of the Island*; 'Sibelius's symphonic ballad *Skogsrået*', pp. 132–3.

20. Tarasti, *Myth and Music*, p. 118.

21. Tawaststjerna/Layton, *Sibelius. Vol. I*, p. 215.

22. Jackson, 'Observations', p. 198.

23. Tarasti, *Myth and Music*, pp. 163–4.

24. Murtomäki, *Symphonic Unity*, pp. 42, 44. Pike argues that this tune does not 'grow out of the previous material', and is therefore a 'gigantic symphonic pause' in which the listener 'merely immerses himself in the gorgeous sounds, since the argument in no way compels attention'; *Beethoven, Sibelius, and the 'Profound Logic'*, p. 177.

25. See Benjamin M. Korstvedt, *Bruckner: Symphony no. 8* (Cambridge: Cambridge University Press, 2000), pp. 54–67.

26. On this aspect of the Strauss see James Hepokoski, 'Fiery-pulsed libertine or domestic hero?: Strauss's *Don Juan* reinvestigated', in Bryan Gilliam (ed.), *Richard Strauss: New Perspectives on the Composer and His Works* (Durham: Duke University Press, 1992), p. 150.

27. Henry Sussman, *The Aesthetic Contract: Statutes of Art and Intellectual Work in Modernity* (Stanford: Stanford University Press, 1997), pp. 146–50.

28. Jean-François Lyotard, 'Answering the question: what is postmodernism?' ('Réponse à la question: qu'est-ce que le postmoderne?'), *Critique* 419 (April 1982), trans. Régis Durand in *The Postmodern Condition: A Report on Knowledge* (Manchester: Manchester University Press, 1984), pp. 71–82 (esp. pp. 77–80).

29. Catherine Coppola, 'The elusive fantasy: genre, form and program in Tchaikovsky's *Francesca da Rimini*', *Nineteenth-Century Music* 22 (1998), pp. 169–79.

30. Lisa Rado, *The Modern Androgyne Imagination: A Failed Sublime* (Charlottesville: University Press of Virginia, 2000), pp. 20–3.

31. Hamsun was in Helsinki from autumn 1898 until the end of the summer of 1899 and made a powerful impression on Sibelius; Tawaststjerna/Layton, *Sibelius. Vol. I*, pp. 217–18.

32. See David Brodbeck, 'Brahms, the Third Symphony, and the New German School', in Walter Frisch (ed.), *Brahms and His World* (Princeton: Princeton University Press, 1990), pp. 65–80 (the allusion is heard in bars 31–5 of the first movement). On the problematising of the 'heroic paradigm' in this symphony see Susan McClary, 'Narrative agendas in "absolute" music: identity and difference in Brahms's Third Symphony', in Ruth Solie (ed.), *Musicology and Difference* (Berkeley: University of California, 1993), pp. 326–44. In a footnote Hepokoski acknowledges that the ancestry of Sibelius's dissonance goes back to Wagner's; 'Sibelius', p. 445, n. 16.

33. Peter Franklin, 'Kullervo's problem – Kullervo's story', in Jackson and Murtomäki (eds.), *Sibelius Studies*, p. 74.

34. Tawaststjerna/Layton, *Sibelius. Vol. I*, pp. 243–4; Tarasti, 'Sibelius and Wagner', p. 71 (where he notes that Krohn draws upon the hermeneutic traditions of Schering's Beethoven

readings and Wolzogen's readings of Wagner); Tarasti, 'An essay in post-colonial analysis: Sibelius as an icon of the Finns and others', in Jackson and Murtomäki (eds.), *Sibelius Studies*, pp. 8–10.

35. For discussions of these well-known aspects see Howell, *Jean Sibelius*, pp. 11ff.; Murtomäki, *Symphonic Unity*, pp. 46ff.; Pike, *Beethoven, Sibelius, and the 'Profound Logic'*, pp. 88ff.

36. On the latter see Jackson, '*The Maiden with a Heart of Ice*: "crystallization" and compositional genesis in Sibelius's *Pohjola's Daughter* and other works', in Murtomäki, Kilpeläinen and Väisänen (eds.), *Sibelius Forum*, pp. 248–9 and his Schenkerian analytical graph of the whole symphony, p. 250.

37. David Haas, 'Sibelius's Second Symphony and the legacy of symphonic lyricism', in Goss (ed.), *Sibelius Companion*, p. 91.

38. Tawaststjerna/Layton, *Sibelius. Vol. I*, p. 248.

39. Reinhold Brinkmann, *Late Idyll: The Second Symphony of Johannes Brahms*, trans. Peter Palmer (Cambridge, MA: Harvard University Press, 1995), p. 200.

40. Theodor Adorno, 'Glosse über Sibelius' (1938); trans. from the Preface to Jackson and Murtomäki (eds.), *Sibelius Studies*, p. xiii.

41. Tarasti, 'An essay in post-colonial analysis', p. 13. See the empty frozen Karelian landscapes in, for example, Pekka Halonen's canvasses *Winter's Day in Karelen* (1896) or *Wilderness* (1899), which are briefly discussed in Shearer West, *Fin de Siècle: Art and Society in an Age of Uncertainty* (London: Bloomsbury, 1993), p. 128.

42. Tawaststjerna/Layton, *Sibelius. Vol. I*, pp. 242, 250.

43. Haas, 'Sibelius's Second Symphony and the legacy of symphonic lyricism', p. 91.

44. Hepokoski, 'Sibelius', p. 429.

45. Brinkmann, *Late Idyll*, p. 219.

46. Tawaststjerna/Layton, *Sibelius. Vol. I*, p. 255.

47. See Timo Virtanen, '*Pohjola's Daughter* – "L'aventure d'un héros"', in Jackson and Murtomäki (eds.), *Sibelius Studies*, pp. 139–74. Jackson reads the tonal structure of this piece as a chromaticised, and hence 'deviant', version of the kind of 'large-scale auxiliary cadence' (VI–V–I) which underlies the teleology linking the final two movements of the Second Symphony: '*The Maiden with a Heart of Ice*', pp. 260–4.

4 The later symphonies

1. Arnold Schoenberg, *Style and Idea*, ed. Leonard Stein, trans. Leo Black (London: Faber, 1975), p. 136.

2. Hepokoski's work on Sibelius includes the following: *Sibelius, Symphony no. 5* (Cambridge: Cambridge University Press, 1993); 'The essence of Sibelius: creation myths and rotational cycles in *Luonnotar*', in *The Sibelius Companion*, ed. Glenda Dawn Goss (Westport: Greenwood, 1996), pp. 121–46; 'Structural tensions in Sibelius's Fifth Symphony: circular stasis, linear progress, and the problem of "traditional" form', in *Sibelius Forum*, ed. Veijo Murtomäki, Kari Kilpeläinen and Risto Väisänen (Helsinki: Sibelius Academy, 1998), pp. 213–36; 'Sibelius', *The New Grove Dictionary of Music and Musicians*, second edn, ed. Stanley Sadie and John Tyrrell (London: Macmillan, 2001), vol. XXIII, pp. 319–47; 'Rotations, sketches, and the Sixth Symphony' in *Sibelius Studies*, ed. Timothy L. Jackson and Veijo Murtomäki (Cambridge: Cambridge University Press, 2001), pp. 322–51.

3. Hepokoski, 'Sibelius', p. 331.

4. See Veijo Murtomäki, *Symphonic Unity. The Development of Formal Thinking in the Symphonies of Sibelius*, trans. Henry Bacon (Helsinki: Helsinki University Press, 1993), p. 62 for specific examples of this folk-like aspect.

5. Hepokoski, 'Sibelius', p. 331.

6. Murtomäki, *Symphonic Unity*, p. 73.

7. Ibid., p. 79.

8. Ibid., p. 81.

9. Edward Laufer, 'On the first movement of Sibelius's Fourth Symphony', in *Schenker Studies 2*, ed. Carl Schachter and Hedi Siegel (Cambridge: Cambridge University Press, 1999), p. 159.

10. Murtomäki, *Symphonic Unity*, p. 133.

11. Ibid., p. 289.

12. Hepokoski, 'Sibelius', p. 333.

13. Ibid., pp. 332–3 and 334.

14. Ibid., pp. 334–5.

15. Ibid., p. 334.

16. Murtomäki, *Symphonic Unity*, p. 142.

17. Ibid., p. 143.

18. Hepokoski, *Sibelius, Symphony no. 5*, p. 58.

19. Ibid., p. 40.

20. Ibid., p. 21.

21. Murtomäki, *Symphonic Unity*, p. 183.

22. Ibid., p. 192.

23. Hepokoski, 'Sibelius', p. 335.

24. Hepokoski, *Sibelius, Symphony no. 5*, p. 59.

25. Ibid., pp. 59–60.

26. Ibid., p. 62.

27. Ibid., pp. 70–1.

28. Ibid., pp. 78–9.

29. Ibid., p. 79.

30. Murtomäki, *Symphonic Unity*, p. 240.

31. Hepokoski, 'Rotations, sketches, and the Sixth Symphony', p. 323.

32. Murtomäki, *Symphonic Unity*, p. 240.

33. Hepokoski, 'Structural tensions in Sibelius's Fifth Symphony', p. 235.

34. Ibid., p. 230.
35. Hepokoski, 'Rotations, sketches, and the Sixth Symphony', p. 350.
36. Murtomäki, *Symphonic Unity*, p. 196.
37. Hepokoski, 'Sibelius', p. 337.
38. Ibid.
39. Jackson, 'Observations on crystallization and entropy in the music of Sibelius and other composers', in Jackson and Murtomäki (eds.), *Sibelius Studies*. The discussion in the following paragraphs adapts my review of *Sibelius Studies* in *The Musical Times* (Spring 2001), pp. 54–6.
40. Jackson, 'Observations on crystallization', pp. 175 and 269.
41. Ibid., p. 179.
42. Ibid., p. 179.
43. Murtomäki, *Symphonic Unity*, p. 243.
44. *Musical Composition in the Twentieth Century* (London: Oxford University Press, 1999), pp. 61–4.
45. Jackson, 'Observations on crystallization', pp. 261 and 260.
46. Ibid., p. 176.
47. Laufer, 'Continuity and design in the Seventh Symphony', p. 355.
48. Murtomäki, *Symphonic Unity*, pp. 249 and 280.
49. Jackson, 'Observations on crystallization', pp. 265 and 272.

5 The genesis of the Violin Concerto
1. Erik Tawaststjerna, *Jean Sibelius. Åren 1893–1904* (Helsinki: Söderström, 1994), pp. 180–1.
2. Letter from 'Janne' (Jean Sibelius) to his uncle Pehr Sibelius, 1 August 1882, published in Jean Sibelius, *The Hämeenlinna Letters. Jean Sibelius ungdomsbrev*, ed. Glenda Dawn Goss (Helsinki: Schildts Förlag, 1997), p. 54.
3. Letter from Jean Sibelius to Aino Järnefelt, 2 November 1890, from Vienna, in Suvi-Sirkku Talas (ed.), *Sydämen aamu, Aino Järnefeltin ja Jean Sibeliuksen kihlausajan kirjeitä* (Helsinki: Suomenlaisen Kirjallisuuden Seura, 2001), p. 27.
4. Letter from Jean Sibelius to Aino Järnefelt, 11 November 1890 from Vienna, ibid., p. 138.
5. The violin concerto plan from 1890 is mentioned in a letter from Jean Sibelius to Aino Järnefelt, 29 October 1890, from Vienna (ibid., p. 138), and the plan from 1898 is mentioned in Sibelius's letter to Adolf Paul, cited in Vesa Sirén's *Aina poltti sikaria, Jean Sibelius aikalaisten silmin*, rev. edn (Helsinki: Otava, 2000), p. 170.
6. Tawaststjerna, *Jean Sibelius. Åren 1914–1919* (Helsinki: Söderström, 1993), p. 74.
7. Tawaststjerna, *Jean Sibelius. Åren 1893–1904*, pp. 178, 181, 206–7.
8. Ibid., p. 210.
9. Ibid., pp. 210–11.

10. Observations concerning the sketches and the drafts for the Violin Concerto are based on manuscript materials in the collections of Helsinki University Library (HUL). The four-digit manuscript codes refer to the catalogue made of the Sibelius collection by Kari Kilpeläinen: *The Jean Sibelius Manuscripts at Helsinki University Library: A Complete Catalogue* (Wiesbaden: Breitkopf und Härtel, 1991). The finale's first subject appears on the thematic memo HUL 1510 and the violin's answer to the second subject on the thematic memo HUL 1507. The manuscript material for the Violin Concerto is among the most extensive for any of Sibelius's works, and it contains a large number of pages with thematic sketches. There are many unknown themes, and it is impossible to know whether Sibelius sketched those for the concerto or for some other purpose. However, the majority of the sketches and drafts contain music that is related to the two versions of the concerto.
11. The dating of the sketches is not unambiguous. It is possible that Sibelius made later additions to earlier thematic memos. In the case of the finale themes, however, it seems they were written before 1902 since they appear alongside themes for the Second Symphony, with no evidence to suggest that the finale themes had been inserted later. However, the dating of the Violin Concerto manuscripts is very problematic. This is because the dating of manuscripts is based on factors such as how the composer's handwriting changed, and which kinds of inks, pens and pencils he used at different times. Such changes are not usually evident, but most of the manuscripts of the Violin Concerto were written in 1902–3; the drafts of the revised version are most likely from spring/summer 1905. For this reason it is impossible to date the compositional process of the concerto in the way Kari Kilpeläinen has done for the Seventh Symphony ('An introduction to the manuscript and printed sources of Sibelius's Seventh Symphony', in Glenda Dawn Goss (ed.), *The Sibelius Companion* [Westport: Greenwood, 1996], pp. 239–70).
12. Tawaststjerna, *Jean Sibelius. Åren 1893–1904*, p. 205.
13. Erik Tawaststjerna invented the name 'dorian melisma' for this melodic figure, which is a prominent characteristic of Sibelius's music.
14. Copland, *What to Listen for in Music*, rev. edn (New York: New American Library, 1957), pp. 27–8.
15. As Tomi Mäkelä has pointed out in his article 'The Sibelius violin concerto and its dramatic virtuosity: a comparative study', *The*

Proceedings of the First International Jean Sibelius Conference, Helsinki, August 1990, ed. Eero Tarasti (Helsinki: Sibelius Academy, 1995), p. 124, 'frequent discussions have centered on defining the second subject in the movement' but 'more emphasis should go to the concept of the second subject area than to the second subject as a closed melodic unit'.

16. The word 'Aino', the name of the composer's wife, can be seen quite frequently in Sibelius's sketches and drafts. This has been the cause of controversy among scholars, some of whom maintain that, where Sibelius has written 'Aino', the music refers to the composer's wife, whereas others maintain that the markings simply represent Sibelius's own characteristic manner of highlighting important features in his manuscripts.

17. Virtanen, '*Pohjola's Daughter* in the light of sketch studies', *Sibelius Forum. Proceedings from the Second International Jean Sibelius Conference. Helsinki, November 25–29, 1999*, ed. Veijo Murtomäki, Kari Kilpeläinen, and Risto Väisänen (Helsinki: Sibelius Academy, 1999), p. 315.

18. Lindgren, 'I've got some lovely themes for a violin concerto', *Finnish Music Quarterly* 3–4 (1990), p. 28.

19. Erkki Salmenhaara has written about this in various texts: see Salmenhaara, liner notes for *Jean Sibelius: Violin Concerto (original and final versions)*, BIS CD-500 (1991); 'Jean Sibelius: Violin Concerto', *Masterpieces of Nordic Music*, ed. Harald Herresthal and Heinrich W. Schwab (Wilhelmshaven: Florian Noetzel Verlag, 1996); 'The Violin Concerto' in Goss (ed.), *Sibelius Companion*; and *Suomen musiikin historia: II. Kansallisromantiikan valtavirta, 1885–1918* (Porvoo: Werner Söderström Osakeyhtiö, 1998), pp. 151–60.

20. Percy Young, *The Concerto* (London: Phoenix House, 1957), p. 109. Young writes that, probably for the reason mentioned above, the concerto is unjustly neglected. Although this was perhaps true in 1957, it certainly does not apply any longer: according to Martti Haapakoski ('The concerto that holds a record', *Finnish Music Quarterly* 3–4 [1990], p. 34), the concerto was recorded more than seventy times during the years 1935–90 (the first recording was made by Jascha Heifetz and Sir Thomas Beecham). During the 1970s and 1980s about twenty recordings were published in each decade, and in the 1990s (as far as 1996), at least thirty appeared. According to Haapakoski, the concerto is the most recorded twentieth-century concerto, and in terms of the number of recordings, only the Tchaikovsky, Beethoven, Mendelssohn, and Brahms concertos are ahead

of Sibelius's work (see Haapakoski, 'The Sibelius Concerto still holds a record', *Finnish Music Quarterly* 4 [1996], pp. 14–15).

21. Burmester's comment is cited in Tawaststjerna, *Jean Sibelius. Åren 1863–1904*, pp. 209–10, and Flodin's comment in Salmenhaara, 'Jean Sibelius, Violin Concerto', p. 19.

22. Hepokoski has been interviewed by Minna Lindgren in 'I've got some lovely themes for a violin concerto', pp. 26–8.

23. Tawaststjerna, *Jean Sibelius. Åren 1893–1904*, p. 211.

24. The term editing is used here in the sense defined by the Bartók scholar László Somfai. He adapts the term to describe the final manuscript stage, where the composer makes small changes and corrections, and not merely proofreading corrections and editorial work. See *Béla Bartók, Composition, Concepts, and Autograph Sources* (Berkeley: University of California Press, 1996).

25. Tawaststjerna, *Sibelius, Vol. I, 1865–1905*, trans. Robert Layton (London: Faber, 1976), p. 278.

26. Tawaststjerna, *Sibelius, Vol. II* (Helsinki: Otava), p. 270, and Alberto Bachmann, *An Encyclopedia of the Violin* (New York: Da Capo Press, 1966 [first published 1925]), p. 347.

27. There are not many examples of performers having a material effect on Sibelius's compositional work. He did not have favourite musicians he would specifically compose music for, with the exception of his songs (many of which were written for his favourite singers, Aino Ackté and Ida Ekman). The different qualities of these singers are obvious in the songs written particularly for them.

28. Tawaststjerna, *Jean Sibelius. Åren 1893–1904*, p. 211.

29. Salmenhaara, 'Jean Sibelius, Violin Concerto', pp. 37–8.

30. Lindgren, 'I've got some lovely themes for a violin concerto', pp. 26–7.

6 *Finlandia* awakens

1. The original version of 'Suomi herää' was first recorded by Tuomas Ollila and the Tampere Philharmonic, 'Sibelius: Complete Karelia Music [and] Press Celebrations Music: World Premiere Recording', Ondine, ODE 913–2 (1998), with liner notes by Jouni Kaipainen, trans. William Moore. Two years later appeared a recording of the original version along with a second version 'with alternative ending (1899?)': Osmo Vänskä, Lahti Symphony Orchestra, 'Finland Awakes: Patriotic Music by Jean Sibelius', BIS CD-1115 [No. 49 of the Complete Sibelius project] (2000), with liner notes by Andrew Barnett.

2. Liszt, *Berlioz und seine 'Harold-Symphonie'*
[1855], in Liszt, *Gesammelte Schriften*, ed.
L. Ramann [1882] (rpt. Hildesheim: Olms,
1978), vol. IV, pp. 69, 60, 48 (translations mine).
Richard Strauss, almost a half-century past his
own programme-music battles of the 1890s,
recalled the slogan of the Lisztian agenda as
'New ideas must seek new forms for themselves'
(*Neue Gedanken müssen sich neue Formen
suchen*), in Strauss, 'Aus meinen Jugend- und
Lehrjahren', *Betrachtungen und Erinnerungen*,
ed. Willi Schuh, first edn (Zurich: Atlantis,
1949), p. 168. A discussion of the symphonic
environment surrounding Liszt's quotation is
available in Hepokoski, 'Beethoven reception:
the symphonic tradition', chapter 15 of *The
Cambridge History of Nineteenth-Century Music*,
ed. Jim Samson (Cambridge: Cambridge
University Press, 2002), pp. 424–59.
3. Quoted in Erik Tawaststjerna, *Sibelius. Vol. II,
1904–14*, trans. Robert Layton (London: Faber,
1986), p. 66.
4. For example, Hepokoski, *Sibelius: Symphony
no. 5* (Cambridge: Cambridge University Press,
1993), pp. 26–7; 'The essence of Sibelius:
creation myths and rotational cycles in
Luonnotar', in *The Sibelius Companion*, ed.
Glenda Dawn Goss (Westport: Greenwood,
1996), pp. 121–46; and 'Sibelius, Jean [Johan]
(Christian Julius)', in *The New Grove Dictionary
of Music and Musicians*, second edn, ed. Stanley
Sadie and John Tyrrell (London: Macmillan,
2001), vol. XXIII, pp. 318–47 (esp. pp. 332,
334).
5. Within the progressive 'logic' of A♭ tonic
creation, notice that the three V$^4_3$ chords are
placed in situations of increasing cadential
implication and strength: bar 110 (not really
introducing a 'cadence' but rather functioning as
the 'weak' last chord of the B section); bar 124
(a subverted attempt at a contrapuntal cadence
at the supposed end of the rounded-binary
form); bars 127–8 (a more emphatic, forcefully
carried out contrapuntal cadence into bar 129,
although still falling short of full A♭ closure via a
perfect authentic cadence – something still to be
attained).
6. On Carpelan, see Tawaststjerna, *Sibelius.
Vol. I, 1865–1905*, trans. Robert Layton
(London: Faber, 1976), p. 222. On the differing
titles, see p. 225.
7. For the descriptions of the tableau, see, e.g.,
Tawaststjerna, *Sibelius. Vol. 1*, pp. 220–2, and the
liner notes provided for the Ondine recording of
'Suomi herää' by Jouni Kaipainen.
8. Kaipainen, liner notes to Ondine recording.

7 The tone poems
1. For further discussion of the importance of
genre in nineteenth-century music, see Carl
Dahlhaus, *Nineteenth-Century Music*, trans.
J. Bradford Robinson (Berkeley: University of
California Press, 1989).
2. Hugh Macdonald, 'The symphonic poem', in
*The New Grove Dictionary of Music and
Musicians*, second edn, ed. Stanley Sadie and
John Tyrrell, vol. XXIV (London: Macmillan,
2001), pp. 802–6. For the sake of the present
discussion, following Macdonald's *Grove* article,
the terms 'symphonic poem' and 'tone poem'
are treated as synonymous.
3. Dahlhaus, *Nineteenth-Century Music*,
pp. 265–76.
4. Ironically, as Dahlhaus notes, Beethoven's
Sixth Symphony serves as the *locus classicus* for
this kind of effect. In *Realism in
Nineteenth-Century Music*, trans. Mary Whittall
(Cambridge: Cambridge University Press, 1985),
Dahlhaus writes (p. 107): 'Since Beethoven, the
law of symphonic motion has been incessant
goal-directedness, but here the law is set in
abeyance while the music expands in a
stationary spread of sound, albeit animated by
interior motion . . . This expanse has in some
respects neither beginning nor end, and its start
is as indeterminate as its close is unmarked.
Musical pictures of nature, in so far as the
categories of beginning, middle and end are in
abeyance in them, are "formless" in a precise
sense of the word.'
5. The term 'sonata deformation' is introduced
by James Hepokoski, in his *Sibelius: Symphony
no. 5* (Cambridge: Cambridge University Press,
1993), to describe the range of common formal
strategies adopted by composers at the end of
the nineteenth century in dialogue with a fixed
schematic understanding of sonata form. See
especially pp. 5–9.
6. Ibid., pp. 19–30.
7. See the relevant sections of Tawaststjerna,
Sibelius. Vol. III, 1914–1957, trans. Robert
Layton (London: Faber, 1997), pp. 15ff.
8. Otto Andersson, 'Jean Sibelius et la musique
finlandaise', in Jarl Werner Söderhjelm, *Finlande
et Finlandais* (Paris: Librarie Armand Edin,
1913), pp. 175–96.
9. Quoted in Tawaststjerna, *Sibelius. Vol. I,
1865–1905*, trans. Robert Layton (London:
Faber, 1976), p. 130.
10. Veijo Murtomäki, 'Sibelius's symphonic
ballad *Skogsrået*: biographical and
programmatic aspects of his early orchestral
music', in Tim L. Jackson and Veijo Murtomäki
(eds.), *Sibelius Studies* (Cambridge: Cambridge
University Press, 2001), pp. 130–1.
11. Tawaststjerna, *Sibelius. Vol. I*, p. 134.
12. Ibid., p. 152.
13. Ibid., p. 163.
14. Murtomäki, 'Sibelius's symphonic ballad
Skogsrået', p. 106.

15. For a brief analysis, see James Hepokoski, 'Sibelius, Jean', *The New Grove Dictionary of Music and Musicians*, second edn, ed. Stanley Sadie and John Tyrrell (London: Macmillan, 2001), vol. XXIII, pp. 326–7.

16. See Daniel Grimley, 'Sibelius's *Lemminkäinen and the Maidens of Saari* op. 22/1: acculturation, Italy and the midsummer night', *Sibelius Forum: Proceedings from the Second International Jean Sibelius Conference* (Helsinki: Sibelius Academy, 1999), pp. 197–207.

17. Hepokoski, *Sibelius: Symphony no. 5*, p. 62.

18. Virtanen, '*Pohjola's daughter* – "L'aventure d'un héros" ', in Jackson and Murtomäki (eds.), *Sibelius Studies*, pp. 139–74.

19. Quoted in Erik Tawaststjerna, *Sibelius. Vol. 2, 1904–14*, trans. Robert Layton (London: Faber, 1986), p. 37.

20. The term is Tawaststjerna's; see Tawaststjerna/Layton, *Sibelius. Vol. II*, p. 56.

21. Timothy L. Jackson, 'Observations on crystallization and entropy in the music of Sibelius and other composers', in Jackson and Murtomäki (eds.), *Sibelius Studies*, pp. 175–272.

22. Virtanen, '*Pohjola's daughter*', pp. 173–4.

23. For a very different approach that suggests many parallels with Sibelius's work, see Julian Johnson's *Webern and the Transformation of Nature* (Cambridge: Cambridge University Press, 1999).

24. Agawu, *Playing with Signs: a Semiotic Interpretation of Classic Music* (Princeton: Princeton University Press, 1991).

25. Tarasti, 'An essay in post-colonial analysis: Sibelius as an icon of the Finns and others', in Jackson and Murtomäki (eds.), *Sibelius Studies*, p. 13.

26. Ibid., p. 12.

27. Mitchell (ed.), *Landscape and Power* (Chicago: University of Chicago Press, 1994), p. 14.

28. Simon Schama, *Landscape and Memory* (London: Harper Collins, 1995), p. 61.

29. Rosa Newmarch, *Jean Sibelius – a Short Story of a Long Friendship* (Boston: Birchard, 1939), p. 68.

30. Tawaststjerna/Layton, *Sibelius. Vol. II*, p. 66.

31. Two significant pieces of anecdotal evidence, quoted by Tawaststjerna, *Sibelius. Åren 1904–1914* (Helsinki: Söderström, 1991), p. 128, reinforce this hearing. According to Karl Ekman, the music was inspired by the sight of dawn at the Coliseum in Rome, where Sibelius had stayed in 1901. Sibelius also suggested to Levas that the music was inspired by the sight of the northern lights during a night-time sleigh journey from Helsinki to Kervo, when 'the whole sky was a boundless sea of colours that shifted and flowed in the most remarkable display until it all ended in a growing clarity'.

32. Tawaststjerna/Layton, *Sibelius. Vol. II*, pp. 139–40.

33. Ibid., p. 241. Sibelius had earlier composed a setting of the poem in his op. 57 collection of Josephson songs.

34. See Daniel Grimley, 'Horn calls and flattened sevenths: Nielsen and Danish musical style', in Harry White and Michael Murphy (eds.), *Musical Constructions of Nationalism: essays on the history and ideology of European musical culture 1800–1945* (Cork: Cork University Press, 2001), pp. 123–41, for discussion of a parallel phenomenon in the music of Carl Nielsen.

35. *The Musical Times* 54 (October 1913), p. 665.

36. James Hepokoski, 'The essence of Sibelius: creation myths and rotational cycles in *Luonnotar*', in Glenda Dawn Goss (ed.), *The Sibelius Companion* (Westport: Greenwood, 1996), pp. 121–46.

37. Ibid., p. 140.

38. Ibid., p. 133.

39. The final cadence could perhaps be understood as the superimposition of a German sixth (on D♮) and the tonic chord of resolution (F♯), but Sibelius also puns on the enharmonic significance of A♯: B♭ has functioned as an alternative key centre throughout the piece.

40. Tawaststjerna/Layton, *Sibelius. Vol. II*, p. 267.

41. Ibid., p. 267.

42. Ibid., p. 269.

43. Hepokoski, 'Sibelius', *New Grove*, pp. 338–9, and Jackson, 'Observations on crystallization', pp. 235–7.

44. Howell, 'Sibelius the progressive', in Jackson and Murtomäki (eds.), *Sibelius Studies*, pp. 46ff.

45. Sibelius treats the opening chord as a German sixth in G♯; it is only later that we hear the chord as IV_3^4 in B minor.

46. Jackson, 'Observations on crystallization', pp. 235–8.

47. Whittall, 'Sibelius' eighth Symphony', *Music Review* 25 (1964), pp. 239–40.

48. Hepokoski, 'The essence of Sibelius', p. 140.

8 Love, sex and style in Sibelius's songs

I wish to thank the Penn Humanities Forum for the generous financial and intellectual support it provided for the early stages of my research on this topic.

1. For more general surveys of the songs, see Valerie Sirén, 'The Songs', in Glenda Dawn Goss (ed.), *The Sibelius Companion* (Westport: Greenwood, 1996), pp. 171–200, and Jukka Tiilikainen's excellent historical introductions to the first two volumes of the fine new critical edition of the songs (Jean Sibelius, *Solo Songs with Piano, Opp. 1, 13, 17, 35, 36, 37, 38, 50, Jean*

Sibelius Complete Works, Series VIII, vol. II
(Wiesbaden: Breitkopf und Härtel, 1998); and
*Solo Songs with Piano, Opp. 57, 61, 72, 86, 88, 90,
Jean Sibelius Complete Works*, Series VIII, vol. III
(Wiesbaden: Breitkopf und Härtel, 2000). Series
VIII, vol. IV, featuring solo songs without opus
numbers, duets, and arrangements for violin
and piano, is due to be published in 2003.
2. On the Tchaikovskian opening of the song,
see Erik Tawaststjerna, *Sibelius* (Helsinki:
Söderström, 1968), p. 357, and Sirén, 'The
Songs', pp. 191–2.
3. That this poem might be interpreted very
differently becomes clear when we compare the
exceptional 1893 setting of it by the Swedish
composer Wilhelm Stenhammar. Stenhammar
offers a more flexible, musically variable reading
of Runeberg's text, one that ultimately places
more stress on the irony of the narrative (she
who deceives her mother herself suffers from the
lies of a loved one) than on morals. For a
modern edition of Stenhammar's song, see
Thirty Songs of Wilhelm Stenhammar, ed.
Annette Johnson (Mt. Morris, New York: Leyerle
Publications, 1999), pp. 20–5. And for a smart
comparison of the Stenhammar and Sibelius
versions, see Bo Wallner, *Wilhelm Stenhammar
och hans tid*, 3 vols. (Stockholm: Norstedts
Förlag, 1991), vol. II, pp. 223–9.
4. Santeri Levas, the composer's secretary,
reported this quotation. See Santeri Levas,
Sibelius: A Personal Portrait, trans. Percy M.
Young (Lewisberg: Bucknell University Press,
1972), p. 85.
5. Erik Tawaststjerna, *Jean Sibelius. Åren
1904–1914* (Keuruu: Atlantis, 1991), p. 208. This
entry from his diary dates from 1910, while he
was sketching an orchestral song on Viktor
Rydberg's translation of Poe's 'The Raven' from
Korpen (a work he would not complete). Except
where noted, all translations in this chapter are
my own.
6. Diary entry from 1912 concerning a planned
opera; Tawaststjerna, *Jean Sibelius. Åren
1904–1914*, p. 281.
7. James Hepokoski, 'Sibelius, Jean', *The New
Grove Dictionary of Music and Musicians*, second
edn, ed. S. Sadie and J. Tyrrell (London:
Macmillan, 2001), vol. XXIII, p. 326.
8. Perhaps Sibelius's most brilliant lyrical
exposition of this technique is the late song
Norden (The North, op. 90/1, 1917), which
insistently repeats a single C-centred rhythmic
ostinato over the entire course of the song.
9. See George C. Schoolfield, 'National
Romanticism – a golden age?', in *A History of
Finland's Literature*, ed. Schoolfield, *Histories of
Scandinavian Literature*, vol. IV (Lincoln and
London: University of Nebraska Press, 1998),
p. 301.

10. For Sibelius we can confirm this variety by
comparing his different musical settings of
Viktor Rydberg's *Skogsrået*. In his first, solo-song
engagement with the poem (dating from 1889, it
is another example from the earlier songs of
Sibelius's tendency to craft more discursive
forms), he set the stanza where the strong and
handsome Björn cavorts erotically with the
wood nymphs to a frisky D♭ major waltz in 6/8
that studiously avoids foreshadowing the dark
consequences of Björn's illicit intercourse. But
the slow C♯ minor waltz that he later wrote for
the orchestral ballade and the melodrama based
on the poem lends an air of greater
portentousness to the encounter between Björn
and the *skogsrå*. On the erotic history of the
waltz, see Sevin H. Yaraman, *Revolving Embrace:
The Waltz as Sex, Steps, and Sound* (Hillsdale,
NY: Pendragon Press, 2002).
11. On the mid-nineteenth-century
development of the concept of 'sexuality', see
Arnold I. Davidson, *The Emergence of Sexuality:
Historical Epistemology and the Formation of
Concepts* (Cambridge, MA: Harvard University
Press, 2001). This paragraph revisits ideas that I
have also explored in 'Sibelius, *Skogsrået*, and the
history of sexuality', in *Proceedings from the
Third International Jean Sibelius Conference*, ed.
Veijo Murtomäki (Helsinki: Sibelius Academy,
forthcoming).
12. Tawaststjerna, *Sibelius*, pp. 365–6.
13. For claims that Sibelius had the
improvisation in mind when he composed
'Teodora', see Tawaststjerna, *Jean Sibelius. Åren
1904–1914*, p. 125, and Sirén, 'The songs',
p. 189.
14. See Carolyn Abbate, 'Opera; or the
envoicing of women', in Ruth A. Solie (ed.),
*Musicology and Difference: Gender and Sexuality
in Music Scholarship* (Berkeley and Los Angeles:
University of California Press, 1993), p. 248. Of
course, the general similarity in subject matter
(transgressive 'oriental' women) might have led
Sibelius to ponder a *Salome*-like sound-world
for 'Teodora'. But he might also have been
inspired when perusing Gripenberg's *Poems
(Dikter)* – the source of 'Teodora' – the first six
poems of which are grouped under the heading
'Songs to Salome' (*Sånger till Salome*).
15. The expressionist trajectory that in the
songs culminates in 'Teodora' can trace its roots
at least as far back as Sibelius's two great
declamatory works from 1903, 'På veranden vid
havet' (On the Veranda by the Sea) and
'Höstkväll' (Autumn Evening), op. 38/1 and 2.
16. In the songs (particularly those written to
Swedish and Finnish texts), these questions of
style also of course intersect profoundly with
questions of national identity, so that the
shifting templates of style also get filtered

through the apparent 'otherness' of Sibelius's
ethnic background (when measured against
the vocal works by Continental composers set
to texts in German, French, Italian, and English).
17. James Hepokoski, *Sibelius: Symphony no. 5*
(Cambridge: Cambridge University Press, 1993),
pp. 1–18.
18. Tawaststjerna, *Jean Sibelius. Åren
1904–1914*, p. 150.
19. Ibid., p. 283.
20. Ibid., p. 309.

9 Sibelius and the miniature
1. In addition to the solo music, Sibelius wrote
more than three hundred pieces with a piano
part: there are 129 original opus-numbered
pieces, plus many pieces without opus number,
two dozen arrangements of orchestral music,
110 songs with piano accompaniment and
several dozen early piano and chamber music
pieces without opus number, dating from his
student period (c. 1881–91).
2. Cecil Gray, *Sibelius* (London: Oxford
University Press, 1931), pp. 118–19.
3. Eric Blom, 'The piano music', in Gerald
Abraham (ed.), *Sibelius. A Symposium* (London:
Oxford University Press, 1952 [1947]), p. 97.
4. Robert Layton, *Sibelius* (London: J. M. Dent
and Sons, 1978 [1965]), p. 143.
5. Guy Rickards, *Jean Sibelius* (London:
Phaidon, 1997), p. 12.
6. Ibid., pp. 21 and 204.
7. 'Ses compositions pour piano sont
médiocres, et parfois de façon alarmante.' Guy
Sacre, *La musique de piano* (Paris: Robert
Laffont, 1998), p. 2695.
8. Ernst T. Tanzberger, *Jean Sibelius*
(Wiesbaden: Breitkopf und Härtel, 1962), p. 245.
9. Bengt de Törne, *Sibelius: A Close-Up*
(London: Faber, 1937), p. 29.
10. Erik Tawaststjerna, *Sibelius. Vol. II,
1904–1914*, trans. Robert Layton (London:
Faber, 1986), p. 109; *Musical Times*, March 1953.
11. Glenn Gould, 'The piano music of Sibelius',
in Tim Page (ed.), *The Glenn Gould Reader* (New
York: Alfred A. Knopf), pp. 103–7.
12. Ilmari Hannikainen, 'Hieman Sibeliuksen
pianosävellyksistä', *Suomen musiikkilehti* 9
(1935), p. 180.
13. Erik Tawaststjerna, *The Pianoforte
Compositions of Sibelius* (Helsinki: Otava, 1957),
pp. 8–9.
14. Erik T. Tawaststjerna, 'The piano music of
Sibelius', in *Finnish Music Quarterly* (1990/3–4),
p. 67.
15. Eero Heinonen, *Sibelius. Published original
works for piano – complete edition*. Finlandia
Records CD 8573–80776–2 (2000), p. 3.
16. Susanna Välimäki, 'Subjektistrategioita
Sibeliuksen *Kyllikissä*', *Musiikki* (2001), p. 18.

17. Erik T. Tawaststjerna, 'The piano music of
Sibelius', p. 67.
18. Heinonen, *Sibelius*, p. 4.
19. Hermann Danuser, 'Gattung', in *Die Musik
in Geschichte und Gegenwart* (hereafter *MGG*),
Sachteil III, ed. Ludwig Finscher (Kassel:
Bärenreiter, 1995), pp. 1059–62.
20. Carl Dahlhaus, 'Zur Problematik der
musikalischen Gattungen im 19. Jahrhundert', in
Gattungen der Musik in Einzeldarstellungen, ed.
Wulf Arlt and others (Bern: A. Francke, 1973
[1968]), p. 853.
21. Christoph-Hellmut Mahling, 'Zur Frage der
"Einheit" der Symphonie', in Christoph-Hellmut
Mahling (ed.), *Über Symphonien* (Tutzing: Hans
Schneider, 1979), pp. 11–12.
22. Ibid., p. 12; Ferdinand Hand, *Ästhetik der
Tonkunst*, vol. II (Jena, 1841), 405.
23. Dahlhaus, 'Zur Problematik der
musikalischen Gattungen', pp. 845 and 867.
24. Ibid., p. 859.
25. Ibid., pp. 861 and 883.
26. Ibid., p. 883.
27. Eero Tarasti, 'An essay in post-colonial
analysis: Sibelius as an icon of the Finns and
others', in Timothy L. Jackson and Veijo
Murtomäki (eds.), *Sibelius Studies* (Cambridge:
Cambridge University Press, 2001), p. 4.
28. Bernhard R. Appel, 'Characterstück', in
MGG, Sachteil II, pp. 636–42.
29. Andreas Ballstaedt, 'Salonmusik', in *MGG*,
Sachteil VIII, includes the following definition
given by J. Chr. Lobe (1855): 'As is well known,
salon music is called phantasies, songs without
words, potpourri, impromptus, bagatelles,
etudes, nocturnes, scherzi, transcriptions,
character pieces, variations, ballads, polonaises,
waltzes, mazurkas, boleros etc.' (p. 862).
30. Gabrielle Busch-Salmen, 'Hausmusik', in
MGG, Sachteil IV, pp. 232–4.
31. Andreas Ballstaedt, 'Unterhaltungsmusik',
in *MGG*, Sachteil IX, pp. 1188–9.
32. According to the Aristotelian view, for
example, music served three functions: as a
means of education, as an instrument of therapy,
and as entertainment.
33. 'Du goût', *Revue musicale*, 15 February 1913.
34. Claude Debussy, 'Du goût', in *Monsieur
Croche et autres écrits*, ed. François Lesure (Paris:
Éditions Gallimard, 1987 [1971]), p. 230.
35. See my forthcoming article: 'Sibelius and
the French orchestral music in the context of
German symphonic tradition', in *Proceedings of
the colloquium La France dans la musique
nordique – Relations musicales franco-nordiques
de 1900 à 1939*, ed. Helena Tyrväinen. Sibelius
gave the following statement to a Finnish
newspaper in 1909 in connection with his visit
to London: 'It is an absolute fact that the
Englishmen . . . now have music which can

compete with that of the Germans – and furthermore, there is not the slightest doubt that English and French music will overtake it in the very near future.' See Vesa Sirén, *Aina poltti sikaria. Jean Sibelius aikalaisten silmin* (Helsinki: Otava, 2000), p. 272.

36. Välimäki, 'Subjektistrategioita Sibeliuksen *Kyllikissä*', pp. 14–15.

37. Blom, 'The piano music', pp. 97–8.

38. Jeffrey Kallberg, *Chopin at the Boundaries* (Cambridge, MA: Harvard University Press, 1998), pp. 30–61.

39. Sibelius himself could play the Finnish national instrument, *kantele*, to some extent, and later he composed for it two solo pieces: *Moderato* in A minor (1896–8), and *Dolcissimo* in A minor (1897–8); in addition to this, he wrote a *Walz* or *Berceuse* in E minor for violin and *kantele* (1899). See *The Hämeenlinna Letters. Jean Sibelius ungdomsbrev*, ed. Glenda Dawn Goss (Helsinki: Schildts Förlag, 1997), p. 102, and Folke Gräsbeck, 'Sibeliuksen kantelesävellykset kantaesitettiin', in *Kantele* (2001/3), pp. 6–8.

40. Ruwim Ostrovsky, 'Some remarks on Sibelius's treatment of the genre and cycle in his Piano Impromptus Op. 5', in *Sibelius Forum, Proceedings from the Second International Jean Sibelius Conference Helsinki November 25–29, 1995*, ed. Veijo Murtomäki, Kari Kilpeläinen and Risto Väisänen (Helsinki: Sibelius Academy, 1998), p. 293.

41. Sirén, *Aina poltti sikaria. Jean Sibelius aikalaisten silmin*, p. 142.

42. Ostrovsky, 'Some remarks on Sibelius's treatment of the genre and cycle in his Piano Impromptus Op. 5', pp. 294–5.

43. Blom, 'The piano music', p. 105.

44. Goddard, 'The chamber music', in *Sibelius. A Symposium*, ed. Gerald Abraham (London: Oxford University Press, 1947), p. 95.

45. Juhani Alesaro, 'Sibelius's Op. 75 No. 4 – "hardly pianoforte music at all"?', in Murtomäki, Kilpeläinen and Väisänen (eds.), *Sibelius Forum*, p. 184.

46. Sibelius's lecture (1896) has been published in a bilingual edition, translated from Swedish into Finnish, 'Några synpunkter beträffande folkmusiken och dess inflytande på tonkonsten', ed. and trans. Ilkka Oramo. *Musiikki* (1980/10:2), pp. 86–105.

47. For the most recent study of this piece, with an extensive list of references, see Välimäki, 'Subjektistrategioita Sibeliuksen *Kyllikissä*'.

48. Layton, *Sibelius*, p. 146.

49. Friedhelm Loesti, 'Die Zehn Klavierstücke op. 58 von Jean Sibelius', in Murtomäki, Kilpeläinen and Väisänen (eds.), *Sibelius Forum*, pp. 282–3 and 291.

50. Tawaststjerna/Layton, *Sibelius. Vol. II*, p. 159.

51. Ibid.

52. Layton, *Sibelius*, p. 148.

53. Sacre, *La musique de piano*, p. 2700.

54. Melinda Scott, 'Performance and contextual issues within selected Sibelius violin and piano "salon" pieces', in Murtomäki, Kilpeläinen and Väisänen (eds.), *Sibelius Forum*, p. 101.

55. Tawaststjerna, *The Pianoforte Compositions of Sibelius*, pp. 84–5.

56. Erik Tawaststjerna, *Sibelius. Vol III, 1914–1957*, ed. and trans. Robert Layton (London: Faber, 1997), p. 248.

57. Heinonen, *Sibelius. Published original works for piano – complete edition*, p. 11.

58. Anybody interested in these marvellous pieces should consult copies of the autograph scores, located in the Sibelius manuscript collection at the Helsinki University Library.

59. Joseph Kon, 'Sibelius's five sketches as a reflection of 20th-century musical-language evolution', in *Proceedings from The First International Jean Sibelius Conference, Helsinki, August 1990*, ed. Eero Tarasti (Helsinki: Sibelius Academy, 1995), p. 103.

60. Ibid., p. 105.

61. Tawaststjerna/Layton, *Sibelius. Vol. III*, p. 305; the full history of composing the 'Funeral Music' can be found in the Swedish edition of the book, *Jean Sibelius. Åren 1920–1957* (Keuru: Söderström, 1993), pp. 300–1.

62. Santeri Levas, *Jean Sibelius. A Personal Portrait*, trans. Percy M. Young (London: J. M. Dent and Sons, 1972 [1968]), p. 87. The original Finnish version was published in two volumes as *Nuori Sibelius* (1957) and *Järvenpään mestari* (1960).

10 Sub umbra sibelii

1. Ernest Pingoud, 'Den yngsta finska musiken' [The youngest Finnish music], *Nya Argus* 18 (1928); Finnish trans. as 'Uusin suomalainen musiikki', in Ernest Pingoud, *Taiteen edistys* [Art's Progress], ed. Kalevi Aho (Helsinki: Gaudeamus, 1995), pp. 197–9.

2. Ernest Pingoud, 'Jean Sibelius', *Montagsblatt der Sankt Petersburger Zeitung*, 8 June 1909; Finnish trans. ibid., pp. 73–5.

3. Walter Niemann, *Die Musik Skandinaviens* (Leipzig: Breitkopf und Härtel, 1906), p. 237.

4. Ernest Pingoud, 'Kansallinen musiikki' [National music], *Ultra* 3 (1922); repr. in Pingoud, *Taiteen edistys*, pp. 246–7.

5. Seppo Nummi, 'Yrjö Kilpinen musiikinhistoriassa ja Suomen säveltaiteessa' [Yrjö Kilpinen in the history of music and in the music of Finland], *Suomen Musiikin Vuosikirja 1968–1969* [Yearbook of Finnish music

1968–1969], ed. I. Oramo (Helsinki: Otava, 1970), p. 11.

6. Yrjö Suomalainen, *Robert Kajanus* (Helsinki: Otava, 1952, p. 98).

7. Ilkka Oramo, 'Beyond nationalism', *Music and Nationalism in 20th-Century Great Britain and Finland*, ed. Tomi Mäkelä (Hamburg: von Boeckel Verlag, 1997), p. 37.

8. Selim Palmgren, *Minusta tuli muusikko* [I became a musician] (Porvoo: Werner Söderström Osakeyhtiö, 1948), pp. 26–7.

9. Erik Tawaststjerna, *Sibelius. Vol. I 1865–1905*, trans. Robert Layton (London: Faber, 1976), p. 103; cf. Veijo Murtomäki, 'Sibelius – composer and patriot', *Sibelius Forum 2. Proceedings from the Third International Jean Sibelius Conference, Helsinki 2000* [forthcoming].

10. See e.g. G. C. Schoolfield, *Helsinki of the Czars* (Columbia, SC: Camden House, 1996), pp. 205–14.

11. Cf. James Hepokoski, 'Sibelius, Jean', *The New Grove Dictionary of Music and Musicians*, second edn, vol. XXIII (London: Macmillan, 2001), pp. 328–9, and Murtomäki, 'Sibelius – composer and patriot'.

12. Joonas Kokkonen, 'Mestarin tie' [The path of the master], *Ilta-Sanomat* 21 (September 1957).

13. Eero Tarasti, 'An essay in post-colonial analysis: Sibelius as an icon of the Finns and others', in Timothy L. Jackson and V. Murtomäki (eds.), *Sibelius Studies* (Cambridge: Cambridge University Press, 2001), p. 4.

14. Leevi Madetoja, 'Jean Sibelius opettajana' [Jean Sibelius as a teacher], *Aulos* (1925). Quoted in Erkki Salmenhaara, *Leevi Madetoja* (Helsinki: Tammi, 1987), p. 43.

15. Ibid., p. 60. A third composer who described himself as Sibelius's student was Bengt von Törne, whose *Sibelius – A Close-up* (London: Faber, 1937) provoked Theodor W. Adorno to write his 'Glosse über Sibelius', originally published in *Zeitschrift für Sozialforschung* 7 (1938), pp. 460–3.

16. Einar Englund, *Sibeliuksen varjossa. Katkelmia säveltäjän elämästä* [In the Shadow of Sibelius. Fragments from a Life of a Composer] (Keuruu: Otava, 1997), pp. 337–8.

17. See e.g. Carl Dahlhaus, *Nineteenth-Century Music*, trans. J. Bradford Robinson (Berkeley and Los Angeles: University of California Press, 1989), and Arnold Whittall, *Musical Composition in the Twentieth Century* (London: Oxford University Press, 1999).

18. Salmenhaara, *Leevi Madetoja*, pp. 148–50, 179–82.

19. Ibid., p. 230.

20. Ibid., p. 340.

21. Ibid., p. 352.

22. Kalevi Aho and Marjo Valkonen, *Uuno Klami. Elämä ja teokset* [Uuno Klami. Life and Works] (Helsinki: Werner Söderström Osakeyhtiö, 2000), p. 215.

23. Seppo Heikinheimo, *Aarre Merikanto. Säveltäjänkohtalo itsenäisessä Suomessa* [Aarre Merikanto. Fate of a Composer in Independent Finland] (Porvoo, Werner Söderström Osakeyhtiö, 1985), p. 266.

24. Ibid., p. 262.

25. Ibid., p. 590.

26. Paavo Heininen, ' "Blow it out and I will light it again". Aarre Merikanto's mutilated *Study* and its reconstruction', *Finnish Music Quarterly* 1 (1986), pp. 60–7.

27. Ibid., p. 62.

28. Erik Tawaststjerna, *Sibelius. Vol. II, 1904–1914*, trans. Robert Layton (London: Faber, 1986), pp. 169–70.

29. For example, Raitio's *Antigone* (1922), Merikanto's *Ekho* (1922) and *Pan* (1924).

30. Such as Pingoud's *Les dernières aventures de Pierrot* (1916) and *La face d'une grande ville* (1937).

31. For example, the *Kalevala Suite* (1933/43) and *The Cobblers on the Heath* overture after Aleksis Kivi (1936).

32. Englund, *Sibeliuksen varjossa*, p. 338.

33. Edward Jurkowski, 'The Symphonies of Joonas Kokkonen', *Tempo* 208 (1999), p. 19.

34. Hepokoski, 'Sibelius, Jean', *New Grove*, p. 334.

35. Ilkka Oramo, 'Lindberg, Magnus', *The New Grove Dictionary of Music and Musicians*, second edn, vol. XIV (London: Macmillan, 2001), p. 711.

11 Sibelius and Germany

1. Original (in German) in the University of Helsinki Library (UHL), Coll. 206: 20.

2. List of the members and the Letter of Invitation of the Comitato 1916 (in Italian): see Finnish National Archives (NA), Coll. Sibelius: 16. Documents quoted without reference to other publications are hitherto unpublished.

3. *Jean Sibelius und Wien*, ed. Hartmut Krones (Vienna: Böhlau, 2003).

4. Sketch of a letter of Sibelius to Robert Lienau 26 May 1910, and of Robert Lienau to Sibelius, 14 January 1911; in NA Coll. Sibelius: 46. There has been some confusion about the location of the world premiere; the information given here is based on primary sources.

5. Sketch of a letter of Sibelius to Wilhelm Hansen, 2 December 1937 (in Swedish); in NA Coll. Sibelius: 45.

6. He may actually have planned to study with Anton Bruckner. Cf. his letter to Aino Järnefelt, 29 October 1890; quoted in Suvi Sirkku Talas

(ed.), *Sydämen aamu. Aino Järnefeltin ja Jean Sibeliuksen kihlausajan kirjeitä* (Helsinki: Suomalaisen kirjallisuuden seura, 2001), p. 26.

7. Tomi Mäkelä, ' "Mein Kopf ist voller Walzer": Jean Sibelius und der Umkreis Pauline Lucas in Wien', in *Jean Sibelius und Wien*, pp. 65–78.

8. Postcard to Sibelius (in German), in UHL Coll. 206: 19.

9. Erik Tawaststjerna, *Jean Sibelius. Åren 1920–1957*, ed. Gitta Henning (Helsinki: Söderström, 1997), p. 140.

10. Ibid., pp. 97–8.

11. NA Coll. Sibelius: 22.

12. Cited in Ruth-Maria Gleißner, *Der unpolitische Komponist als Politikum. Die Rezeption von Jean Sibelius im NS-Staat* (Frankfurt am Main: Peter Lang, 2002), p. 85.

13. Tawaststjerna, *Sibelius. Åren 1920–1957*, pp. 334–5.

14. NA Coll. Sibelius: 34, reproduced in Tomi Mäkelä, 'Jean Sibelius, politiikka ja Theodor W. Adorno – vastaväittäjän puheenvuoro, lausunto ja loppukaneetti', *Musiikki* 31/1 (2001), pp. 39–64.

15. Reproduced in Erik Tawaststjerna *Sibelius*, ed. Erik T. Tawaststjerna (Helsinki: Otava, 1997), p. 288.

16. UHL Coll. 206: 62. Letter to Alf Klingenberg, 28 February 1920 (in Swedish). Quoted in Tawaststjerna, *Sibelius. Åren 1920–1957*, p. 34 – omitting the original '(!)'.

17. Glenda D. Goss, *Jean Sibelius and Olin Downes. Music, Friendship, Criticism* (Boston: Northeastern University Press, 1995), pp. 39–121.

18. Georg Göhler, 'Orchesterkompositionen von Jean Sibelius', in *Der Kunstwart*, September 1908, p. 262.

19. Cf. R. Batka, 'Sibelius als Liederkomponist', in *Der Kunstwart*, July 1907, pp. 457–9.

20. Reinhold Sietz, 'Niemann', in *Die Musik in Geschichte und Gegenwart. Allgemeine Enzyklopädie der Musik*, ed. Friedrich Blume (Kassel: Bärenreiter, 1961), p. 1519.

21. Quoted in Erik Tawaststjerna, *Jean Sibelius. Åren 1904–1914*, ed. Gitta Henning (Helsinki: Söderström, 1991), p. 332.

22. UHL Coll. 206: 2 (in Finnish).

23. 'Fußnote zu Sibelius und Hamsun', in *Theodor W. Adorno: Gesammelte Schriften*, ed. Rolf Tiedemann (Frankfurt: Suhrkamp, 1986), vol. XX/ii, p. 804. 'Glosse über Sibelius', in *Gesammelte Schriften*, vol. XVII, pp. 247–52.

24. Theodor W. Adorno, *Introduction to the Sociology of Music*, trans. E. B. Ashton (New York: Seabury, 1976). The Sibelius–Newman anecdote is on pp. 172–3, and runs as follows: 'More than thirty years ago I once asked Ernest Newman, the initiator of Sibelius's fame, about the qualities of the Finnish composer. After all, I said, he had adopted none of the advances in compositorial techniques that had been made throughout Europe; his symphonics [sic] combined meaningless and trivial elements with alogical and profoundly unintelligible ones; he mistook esthetic formlessness for the voice of nature. Newman, from whose urbane all-round skepticism someone bred in the German tradition had much to learn, replied with a smile that the qualities I had just criticized – and which he was not denying – were just what appealed to the British.'

25. Theodor Adorno, *Aesthetic Theory*, trans. C. Lenhardt, ed. Gretel Adorno and Rolf Tiedemann (London and New York: Routledge and Kegan Paul, 1984 [1970]), p. 61.

26. Reinhold Brinkmann and Wolfgang Rihm have recently discussed Adorno's influence on the German Sibelius debate, in Brinkmann and Rihm, *Musik Nachdenken* (Regensburg: Con Brio, 2001), pp. 139ff. Rihm seems to believe in Adorno's impact whereas Brinkmann obviously has his doubts.

27. NA Coll. Sibelius: 31 (in German).

28. NA Coll. Sibelius: 31.

29. Ernst Tanzberger, *Jean Sibelius. Eine Monographie* (Wiesbaden: Breitkopf und Härtel, 1962), p. 253.

30. NA Coll. Sibelius: 23 (in German).

31. Letter of von Hase, 11 August 1942; photocopy in the Sibelius Museum; the original in Wiesbaden (in German).

32. Ernst Gerhard Welcke, the Leipzig conductor and husband of the Finnish soprano Lea Piltti, recalls that, in spite of his earlier experience with the composer, Niemann apparently considered a new book on Sibelius as early as 1933 (UHL Coll. 206: 40, in Finnish). Sibelius's reaction to the prospect of Niemann's book is not known but easy to imagine.

33. Ernst Tanzberger, *Die symphonischen Dichtungen von Jean Sibelius. Eine inhalts- und formanalytische Studie* (Würzburg: Konrad Triltsch, 1943), p. v.

34. UHL Coll. 206: 42.

35. Tanzberger, *Die symphonischen Dichtungen*, p. 1.

36. NA Coll. Sibelius: 33 (documentation in Finnish).

37. Tanzberger, *Eine Monographie*, p. 1.

38. Quoted in Tanzberger, *Eine Monographie*, pp. 17–18.

39. René Leibowitz, *Sibelius, le plus mauvais compositeur du monde* (Liège: Dynamo, 1955). Tanzberger, *Eine Monographie*, p. 65.

40. Cf. footnote of the Editor in Adorno, 'Fußnote zu Sibelius und Hamsun', in *Gesammelte Schriften*, Band 20/2, *Vermischte*

Schriften II, ed. Rolf Tiedemann (Frankfurt am
Main: Suhrkamp, 1986), p. 804.
41. UHL Coll. 206: 24 (in Swedish).
42. Tawaststjerna, *Jean Sibelius. Åren
1893–1904*, ed. Gitta Henning (Helsinki:
Söderström, 1993), p. 122 and illustration before
p. 65.
43. Tawaststjerna, *Jean Sibelius. Åren
1920–1957*, p. 268.
44. Adorno, 'Glosse über Sibelius', in
Gesammelte Schriften, Band 17, *Musikalische
Schriften IV*, ed. Rolf Tiedemann (Frankfurt am
Main: Suhrkamp, 1982), pp. 247–52.
Tawaststjerna, 'Über Adornos Sibelius-Kritik', in
*Adorno und die Musik (Studien zur
Wertungsforschung*, Band 12), ed. Otto
Kolleritsch (Wien: Universal Edition –
Hochschule für Musik und darstellende Kunst,
1979), pp. 112–24; Tomi Mäkelä, 'Jean Sibelius
contra Theodor W. Adorno – "Das Prinzip des
Stars ist totalitär geworden"', in *Finnish Music
Quarterly* (special German issue, 1994),
pp. 16–19ff.
45. Hans H. Hofstätter, *Idealismus und
Symbolismus* (Vienna and Munich: Anton
Schroll, 1972), p. 24.
46. Hofstätter, *Idealismus und Symbolismus*,
p. 6f.
47. Hofstätter, *Idealismus und Symbolismus*,
p. 56.
48. Wolfgang Welsch, *Ästhetisches Denken*
(Stuttgart: Reclam, 1990), pp. 114–56. Tomi
Mäkelä, 'Natur und Heimat in der
Sibelius-Rezeption. Walter Niemann, Theodor
W. Adorno und die "postmoderne Moderne"'
(in *Proceedings of the International Sibelius
Conference in Helsinki, 2000*, forthcoming).
49. Tawaststjerna, *Jean Sibelius. Åren
1914–1919*, ed. Gitta Henning (Helsinki:
Söderström, 1993), p. 297.
50. Cf. Timothy L. Jackson and Veijo
Murtomäki (eds.), *Sibelius Studies* (Cambridge:
Cambridge University Press), 2001, p. xii.
51. Adorno, 'Glosse über Sibelius', p. 249.
52. For a similar argument, see Kaikhosru
Sorabji, *Mi contra Fa* (London, 1947), pp. 49ff,
discussed in Tomi Mäkelä, 'Nationalismus und
Kontinentalismus – "Britizismus" und
Modernismus. Zur stilistischen und nationalen
Orientierung Britischer Komponisten nach
1914', in *Französische und deutsche Musik im 20.
Jahrhundert*, ed. Giselher Schubert (Mainz:
Schott, 2001), pp. 84–5.
53. Bengt de Törne, *Sibelius: A Close-Up*
(London: Faber, 1937), pp. 88, 103.
54. NA Coll. Sibelius: 17 (in German).

12 Sibelius in Britain
1. Mellers, *Man and his Music. The Story of
Musical Experience in the West*, Part IV:

'Romanticism and the twentieth century'
(London: Barrie and Jenkins, 1969), p. 130.
2. Ibid.
3. BBC Radio recording, 11 March 1941.
Reissued as track 23 on CD *Bantock: The Song of
Songs and other historical recordings*, Dutton,
CDLX 7043, 2000.
4. H. Orsmond Anderton, *Granville Bantock*
('Living Masters of Music', ed. Rosa Newmarch,
London: The Bodley Head, 1915), p. 2.
5. Tawaststjerna, *Sibelius. Vol. II: 1904–1914*,
trans. Robert Layton (London: Faber, 1986),
p. 40.
6. Constant Lambert, *Music Ho! A Study of
Music in Decline* (London: Faber, 1934 [revised
edn. 1937 and subsequent reprints]), p. 215.
7. Tawaststjerna/Layton, *Sibelius. Vol. II*, p. 40,
and Rosa Newmarch, *Jean Sibelius. A Short Story
of a Long Friendship* (London: Goodwin and
Tabb, 1944), p. 8.
8. Scholes, Percy A., *The Mirror of Music
1844–1944*, Vol. I (London: Novello and Oxford
University Press, 1947), p. 448.
9. Tawaststjerna/Layton, *Sibelius. Vol. II*, p. 42.
10. Ibid., p. 39.
11. Newmarch, *Jean Sibelius. A Short Story of a
Long Friendship*, p. 10.
12. Tawaststjerna/Layton, *Sibelius. Vol. II*, p. 42;
Newmarch, *Jean Sibelius. A Short Story of a Long
Friendship*, pp. 5 and 8.
13. Newmarch, *Jean Sibelius. Ein finnländische
Komponist* (Leipzig, Breitkopf und Härtel,
1906 – it contains an advertisement at the back
for W. Niemann, *Die Musik Skandinaviens*).
14. Tawaststjerna/Layton, *Sibelius. Vol. II*,
p. 87.
15. Ibid., p. 105.
16. Ibid., p. 111.
17. Ibid., p. 107.
18. Ibid., p. 112.
19. Ibid., p. 105.
20. Broad Meadow (which Bantock bought in
1913) is described in M. Bantock, *Granville
Bantock, a personal portrait* (London: Dent,
1972), pp. 10–14; for Myrrha Bantock on
Sibelius, see ibid., pp. 22–3, 46–7 and 126–7.
21. Tawaststjerna/Layton, *Sibelius. Vol. II*,
p. 107.
22. Ibid., p. 219.
23. Newmarch, *Jean Sibelius. A Short Story of a
Long Friendship*, p. 32.
24. Tawaststjerna/Layton, *Sibelius. Vol. II*,
p. 106.
25. Ibid., p. 243.
26. Mellers, *Man and his Music*, Part IV,
p. 129.
27. J. Cuthbert Hadden, *Modern Musicians. A
Book for Players, Singers and Listeners* (London
and Edinburgh: T. N. Foulis, 1913), chapter 5,
pp. 33–4.

28. David Cox, *The Henry Wood 'Proms'* (London: BBC, 1980), p. 325.

29. Newmarch, R. *Jean Sibelius. Ein finnländische Komponist*, p. 22 (my translation).

30. Tawaststjerna, *Sibelius. Vol. III: 1914–1957*, trans. R. Layton (London: Faber, 1997), p. 34.

31. Ibid., p. 197.

32. Newmarch, *Jean Sibelius. A Short Story of a Long Friendship*, pp. 42–3; Tawaststjerna/Layton, *Sibelius. Vol. III*, pp. 199–200.

33. Ibid., pp. 200–2.

34. Ibid., pp. 202–5.

35. Blom, 'Sibelius, Jean', in H. C. Colles (ed.), *Grove's Dictionary of Music and Musicians*, 3rd edn. (London: Macmillan, 1928), pp. 749–51.

36. V. Murtomäki, K. Kilpenäinen, and R. Väisänen (eds.), *Sibelius Forum. Proceedings from the Second International Jean Sibelius Conference, Helsinki November 25–29 1995* (Helsinki: Sibelius Academy, 1998), p. 71.

37. Cecil Gray, *Sibelius*, 2nd edn. (Oxford: Oxford University Press, 1934), p. 172.

38. Ibid., p. 173.

39. Ibid., p. 176.

40. Ibid., p. 175.

41. Ibid., p. 176.

42. Lambert, *Music Ho!*, p. 11.

43. Ibid., p. 231.

44. Ibid., p. 216.

45. Ibid., p. 230.

46. Ibid., p. 230.

47. Tovey's essays would be collected in his six-volume series of *Essays in Music Analysis*, 1935–9.

48. *The Musical Times*, March 1935, p. 219.

49. D. F. Tovey, *Essays in Musical Analysis, vol. VI, Supplementary Essays, Glossary and Index* (London: Oxford University Press, 1939), pp. 89–90.

50. S. Lloyd, *William Walton: Muse of Fire* (Woodbridge: Boydell, 2001), p. 162.

51. See R. Layton, *Sibelius* (Master Musicians series, London: Dent, 1965 [and subsequent editions]).

52. From Britten's article 'England and the Folk-art Problem' (*Modern Music* 8, Jan./Feb. 1941), quoted in D. Mitchell, and P. Reed, *Letters from a Life. Selected Letters and Diaries of Benjamin Britten, Vol. 2: 1939–1945* (London: Faber, 1991), p. 924.

53. Lionel Carley, *Delius. A Life in Letters 1909–1934* (Aldershot: Scolar Press, 1988), p. 421.

13 Sibelius and contemporary music

1. Since 2000, Boulez has conducted several performances of Janáček's *Sinfonietta* and the *Glagolitic Mass* with, amongst others, the Chicago Symphony Orchestra. He has not to date conducted any Sibelius or Nielsen.

2. George Benjamin, a pupil from the 1970s, remembers Messiaen's repeated criticisms of serialism in his classes, not least for its avoidance of octaves and the lower, consonant partials of the harmonic series generally. Messiaen's own more extreme pieces from this period such as the *Livre d'orgue* were not exempt from his censure.

3. Any serious student of Stockhausen and Boulez will immediately object that they did indeed show considerable interest in these phenomena in their music. However, what concerns us is that at this time their handling of these things was not as immediately apparent as a seeming indifference to them in the resultant music. See Grisey's treatise, 'Tempus ex machina – Reflexions sur le temps musical', in *Entretemps – Grisey/Murail* (Paris, 1989).

4. In acoustic terminology, an inharmonic spectrum is a sound whose partials do not conform to the standard pattern of the harmonic series, but rather to an irregular pattern – often lacking any one fundamental note. Metallic instruments such as bells and gongs feature varying degrees of inharmonicity. Natural sounds, such as waterfalls, waves or storms (evoked here by Sibelius) feature a strong degree of inharmonicity bordering on noise. Inharmonic spectra were a particular source of fascination to Grisey and Murail.

5. See James Hepokoski, *Sibelius: Symphony no. 5* (Cambridge: Cambridge University Press, 1993), p. 28. Hepokoski himself calls such moments in Sibelius 'proto-minimalist' – presumably the nearest he could get to asserting the influence of such passages on contemporary music. As an American-based musicologist, Hepokoski was probably unaware of spectral music at this time: it has only begun to make its influence felt in America since Murail became Professor of Composition at Columbia University in 1997.

6. See Rosa Newmarch, *Sibelius: A Short Story of a Long Friendship* (London: Goodwin and Tabb, 1945). A photo (opposite page 19) taken by the author in this book actually shows Sibelius listening to the vibrations of the waters of Lake Saimaa. Most significantly for the present article, Newmarch's commentary remarks that 'Sibelius had at that time a passion for trying to catch the pedal notes of natural forces.'

7. In conversation with the author, August 2002.

8. The group comprised a performing ensemble, plus five composers: Murail, Grisey, Dufourt, Michael Levinas and Roger Tessier. It was founded by Murail and Levinas in 1973.

9. Dufourt, programme note to the commercial recording of *Saturne* (1979, Sappho 004).

10. See Dufourt, 'L'œuvre et l'histoire', in *Musique, Pouvoir, Écriture* (Paris: Bourgois, 1991), p. 324.

11. The scoring also reveals the influence, as the composer readily confesses, of 1970s punk rock.

12. According to his pupil Magnus Lindberg. Lindberg adds that amongst younger French composers Sibelius's Seventh was 'truly a cult piece at that time!' See the interview with Peter Szendy in *Magnus Lindberg* (originally published by IRCAM, 1993, Eng. trans. published by the Finnish Music Information Centre), page 10.

13. *Partiels* and *Transitoires* are both from Grisey's ambitious cycle of six large pieces *Les espaces acoustiques* (1974–85), each of which can be played on its own or as part of the whole cycle.

14. Conversation with the author in August 2002.

15. According to Murail, his original ambition had been to include *Lemminkäinen in Tuonela*, but this did not fill out the programme enough, so the Seventh was substituted. Although Murail admired this symphony, its inclusion was actually suggested by the series producer – none other than Alain Banquart (see below).

16. Harry Halbreich, review in *La Croix*, December 1980 in the archives of the CDMC, Paris, exact date not indicated.

17. It was shortlisted at the 1981 Unesco International Rostrum of Composers, and as a result was broadcast by most major radio stations (including BBC Radio 3, in March 1982).

18. See Banquart, 'Quelques années fructueuses', in *Vingt-cinq ans de création musicale contemporaine – L'itinéraire en temps réel*, ed. Danielle Cohen-Levinas (Paris: L' Harmattan, 1998), pp. 221–4.

19. *The Forest's Mighty God* (British Sibelius Society, 1997), p. 61. This tribute is printed in English, although whether the composer's or that of a translator is not stated. Either way, the language is somewhat confused, which accounts for my use here of my own paraphrases (attempting to make sense of it) rather than exact quotations from the tribute itself.

20. This letter and Sibelius's reply are quoted in full in the composer's own translation in *The Forest's Mighty God*, pp. 66–8.

21. Interview with Roger Wright, BBC Radio 3, November 1984.

22. See Gefors article 'Make change your choice!', in *Per Nørgård – 14 Interpretative Essays*, ed. Anders Beyer (Aldershot: Scolar Press, 1996).

23. See Hepokoski, *Sibelius: Symphony no. 5*, p. 37.

24. See Gefors, 'Make change your choice!', p. 39. Gefors's analysis here corresponds exactly

in its technical terminology and substance to the one I heard Nørgård give of the passage in composition classes at Dartington in August 1990. It must therefore be the result of Gefors's own period of study with Nørgård in the early seventies when, significantly, his use of infinity row techniques was at its height in the composition of the huge *Third Symphony* (1972–5).

25. For technical details, see Erling Kulberg's article 'Beyond infinity' in Beyer, *Per Nørgård*, pp. 71–94.

26. Both in its irregular, unpredictable contours and its endless self-reproduction the infinity row is closely related to the well-known fractals of chaos theory, such as the Mandelbrot set. It is, in fact, one of the earliest fractals discovered, since in 1959 chaos theory was in its infancy.

27. For a more detailed survey of these similarities, see Julian Anderson, 'Perception and deception', in Beyer, *Per Nørgård*.

28. See Szendy, *Magnus Lindberg*, p. 11.

29. For further details on this and other technical questions in Lindberg's music, see Julian Anderson, 'The spectral sounds of Magnus Lindberg' in *The Musical Times*, November 1992; and Peter Szendy 'The point of style: *Joy*', in *Magnus Lindberg*.

30. This is actually a quote from Lindberg's programme note to *Kinetics*, completed two years previously, but it applies even more to the harmonic structure and orchestration of *Joy*.

31. Lindberg, programme note in the full score of *Aura*, Chester Music 1995.

32. This sketch was printed on the front of Timothy L. Jackson and Veijo Murtomäki (eds.), *Sibelius Studies* (Cambridge: Cambridge University Press, 1999).

33. Due precisely to the presence of an exceptional team of BBC producers such as Robert Simpson, Hans Keller and Alexander Goehr.

34. See *The Forest's Mighty God*, p. 69.

35. Interview with Maxwell Davies in Richard Duffallo, *Trackings* (London: Oxford University Press, 1987), pp. 153–4.

36. R. Murray Schaefer, *British Composers in Interview* (London: Faber, 1962).

37. A phrase found in the writings of both Peter J. Pirie and Stephen Pruslin, to name but two.

38. In *Peter Maxwell Davies – Studies from Two Decades*, ed. Stephen Pruslin (*Tempo* Booklet No. 2, Boosey and Hawkes, 1979), p. 4. He was not alone in his wonderment. Anecdotally, it may surprise some readers to know that the 1978 premiere of the work was featured on that night's BBC *Nine O'Clock News* – the fact that a composer of avant-garde leanings should have

produced a symphony was regarded as sufficiently rare to be newsworthy.

39. See Davies's programme note in Stephen Pruslin, pp. 94–7.

40. In conversation with the author, November 2002.

41. Ibid.

42. In conversation with the author, November 2002.

43. Published in *Morton Feldman – Essays*, ed. Walter Zimmerman (Cologne: Beginner Press, 1985), pp. 181–213. Except where indicated, all quotations from Feldman are from this lecture.

44. 'Their lack of interest in Stravinsky is very, very sad . . .Without Stravinsky in your life, you have no feeling for instruments.'

45. Sibelius's remarks, as quoted by Bengt de Törne, run as follows: 'The orchestra, you see, is a wonderful instrument which has got everything – except the pedal. You must always bear this in mind. You see, if you don't create an artificial pedal for your orchestration, there will be holes in it, and some passages will sound ragged.' See Bengt de Törne, *Sibelius: A Close-Up* (London: Faber, 1937), pp. 30–1.

46. Programme note to the score of *Coptic Light* (Universal Edition, London, 1985).

47. I am indebted to Harry Halbreich, for filling out details of the role he played in the dissemination of Sibelius in Central Europe. My thanks to the CDMC, Paris, for their extensive help in providing copies from their archives of relevant programme notes, articles and reviews from the past thirty years. Thanks also to Bayan Northcott for discussions on Sibelius generally and especially for locating the exact source quotation in Bengt de Törne's book for Feldman's reference to Sibelius in *Coptic Light*.

14 Interpreting Sibelius on record

1. H. E. Johnson, *Jean Sibelius* (New York: Knopf, 1959), p. 172. Johnson considered this issue significant enough to write a separate book on it: *Jean Sibelius: The Recorded Music* (Helsinki: Westerlund, 1957).

2. See L. Gray, 'Sibelius and England', in Glenda Dawn Goss (ed.), *The Sibelius Companion* (Westport: Greenwood, 1996), pp. 281–96. The most salient contemporary statement of these preferences is Constant Lambert, *Music Ho! A Study of Music in Decline* (London: Hogarth Press, 1985 [first publ. 1934]).

3. S. Goddard, 'Sibelius's Second Symphony', *Music and Letters* 12 (1931), pp. 156–63; p. 156.

4. C. Mackenzie, Editorial, *Gramophone* (May 1941), pp. 263–5; p. 263.

5. R. Väisänen, 'Problems in performance studies', in *Sibelius Forum: Proceedings from the*

Second International Jean Sibelius Conference, ed. V. Murtomäki, K. Kilpeläinen and R. Väisänen (Helsinki: Sibelius Academy, 1998), pp. 129–41, discusses the *Andante festivo* recording that is our only record of Sibelius's conducting.

6. Translated into English as *Jean Sibelius: His Life and Personality* (London: Alan Wilmer, 1936).

7. M. Huttunen, 'The usefulness of historical knowledge in musical interpretation', unpublished paper given at *Performance 2000* conference, University of Southampton, April 2000, p. 5.

8. Huttunen, 'The usefulness of historical knowledge', p. 6.

9. Otter and Bengt Forsberg give us vol. 1 (BIS CD-457, 1990), which includes opp. 17, 36, 37, and 88, and vol. 3 (BIS CD-757, 1996), which includes opp. 13, 50, and 90, whilst Groop and Love Derwinger appear on vol. 2 (BIS CD-657, 1994) with opp. 1, 57, 86 and others.

10. Robert Layton, 'From Kajanus to Karajan: Sibelius on record', in T. L. Jackson and V. Murtomäki (eds.), *Sibelius Studies* (Cambridge: Cambridge University Press, 2001), pp. 14–34; p. 32.

11. K. Borg, 'How to sing them: some thoughts on the interpretation of Sibelius's songs', *Finnish Music Quarterly* (1990), nos. 3–4, pp. 58–61; p. 60.

12. Robert Keane points out that in 1946 the composer forbade Finnish Radio to broadcast his songs other than in the original version with piano, saying that 'I don't want them orchestrated . . . One can't express little ideas by means of a large orchestra' (quoted in Robert Layton, *Sibelius* [London: Dent, 1965], p. 162). That he did, nonetheless, orchestrate some of them is typical of Sibelius's elusive and contradictory poietics.

13. The principal culprit has been Astra Desmond in her article 'The songs', in *Sibelius: A Symposium*, ed. Gerald Abraham (London: Lindsay Drummond, 1947), pp. 108–36; see, for example, pp. 108 and 128. Desmond has been set up as something of a straw man by later writers, since her principal point has been that Sibelius's songs are distinctive in style and should not be compared to the German lied (pp. 108, 135).

14. See Gray, *Sibelius* (London: Oxford University Press, 1935), p. 118: 'What is surprising . . . is that he should have written so much for an instrument which he does not seem to understand, and even appears positively to dislike and despise.'

15. These valuable recordings have now been rereleased on CD: the First and Second Symphonies on Koch 37127-2, and the Third and Fifth Symphonies on Koch 37133-2.

16. B. de Törne, *Sibelius: A Close-Up* (London: Faber, 1937), p. 14.

17. Ibid.

18. R. Philip, *Early Recordings and Musical Style: Changing Tastes in Instrumental Performance 1900–1950* (Cambridge: Cambridge University Press, 1992), p. 6.

19. G. Thomas, *The Symphonies of Jean Sibelius: A Discography and Discussion* (Bloomington, Indiana University School of Music, 1990), p. 8.

20. The term 'rubato' is falling out of favour due to controversies and misconceptions traditionally surrounding it, in particular the notion that time 'robbed' (through *rallentando*) must necessarily be 'paid back' (through acceleration) elsewhere. For this reason, more recent writers prefer to refer to tempo 'flexibility' or 'fluctuation'. The historical background to the debate and the pioneering empirical work of John McEwan and others are described in Philip, *Early Recordings*, pp. 37–69.

21. J. Bowen, 'Tempo, duration and flexibility: techniques in the analysis of performance', *Journal of Musicological Research* 16 (1996), pp. 111–56; p. 154 and p. 156.

22. Ibid., p. 115.

23. Details of these records are as follows: Serge Koussevitzky and the Boston Symphony Orchestra (HMV DB3168-71, 1940 – now also on CD, Pearl EEMM CD59408); Erich Leinsdorf and the LPO (Decca AK2193-6, 1949); Erik Tuxen and the Danish Radio Orchestra (Decca LXT2744, 1952); and Anthony Collins and the LSO (Decca LXT5083, 1955).

24. Leonard Bernstein and the New York Philharmonic Orchestra (CBS BRG72356, 1966). In Bernstein's later recording of the Fifth Symphony with the Vienna Philharmonic in 1987 (DG427 647–2) this influence has been somewhat muted.

25. N. Lebrecht, *The Maestro Myth: Great Conductors in Pursuit of Power* (London: Simon and Schuster, 1991), pp. 136–7.

26. E. Greenfield, I. March, and D. Stevens, *The Stereo Record Guide*, vol. II (London: The Long Playing Record Library Ltd, 1961), p. 498. Since the contributor Ivan March is listed as having interests in 'symphonies of Dvořák, Sibelius and Tchaikovsky', this review could confidently be attributed to him.

27. Robert Layton, Review, *Gramophone* 61 no. 722 (July 1983), p. 154.

28. Alexander Gibson and the Scottish National Orchestra in 1975 (CFP40218), and a 1983 recording also with the SNO (Chandos CHAN8388).

29. R. Osborne, *Conversations with Karajan* (Oxford: Oxford University Press, 1991), pp. 96–7.

30. See 'The pastness of the present and the presence of the past', in N. Kenyon (ed.), *Authenticity and Early Music* (Oxford: Oxford University Press, 1988), pp. 137–207.

31. Thomas, *The Symphonies of Jean Sibelius*, p. 17. Thomas is referring to Karajan's 1968 performance with the Berlin Philharmonic (DG SLPM139032).

32. There are four recordings of the Fifth Symphony under Karajan, two with the Philharmonia (1953, 1961) and two with the Berlin Philharmonic (1965, 1978); of these perhaps the most notable is the third, DG LPM18973.

33. These recordings are Georges Prêtre and the NPO (RCA Victor SB6775, 1968); Colin Davis and the Boston Symphony Orchestra (Philips 6500 959, 1975); Vladimir Ashkenazy and the Philharmonia (Decca SXDL7541, 1981); Esa-Pekka Salonen and the Philharmonia (CBSM42366, 1987), and Herbert Blomstedt and the San Francisco Symphony Orchestra (DG425 858-2, 1993).

34. All these variations in performance style and outline are presented, discussed and illustrated in more depth in B. Lowe, 'Performance, analysis, and interpretation in Sibelius's Fifth Symphony', Ph.D. thesis, University of Southampton (2000), pp. 187–246, where the reasons for a change in style are considered on pp. 223–6.

35. The intended metronome markings were not written in the published score, but were published separately later in a Finnish journal in 1943 and in D. Cherniavsky, 'Sibelius's tempo corrections', *Music and Letters* 31 (1950), pp. 53–5. Although these suggestions were well circulated before any of the performances discussed in this section took place, part of the interpretative diversity may stem from certain of the orchestral materials in circulation, which still bore the suggestion of $\downarrow$. = 40 from the second, 1916, version of the symphony (see Väisänen, 'Problems in performance studies', pp. 137–8).

36. For example, Kyrill Kondrashin and the Concertgebouw Orchestra (Philips 412069-1PH, performed in 1976), Gennadi Rozhdestvensky and the Moscow Radio Symphony Orchestra (HMV Melodiya ASD3780, 1980), and Jascha Horenstein and the BBC Northern Symphony Orchestra (Intaglio INCD7331, performed in 1971).

37. For example, Sergiu Celibidache and the Danish Radio Symphony Orchestra's version of the Fifth Symphony (SH863, performed in 1971).

38. Paavo Berglund has recorded the Sibelius symphonies with the Bournemouth Symphony Orchestra, the Helsinki Philharmonic Orchestra, and the Chamber Orchestra of Europe. All are

excellent, but perhaps the most colourful and interesting are those with the Helsinki Philharmonic: Symphonies 1–4 (EMI CZS5 68643-2, recorded in 1984) and Symphonies 5–7 (EMI CZS 68646-2, recorded in 1986). It goes without saying that I do not support Robert Layton's judgement of these performances as 'selfless and literal' (Layton, 'Sibelius on record', p. 30 n. 47).

39. M. Haapakoski, 'The concerto that holds a record: the Sibelius Violin Concerto on disc', *Finnish Music Quarterly* (1990), nos. 3–4, p. 34.

40. M. Haapakoski, 'The Sibelius Concerto still holds a record: discography of the recordings released in the 1990s', *Finnish Music Quarterly* (1996), no. 4, pp. 14–15.

41. *RED Classical Catalogue*, master edition 2001/2 (London: RED Publishing/Gramophone, 2001).

42. For example, Ondine's *Early Chamber Music, vol. 1* (ODE 826-2, 1995) contains worthwhile recordings of the F major Violin Sonata (1889), String Trios in A major (1889) and G minor (1893–4), and Piano Quartet in C minor (1891).

43. M. Haapakoski, 'Select discography of Finnish choral music', *Finnish Music Quarterly* (1987), no. 2, p. 71. More recent releases of the YL performing these two major works with Paavo Berglund and the Helsinki Philharmonic Orchestra can be found on EMI EX 27 0336 3/CDS 747 4968, whilst the part-songs can be found on Finlandia FAD 206/FACD 206 under Matti Hyökki.

44. The original Fifth Symphony is on BIS CD-863 (1997), and the original Violin Concerto, with Leonidas Kavakos as soloist, on BIS CD-500 (1991).

45. I would like to thank Chris Mobbs and Tim Day of the National Sound Archive, Elizabeth Berry, and Daniel Grimley for their generous help in preparing this chapter.

15 Performing Sibelius: Sir Colin Davis and Osmo Vänskä

1. The single surviving recording of Sibelius conducting his own work is a radio broadcast of a glowing performance of the *Andante festivo*, dating significantly from the eve of war in 1939.

2. Compare Robert Layton's discussion, 'Nielsen and the gramophone', in Mina Miller (ed.), *The Nielsen Companion* (London: Faber, 1994), pp. 116–47.

Select bibliography

Correspondence and primary sources

Sibelius, Jean, *The Hämeenlinna Letters. Jean Sibelius ungdomsbrev*, ed. Glenda Dawn Goss (Helsinki: Schildts Förlag, 1997).

Sibelius, Jean, Symphony no. 2, ed. Kari Kilpeläinen, *Jean Sibelius Complete Works* (Wiesbaden: Breitkopf und Härtel, 2000).

Sibelius, Jean, Solo Songs with Piano, opp. 1, 13, 17, 35, 36, 37, 38, 50, *Jean Sibelius Complete Works*, Series VIII, vol. 2 (Wiesbaden: Breitkopf und Härtel, 1998).

Sibelius, Jean, Solo Songs with Piano, opp. 57, 61, 72, 86, 88, 90, *Jean Sibelius Complete Works*, Series VIII, vol. 3 (Wiesbaden: Breitkopf und Härtel, 2000).

Secondary literature

Abraham, Gerald (ed.), *Sibelius. A Symposium* (London: Oxford University Press, 1947).

Adorno, Theodor W., 'Glosse über Sibelius', reprinted as part of the *Impromptus*, in *Gesammelte Schriften*, vol. XVII (*Musikalische Schriften IV*), (Frankfurt: Suhrkamp, 1982), pp. 247–52; first publ. 1938 (in German).

Dahlhaus, Carl, *Nineteenth-Century Music*, trans. J. Bradford Robinson (Berkeley: University of California Press, 1989); first publ. 1980 (in German).

Ekman, K., *Jean Sibelius. His Life and Personality*, trans. E. Birse (London: Alan Wilmer, 1936 [New York: Tudor, 1946 (originally Knopf, 1938)]).

Furuhjelm, Erik, *Jean Sibelius: Hans tondiktning och drag ur hans liv* (Borgå, 1916).

Goss, Glenda Dawn, *Jean Sibelius: A Guide to Research* (New York and London: Garland, 1998).

Goss, Glenda Dawn, *Jean Sibelius and Olin Downes. Friendship, Music, Criticism* (Boston: Northeastern University Press, 1995).

Goss, Glenda Dawn (ed.), *The Sibelius Companion* (Westport: Greenwood, 1996).

Gray, Cecil, *Sibelius*, second edn (London: Oxford University Press, 1934); first publ. 1931.

Grimley, Daniel, 'Sibelius's *Lemminkäinen and the Maidens of Saari* op. 22/1: acculturation, Italy and the midsummer night', in *Sibelius Forum. Proceedings from the Second International Jean Sibelius Conference. Helsinki, November 25–29, 1999*, ed. Veijo Murtomäki, Kari Kilpeläinen, and Risto Väisänen (Helsinki: Sibelius Academy, 1999), pp. 197–207.

Hepokoski, James, *Sibelius: Symphony no. 5* (Cambridge: Cambridge University Press, 1993).

Hepokoski, James, 'Sibelius', in *The Nineteenth-Century Symphony*, ed. D. Kern Holoman (New York: Schirmer, 1997).

Hepokoski, James, 'Sibelius, Jean', in *The New Grove Dictionary of Music and Musicians*, second edn, ed. Stanley Sadie and John Tyrrell (London: Macmillan, 2001), vol. XXIII, pp. 319–47.

Howell, Tim, *Jean Sibelius: Progressive Techniques in the Symphonies and Tone Poems* (New York and London: Garland, 1989).

Huttunen, Matti, 'How Sibelius became a classic in Finland', in *Sibelius Forum. Proceedings from the Second International Jean Sibelius Conference. Helsinki, November 25–29, 1999*, ed. Veijo Murtomäki, Kari Kilpeläinen, and Risto Väisänen (Helsinki: Sibelius Academy, 1999), pp. 73–81.

Huttunen, Matti, *Jean Sibelius: pienois-elämäkerta (An illustrated life)*. English text by Michael Wynne-Ellis (Porvoo: Werner Söderström, 1999).

Jackson, Timothy L., and Veijo Murtomäki (eds.), *Sibelius Studies* (Cambridge: Cambridge University Press, 2001).

Jussila, Osmo, Seppo Hentilä and Jukka Nevakivi, *From Grand Duchy to a Modern State: A Political History of Finland since 1809* (London: Hurst and Co., 1999), first published as *Suomen Poliittinen historia, 1809–1995* (Helsinki: Wener Söderström Oy, 1995).

Kilpeläinen, Kari, *The Jean Sibelius Musical Manuscripts at Helsinki University Library: A Complete Catalogue* (Wiesbaden: Breitkopf und Härtel, 1991).

Laufer, Edward, 'On the first movement of Sibelius's Fourth Symphony', in *Schenker Studies 2*, ed. Carl Schachter and Hedi Siegel (Cambridge: Cambridge University Press, 1999), pp. 127–59.

Layton, Robert, *Sibelius*, rev. edn (London: Dent, 1978).

Levas, Santeri, *Sibelius: a personal portrait*, trans. Percy M. Young (London: Dent, 1972).

Luyken, Lorenz, *"– aus dem Nichtigen eine Welt schaffen –". Studien zur Dramaturgie im symphonischen Spätwerk von Jean Sibelius*. Kölner Beiträge zur Musikforschung 190 (Kassel: Bosse, 1995).

Mäkelä, Tomi (ed.), *Music and Nationalism in Twentieth-century Great Britain and Finland* (Hamburg: von Bockel, 1997).

Murtomäki, Veijo, *Symphonic Unity. The Development of Formal Thinking in the Symphonies of Sibelius*, trans. Henry Bacon, Studia Musicologica Universitatis Helsingiensis 5 (Helsinki: University of Helsinki Press, 1993).

Murtomäki, Veijo, Kari Kilpeläinen, and Risto Väisänen (eds.), *Sibelius Forum. Proceedings from the Second International Jean Sibelius Conference. Helsinki, November 25–29, 1999* (Helsinki: Sibelius Academy, 1999).

Newmarch, Rosa, *Jean Sibelius: a Short Story of a Long Friendship* (Boston: Birchard, 1934).

Niemann, Walter, *Die Musik skandinaviens: ein Führer durch die Volks- und Kunstmusik* (Leipzig: Breitkopf und Härtel, 1906).

Niemann, Walter, *Jean Sibelius* (Leipzig: Breitkopf und Härtel, 1917).

Parmet, Simon, *The Symphonies of Sibelius: A Study in Musical Appreciation*, trans. Kingsley A. Hart (London: Cassell, 1959); first publ. 1955 (in Swedish).

Rickards, Guy, *Jean Sibelius* (London: Phaidon, 1997).

Salmenhaara, Erkki, *Jean Sibelius* (Helsinki: Tammi, 1984).

Simpson, Robert, *Carl Nielsen: Symphonist*, rev. edn (London: Kahn and Averill, 1979).

Tanzberger, Ernst, *Jean Sibelius: Eine Monographie* (Wiesbaden: Breitkopf und Härtel, 1962).

Tarasti, Eero, *Myth and Music. A Semiotic Approach to the Aesthetics of Myth in Music, Especially that of Wagner, Sibelius and Stravinsky*. Acta Musicologica Fennica 11 (Helsinki: Suomen musiikkitieteellinen seura, 1978).

Tarasti, Eero (ed.), *The Proceedings of the First International Jean Sibelius Conference, Helsinki, August 1990* (Helsinki: Sibelius Academy, 1995).

Tawaststjerna, Erik, *Jean Sibelius*, 5 vols. (Helsinki: Otava, 1965–88; vol. 1 rev. 1989), trans. into Finnish from the original Swedish by Tuomas Anhava, Jaija Mattila, and Erkki Salmenhaara; Swedish version published by Söderström, 1994.

Tawaststjerna, Erik, *Sibelius*, abridged version of above, trans. Robert Layton, 3 vols. (London: Faber, 1976, 1986, 1997).

Törne, Bengt de, *Sibelius: A Close-Up* (London: Faber, 1937).

Wallner, Bo, *Wilhelm Stenhammar och hans tid*, 3 vols. (Stockholm: Norstedts Förlag, 1991).

Whittall, Arnold, *Musical Composition in the Twentieth Century* (London: Oxford University Press, 1999).

Index

Cambridge Companions to Music

Topics

The Cambridge Companion to Blues and Gospel Music
Edited by Allan Moore

The Cambridge Companion to Conducting
Edited by José Antonio Bowen

The Cambridge Companion to Grand Opera
Edited by David Charlton

The Cambridge Companion to Jazz
Edited by Mervyn Cooke and David Horn

The Cambridge Companion to the Musical
Edited by William Everett and Paul Laird

The Cambridge Companion to the Orchestra
Edited by Colin Lawson

The Cambridge Companion to Pop and Rock
Edited by Simon Frith, Will Straw and John Street

The Cambridge Companion to the String Quartet
Edited by Robin Stowell

Composers

The Cambridge Companion to Bach
Edited by John Butt

The Cambridge Companion to Bartók
Edited by Amanda Bayley

The Cambridge Companion to Beethoven
Edited by Glenn Stanley

The Cambridge Companion to Benjamin Britten
Edited by Mervyn Cooke

The Cambridge Companion to Berg
Edited by Anthony Pople

The Cambridge Companion to Berlioz
Edited by Peter Bloom

The Cambridge Companion to Brahms
Edited by Michael Musgrave

The Cambridge Companion to Bruckner
Edited by John Williamson

The Cambridge Companion to John Cage
Edited by David Nicholls

The Cambridge Companion to Chopin
Edited by Jim Samson

The Cambridge Companion to Debussy
Edited by Simon Trezise